AF291809

AGRARIAN STUDIES 6

WOMEN AND WORK IN RURAL INDIA

Edited by
Madhura Swaminathan
Shruti Nagbhushan
V. K. Ramachandran

Tulika Books

Published by
Tulika Books
44, first floor, Shahpur Jat, New Delhi 110 049, India
www.tulikabooks.in

© Madhura Swaminathan, Shruti Nagbhushan,
and V. K. Ramachandran 2020

First edition (hardback) 2020

ISBN: 981-81-939269-6-3

Printed at Chaman Offset, Delhi 110 002

Contents

Foreword   vii

Preface   ix

Introduction *Madhura Swaminathan and V. K. Ramachandran*   xi

I Conceptual, Theoretical, and Methodological Issues in Understanding Women's Work

1 Work, Employment, and Labour Underutilisation: What the ILO
  Resolution Means for India
  Indira Hirway   3

2 Measuring Women's Work with Time-Use Data: An Illustration
  from Two Villages of Karnataka
  Madhura Swaminathan   19

3 An Augmented Definition of Work Participation in Rural India
  Yoshifumi Usami, with Subhajit Patra and Abhinav Kapoor   40

4 Proletarianisation and Women's Work: Notes on Rural India
  V. K. Ramachandran   67

II Women's Work in Agriculture and Allied Sectors

5 Sectoral Shifts and Declining Labour Participation Rate of Women
  Jayan Jose Thomas   85

6 Women in the Rice Economy of India: Evidence from Village
  Studies
  S. Niyati   109

7 Forms of Wages in the Assam–Dooar Plantations: A Historical
  Perspective
  Jeta Sankrityayana   134

8 Women in Livestock-Rearing
  R. Vijayamba   167

III CASTE AND CLASS ISSUES

9 Scheduled Caste Women in India's Periodic Labour Force Survey
Khalid Khan and Sukhadeo Thorat   189

10 Employment Trends among Scheduled Tribe Women
Athary Janiso   209

11 Employment and Unemployment in Manual Worker Households
Shruti Nagbhushan   221

IV WOMEN IN NON-AGRICULTURAL WORK

12 Conditions of Work among "Scheme Workers"
K. Hemalata   237

13 Women's Participation in NREGA: A Review of the Literature
Smita Ramnarain and Smriti Rao   256

V WOMEN'S WAGES AND EARNINGS

14 Women's Work and Earnings in Nineteenth-Century Rural Bihar
Madhavi Jha   281

15 Trends in Male and Female Wage Rates
Arindam Das   298

16 The Gender Gap in Wage Rates: Exploring the Role of Female
Labour Supply with Evidence from PARI Villages
Arindam Das   322

VI ACCESS TO FINANCE

17 Women's Access to Banking in India: Policy Context, Trends,
and Predictors
Pallavi Chavan   343

List of Contributors   375

Index   377

Foreword

Women and Work in Rural India is the sixth book in the Agrarian Studies Series published by the Foundation for Agrarian Studies (FAS).

The origin of this book is in a two-year research project on women's work in rural production systems conducted by the FAS with funding from the Rosa Luxemburg Stiftung (RLS). The empirical study of women in rural production systems in India is inadequate, and the project was designed to address that gap in scholarship.

The book draws on empirical evidence from a wide range of sources of data, secondary and primary. The database includes material from a small-scale intensive time-use survey conducted by FAS in two villages of Karnataka. The results of this survey were crucial in contributing to the debate on the definition of work (paid and unpaid), and in evaluating the actual participation of rural women in the production process.

The research brought together in this volume was first presented at an international conference titled "Women's Work in Rural Economies" organised by FAS and held at Vayalar, Kerala, in December 2018. The studies deal with a very wide range of activities in which rural women participate, and show up, in no uncertain terms, the scarcity of well-paid employment for women in rural India.

Women and Work in Rural India is published in collaboration with Tulika Books, New Delhi. The book is designed by TNQ Books and Journals.

V. K. Ramachandran
General Editor, Agrarian Studies Series

Preface

In 2017 the Foundation for Agrarian Studies began a project to study women's work in rural production. Most of the chapters in this book came either from the research project or were presented at the conference with which the project concluded.

Judith Heyer provided ideas when the project was in its planning stages. Sandipan Baksi steered the project through its two years and led the effort to organise the project and conference.

The organisation of the international conference titled "Women's Work in Rural Economies" was coordinated by Shruti Nagbhushan with support from Sanjukta Chakraborty, Arindam Das, Divya Devadiga, Pushpita Dhar, Titas Dutta, Ritam Dutta, Pinki Ghosh, Deepak Johnson, Abhinav Kapoor, Veydaant Khanna, L. Vijay Kumar, Rakesh Kumar Mahato, Tapas Modak, and Subhajit Patra. Ranjini Basu, Aardra Surendran, S. Niyati, and Ashmita Sharma served as conference rapporteurs.

The Rosa Luxemberg Stiftung (RLS) supported the project from its inception. The conference received financial support from the Indian Council of Social Science Research, the M. S. Swaminathan Research Foundation, the Rosa Luxemburg Stiftung, and TNQ Books and Journals.

Chapter readers and commentators include Aparajita Bakshi, Gaurav Bansal, Amit Basole, Riya Cherian, S. Mahendra Dev, Indira Hirway, Praveen Jha, A. V. Jose, Aasha Kapur Mehta, Parvathi Menon, D. Narayana, Sony Pellissery, Smita Ramnarain, Smriti Rao, Smita Sirohi, Jeemol Unni, and Yoshifumi Usami. Mansi Goyal edited all the chapters.

The Editorial Board of the *Review of Agrarian Studies* allowed us to republish three articles from the journal. Mariam Ram and Samson Duraisamy of TNQ Books and Journals designed the cover. Indira Chandrasekhar and her team at Tulika Books prepared the manuscript for publication during the lockdown.

We are deeply grateful to all of them.

Bengaluru
5 June 2020

MADHURA SWAMINATHAN
SHRUTI NAGBHUSHAN
V. K. RAMACHANDRAN

Introduction

Madhura Swaminathan and V. K. Ramachandran

The empirical study of women's work and of women in the diverse labour processes that exist in rural India is meagre. This is unfortunate, since a necessary condition for India's development transition is the participation and leadership of its working women, most of whom live in the countryside. This neglect reflects the undervaluation of women's contribution to economic production by academics and policy makers, and conditions the public perception of women's work and agency.

This book seeks to broaden our understanding of the nature of women's work in different sectors of the rural economy. It does so by drawing on novel concepts and definitions and multiple sources of data, in particular, time-use surveys and gender-disaggregated data from village surveys.

At the Census of 2011, there were 275 million women aged 15 and above in rural India. By official count, 35 per cent – or 96 million rural women – were in the work force. By augmenting the official definition of workers to include women engaged in a range of activities relating to agricultural production, processing, collection of firewood and other products that have economic benefits, the number doubles. In other words, although over 190 million rural women engage in different forms of economic activities, we have serial data on some variables (sector of employment, occupation, days of employment and unemployment, and wage rates and wage earnings) for only half these women.

The quality of data in the work force, the number of days worked and unemployed, and wage rates and wage earnings are impaired by problems of infrequency and irregularity, and of survey method. Data users have limited access to disaggregated unit-level data in these fields. Problems of quality and ease of access are worse with respect to data on the female work force than with respect to data on the male work force.

There thus is a huge gap in our understanding of rural women's work. What are the economic activities in which this population is engaged? In what ways do rural women participate in agricultural and non-farm production? What are the relations into which they enter in the process of production? How do class and caste affect the world of women's work? How do the agrarian crises of work and livelihood specifically affect women? Our understanding of the agrarian economy and of our society will be determined by the answers to such questions.

In official data, undercounting of women in the work force begins with the definition of "work" itself. A major consequence of the failure to conceptualise, define, and measure women's work accurately is that official statistics show low and declining female work participation in economic activity in India. This statistical outcome (often termed a "puzzle") in official data has led to the generation of a huge literature on the "withdrawal" of women from the labour force, supposedly on account of higher incomes and better educational achievements. Evidence from the ground suggests otherwise. At the Vayalar conference, at which most of the papers in this volume were first presented, Brinda Karat presented the view of frontline women activists on this issue. She pointed out that the reality was not of women *opting out* of the work force but of *a crisis of regular employment*, leading to further invisibility of women's work and greater vulnerability among women who sought work outside their villages.

Data on women are lost in aggregates or in the specifics of data collection methods. An important example is work in tending animal resources and dairying. In general, most family labour on animal resources – and perhaps more than 90 per cent of labour time on animal resource maintenance – is expended by women. The labour of women at these tasks, however, is not necessarily expended in continuous stretches of labour but in short, discontinuous stretches. These tasks are often unrecorded.

Data that deal with women as separate participants in labour processes and in production relations in rural India do not exist if they are not collected by scholars. Such data are nevertheless essential if we are to understand the part played by women in the economy. Studies of classes and their socio-economic characteristics in the countryside deal typically with *households* and the classes to which *households* belong. When our attention is on households as a whole, we miss the specific features of the deployment of labour of women within them, features that call for specific attention and study.

To understand the lives and labour of hundreds of millions of rural women, we thus need to explore new concepts, new definitions, and, very importantly, new sources of data. In order to understand women's work in rural India better, the papers in this volume draw not only on official labour force surveys, but also on alternative sources of data, including government reports and records, large and micro-level time-use surveys, and village-level, household-level, and worker-level data from the archive of the Foundation for Agrarian Studies.[1]

---

[1] Several chapters in this volume draw on the village data archive of the Project on Agrarian Relations in India (PARI) of the Foundation for Agrarian Studies (see www.fas.org.in).

Some Major Themes

In sum, this book challenges the prevalent notion of "low" work participation of women in rural India and their growing "withdrawal" from the labour force. The evidence from academic research as well as from the experience of activists demonstrate clearly that women are facing a crisis of regular employment while actually working very long hours in production-related activities.

Secondly, the book examines the relations into which workers in poor peasant and manual worker households enter in the process of production – separately for men and women. A clear conclusion of the analysis is that women and men in the same household deploy their labour very differently, and that specific demands have to be raised for women workers in every socio-economic class.

Thirdly, the gender gap in agricultural wages remains large and has narrowed only a little over the last few decades. The gender gap is the widest in respect of new employment opportunities, that is, in the non-agricultural sector. This issue is of particular relevance to women from the Scheduled Castes and Tribes who constitute the bulk of the rural labour force.

Fourthly, more than a decade after the implementation of a policy of financial inclusion, rural women remain at a big disadvantage with respect to access to credit from banking institutions. Micro-credit, it turns out, is not a serious alternative, accounting for a minuscule proportion of total credit in the economy.

Conceptual and Methodological Issues

The first set of chapters in this volume deals with conceptual and methodological issues in measuring women's work in rural areas. The basic premise of the chapters here is that existing labour force surveys and concepts and definitions do not adequately capture the work undertaken by women in rural and informal settings. Indeed, several chapters take the underestimation of women workers in official statistics and the lack of recognition of women's work as the starting point of their analysis.

The 19th International Conference of Labour Statisticians, held in 2013, proposed major changes in the concept of work and in definitions of employment and unemployment. Indira Hirway explains the major changes proposed by the ILO recommendations, their implications for the work of women, and ways in which these recommendations can be implemented in India.

Time-use surveys are an important tool in studying women's work because they include all activities undertaken in a certain time period, usually 24 hours, rather than covering only "economic" activities. As of now, data are available for only one pilot time-use survey, completed 20 years ago. Madhura Swaminathan uses data from village-level time-use surveys on time spent by women in different activities during the reference week (24-hour data for seven days consecutively) to identify workers. There are clear patterns of seasonality in the hours spent in economic activity (that is, activity within the production boundary or System of National Accounts). A finding of major significance is that, during the peak or harvest season, almost all rural women fell within the definition of "worker."

In order better to evaluate women's work with data from existing labour force surveys conducted by the National Sample Survey Organisation (NSSO), Yoshifumi Usami defines and estimates an "augmented work participation rate." He does so by adding women's engagement in specified activities, such as activity connected with tending household poultry and livestock, to the standard definition of workers based on usual principal and subsidiary activity status. Not surprisingly, he finds distinctly higher rates of work participation with the augmented definition. He uses panel data from three villages of West Bengal for 2010 and 2015 as a way of ground-truthing his observations on levels and trends in women's work participation.

The basic unit of investigation in studies of agrarian classes in India has been the household. The database generated by the Project on Agrarian Relations in India (PARI) permits us to examine production relations as they affect men and women in households separately. The chapter by V. K. Ramachandran in this volume is on poor peasant and manual worker households in 16 villages in different parts of India. It finds significant differences in the deployment of male and female labour time in households, and, further, that processes of proletarianisation among men and women have distinct features. These findings, in turn, have important implications for theory and practice.

SECTORAL STUDIES

The chapters in the second section explore women's work in different sectors of the rural economy, using official statistics and primary village-level studies. The chapter by Jayan Jose Thomas, which uses data from the National Sample Surveys, deals with national and State-level inter-sectoral shifts in employment. Thomas argues that one of the reasons for low and falling women's employment is that non-agricultural employment opportunities were not available to women as demand for labour in agriculture declined.

Tea plantations in eastern India have historically employed men and women in family units. Jeta Sankrityayana examines changes in the Assam–Dooars tea plantation economy over a long time period, and analyses the effects of a structural shift from large tea plantations to small-holder tea production units on women workers. He argues that women workers have been made "invisible" as they shifted from wage work on plantations to family labour on small tea gardens.

Although women have been the backbone of the rice economy of Asia, in recent times, there has been surprisingly little scholarship on women's changing roles in rice production. Drawing on detailed evidence from seven villages surveyed by PARI, S. Niyati examines women's work in specific field operations in rice cultivation. Her main findings are of relatively low use of female labour in villages with high rice productivity on account of mechanisation and displacement of female labour. While many scholars have noted the spread of piece-rate contracts in agricultural field operations, Niyati discusses the ways in which this change affects the gender division of labour.

When a household owns livestock, women invariably spend two or more hours each day on animal care. Using an augmented work participation approach, R. Vijayamba estimates that in 2012, nearly 50 million women (of a total of 275 million adult rural women) were involved in livestock-rearing in different degrees, making this one of the most significant occupations today for rural women.

Class, Caste, and Scheduled Tribes

Women's occupations are marked by different types of sectional social distinctions. The three chapters in the third section focus on women from the Scheduled Castes, the Scheduled Tribes, and manual worker households, and build a picture of work and employment opportunities among oppressed sections of the rural population.

Khalid Khan and Sukhadeo Thorat use data from the Periodic Labour Force Survey (PLFS), 2017–18, to demonstrate inequalities across social groups in respect of employment by industry and occupation. Although the employment rate is high among Scheduled Caste women, they are disproportionately employed in occupations with the lowest skill levels,[2] that is, they must work in unskilled and poorly paid jobs to secure their day-to-day survival.

Janiso Athary examines all-India and State-level trends in employment among Scheduled Tribe women from 1983 to 2017–18. Although there has

---

[2] In the National Classification of Occupations 2004, the lowest skill level refers to performance of simple and routine physical or manual tasks, and is associated with minimal educational requirements.

been a clear decline in the work participation rate among women over this 35-year period (according to data from standard labour force surveys), the absolute level of employment among Scheduled Tribe women remains higher than among any other social group. More than 90 per cent of Scheduled Tribe women were employed in agriculture (either as self-employed or casual workers), reflecting the absence of opportunities for occupational diversification.

The final chapter in this section, by Shruti Nagbhushan, looks at features of employment among women in manual worker households, that is, households dependent primarily on incomes from wage labour. Her study is based on data for 21 villages from the PARI archive, a data-set that provides for a socio-economic classification of households. One of the striking findings of her study is that, in manual worker households, there are often an equal number of men and women workers. That does not, of course, imply availability of adequate and suitable employment for them.

STATE-DRIVEN EMPLOYMENT

There is a broad consensus, based on official sources of data as well as village surveys, that agriculture is the main employer of women in India at present, and that low levels of employment among rural women reflect, in large part, the lack of suitable non-agricultural jobs. In the last few decades, the two main sources of new employment for women in rural areas have been engagement as "scheme workers" (that is, workers who implement government schemes at the ground level) and public works employment generated by the National Rural Employment Guarantee Scheme (NREGS).

In the fourth section, K. Hemalata documents the nature of work contracts among a range of scheme workers in India. There are about 8 million scheme workers in India; their official work status is that of "volunteers," not workers; and their remuneration is considered an honorarium, not a wage. This chapter, by an author who has years of trade union experience, provides a detailed and first-hand account of the dismal conditions of work that they must endure.

Smita Ramnarain and Smriti Rao contribute to the existing literature on the National Rural Employment Guarantee Act (NREGA) by examining the conditions that led to large-scale participation, much above the required 33 per cent quota, of women in the programme. While it is known that the NREGA came about in response to widespread agrarian distress and unemployment, the class and gender factors affecting participation in it have not been studied in detail. This chapter explores factors such as women's reproductive burden and male–female differences in employment within households, and proposes areas for further research.

Wage Rates and Earnings, Historical and Contemporary

The chapters in the fifth section of the book focus on wage rates and earnings of women in rural India.

Madhavi Jha provides an account of women's labour in nineteenth-century Bihar: work on the fields, in grain processing after harvest, and in fuel collection and preparation. For each of these activities she identifies the remuneration, and argues that women's paid work was a significant and often critical component of the earnings of a labouring household.

Arindam Das analyses trends in wage rates for different crop operations as well as for unskilled non-agricultural labour for a two-decade period, from 1998–99 to 2018–19, drawing on data from *Wage Rates in Rural India*. His study shows that, after a long period of stagnation, real wage rates grew substantially from 2006–07 to 2015. Over the last few years, however, the rate of growth of real wages slowed down, and even declined in some States. The wage gap itself remained wide (although it narrowed somewhat during the period of growth in wage rates), and was the highest for non-agricultural jobs. This is a matter of some policy importance, since the non-agricultural sector (where wage rates are higher than in agriculture) is where future employment opportunities are expected.

In an exploratory companion piece, Arindam Das uses village-level data from 16 PARI villages to examine wage rates for women and the gender gap in wage rates at a more disaggregated level – for example, at the level of individual crops, crop combinations, and crop operations. He suggests that the size of the female agricultural labour force or labour supply at the village level plays a role in determining the level of wages and the gender wage gap, a hypothesis that needs further testing.

Financial Inclusion

The lack of recognition of women's engagement in economic activity is reflected in the exclusion of women from credit advanced by formal financial institutions. In the last chapter of this volume, Pallavi Chavan reveals the huge gender gap, a decade after the introduction of a policy of financial inclusion, in access to credit from banks. Women's access to credit was much lower than their contribution to savings through bank deposits. Further, counting all loans received by women – from banks, microfinance institutions, and self-help groups – women's share in total credit from the banking system in India was a mere 8 per cent.

Ways Ahead

First, we need to count women workers better, with new concepts and definitions and multiple data sources in addition to standard labour force surveys. More specifically, data collection on employment and unemployment in India needs to take cognition of the new ILO proposals, in particular, the concept of potential labour force. Using existing labour force surveys, estimates of women workers were much higher with the augmented definition of work participation. Unfortunately, the new Periodic Labour Force Survey (PLFS) has dropped the collection of data on "specified activity," the component used to define augmented work participation. Time-use surveys suggest huge underemployment among rural women. A national time-use survey was conducted in 2019 – the results must be released soon, and such surveys should be conducted regularly.

Secondly, we need further study of women's labour in the current context of development of capitalist agriculture and associated changes in agrarian relations in different regions of the country. The Project on Agrarian Relations in India (PARI) has village-level data for more than 25 villages, a data-set that has information on socio-economic classes and gender-disaggregated data on forms of employment. Drawing on this archive, some features of women's work among peasant and worker households are explored in this volume. More such studies are needed to understand the effect of socio-economic hierarchies and caste–class interactions on women's work. Such research is also critical to address the problems of women of the Scheduled Castes and Scheduled Tribes.

Thirdly, this volume highlights sectors of the rural economy or occupations where millions of women work – in agricultural and allied sectors such as rice cultivation, animal-rearing, and tea gardens, as well as in non-agricultural occupations such as scheme work and public works under the National Rural Employment Guarantee Scheme (NREGS). Research must engage with the sector-specific characteristics and concerns of women workers, including those relating to working hours, wages and remuneration, and work contracts.

Put together, this volume speaks of a serious crisis of employment and livelihoods for rural women, one that can no longer remain unheeded or understudied.

I

Conceptual, Theoretical, and Methodological Issues in Understanding Women's Work

1

Work, Employment, and Labour Underutilisation
What the ILO Resolution Means for India

Indira Hirway

This chapter presents the ILO Resolution on Statistics on Work, Employment, and Labour Underutilisation (adopted by the Nineteenth International Conference of Labour Statisticians) and illustrates its importance with regard to women's work, particularly in the agriculture and allied sector as well as in subsistence agriculture and unpaid domestic services including unpaid care work.[1] It also discusses issues pertaining to data for implementing the resolution.

This groundbreaking resolution was passed in 2013 by the Nineteenth International Conference on Labour Statistics (ICLS) of the International Labour Organization (ILO) mainly because: (1) there was a need to broaden the concept of "work" to include all "economic activities," i.e. all forms of work; (2) the definition of employment was viewed as "too broad"; and (3) the concept of unemployment did not provide adequate information on characteristics of unemployment.

In previous standards, the term "work" referred only to those activities included in the production boundary and counted in national accounts. This is a narrow definition as it excludes other important categories such as unpaid domestic services, care, and voluntary work.[2] At the same time, the concept of "employment" was too broad, as it included not only work performed for pay or profit, but also some non-market work (but not all non-market work)

---

[1] This chapter is based on ILO (2013).

[2] According to the United Nations' System of National Accounts (UNSNA), there are SNA and non-SNA economic activities; the distinction made between the two is an arbitrary decision (UN 2008).

performed without any direct pay or profit. Again, the term "unemployment" did not adequately capture the characteristics of unemployment, such as the duration for which one is underemployed, employed or seeking employment. It was decided therefore to develop a new resolution on work, employment, and labour underutilisation, in order to facilitate the integration of labour statistics with other domains and to respond to emerging social and economic information needs (labour market dynamics, job creation, household livelihoods, well-being beyond GDP indicators).

This ILO resolution aims

> to set new standards for work statistics to guide countries in updating and integrating their existing statistical programmes in the field. It defines statistical concept of work for reference purposes and provides operational concepts, definitions and guidelines for forms of work, labour force status and measures of labour underutilisation. (ILO 2013)

A New Definition and New Forms of Work

"Work" is defined under this resolution as "any activity performed by persons of any sex and age to produce goods or to provide services for use by others or for own use" (*ibid.*). This definition is consistent with the concept of general production boundary under the System of National Accounts (SNA), and excludes those activities that do not satisfy the third person criterion (non-delegable activities) and activities that do not produce goods or services, such as begging and theft. The resolution distinguishes five forms of work – own-use production work, employment work, unpaid trainee work, volunteer work, and other work activities. An important achievement for women is the category of own-use production, which recognises subsistence work and unpaid domestic services – both largely performed by women, especially in a country like India. Formal recognition of women's unpaid services as "work" has been a long-standing demand of women's movements. This makes it mandatory for governments to collect data for policy-making.

Figure 1.1 shows how the new conceptual framework is compatible with the 2008 SNA. Own-use production of goods, employment, unpaid trainee work, select volunteer work, and other work activities form the basis for the preparation of national production accounts within the 2008 SNA production boundary. Own-use provision of services and the remaining voluntary work fall within the general production boundary but outside the production boundary.

The different categories of work are described below.

Figure 1.1 *Forms of work and the System of National Accounts (SNA), 2008*

Intended destination of production	*for own final use*		*for use by others*					
Forms of work	**Own-use production work**		**Employment (work for pay or profit)**	**Unpaid trainee work**	**Other work activities**	**Volunteer work**		
	of services	*of goods*				in market and non-market units	in households producing	
							goods	services
Relation to 2008 SNA	*Activities within the SNA production boundary*							
	Activities inside the SNA General production boundary							

Source: ILO (2013).

Employment

Persons in employment are defined as "all those of working age who, during a short reference period (generally a week or seven days), were engaged in any activity to produce goods or provide services for pay or profit." They comprise employed persons "at work," i.e. who worked in a job for at least one hour during the reference period, and employed persons "not at work" due to temporary absence or to particular time arrangements (such as shift work, flexitime, and compensatory leave for overtime). "For pay or profit" refers to work done as part of a transaction in exchange for remuneration payable in the form of wages or salaries for time worked or work done, or in the form of profits derived from the goods and services produced through market transactions, specified in the most recent international statistical standards concerning employment-related income.

Employed persons on "temporary absence" during the short reference period refers to those who, having already worked in their present job, were "not at work" for a short duration but maintained job attachment during their absence.[3] Employed persons also include workers on paid programmes for

---

[3] In such cases "job attachment" is established on the basis of reasons for absence, which include: (1) those for which the continued remuneration is received; (2) those that are usually of short duration and where "job attachment" is maintained; and (3) those where the "job attachment" requires further assessment – for example, in cases of parental leave, educational leave, care for others, other personal absences, strikes or lockouts, and reduction in economic activity.

training or skills; apprentices, interns or trainees who work for pay in cash or in kind; persons who work for pay or profit through employment promotion programmes; persons who work in their own economic units to produce goods intended mainly for sale or barter; and persons with seasonal jobs during the off season if they continue to perform some tasks and duties of the job.

Women's presence is limited in "employment" because a significant number of them are subsistence workers and/or unpaid domestic and care workers. This exclusion reflects clearly the inferior status of women in the labour market.

Own-Use Production Work

Own-use production work refers to work that produces goods and provides services for workers' own household use. These workers are defined as "all those of working age who, during a short reference period, performed any activity to produce goods or provide services for own final use." An activity here is recognised as own production work if at least one hour is spent on it during the reference period.

While own-use production work for goods is included within the 2008 production boundary (i.e. in national accounts), services is not. Production of goods, most of which is performed by women, covers producing and/or processing for storage of agricultural, fishing, hunting and gathering products; collecting and/or processing for storage of mining and forestry products, including firewood and other fuels; fetching water from natural and other sources; manufacturing household goods (such as furniture, textiles, clothing, footwear, and pottery).

Own-use production of services which is outside the 2008 SNA production boundary but inside the general production boundary covers unpaid household upkeep and unpaid care that is mainly performed by women.[4] Household upkeep includes: (1) household accounting and management, shopping for own household, and providing transportation services to own household;

---

[4] The UNSNA document argues that unpaid services are excluded from the production boundary because (1) these non-monetary flows have little relevance for the macroeconomy; (2) inclusion of unpaid work will swamp national accounts; and (3) inclusion will imply the condition of full employment in the economy, which does not make much sense (UN *et al.* 2008). These arguments do not appear to be valid for several reasons. First, non-SNA or non-monetary flows have strong linkages with market flows — in fact, as will be discussed, macroeconomic forces have a significant influence on the size and characteristics of non-SNA activities. Secondly, unpaid work is significant and therefore cannot be excluded from the total economy, irrespective of the fact that it swamps or does not swamp national accounts. Thirdly, inclusion of unpaid work requires modified concepts (e.g., work force, labour force) and new analytical tools, and not the *exclusion of unpaid work* from the production boundary.

(2) preparing and/or serving meals, household waste disposal, and recycling; (3) cleaning, decorating, maintenance, and gardening; and (4) child care and instruction as well as transporting and caring for elderly, dependent or other household members, and domestic animals or pets. Household unpaid care includes care of children, the elderly, sick, and disabled of the household. Women in India are predominantly engaged in these activities, as Madhura Swaminathan discusses in this volume (chapter 2).

This is for the first time that the ILO has officially recognised unpaid domestic services as "work." Also, subsistence work that involves the production of goods for self-consumption is an important component of own-household production of goods. It includes goods related to agriculture, fishing, hunting or gathering that contribute to the livelihood of the household or family. However, it excludes work performed for recreational or leisure purposes (for example, fishing as a hobby). For operational purposes, it is important to assess the subsistence nature of the activity in which workers are not hired for pay or profit.

Unpaid Trainee Work

Unpaid trainee workers produce goods and services for others without pay to acquire workplace experience or skills. Persons in unpaid trainee work are defined as "all those of working age who, during a short reference period, performed any unpaid activity to produce goods or provide services for others, in order to acquire workplace experience or skills in a trade or profession." An activity here is recognised as unpaid trainee work if at least one hour is spent on it during the reference period. These workers nevertheless may receive some form of support, such as education stipends or grants, or occasional in-cash or in-kind support (e.g., a meal).

Unpaid trainee workers includes (1) persons in traineeships, apprenticeships, internships or other types of programmes wherein their engagement in the production process of the economic unit is unpaid; and persons in (2) unpaid skills training or retraining schemes within employment promotion programmes who are engaged in the production process of the economic unit. Unpaid workers learning skills in traditional trades and industries under household businesses may also be treated as unpaid trainees.

Voluntary Work

Voluntary work is performed for producing goods and services without pay or profit. Persons in volunteer work are defined as "all those of working age who, during a short reference period, performed any unpaid, non-compulsory activity to produce goods or provide services for others." An activity is recognised as voluntary if at least one hour is spent on it in the short reference period. Volunteer workers may receive a small form of support or stipend in cash, below one-third of the local market wages, for out-of-pocket expenses or to cover living expenses incurred for the activity, or in kind (e.g. meals, transportation, symbolic gifts).

"Unpaid" is interpreted as the absence of remuneration in cash or in kind for work done or hours worked. Production "for others" refers to work performed (1) through or for organisations comprising market and non-market units (i.e. organisation-based volunteering), including through or for self-help, mutual aid or community-based groups of which the volunteer is a member; and (2) for households other than the household of the volunteer worker or those of related family members (i.e. direct volunteering).

Organisation-based voluntary work and the production of goods for household-based voluntary work are included in the production boundary, and are thus counted in national income accounts, while production of services for household-based voluntary work is excluded from the production boundary. Time-use surveys have shown few people spending time on voluntary services in developing countries as compared to those in developed countries. This, as observed by experts, is due to the fact that help extended to neighbours and friends in developing countries is usually not reported as voluntary services.

The instance of "scheme workers" given by K. Hemalata (see chapter 12 in this volume) exemplifies the necessity of this category of work, particularly for women. Scheme workers such as *anganwadi* helpers often perform voluntary care services as they are not recognised as formal employees.

New Labour Force Status Classification

Another important contribution of the ILO resolution is a new labour force status classification that refers to the "working age population." In principle, the national system of work statistics should cover activities of the population in all age groups. To serve different policy concerns, however, separate statistics are needed for the working age population and for others (children) in productive activities. To determine the working age population figure, the lower age limit should match that established either in national laws/regulations or the age after compulsory schooling. There is no need to set an upper age limit; this will permit comprehensive coverage of work activities of the adult population and allow the transition between employment and retirement to be examined.

The resolution presents labour force status for the working age population in mutually exclusive and exhaustive categories of work status. These categories are persons in employment, persons in unemployment and persons outside labour force, as will be discussed below.

Persons in Unemployment

This category is defined as "all those of working age who were not employed, carried out activities to seek employment during a specified recent period and were currently available to take up employment given a job opportunity." "Not in employment" is assessed with respect to the short reference period (e.g., one week) as a standard measure. To "seek employment" refers to being engaged in any activity, during a specified recent period of the past four weeks, having the purpose of finding a job, setting up a business or an agricultural undertaking which includes part-time jobs and informal, temporary, seasonal or casual employment. Availability is assessed during the reference period for "not in employment" plus the following two weeks.

Examples of such activities are: arranging for financial resources; applying for permits or licenses; looking for land, premises, machinery, supplies or farming inputs; seeking the assistance of friends, relatives or other types of intermediaries; applying to employers directly or inquiring at worksites, farms, factory gates, markets or other assembly places. Included in "unemployment" are:

- future starters defined as persons "not in employment" and "currently available" who did not "seek employment" because they had made arrangements already to start a job within a short subsequent period (generally not greater that three months);
- participants in skills training or retraining schemes within employment promotion programmes who are "not in employment," not "currently available," and did not "seek employment" because they already had a job offer; and
- persons not in employment who carried out activities to migrate abroad in order to work for pay or profit but were still waiting for the opportunity to leave.

For a structural analysis of unemployment, it may be useful to collect information on the duration of the search for employment, measured from when unemployed persons began carrying out activities to "seek employment" or from the end of their last job, whichever is shorter. Also, it may be useful to separately identify, from among persons in unemployment, those in long-term unemployment, that is, those searching for employment for twelve months or more including the reference period. To monitor policies related to provision of social benefits, a shorter duration limit may be used (i.e. six months or more).

Persons Outside the Labour Force

Persons outside the labour force are "those neither of working age population who are employed nor in unemployment in the short reference period." They also include a specific group identified as potential labour force, i.e. persons outside the labour force seeking employment but not "currently available" (or unavailable job seekers), and those not seeking employment but wanting employment and currently available (or available potential job seekers).

The resolution precisely defines the term "potential labour force" and describes its scope in detail. Potential labour force is defined as "all persons of working age who, during the short reference period, were neither in employment nor in unemployment." It also includes both those seeking employment who are not currently available for work but would become available within a short subsequent period established in light of national circumstances (or unavailable job seekers), and those not seeking employment but wanting employment and "currently available" (or available potential job seekers). The latter includes persons identified as discouraged job seekers, i.e. those who failed in getting work due to market-related reasons (such as past failure to find a suitable job, lack of experience, skills matching, lack of jobs in the area).

A separate group expressing interest in employment not included within the potential labour force but relevant for social and gender analysis in specific contexts is that of willing non-job seekers, defined as those "not in employment" who wanted employment but did not "seek employment" and were not currently available. In order to identify the two categories of potential labour force as well as willing non-job seekers, questions on the activities undertaken to "seek employment" and current availability should be asked of all persons "not in employment" in the short reference period. Questions to determine whether persons wanted employment should only be asked to those who did not carry out activities to "seek employment." The term "extended labour force" can be defined by the sum of the labour force and the potential labour force.

It also needs to be noted that the sum of persons in the first two categories constitute the labour force and the rest are outside of it. In this category, priority is to be given to employment over the other two categories and to unemployment over the "outside labour force."

This new labour force status classification is important for women in several ways. To start with, there are likely to be many women who are willing to work but who do not look for employment because no work is available for them in the labour market. Again, more women than men look for part-time, informal, temporary or seasonal jobs, or casual employment. Availability is assessed during the reference period for "not in employment," plus the following two weeks.

Also, the term "potential labour force" is likely to be more relevant to women than to men. That is, both categories of potential labour force – (1) persons outside the labour force and seeking employment but not "currently available" and (2) available potential job seekers – are more applicable to women than to men. This is because women, particularly rural women, frequently have constraints such as mobility given their reproductive responsibilities, which prevent them from entering the labour market in nearby towns, or they are discouraged due to the unavailability of jobs for them in and around their village of residence.

LABOUR UNDERUTILISATION

For the first time in the ILO classification, the resolution has introduced a new concept of labour underutilisation which refers to "mismatches between labour supply and demand, which translate into an unmet need for employment among the population." Measures of labour underutilisation include: (1) time-related underemployment, when the working time of persons in employment is insufficient in relation to alternative employment situations in which they are willing and available to engage; (2) unemployment, reflecting an active job search by persons not in employment who are available for this form of work; and (3) the potential labour force, i.e. persons not in employment but who are willing to work under specific conditions. Once again, this concept is very relevant to women workers, of whom a significant number do not receive full-time employment.

For a more comprehensive assessment of labour underutilisation, other indicators can be used. These include: (1) work in the informal economy, especially informal sector employment and informal employment, according to the relevant international statistical standards; (2) activities to "seek employment" by persons in employment, indicating pressure on the labour market; (3) inadequate employment situations due to skills, income or excessive working time, according to the relevant international statistical standards; (4) slack work (reduction in economic activity during lean season) among the self-employed; and (5) gross labour market flows between labour force statuses and within employment.

Persons in time-related underemployment are defined as "all persons in employment who, during a short reference period, wanted to work additional hours, whose working time in all jobs was less than a specified hours threshold, and who were available to work additional hours given an opportunity for more work." The "working time" concept is hours actually or usually worked, dependent on the measurement objective (short- or long-term situations) and in accordance with the international statistical standards on the topic. Established for specific worker groups, the "hours threshold" is based on: (1) the boundary between full- and part-time employment, (2) the median or mode values of the hours usually worked of all persons in employment, (3) the working-time norms according to relevant legislation or national practice. Instead of using the categories part-time workers and full-time workers, the ILO now recognises all workers who work for less than the "hours threshold." Depending on the working time concept applied and among persons both in the time concept applied and in time-related underemployment (i.e. those wanting and "available" to work "additional hours"), it is possible to identify the following groups:

- persons whose hours usually and actually worked were below the "hours threshold";
- persons whose hours usually worked were below the "hours threshold" but whose hours actually worked were above the threshold; and
- persons "not at work" or whose hours actually worked were below the "hours threshold" due to economic reasons (e.g., a reduction in economic activity including temporary lay-off, slack work or the effect of the low season).

Requirements for Implementing the New Standards

There are several implications of these new standards under the ILO resolution. First, all forms of work must be investigated so as (1) to identify all forms of work for all persons of working age, and (2) to measure working hours in all forms.

The resolution has contributed significantly to recognising women's work, which was previously invisible in most data and policies. Women's unpaid domestic services now receive visibility in national statistical systems as well as in national policy-making. This is likely to give a big push to both the movement for gender equality and women's empowerment, and research on the role of women's work in the larger economy.

Defining Data

According to the resolution, each country should aim to develop in its national data system, labour statistics keeping in mind its various uses: (1) comprehensive measurement of participation in all forms of work in order to estimate volume of work or labour input for national production accounts, including "satellite accounts"; (2) comprehensive measurement of the contribution of all forms of work to economic development, including household livelihoods and individual and societal well-being; (3) assessing participation in different forms of work among population groups such as women and men, young people, children, migrants, and other groups of particular policy concern; and (4) monitoring labour markets and labour underutilisation including unemployment for economic and social policies and programmes related to employment generation, skill development, income generation, and decent work.

A national data collection strategy should be established that allows different sets of relevant statistics to be reported at different frequencies. First, sub-annual or short-term surveys should collect data on main aggregates of employment, the labour force, labour underutilisation including unemployment, and subsistence producers, in order to monitor short-term trends and seasonal variations (i.e. high and low season, quarterly). These surveys would throw light on seasonal and other temporal variations in work activity patterns. Secondly, an annual survey should collect detailed statistics of the labour force and of labour underutilisation including unemployment. This would permit a structural analysis of labour markets and statistics of working time in relation to the total number of jobs/work activities contributing to production within the SNA production boundary in order to compile national accounts. Finally, on a less frequent basis, other surveys can generate benchmarking and comprehensive macro socio-economic estimates, and include statistics on participation and time spent on own-use production work, unpaid trainee work, and volunteer work. These surveys would cover particular topics such as labour migration, child labour, transition in and out of employment, youth, gender issues in work, household characteristics, work in rural areas, and the relationship between employment and income.

The Labour Force Survey

As stated in the ILO resolution, labour force surveys will be the main source of data for its implementation; however, the standard survey requires significant modification. Though we are not focusing on the changes needed in labour force surveys in this chapter, it would be pertinent to discuss the required characteristics of labour force surveys if time-use surveys are to complement them, for the purpose of implementing the resolution. A national labour force survey will have to provide data on employment, unemployment, labour underutilisation (e.g., whether the person wants to take additional work), and potential labour force (by asking probing questions). It must also collect data on all forms of work, i.e. own-use production of goods, own-use production of services, voluntary work within SNA, voluntary work outside the production boundary and unpaid trainee work, and short- and long-term employment. This survey is expected to use short supplementary modules for own-use production work, unpaid trainee work, and voluntary work if required for a sub-sample of the respondents, keeping in mind respondent burdens as well as survey quality including sampling and non-sampling errors. In addition, specialised household surveys will be needed on specific subjects like education and training, volunteering, child labour, migration, and time use. Of these, time-use surveys will be of particular importance. Other sources of data required for implementing the resolution will be: (1) administrative records, (2) population and economic censuses, and (3) establishment and mixed surveys.

Time-use surveys provide comprehensive and detailed information on how individuals spend their time on different activities, on a daily or weekly basis. These activities include both those that fall within the production boundary of the SNA and outside the production boundary but within the general production boundary, as well as personal activities that are non-delegable. Time-use statistics are thus quantitative summaries of time allocation by people in their different activities. These surveys thus can help implement parts of the resolution in multiple ways. Time-use statistics are likely to improve the existing estimates and provide fresh estimates of the various categories of work.

There are several advantages of time-use data in producing correct estimates of the different categories of work as defined by the ILO. For example, time-use data can help estimate scattered, intermittent, seasonal, temporary or unstable work performed by workers in the economy. Because labour force surveys are not equipped to collect information on multiple jobs, jobs of a scattered nature or those with flexible work-time arrangements, time-use surveys (TUS) can be used to fill these lacunae. TUS collect data on intensity of employment (in hours per day) and multiple jobs performed by people (particularly important in the case of women), and provide insight into the scattered nature of their jobs or flexible work-time arrangements. Time-use surveys are equipped to cover all employment activities as well as characteristics of employment (see Madhura Swaminathan, chapter 2 in this volume). Our study in India has shown that time-use surveys are able to overcome these problems and provide improved estimates as well as additional information on the work force/labour force in an economy (Hirway and Jose 2011). Again, time-use surveys can collect data on own-use production of goods, i.e. subsistence production, as no labour force survey has ever collected this information on this category of work though some have attempted to collect information on a few subsistence activities (in addition to agricultural production). As the OECD (Organisation for Economic Cooperation and Development) has suggested, the time-use survey is best suited to collect information on subsistence work.[5] As seen in the case of other work, time-use statistics provide information on the scattered nature of and time spent on this work. Similarly, time-use surveys collect data on own-use production of services as, once again, labour force surveys are not equipped (nor do they aim) to collect information on production of own-use services, which is supposedly outside their purview. Finally, time-use surveys are also equipped to collect data on unpaid trainee work and voluntary services.

In the case of labour underutilisation, time-use data are essential to estimate time-related underemployment, unemployment, and potential labour force. In short, though (modified) labour force surveys are the main source of data needed to implement the resolution, time-use surveys provide essential and complementary data.

Implementation of the ILO Resolution in India

Though the resolution was passed in 2013, not many countries have been able to implement it to date owing to the fact that it takes time for countries to understand the intricacies of the new concepts and their measurement. As a member of the ILO, India intends to implement this new resolution; however, not much progress has been achieved so far. For instance, India's labour force survey has not yet adopted the new concepts and methods.

As mentioned earlier, this resolution is crucial for obtaining estimates of women's paid and unpaid work in India, particularly of their work in agriculture and in the rural economy. These data can be very useful in improving the conditions of women workers in agriculture and allied sectors. Data on men's and women's unpaid work help in estimating and understanding gender inequalities prevailing in the economy, which can be a useful input in designing interventions to improve agriculture in general as well as women's productivity in agriculture.

An all-India time-use survey began in December 2018. However, the

---

[5] This is firstly because only time-use surveys are able to capture this work, and secondly because the time spent on these activities reflects the real effort that has gone into performing these.

design of this time-use survey is not suited to the implementation of the ILO resolution as it does not follow the appropriate sampling, activity classification or data collection methods. One reason for this lies in the fact that the ILO or UNSD (United Nations Statistics Division) has not standardised the methodology of conducting time-use surveys. Despite this, many countries are attempting to implement the resolution empirically.

It seems that the Indian government is interested in implementing the resolution but is not yet ready to do so. Also, the time-use survey has not been designed according to the sustainable development goals (SDGs) to which the Indian government is committed. Overall, it appears that India is not yet ready to adopt the recent changes into its national database.

In closing, we reiterate the fact that the ILO Resolution on Statistics on Work, Employment, and Labour Underutilisation (adopted by the Nineteenth International Conference of Labour Statisticians) has broadened the concept of "work" such that women's paid and unpaid work are rendered visible, and narrowed the concept of "employment" to exclude unpaid work. These modifications can enable policy-makers to formulate development policies for women's employment as well as for addressing the highly unequal burden of total work upon women.

BIBLIOGRAPHY

Budlender, Debbie (2007), "A Critical Review of Selected Time Use Surveys," Gender and Development Programme Paper no. 2, United Nations Research Institute for Social Development (UNRISD), Geneva, June.

Central Statistical Organisation (CSO) (2000), "Report of the Time Use Survey," Ministry of Statistics and Programme Implementation (MoSPI), Government of India, New Delhi.

Charmes, Jacques (2004) "Data Collection on the Informal Sector: A Review of Concepts and Methods Use since the Adoption of an International Definition towards a Better Comparability of Available Statistics," Delhi Group on Informal Sector Statistics, International Labour Organization (ILO), Bangkok, February.

Gershuny, Jonathan (2014), "Conducting Time Use Survey for Seven Consecutive Days," presentation made at the 36th Annual Conference of the International Association for Time Use Research (IATUR), Turku, Finland.

Gloriex, Ignace, Minnen, Joeri, van Tienoven, Theun Pieter, Deyaert, Jef, and Mészáros, Eszter (2014), "Labour Force Survey and Time: Towards a Better Measurement of Working Times," presentation made at the 37th Annual Conference of the International Association for Time Use Research (IATUR), Ankara, Turkey.

Hirway, Indira (2003), "Indian Experience in Time Use Surveys in Applications of Time Use Statistics," Central Statistical Organisation (CSO), Government of India, New Delhi.

Hirway, Indira and Charmes, Jacques (2006), "Estimating and Understanding Informal Employment through Time Use Studies," presentation made at the Delhi Group Meeting, New Delhi.

Hirway, Indira and Jose, Sunny (2011), "Understanding Women's Work Using Time-Use Statistics: The Case of India," *Feminist Economics*, vol. 17, no. 4, October, pp. 67–92.

International Labour Organization (ILO) (2013), "Resolution on Statistics on Work, Employment and Labour Underutilisation," Nineteenth International Council of Labour Statistics, ILO, Geneva.

Ironmonger, Duncan (2008), "Multiple Uses of Time Use Statistics in Developing Countries," in Indira Hirway (ed.), *Mainstreaming Time Use Survey in National Statistical Systems*, Government of India.

Jain, Devaki (1983), "Report of the Time Use Survey of Villages in India," Institute of Social Studies Trust, New Delhi.

Organisation for Economic Cooperation and Development (OECD) (2002), "Measuring the Non-Observed Economy," Paris, France, available at https://www.oecd.org/sdd/na/1963116.pdf, viewed on 7 August 2019.

Pakkonnen, Hannu (2012), "Time Use Survey with a Week Diary and Time Grid," presentation made at the 36th Annual Conference of the International Association for Time Use Research (IATUR), Turku, Finland.

Pandey, R.N. (2000), "Sampling Issues in Time Use Survey: Indian Experience," paper prepared for Expert Group Meeting on Time Use Survey, New York, 23–27 October.

United Nations (UN) (2009), *System of National Accounts 2008*, New York, available at https://unstats.un.org/unsd/nationalaccount/docs/SNA2008.pdf, viewed on 7 August 2019.

United Nations Statistics Division (UNSD) (1997), "Trial International Classification of Activities for Time-Use Statistics," New York.

United Nations Statistics Division (UNSD) (2016), "International Classification of Activities for Time-Use Statistics," New York.

APPENDIX

The composite measures of labour underutilisation as per ILO (2013) are of four categories:

LU1: Unemployed
LU2: Time-related underemployed + unemployed
LU3: Unemployed + potential labour force
LU4: Time-related underemployed + unemployed + potential labour force

As previously mentioned, potential labour force includes "seeking not available" + "available not seeking."

The composite measures of labour underutilisation can be translated into the following rates of labour underutilisation:

LU1
= Unemployment rate
$$= \frac{\text{Persons in unemployment} \times 100}{\text{Labour force}}$$

LU2
= Combined rate of time – related underemployment and unemployment
$$= \frac{(\text{Persons in time-related underemployment} + \text{persons in unemployment}) \times 100}{\text{Labour force}}$$

LU3
= Combined rate of unemployment and potential labour force
$$= \frac{(\text{Persons in unemployment} + \text{potential labour force}) \times 100}{\text{Extended labour force}}$$

LU4
= Composite measure of labour underutilisation
$$= \frac{(\text{Persons in time-related underemployment} + \text{persons unemployed} + \text{potential labour force}) \times 100}{\text{Extended labour force}}$$

2

Measuring Women's Work with Time-Use Data

An Illustration from Two Villages of Karnataka

Madhura Swaminathan

Drawing on repeated time-use surveys of 36 women in two villages of Karnataka, India in 2017–18, this chapter argues that not only is women's work participation in rural areas high, but also that women bear a heavy burden of work in terms of hours worked a week. The motivation for this paper comes from the fact that there are very few time-use studies of rural women's work patterns and work load in the contemporary period. The only time-use data available nationally in India are from a pilot survey conducted in 1998–99, more than 20 years ago.

Official statistics in India claim that the work participation rate among rural women (and urban women, for that matter) is not only low, but also declining. According to the Employment and Unemployment Survey of the NSSO (National Sample Survey Office), the work participation rate for women above the age of 15 in rural India was 48.5 per cent in 2004–05 and fell to 35 per cent in 2011–12. It fell to 30 per cent in 2015–16, according to the Labour Bureau (Usami 2018).[1] Further, according to the Periodic Labour Force Survey of 2017–18, work participation among rural women has fallen to 23.6 per cent. This picture of low work participation, I argue, is a gross misrepresentation on account of two factors. First, as is well known, standard labour force surveys fail to capture many women engaged in economic activity that is largely informal and often within the family farm or homestead. As noted by scholars, official surveys very likely underestimate women's participation in economic activity. Secondly, there are issues in the very definitions of "work" and "economic activity" as counted in the System of National Accounts (SNA). In 2013, the International Labour Organization (ILO) recommended broadening the concept of work and demarcating it

---

[1] This refers to usual principal and subsidiary status.

from employment, as discussed at length by Indira Hirway (chapter 1 in this volume). Time-use surveys, while not a replacement for standard labour force surveys, can address some of the problems raised above. Time-use surveys typically collect information on all activities undertaken during a short reference period, usually one day, and are thus able to capture activities that may be unpaid or within the homestead or undertaken for a short period. Given information on all activities, it is also possible to identify those falling within the SNA and extended SNA (care activities, for example) boundary.

The specific questions asked in this paper are: what can we learn from time-use data about women's participation in economic activity (or SNA activity), about seasonal variations in work participation, and about the total number of hours spent by women working in SNA and extended SNA activities? These questions are answered with time-use data for women in two villages in different seasons, using current weekly status and current daily status definitions of employment.

The paper argues that a daily status definition of employment brings out the reality of rural women, showing very high work participation during seasons when work is available and lower work participation when work is not available. The paper also brings to light problems that can arise when applying the concepts and definitions proposed by ILO (2013) in practice. Lastly, the data point to the enormous burden of work on rural women. The data used in this paper relate to a small number of women, but are reliable and can help identify issues for further research.

SURVEY METHOD

Several scholars have argued that time-use surveys are better than labour force surveys in being able to capture women's work in economies such as that of India, where a large part of the economy is in the informal sector comprising household-level enterprises. As Hirway and Jose (2011, p. 68) note, "informal employment therefore is sometimes scattered and intermittent, temporary or short term; and it is home-based, so it is frequently categorised with unpaid household work." A regular labour force survey may not capture such informal employment both because of (i) the conceptual problems in separating informal employment from household work and (ii) other factors such as investigator bias or respondent bias (*ibid.*).

By contrast, "a major advantage of time-use surveys is that they do not ask any direct question to respondents about whether they are 'workers' or are engaged in any 'economically productive activity.' Instead, information is collected on how respondents spend their time on different activities, including multiple and simultaneous activities" (Hirway and Jose 2011). A time-use survey can thus address both problems listed above.

In 1998–99, the NSSO conducted a pilot Time Use Survey (TUS) in six States. Combining the data for the six States, Hirway and Jose (2011) estimated the work participation rate for rural women with the current weekly status definition to be 58.2 per cent,[2] as compared to an estimate of 25.3 per cent from the Employment and Unemployment Survey of 1999–2000. In spite of the important and interesting insights into women's work that emerged from the TUS, there has been no further national survey, although a new large-scale time-use survey is currently underway.

CONCEPTS AND DEFINITIONS

Work and Economic Activity

A worker is a person engaged in economic activity for a certain time period. One of the critical issues, then, is setting the boundaries of economic activity. Typically, the boundary is set by the United Nations' System of National Accounts (UNSNA), and includes all activities whose contribution is counted in national income. The United Nations introduced the concept of extended SNA in 1968, which refers to activities that contribute to household reproduction such as household maintenance, child care, and elderly care. The Indian government has adopted the UN recommendations though there remain a few differences between the Indian SNA (ISNA) and the UNSNA (last modified in 2008).

To classify activities undertaken by women into either SNA or extended SNA in our survey, we used the activity classification used for the NSSO's pilot Time Use Survey, based on the National Classification of Occupations. SNA activities comprise primary production activities (Code I), secondary activities (Code II), and trade, business, and service activities (Code III). All activities under Code IV (household maintenance, management, and shopping for own household), Code V (care for children, the sick, elderly, and the disabled for own household), and Code VI (community service and help to other households) were included in the extended SNA. Learning (Code VII), social and cultural activities (Code VIII), and personal care (code IX) were termed non-SNA.

A different approach has been taken by the International Conference of Labour Statisticians (ICLS) in redefining the concept of work (ILO 2013). It has identified five mutually exclusive forms of work:

[2] They used an arbitrary cut-off of eight hours during the reference week rather than one hour to identify workers.

- employment work comprising work performed in exchange for pay or profit (this could be termed self-employment and wage-employment);
- own-use production work comprising production of goods and services for own final use;
- unpaid trainee work;
- volunteer work; and
- other work activities.

With this approach, the concept of employment has been restricted to the production of goods and services for pay or profit (that is, the first category). At the same time, the concept of work has been broadened – for example, by including unpaid trainee and volunteer work in addition to own-use production in the definition of work.

These new categories of work are mapped with the SNA production boundary and extended SNA (or general) production boundary (as shown in chapter 1 by Hirway, in this volume). We propose to map activities reported in our survey using this five-fold format as well.

Definition of Employment

There are many definitions of work and employment used in India, depending on the reference period (a year, a week, etc.).[3] Estimates of work participation from time-use surveys are typically based on the reference week.

Our first definition of worker, drawing on NSSO reports as well as ILO (2013), based on "current weekly status," is as follows:

(i) A worker is any person who has engaged in economic activity for at least one hour a day on any one day of the previous week.

The second definition is based on "major time spent" during the reference week or the current daily status approach, which captures the activity status on each day of the reference week.[4] For each day during the reference week, we can define a half-day (from one to four hours) and full day (four or more hours) of work. To ascertain major time during the reference period, half-days and full-days during the reference week are aggregated, and a person is termed a worker

---

[3] Note that there is one difference between our data and that of the NSSO, namely that we have not asked about seeking work and therefore cannot identify the unemployed. So, strictly speaking, this is not comparable to the Employment and Unemployment Survey (EUS) definition.

[4] This is a flow rate and as given in Krishna (1984): "The daily status flow rate is evidently the most inclusive, covering open as well as partial unemployment. It is therefore the rate which is most relevant for policy-making."

if 3.5 or more days (major time) were spent on SNA activity.[5] The second definition of worker using the "current daily status" approach is as follows:

(ii) Any person who engaged in economic activity for the major part of the reference week, that is, for more than three days during the reference week.

Field Data

The data for this chapter come from a project to study women's work in rural production, initiated by the Foundation for Agrarian Studies (FAS) in 2017.[6] The project undertook time-use surveys in two villages of Karnataka. The two villages were selected purposively because they had been surveyed by FAS in 2009, and re-surveyed briefly in 2014 (Swaminathan and Das, eds. 2016). Both villages are easily accessible from Bangalore.

For each respondent, information was collected twice a day at 12-hour intervals, and covers all activities during a 24-hour reference period for seven consecutive days.[7] Further, seasonality was captured by two or three re-surveys during the year. The time-use survey method was used to collect data from 14 women in Siresandra village of Kolar district across two seasons, and from 22 women in Alabujanahalli village of Mandya district across three seasons in 2017–18. A household-level questionnaire was also canvassed so as to collect information on the economic conditions of the household to which each respondent belonged.

Siresandra village is 20 kilometres from Kolar town. The major caste group in this village was Vokkaliga, which was also the major landowning caste in the village. There were 79 households in the 2009 FAS survey, of which 37 per cent were Adi Karnataka (Scheduled Caste) and the remaining 63 per cent were Vokkaliga (classified as Other Backward Class or OBC). This village belongs to the semi-dry rainfed region of southeastern Karnataka. Sericulture and dairying were two important activities in the villages.

Based on the 2009 survey data, we chose women from different castes and socio-economic classes, and covered younger (18–35 years) as well as older (36–65 years) women (Tables 2.1 and 2.2).[8]

---

[5] In terms of hours a week, this would be at least seven hours a week (assuming the minimum of one hour a day on each day, or seven half-days of work).

[6] I was part of this project and fieldwork.

[7] To my knowledge, this is unique among time-use surveys, which usually have a 24-hour reference period for one day only.

[8] For details of the socio-economic classes, see Swaminathan and Das, eds. (2016).

Figure 2.1 *Map of Karnataka with agroclimatic zones and location of study villages*

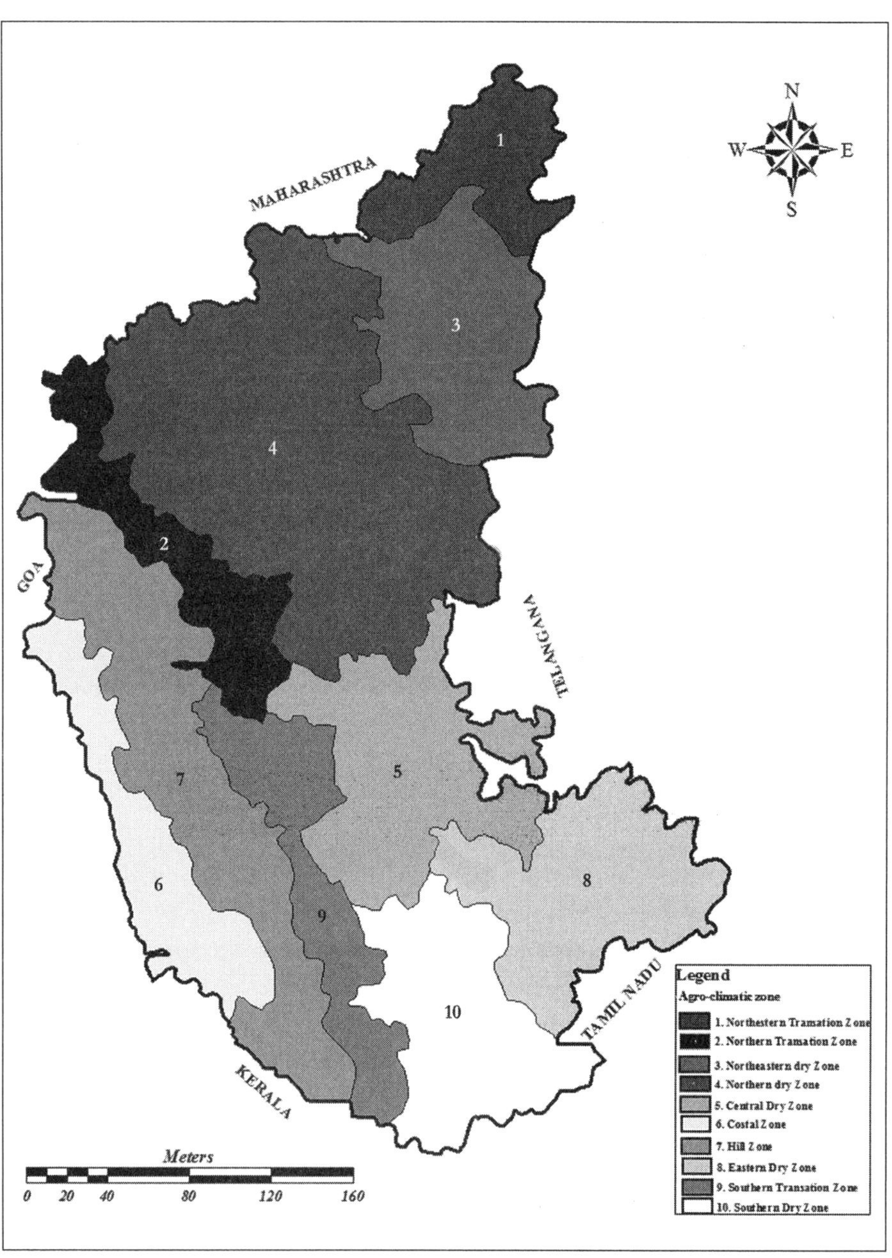

Source: University of Agricultural Sciences, Bangalore.

Table 2.1 *Sample size and survey dates, Siresandra village*

Visit	Season	Date	No. of households	No. of women
1	Lean	12–18 May 2017	10	14
2	Harvest	13–19 December 2017	10	12

Source: Survey data.

Table 2.2 *Socio-economic class of selected women, Siresandra village*

Category	Number of households	Number of women
Manual worker	3	3
Poor peasant	2	3
Middle peasant	2	2
Rich peasant	2	5
Salaried	1	1

Notes: The village comprised mainly peasant households, who were classified into three groups: rich, middle, and poor peasants. Moving from rich to poor peasant, the value of assets including means of production declines, and the share of family labour to total labour rises. Manual worker households rely on incomes from wage labour.
Source: Survey data.

We surveyed 14 women from 10 households during visit 1 (lean season) and 12 respondents during visit 2 (harvest season); two women had gone to their maternal homes for child delivery and were not available in the second round. In total, we have 182 daily observations for Siresandra. Of the 14 women, 12 belonged to the Vokkaliga caste and two to Scheduled Caste (Adi Karnataka).

The second village was Alabujanahalli, in Maddur taluk of Mandya district. The village is located at a distance of 15 kilometres from Maddur and Mandya. This is a multi-caste village. According to the 2009 survey data, there were 243 households in Alabujanahalli, of whom 14 per cent were Adi Karnataka (Scheduled Caste) and the remaining 63 per cent were mainly Vokkaliga. The village belongs to the Cauvery-irrigated region of south Karnataka. Major crops are sugarcane, rice, and finger millet, while the commercial crops being cultivated include banana, coconut, and papaya. Animal rearing (dairying) and sericulture were important occupations in the village apart from crop farming activities (for details, see Swaminathan and Das, eds. 2016).

In Alabujanahalli village, visit 1 was during the sowing season (13–19 September 2017), when a total of 22 women from 20 households were interviewed (Table 2.3). Visit 2 was during the harvest period, 4–10 January

2018, and the same 22 women were interviewed. Visit 3 of the survey was during the lean season, 18–24 May 2018, when only 20 women were interviewed as one woman had gone to her natal home for childbirth and another had left for a medical emergency. In total, we have 448 daily observations for the women from Alabujanahalli village. Of the 22 women, seven were from Scheduled Castes and the remaining were from Other Backward Classes (mainly Vokkaliga). The distribution of sample women across socio-economic classes is shown in Table 2.4.

In total, combining the two villages and seasons, we have observations on 90 women and 630 24-hour days. The time-use data are unique in capturing activities over 24 hours for seven days continuously. The collection and processing of data were done by a small and dedicated team, ensuring good quality of data.[9]

Table 2.3 *Sample size and survey dates, Alabujanahalli village*

Visit	Season	Date	No. of households	No. of women
1	Sowing	13–19 September 2017	20	22
2	Harvesting	4–10 January 2018	20	22
3	Lean	18–24 May 2018	18	20

Source: Survey data.

Table 2.4 *Socio-economic class of selected women, Alabujanahalli village*

Category	Number of households	Number of women
Rich capitalist farmer	2	2
Peasant 1	2	2
Peasant 2	3	4
Manual worker 1	4	5
Manual worker 2	4	4
Salaried and business	5	5

Notes: The socio-economic categories in this village included capitalist farmers, peasants, manual workers, and households with business and salary incomes. "Manual worker 1" also cultivated land whereas "manual worker 2" had no operational holdings. "Peasant 1" households were demarcated from "peasant 2" households by a higher level of means of production and lower use of family labour.
Source: Survey data.

---

[9] I am grateful to the entire fieldwork and data team at the Foundation for Agrarian Studies.

Results and Discussion

High Worker–Population Ratio

First, using the weekly status definition of a worker – that is, any person who has worked at least one hour during any day of the reference week in any activity within the production boundary – we observe extremely high worker–population ratios or WPRs among women in these two villages. By this definition, *all women in Siresandra and Alabujanahalli villages were workers.*

Using the above-mentioned definition (ii) of the current daily status approach, we first identified half-days and full-days during the reference week, as illustrated for Siresandra village in Appendix Table 2.1. Workers were then identified based on major time during the reference week. The results for Siresandra village are summarised in Table 2.5.

In the lean season in Siresandra village, 9 out of 14 women can be classified as workers.[10] In the harvest season, 11 out of 12 or 92 per cent of the women surveyed can be classified as workers. In short, during the harvest season, all but one woman was termed a worker. The exception was KA, who was a manual worker in the 2009 survey but is now engaged only in domestic tasks. After her husband took a job as an employee of the taluk panchayat, she decided not to engage in manual labour. Thus, by the second and more stringent definition, we observe a very high worker–population ratio during the harvest season. The WPR observed during the lean season (64 per cent) was similar to the WPR for the village reported in the Census of 2011 (63 per cent).

A similar analysis was done for Alabujanahalli village using the daily status definition (Table 2.6). In the first visit during the sowing season, 15 of the 22

Table 2.5 *Women workers by current daily status approach during reference week, Siresandra village, May/December 2017*

Season (visit)	No. of women workers	No. of women	Worker–population ratio
Lean (1)	9	14	64
Harvesting (2)	11	12	92
Combined	11	14	79

Note: The definition of workers for the combined season refers to those who spent their major time in economic activity during the two reference weeks put together.
Source: Survey data.

[10] This assumes that all seven days can be working days. If we take the major time spent criterion with six days only, the WPR increases to 71 per cent in the lean season.

Table 2.6 *Workers by current daily status approach during reference week, Alabujanahalli village, September 2017 and January/May 2018*

Visit (season)	No. of women workers	All women	Worker–population ratio
1 (Sowing)	15	22	68
2 (Harvesting)	18	22	82
3 (Lean)	14	20	70
Combined	15	22	68

Note: The definition of workers for the combined season refers to those who spent their major time in economic activity during the three reference weeks put together.
Source: Survey data.

women (68 per cent) were classified as workers. In the second visit during the harvest, 18 out of 22 women (82 per cent) were classified as workers; and in the third visit, during the lean season, 14 out of 20 women (70 per cent) were classified as workers.[11] Work participation was lower in the lean and sowing seasons than in the harvest season. Only four women in Alabujanahalli were classified as non-workers during the harvest season: one was a student, another was seeking employment, a third had full-time child-care duties on account of a handicapped child, and the fourth was from a rich peasant family who only undertook domestic tasks.

To summarise, using a definition of work based on daily status and the intensity of activity during the reference week, there was near-universal work participation in the peak or harvesting season. The second important observation with respect to identification of work and workers is the huge seasonal fluctuation in worker–population ratio. This suggests that work participation in the lean season may be low on account of the lack of suitable work/job opportunities. Thirdly, census data, based on one-year recall, appear to capture the worker–population ratio in the lean season and not the harvest season.

Reviewing the ILO Concept of Work and Employment

A feature of women's work in rural India that has been noted in the scholarly literature but which emerges clearly from a time-use survey is that most women participate in production activities as part of unpaid family labour or tasks in household-level production activities. When the goods produced from these activities are not marketed (such as rearing of goats and poultry for home consumption), women may not be counted as workers in the official statistics.

---

[11] According to the Census of 2011, the WPR in Alabujanahalli was 58 per cent.

Using our detailed time-use data, we can classify workers as per the new classification of activities proposed by ILO (2013) specifically into the following four categories (out of six):

- own-use production work
- employment for profit (self-employment)
- employment for pay (wage employment)
- volunteer work.

We did not find any unpaid trainee worker or person engaged in "other work" in the two villages.

Using this classification, the data for women workers in Siresandra village is shown in Table 2.7 (we have taken the average over both seasons). First, all the women spent some hours a week, ranging from 5 to 31 hours, on own-use production of goods. Secondly, only three women were found to be in wage employment (all came from households of manual workers). Most of the women from peasant households were in self-employment (their own farm, sericulture or dairying). Two women volunteered time for their self-help group.

The situation was more complex in Alabujanahalli (Table 2.8). More than ten women were reported as wage or salary earners. Among them, five women

Table 2.7 *Average time spent on different production activities by women workers, Siresandra village, May/December 2017* in hours per week

Name	Own-use production Goods	Employment		Volunteer Outside the house	SNA production boundary
		Self	Wage		
NG	7	14	0	0	21
PU	7	14	0	2	23
AM	14	2	7	0	23
AG	11	13	0	0	24
SN	5	22	0	0	26
AR	27	11	0	0	38
VT	13	5	24	0	43
NA	8	13	22	0	43
PA	4	38	0	5	47
SM	31	25	0	0	57
GW	8	57	0	0	65

Note: The data are for the 11 women identified as workers according to the current daily status definition (all names have been initialised to ensure anonymity).
Source: Survey data.

Table 2.8 *Average time spent on different production activities by women workers, Alabujana-halli village, September 2017 and January/May 2018* in hours per week

| Name | Own-use production | Employment | | Volunteer | SNA production |
	Goods	Self	Wage	Outside the house	boundary
SO	5	12	0	1	17
RA	5	16	0	1	22
NL	4	20	0	1	24
LD	7	10	1	9	27
LS	7	10	21	1	39
JA	3	9	27	0	39
AR	0	0	39	0	40
TH	2	2	33	4	40
SA	8	21	2	8	40
LM	3	4	29	4	40
AN	14	27	3	1	45
BM	7	38	0	3	47
SU	9	36	2	2	49
AS	3	27	15	5	50
PU	15	42	0	0	57
NA	0	0	52	10	63

Note: The data are for the 16 women identified as workers according to the current daily status definition in all three rounds (all names have been initialised to ensure anonymity). *Source*: Survey data.

were engaged as wage/salaried workers in the services sector (as a cook, health or ASHA worker, home guard, laboratory technician, and domestic worker), and also engaged in family labour on their fields or in animal care. They belonged to poor peasant, manual worker, and business and salaried households. There were also other forms of wage employment including in agriculture and construction. Thus, in this larger village with better urban connectivity as well as a more differentiated economic structure, more women were in wage employment. However, most women in wage employment were also engaged in some self-employment or family labour in SNA activities. Again, almost all the women spent some time in the reference week producing goods for own use.

An interesting association emerges between the extent of wage employment and all other forms of employment (self-employment and own-use production, mainly), as shown in Figure 2.2. In both the villages, there were some women who engaged only in own-use production and self-employment, that is, did not work outside the family home or enterprise (with hours of wage employment equal to zero in Figure 2.2). Whereas those who engaged in wage or salaried employment also engaged in self-employment, depending on the available opportunities (when hours of wage employment were more and those of self-employment were less, and vice versa).

These observations raise questions about the newly established distinction between work and employment in the 2013 ILO report, where only work for pay or profit is counted as employment. I argue that this distinction can be

Figure 2.2 *Scatter plot of hours of wage employment and self-employment for women workers in Alabujanahalli and Siresandra villages*

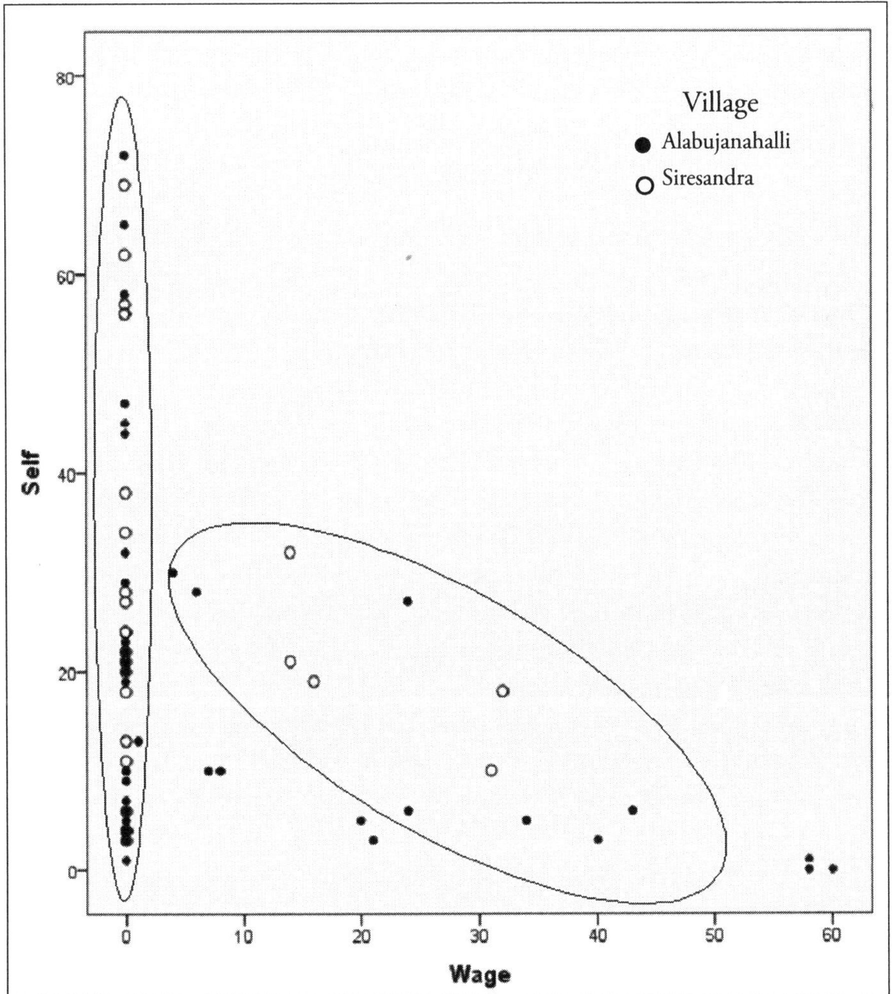

Source: Survey data.

fluid and seasonal. To take one example, in a situation of unemployment and absence of job opportunities, women may engage in own-use production of goods and services. In short, it may be lack of employment that leads a woman to not engage in wage employment or self-employment. To take another example, dairying could be self-employment in times when the output (milk) is sold and for own-use production at other times. To put it differently, the line between own-use production and production for profit (self-employment) is blurred, and can vary across time and differentially across households. For example, a bad harvest could reduce the sale of rice to the market or an illness could reduce the sale of milk and other animal products; these situations do not necessarily affect all households at the same time. A person characterised as "employed" when engaged in the production of goods for the market would be termed as not-employed when there is no sale of output. We argue that this division is particularly unstable for women who are largely engaged in home- or family-based activities such as family farming and animal rearing.

The Burden of Work

Each woman in the survey worked very long hours, be it in production (SNA) or extended production (extended SNA), and this raises concerns about women's well-being and work–life balance. Though the focus is on SNA activities in this paper, I begin with data on hours per week reported by each woman in SNA and extended SNA. I illustrate the point with data for women in Siresandra village (Table 2.9) during visit 1 (lean season).

In Siresandra village, three women engaged in production activities for more than 50 hours in the lean season (one was a manual worker in agriculture; the second was from a poor peasant family and engaged in livestock care; and the third, from a rich peasant family, was engaged in sericulture). Similarly, in the harvest season, three women spent more than 50 hours during the reference week in production activities (two of these were the same women in both seasons; see Appendix Table 2.2).

According to global statistics, in 2016, the average work week was 32 hours in the UK and 24 hours in Germany. Eight women in Siresandra worked for more than 24 hours a week in SNA activities in the lean and harvest seasons. Further, if we take the entire "work" burden of women, that is, in production or SNA and extended SNA activities, then the hours of work ranged from 61 to 88 a week in the lean season, and from 57 to 91 a week in the peak season. This is very high by any historical standard. It also shows that after allowing for sleep and basic personal care, there is not much time left for leisure.

Table 2.9 *Time spent on different activities by workers, Siresandra village, May 2017 (lean season)* in hours per week

Name	SNA	Extended SNA	SNA + Extended SNA
SN	4	82	86
JY	4	81	84
KA	6	72	78
AM	11	65	76
PU	17	44	61
NG	22	43	64
AG	24	57	81
PA	27	39	66
SR	34	54	88
AR	38	29	67
NA	41	45	86
VT	50	30	80
SM	58	12	70
GW	62	15	77

Note: The women have been ranked in ascending order of hours spent in SNA activity.
Source: Survey data.

Seasonal Variation

We have already noted a clear difference in the number of women workers across seasons. We now turn to differences in hours of SNA activity across seasons. Data in Table 2.10 for Alabujanahalli show that the range of hours worked (in SNA) during the reference week was large, with the maximum being 79 hours during visit 1 (LM worked as an agricultural labourer at sugarcane harvesting), 65 hours during visit 2 (SU was a poor peasant who worked in agricultural fields and tended cattle), and 72 hours during visit 3 (PU was a Scheduled Caste manual worker who laboured in the fields and tended one milch animal). Further, 11 women worked more than 32 hours a week during visits 1 and 3; the corresponding number was 9 women during visit 2 .

While more women worked longer hours during the harvest season, there is also a lot of fluctuation in the hours worked by any woman over the three seasons. NA, a woman from a manual worker household, showed consistently high hours of work (60 or more hours) in all three seasons. BM, a woman from a rich peasant household, worked long hours in the sowing and harvest seasons but less in the lean season.

Table 2.10 *Time spent on SNA by visit (season), Alabujanahalli village* in hours per week

Name	Visit 1 (Sowing)	Visit 2 (Harvest)	Visit 3 (Lean)
SU	48	65	35
NA	64	64	60
TH	15	63	43
AR	1	60	58
AS	67	53	31
BM	58	52	32
PU	52	47	72
RA	15	44	6
LM	32	35	52
JA	49	31	39
AN	50	27	58
HM	3	23	5
SA	51	23	45
NJ	17	23	6
LS	79	22	18
NL	32	21	20
SO	17	19	15
LD	31	16	35
GN	9	7	5
BC	2	4	9
CD	4	3	NA
DI	7	1	NA

Notes: The data are sorted in descending order by hours worked during visit 2, the harvest season. NA = respondent not available.
Source: Survey data.

Variations in Hours of Work

Hours of work (in SNA) are likely to depend on several demographic, economic, and social factors. Women spend many hours in extended SNA or care work. In both the study villages, there was a strong negative correlation between hours worked in SNA and in extended SNA (in other words, women who spent less time in SNA activities spent, not surprisingly, more time in extended SNA activities).

In both villages, hours of SNA activity in the reference week were positively correlated with age and negatively with years of schooling (Table 2.11). Older women with fewer years of formal education spent more time in SNA activity as compared to younger women. This was partly on account of the younger (more

Table 2.11 *Correlation coefficients between hours of work in SNA and various factors, Siresandra and Alabujanahalli villages*

Factor	Siresandra		Alabujanahalli		Combined	
	Coefficient	p-value	Coefficient	p-value	Coefficient	p-value
Extended SNA	−0.897	0.00	−0.663	0.00	−0.72	0.00
Age	0.6882	0.00	0.193	0.124	0.333	0.001
Years of schooling	−0.719	0.00	−0.192	0.127	−0.334	0.001
Caste	−0.043	0.831	−0.106	0.402	−0.083	0.43
Economic class	0.085	0.679	0.197	0.117	0.169	0.1
Household size	0.128	0.53	−0.082	0.516	0.033	0.75
Household structure	−0.033	0.86	0.898	0.898	0.051	0.6271
Number of women	0.172	0.39	−0.016	0.898	0.068	0.5231

Source: Survey data.

educated) women bearing more child-care responsibilities and having young families, but it also, perhaps, reflects their aspirations towards non-manual jobs.

In both villages, the sign of the caste coefficient was negative (though not significant), implying that women from non-Scheduled Caste families reported fewer hours of SNA activity than women from Scheduled Caste families. At the same time, the economic class variable had a positive coefficient (again, not significant), implying that moving up the class hierarchy, from manual workers to peasants and capitalist farmers, the hours of SNA rose. There are two opposing tendencies here: Scheduled Caste women from manual worker households rely on wage employment and this is reflected in their hours of work; however, they may not have regular employment during the week. By contrast, in both villages women from peasant families spent long hours on dairying, sericulture, and other household enterprises or activities that occurred on all days of the week.

We did not find a stable or significant correlation between hours of SNA per week and household size, household structure (whether joint or nuclear family), and number of women in the household in either of the two villages. A larger household (generally among rich peasant and capitalist farmer families) usually has more than one woman, so the additional burden of work on account of more members may be countered by a joint family structure and more women to share the work burden.

A multiple regression analysis was undertaken to understand the combined effect of different factors on hours of SNA work per week (Appendix Table 2.3). The two statistically significant variables were education and class (and all the others had the expected signs). Hours of SNA were lower for women with higher education, reflecting the fact that more educated women were "seeking" better jobs than were available in the village. Secondly, the economic class variable was positive, indicating that peasant women put in more hours of SNA work than women from manual worker families. This reflects the lack of wage employment for manual workers, on the one hand, and the burden of agriculture and allied home-based activities such as dairying and sericulture on women in peasant families, on the other hand.

CONCLUSION

In this paper, we have attempted to explore issues in the measurement of women's work using illustrative data from time-use surveys of selected women in two villages of Karnataka in south India. Although the number of women surveyed was small, the data are unique in capturing time use for a seven-day consecutive period in multiple seasons. We applied the current weekly status and current daily status approaches to identify workers. We also categorised workers using the new ILO classification of activities (ILO 2013).

We have two striking findings on work participation. First, by the weekly status definition (at least one hour spent in SNA activity during the reference week), all the women were workers. Secondly, using the daily status approach and major time spent criterion, work participation varied by season. It was higher and near-universal during the harvest season than in the lean season. This finding is compatible with the view that women withdraw from the work force when there are no suitable job opportunities (see Swaminathan 2020). These observations also endorse the need for time-use surveys in addition to standard labour force surveys to capture women's work in rural areas.

The new ILO recommendation (ILO 2013) broadens the concept of work but narrows the concept of employment, as only economic activity for pay or profit is counted as employment. Our data show that most women in the two villages were not engaged in wage employment; this could reflect a lack of job opportunities. Women are constrained by care work and safety issues in travelling far for employment. Most women were self-employed in family or farm enterprises, and engaged in own-use production of goods. The line separating production activity for own use and the market is a blurred one, we argue, and can vary over time. Similarly, the shifts between engaging in production for own use, wage employment, and self-employment are likely to be determined by availability of wage employment. To put it differently, women in rural areas move between own-use production, self-employment, and wage employment depending on the season, opportunities available, and other household-specific characteristics and responsibilities. The ILO recommendation assumes five mutually exclusive forms of work, but in the lives of most rural women, there is movement between these forms of work, and this can create problems in any fixed identification based on data from a single survey or selected time period.[12]

Our last finding, of most serious concern, is the extremely long hours of work put in by rural women, be it in SNA or extended SNA activities. If SNA and extended SNA are combined, no woman puts in less than 60 hours a week. Not surprisingly, there was a negative correlation between SNA and extended SNA activity. Hours of SNA activity per week were positively correlated with age and negatively correlated with years of schooling, implying that younger and more educated women had lower hours of SNA than older, less educated women. Women from Scheduled Castes reported higher hours of SNA than women from other social groups. At the same time, peasant women reported higher hours of SNA than women from manual worker households, reflecting the lack of employment among the latter, and the multiple tasks related to family and farm enterprises of the former.

It appears that women are always engaged in some activity and hours of leisure are low. It was surprising to find that not one woman was engaged in any learning activity. The lack of time for self-care and recreation needs to be understood better in order to improve women's well-being and work–life balance. Also, since the home and homestead are often the place of work for women, improving working conditions requires improving living and housing conditions, including ways of accelerating the automation of domestic work in rural areas.

I am grateful to Sanjukta Chakravarty and L. Vijay Kumar for processing the data, preparing the tables, and giving inputs while I was writing up the paper. Vijay Kumar undertook the correlation and regression analysis. I thank Yoshifumi Usami for his comments on the paper.

Bibliography

Hirway, Indira and Jose, Sunny (2011), "Understanding Women's Work Using Time-Use Statistics: The Case of India," *Feminist Economics*, vol. 17, no. 4, October, pp. 67–92.

International Labour Organization (ILO) (2013), "Resolution on Statistics on Work, Employment and Labour Underutilization," Nineteenth International Council of Labour Statistics, ILO, Geneva, available at https://www.ilo.org/wcmsp5/groups/public/---dgreports/---stat/documents/normativeinstrument/wcms_230304.pdf, viewed on 25 November 2019.

---

[12] Specifically, seasonal factors are likely to strongly affect the extent of employment observed.

Krishna, Raj (1984), "The Growth of Aggregate Unemployment in India: Trends, Sources, and Macroeconomic Policy Options," Staff Working Papers, No. 638, The World Bank, Washington, D.C., 31 March.
Swaminathan, Madhura (2020), "Features of Rural Workers Today with a Focus on Gender and Caste," *Indian Journal of Labour Economics*, vol. 63, no. 1, January–March.
Swaminathan, Madhura, and Das, Arindam (eds.) (2017), *Socioeconomic Surveys of Three Villages of Karnataka: A Study of Agrarian Relations*, Tulika Books, New Delhi.
Swaminathan, Madhura, and Usami, Yoshifumi (2016), "Women's Role in the Livestock Economy," *Review of Agrarian Studies*, vol. 6, no. 2, pp. 123–34.
Usami, Yoshifumi, with Subhjit Patra and Abhinav Kapoor (2018), "Measuring Female Work Participation in Rural India," *Review of Agrarian Studies*, vol. 8, no. 2, July–December, pp. 3–31.

APPENDIX

Appendix Table 2.1 *Daily activity status by intensity of work (half-day and full-day) in the production boundary, Siresandra village, May 2017*

Name	Day 1	Day 2	Day 3	Day 4	Day 5	Day 6	Day 7	Total activity days
JY	0	0.5	0	0.5	0	0	0.5	1.5
SN	0.5	0.5	0	0	0.5	0.5	0	2
KA	0	0	0.5	0.5	0	0.5	0.5	2
AMa	0	0.5	0.5	0.5	0	1	0.5	3
PU	0.5	0.5	0.5	0.5	0.5	0.5	0.5	3.5
PA	0.5	1	0.5	1	0.5	0.5	0.5	4.5
AG	0.5	0.5	1	1	0.5	0.5	1	5
NG	1	0.5	0.5	1	0.5	1	0.5	5
AR	0.5	0.5	1	0.5	1	1	1	5.5
NA	1	1	1	1	0.5	1	0.5	6
SR	1	1	1	1	0.5	1	0.5	6
VT	1	1	1	1	1	0.5	1	6.5
SM	1	1	1	1	1	1	1	7
GW	1	1	1	1	1	1	1	7

Note: A person who works for more than four hours a day is assigned a work intensity of 1 whereas anyone working between one to four hours a day is assigned an intensity of 0.5.

Appendix Table 2.2 *Time spent on SNA and extended SNA activities, Siresandra village, December 2017 (harvest season)* in hours per week

Name	SNA	Extended SNA	SNA + Extended SNA
KA	3	60	63
SR	18	69	87
NG	20	54	74
SN	21	68	89
AG	24	67	91
PU	28	50	79
AM	35	52	87
VT	35	22	57
NA	45	33	78
SM	56	11	67
PA	67	7	73
GW	69	12	81

Note: The data are sorted by hours spent in SNA activity.

Appendix Table 2.3 *Ordinary Least Squares Regression results to explain hours of SNA activity per week, two villages of Karnataka*

Variable	Coefficient	Standard error	t value	p value
Intercept	32.5451	17.2953	1.882	0.0634
Caste	–3.7198	4.8763	–0.763	0.4478
Class	3.1953	1.5457	2.067	0.0419
Age	0.1648	0.2613	0.631	0.53
Education	–1.282	0.6053	–2.118	0.0372
Household size	0.2998	0.8053	0.372	0.7106
Household type: nuclear/joint	2.903	5.0882	0.571	0.5699
Village dummy	–5.0949	4.9822	–1.023	0.3095

Notes: (i) Residual standard error: 19.11 on 82 degrees of freedom. (ii) Multiple R-squared: 0.196, Adjusted R-squared: 0.127. (iii) F-statistic: 2.865 on 7 and 82 DF, p-value: 0.0099.

The continuous variables are: (i) Age in years. (ii) Education in years of schooling. (iii) Household size in numbers.

The dummy variables are: (i) Caste (Scheduled Caste=0, Others=1). (ii) Class (Manual worker=0, Poor peasant=1, Rich peasant/capitalist farmer=2, Business and salaried=3). (iii) Household type (Nuclear=0, Joint=1). Village dummy (Siresandra=0, Alabujanahalli=1).

3

An Augmented Definition of Work Participation in Rural India

Yoshifumi Usami[1]
with Subhajit Patra and Abhinav Kapoor

There has been a decline in the female worker–population ratio (WPR) and labour force participation ratio (LFPR) in rural India over the last two to three decades.[2] This is an issue of serious concern in a period of rapid economic growth. One set of studies on this topic – "mainstream" studies – has focused on structural changes in the Indian economy, specifically the U-shaped relationship between economic development and women's participation in the labour market. According to this approach, improvements in school attendance, income effects, and social restrictions are the major factors influencing female WPR. These studies, particularly econometric analyses, use the Employment and Unemployment Survey (EUS) of the National Sample Survey Organisation (NSSO), and combine usual principal status (UPS) and usual subsidiary status (USS) workers to calculate the WPR; further, they include unemployment to estimate the LFPR. Differences between UPS and USS workers, or between different employment status (own account worker, unpaid family helper, regular wage/salaried worker, and casual labourer), are not taken into account. In short, the movement of workers across these categories is ignored.

A second set of studies has raised doubts about the concept of female workers in the Employment and Unemployment Survey of the NSSO. The problem relates to the delineation of the production boundary, and emerges from the cut-off used to separate activities within and outside the production boundary especially as it affects a wide range of activities undertaken by

---

[1] This article was first published in *Review of Agrarian Studies*, vol. 8, no. 2, July–December 2018.
[2] Ever since P. Visaria and others criticised the reliability of economic tables of the Population Census, most studies on employment and/or the labour market have used the NSSO's Employment and Unemployment Survey. Unfortunately, there are few studies that analyse employment during the post-reform period using Population Census data. The review of research literature by Mehrotra and Sinha (2017b) is quite extensive.

women. The production boundary as defined by the United Nations' System of National Accounts (UNSNA) is much wider than that of the EUS of the NSSO. As compared to the former, the latter uses a rather narrow concept of economic activity and excludes various kinds of activities from the ambit of economic production. However, the EUS collects information on women's participation in various specific activities and publishes these results; but none of the 12 specified activities is taken into account in the calculation of WPR. This strand of the literature suggests that a time-use survey is the only way to capture the work participation of rural women.

In spite of the substantial literature on WPR, two major questions remain. The first is whether the low observed female labour force participation ratio of Indian women is real. It is not clear if the official EUS data manage to capture rural women's participation in economic activities where there is no participation in the labour market. Secondly, there is the question of whether there has been a real and rapid decline in female WPR or LFPR since 2004–05. The WPR is a head count ratio, assigning the weight as either worker = 1 or non-worker = 0 for each person. A change in the duration of work, such as between principal and subsidiary activities, is not taken into consideration.

In order to address these questions, the next section of this chapter examines the concept of "worker," and modifies the female WPR by taking account of information on specific activities. It also examines issues of measurement in the NSSO's EUS. To examine trends in WPR beyond 2011–12, we use unit-level data of the EUS conducted by the Labour Bureau (LB) in 2015–16 after checking for comparability with the NSSO (in the third section of the chapter).

Lastly, we examine village-level data on workers from the survey of three villages in West Bengal conducted by the Foundation for Agrarian Studies (FAS). The FAS surveys provide us panel data with a five-year interval, which permits us to look at changes in the employment situation at the village level. West Bengal is a State with a very low female work participation rate according to the NSSO's EUS, but the WPR is substantially higher if economic activities in the secondary and tertiary status are considered. This exercise provides us with valuable insights on measuring different aspects of women's participation in economic activities.

REDEFINING FEMALE WORK PARTICIPATION

Following Kapsos *et al.* (2014), some researchers have talked of an augmented labour force participation ratio (LFPR). Nevertheless, most studies use the worker/non-worker dichotomy given by the NSSO, without differentiating between usual principal status (UPS) workers and usual subsidiary status (USS) workers.

The United Nations' System of National Accounts (UNSNA) includes the following types of production by households within the production boundary, whether intended for own final consumption or not.

(i) The production of agricultural products and their subsequent storage; the gathering of berries or other uncultivated crops; forestry; wood-cutting and the collection of firewood; and hunting and fishing.

(ii) The process of production of other primary products, such as mining salt, cutting peat, supply of water, etc.

(iii) The processing of agricultural products; the production of grain by threshing; the production of flour by milling; the curing of skins and the production of leather; the production and preservation of meat and fish products; the preservation of fruit by drying, bottling, etc.; the production of dairy products such as butter or cheese; the production of beer, wine or spirits; the production of baskets or mats.

(iv) Other kinds of production processes such as weaving cloth; dress-making and tailoring; production of footwear; production of pottery, utensils or durables; making furniture or furnishings. (UN SNA 1993; 2008).

On the other hand, the term "economic activity" as defined in the EUS of the NSSO includes:

(i) all market activities performed for pay or profit that result in production of goods and services for exchange;

(ii) non-market activities;

(iii) all activities related to the agriculture, forestry, fishing, mining, and quarrying sectors (i.e. industry divisions 01 to 09 of NIC-2008) that result in the production of primary goods for own consumption (including free collection of uncultivated crops and firewood, forestry, hunting, fishing, mining, quarrying, etc.); and

(iv) activities related to own-account production of fixed assets, which includes production of fixed assets such as construction of own house, roads, wells, etc., and of machinery, tools for household enterprise, and construction of any private or community facilities, free of charge. A person may be engaged in own account construction in the capacity of either a labourer or a supervisor (NSSO 2014a).

In addition, information on women engaged in specified activities, as listed below, is separately collected by the EUS of the NSSO.

Category (i): Activities relating to agricultural production, such as maintenance of kitchen garden, work in household poultry, dairy, etc., including free collection of agricultural products for household consumption.

Category (ii): Processing of primary products for household consumption.

Category (iii): Other activities for own consumption but resulting in economic benefits to the household (NSSO 2014b).

Activities listed under category (i) fall within the production boundary defined by the United Nations' System of National Accounts, 2008 (henceforth SNA 2008) as well as the Indian System of National Accounts (ISNA). However, if women performed these activities *nominally*, they were not considered to be usual principal status or usual subsidiary status workers. Activities under category (ii) are viewed as economic activities according to the recommendations of SNA 2008, but the ISNA has not, so far, considered them as economic activities if they are carried out for own consumption. Some activities under category (iii), such as preparing cowdung cakes and fetching water from beyond the premises of the household, when pursued for own consumption, are within the production boundary of SNA 2008. Other activities under category (iii) are not considered economic activities either by SNA 2008 or by the ISNA (NSSO 2014b).

It is clear that the activities listed under category (i) are conceptually within the production boundary and more specifically agriculture, in a broad sense. This raises the question as to how women are classified as workers or non-workers. Let us illustrate with the case of livestock rearing, a specified activity (SA02). Depending on the number of work days, a woman who is more or less regularly engaged in animal husbandry (SA02) will be categorised as a worker in agriculture, either self-employed (11) or a family helper (21), or a "non-worker but a specified activity participant." She could be placed in any of the following three categories:

(1) Usual principal status (UPS) worker in animal husbandry;
(2) Usual subsidiary status (USS) worker in animal husbandry;
(3) Non-worker with participation in animal husbandry as a specified activity (SA).

In practice, however, it is very difficult to differentiate the status of a woman worker as between categories (2) and (3). Besides, the EUS is not a time-use survey, and, as a result, recall errors and arbitrariness may arise in classifying a woman as a worker, a non-worker or an SA participant.

Table 3.1 shows the estimated number of USS workers in self-employed status (i.e. NSS category of 11, 12, and 21, including employer and family helper), and SA02 participants among them. It also shows the number of non-workers who participated in SA. It is seen that a majority of USS workers (self-

Table 3.1 *Estimates of usual subsidiary status (USS) self-employed workers in agriculture who are also engaged in a specified activity (animal husbandry), and non-workers who are participants in a specified activity (animal husbandry), 1993–94 to 2011–12 in number and per cent*

| | USS workers | | | Non-workers | |
| | Self-employed in agriculture | Participants in animal husbandry as SA | | Number of participants in animal husbandry as SA without USS work | |
Year	Total (in million)	Total (in million)	Share	Total (in million)	Proportion of women engaged in domestic duties
(1)	(2)	(3)	(4) = (3/2)	(5)	(6)
1993–94	17.9	11.6	64.9	24.9	30.1
1999–2000	15.9	10.3	64.6	24.8	26.6
2004–05	21.5	14.9	69.6	23.3	25.3
2009–10	13	8.3	63.7	26.1	21.3
2011–12	16.1	8.1	50.4	24.2	18.4

Note: Estimated using unit data of NSSO's EUS, various rounds, for rural areas only, and for females aged 15 years and above. Figures have not been adjusted to the census population.
Source: NSSO, Employment and Unemployment Survey (EUS), various years.

employed) in agriculture were also engaged in the specified activity of animal husbandry. Thus, in 2004–05, out of 21.5 million USS women workers who were self-employed in agriculture, 14.9 million (about 70 per cent) were also engaged in animal husbandry as a specified activity. Except in 2011–12, the proportion of USS workers engaged in animal husbandry varied between 64 and 70 per cent. It is not clear how these women were categorised as USS workers since they worked more than 30 days in animal husbandry or as workers in crop cultivation, but also engaged in household poultry or dairy.

Table 3.2 shows the number of UPS and USS workers who were engaged in crop cultivation and animal husbandry. USS workers are categorised as workers if they worked for more than 30 days in agriculture. For example, in 1993–94, a total of 34.3 million workers were categorised as USS self-employed in agriculture, of whom 10.8 million were USS workers engaged in animal husbandry for a period exceeding 30 days.

Now, let us compare the number of USS workers with animal husbandry as specified activity (SA) in Table 3.1 with USS workers (self-employed) in animal husbandry in Table 3.2. In 1993–94, for example, out of 11.6 million USS workers with SA animal husbandry, 10.8 million were "USS animal husbandry workers." The difference of 0.9 million women could be those

Table 3.2 *Female workers engaged in agriculture, usual principal status and usual subsidiary status, 1993–94 to 2011–12* in numbers

	Usual principal status (UPS) workers			Usual subsidiary status (USS) workers		
	Self-employed workers (codes: 11, 12, 21)					
Period	Total employed in agriculture (in million)	Total employed in crop cultivation (in million)	Total employed in animal husbandry (in million)	Total employed in agriculture (in million)	Total employed in crop cultivation (in million)	Total employed in animal husbandry (in million)
(1)	(2)	(3)	(4)	(5)	(6)	(7)
1993–94	28.3	24.5	3.2	34.3	22.5	10.8
1999–2000	30.3	27.6	2.5	16.2	9.5	6.4
2004–05	39.5	33.9	5.2	22.9	12.5	10.1
2009–10	29.9	26.4	3.3	14	8.2	5.5
2011–12	26.4	25.4	2.4	17	10.5	5.8

Note: See Table 3.1.
Source: NSSO, Employment and Unemployment Survey (EUS), various years.

Table 3.3 *Estimates of various categories of female workers in animal husbandry* in numbers

Period	USS workers in animal husbandry (AH) (in millions)	Participants with AH as SA (in millions)	USS workers with SA (AH) (in millions)	Non-workers with SA (AH) (in millions)
1993–94	10.8	11.6	0.9	24.9
1999–2000	6.4	10.3	3.9	24.8
2004–05	10.1	14.9	4.9	23.3
2009–10	5.5	8.3	2.8	26.1
2011–12	5.8	8.1	2.3	24.2

Note: See Tables 3.1 and 3.2.
Source: NSSO, Employment and Unemployment Survey (EUS), various years.

engaged in animal husbandry (AH) as a specified activity (SA), in short, "USS workers with SA (AH)."

We next look at the change in the number of workers for these three categories over the last 20 years: (1) USS animal husbandry workers (Table 3.2, column 7); (2) USS workers with SA (AH) (Table 3.1, column 3); and (3) non-workers with SA (AH) (Table 3.1, column 5).

The fluctuation in numbers of these three categories of workers was substantial between 1993–94 and 2009–10. About 3–4 million animal husbandry workers became USS workers with SA (AH) between 1993–94 and 1999–2000. Between 1999–2000 and 2004–05, there was a substantial increase in the number of workers in animal husbandry. The number of USS animal husbandry workers increased by 3.6 million, and that of USS workers with SA (AH) by 1 million. In the same period, the number of UPS workers in animal husbandry also increased by 2.6 million. In contrast, the number of animal husbandry workers fell between 2004–05 and 2009–10. USS animal husbandry workers decreased by 4.6 million and USS workers with SA (AH) fell by 2 million. This abnormal fluctuation in the number of workers in animal husbandry and SA02 participants, we argue, caused the rise and fall in female WPR in this period. It is not clear if this change was real, or due to errors in the classification of workers and non-workers. This exercise points towards a probable scenario but does not offer enough evidence to resolve measurement issues.

EXTENDING THE TREND IN FEMALE WPR BEYOND 2011–12

We now turn to a survey conducted by the Labour Bureau, and compare it with the EUS of the NSSO (Table 3.4). The sampling method is similar in

Table 3.4 *Comparison of the EUS survey method of the NSSO and the Labour Bureau*

	NSSO	Labour Bureau
Method	Stratified multistage sampling design	Stratified multistage sampling design
Sampling frame	2001 census villages/urban frame sample blocks	2011 census villages/urban frame sampling blocks
Stratification	Rural and urban, and sub-stratum formed (Rural) probability proportional to size with replacement (Urban) simple random sampling without replacement Hamlet group/sub-block formation for big villages/urban blocks	Rural and urban stratum, no sub-stratum formed Circular systematic sampling technique with probability proportional to size Hamlet group/sub-block formation for big villages/urban blocks
No. of villages and urban blocks allocated (surveyed)	7,508 (7,469) villages and 5,276 (5,268) urban blocks	7,412 (7,405) villages and 5,660 (5,654) urban blocks
Ultimate stage unit (USU)	Households	Households
Sampling frame	All households listed	All households listed
Second stage strata (SSS) formation	SSS1: Relatively affluent households SSS2: The remaining households have principal earning from non-agricultural activity SSS3: Other households 8 households (SSS1, 2; SSS2, 4; SSS3, 2)/village	Number of household members aged 15 years and above SSS1: 1 SSS2: 2–3 SSS3: 4–5 SSS4: 6 and above 12 households/village (SSS1, 1; SSS2, 3; SSS3, 4; SSS4, 4)
No. of households surveyed	59,700 (rural) and 42,024 (urban) households	88,783 (rural) and 67,780 (urban) households
Classification of persons by usual activity status		
Usual principal worker	Major time criterion by number of months worked The number of months employed, unemployed, and not in labour force are first enquired, and based on this information the category code number is recorded	Major time criterion by number of months worked The number of months employed, unemployed, and not in labour force are first recorded, and then particulars of each month are recorded. Major time criterion by the number of days worked is applied to each month

(*continued*)

Table 3.4 *continued*

NSSO	Labour Bureau
Usual subsidiary status worker	
A person will be considered to have worked in the subsidiary capacity if he/she has worked for a minimum period of 30 days, not necessarily continuously, during the last 365 days	
(A person who worked five days in each month for six months is categorised as a subsidiary worker.)	(A person who worked five days in each month for six months may not be categorised as a subsidiary worker.)
	As a result, there may be underenumeration of subsidiary status workers

Source: Prepared by the authors.

the two stages: namely, a multistage stratified sampling method with villages/ urban blocks as the first stage units and households as the ultimate stage units. As for sample size, the number of sample villages/urban blocks was almost the same, while the number of households was larger in the Labour Bureau's survey (12 households) than in the NSSO's survey (eight households).

The major differences between the NSSO and the Labour Bureau are as follows:

1. *Formation of second stage strata.* In the NSSO, there are three second stage strata (SSS): SSS1 comprises relatively affluent households; SSS2 comprises households that have principal earnings from non-agricultural activity; and SSS3 comprises other households. On the other hand, the Employment and Unemployment Survey of the Labour Bureau has four second stage strata, formed on the basis of number of household members above the age of 15. These four strata are: SSS1 with 1 person; SSS2 with 2–3 persons; SSS3 with 4–5 persons; and SSS4 with 6 persons and above. The two surveys have very different second stage strata.

2. *Definition of usual subsidiary status workers.* The NSSO makes it clear that a subsidiary worker is one who has worked for a minimum of 30 days during the 365 days prior to the survey, though not necessarily for a continuous period. In the Labour Bureau's questionnaire schedule, there is a question on the number of months a person is available for work and his/her employment status in the last 12 months. Further, there is a question on the particulars for each month (whether employed, unemployed or not in the labour force). Thus,

a person who has worked five days every month for a period of six months is categorised as a usual subsidiary status worker according to the NSSO, but he/she may not be so categorised in the Labour Bureau's EUS. This may result in underenumeration of USS workers in the Labour Bureau's EUS, as we show later. We provide some estimates based on the two employment surveys in Table 3.5.

We observe a difference in the estimated size of households as between the NSSO and the Labour Bureau, but the Labour Bureau's estimate is closer to the 2011 Census figures.[3] The proportions of Scheduled Caste (SC) and Scheduled Tribe (ST) workers in the Labour Bureau's EUS are higher than in the NSSO estimates and the Census. A more detailed analysis is required to judge the difference between the two surveys, but our preliminary analysis suggests that the Labour Bureau's EUS is comparable in a broad sense with

Table 3.5 *Comparison of some EUS estimates between the NSSO and the Labour Bureau*

(A) Size of household

	NSSO	Labour Bureau	Census 2011
Rural	4.6	5.0	4.9
Urban	4.1	4.4	4.6

(B) Distribution of population by sex (15 years and above)

	NSSO (percentage)		Labour Bureau (percentage)		
	Male	Female	Male	Female	Transgender
Rural	50.4	49.6	52.0	47.9	0.1
Urban	51.5	48.5	51.53	48.4	0.1

(C) Distribution of population by social group

	Rural (percentage)			Urban (percentage)		
	NSSO	Labour Bureau	Census	NSSO	Labour Bureau	Census
ST (Scheduled Tribe)	10.8	11.5	11.3	3.4	4.6	2.8
SC (Scheduled Caste)	20.7	22.4	18.5	14.3	13.9	12.6
OBC (Other Backward Classes)	45.1	40.9		41.4	40.1	
Others	23.4	25.2	70.3	40.8	41.4	84.6
All	100	100	100	100	100	100

Sources: NSSO 2011; Labour Bureau 2011; Census 2011.

[3] Interestingly, the Labour Bureau's EUS has captured the size of the transgender population in India.

Table 3.6 *Worker–population ratio for women, by activity status and industry, 2004–05 to 2015–16* in per cent

Rural	Usual principal and subsidiary status (UPSS)				Usual principal status (UPS)				Usual subsidiary status (USS)			
	2004–05	2009–10	2011–12	2015–16	2004–05	2009–10	2011–12	2015–16	2004–05	2009–10	2011–12	2015–16
111	26.1	17.3	17	11.1	16.6	11.9	10.7	8.2	9.5	5.4	6.3	2.9
112	3.1	2	2.6	1.3	2.3	1.6	1.6	1	0.8	0.4	1	0.2
113	0	0	0	0	0	0	0	0	0	0	0	0.
114	1.7	1.3	1.2	1.2	1.4	1.1	1	1	0.3	0.2	0.2	0.2
311	0.2	0.1	0.2	0.1	0.2	0.1	0.2	0.1	0	0	0	0
312	0.3	0.2	0.3	0.5	0.3	0.2	0.3	0.4	0	0	0	0
313	0	0	0	0.1	0	0	0	0	0	0	0	0
314	1.3	1.3	1.5	2.3	1.2	1.3	1.4	2.3	0.1	0	0.1	0
511	14.2	12.1	9.3	10.4	12.5	10.9	7.8	9.2	1.7	1.2	1.5	1.2
512	0.7	0.6	0.6	0.7	0.6	0.5	0.5	0.7	0.1	0.1	0.1	0.1
513	0.7	1.9	2.3	2.1	0.6	1.2	1.3	1.2	0.1	0.7	1.1	0.9
514	0.2	0.3	0.2	0.4	0.2	0.2	0.2	0.3	0	0	0	0.1
All	48.5	37.1	35.2	30.2	35.9	29	25	24.4	12.6	8	10.3	5.6
SA1–4	20.1	26.5	26.7									
SA1–12	29.2	34.8	33.6									

Note: The codes are: 111 – self-employed in agriculture; 112 – self-employed in manufacturing; 113 – self-employed in construction; 114 – self-employed in service sector; 311 – regular wage workers in agriculture; 312 – regular wage workers in manufacturing; 313 – regular wage workers in construction; 314 – regular wage workers in service sector; 511 – casual labour in agriculture; 512 – casual labour in manufacturing; 513 – casual labour in construction; and 514 – casual labour in service sectors.
Source: NSSO, Employment and Unemployment Survey, various years.

the NSSO's EUS at the all-India level. Care would be required when estimates of USS workers are compared, however, as the Labour Bureau's estimates are liable to be underestimates.

Table 3.6 shows the trend in female WPR in rural India separately for UPS and USS workers, and by status (two digits) and industry (one digit). Industry is classified into four groups, with the following codes: agriculture – 1; manufacturing – 2; construction – 3; service sector – 4. Thus, code 111 stands for self-employed (11) in agriculture (1). Similarly, 312 stands for regular wage worker (31) in manufacturing industry (2), and 513 stands for casual labourer (51) in construction (3).

We examined the WPRs of usual principal and subsidiary status (UPSS) workers, but also separately for UPS and USS workers. The decline in WPRs between 2004–05 and 2011–12 was different for principal and secondary status workers. The WPRs of UPS declined by 10.9 percentage points, from 35.9 per cent to 25 per cent, in this period, while the WPRs of USS workers declined from 12.6 per cent to 10.3 per cent, just 2.3 percentage points, in the same period.

Secondly, when we look at the change in WPR by employment status and industry, it is evident that WPR declined the most for those who were self-employed in agriculture (including 111, 121, and 211) and casual labourers in agriculture (511).

For WPRs of usual subsidiary status workers, casual labour in agriculture remained at a similar level but casual labour in construction rose by 1 percentage point. The WPR of casual labour in construction rose for both the UPS and USS groups.

When the WPR of specified activity (1–4) is added, there is a finding of interest. The WPR for those who were self-employed in agriculture declined by 9.1 percentage points, but that for SA (1–4) rose by 6.6 percentage points. Again, it is not clear if this change did in fact occur or if it is due to measurement errors.

In short, extending the trend analysis from 2011–12 to 2015–16 using the Labour Bureau surveys to understand women's WPR remains problematic. Using usual principal status (UPS) workers, the decline in WPR is small; it is more evident using usual subsidiary status (USS) workers. However, a comparison between 2011–12 and 2015–16 is complicated by the inclusion of a separate category called specified activity (SA) in the NSSO, which is absent in the Labour Bureau.

Evidence from Village Surveys

The Foundation for Agrarian Studies (FAS), as part of its Project on Agrarian Relations in India (PARI), carried out a census survey of three villages of West Bengal in 2010, and a sample of households in the same villages was resurveyed in 2015. The number of households and persons surveyed are given in Table 3.7. We have panel data on 214 households with an interval of five years, 2010 and 2015. In this paper, we identify workers using usual status occupation/activity data of 371 women of age 15 years and above among the sample households.[4]

In the survey schedule, information was collected from each person on multiple activities or occupation status, i.e. primary, secondary, tertiary, and other employment. The ordering of activity status is according to the respondent's perception rather than major time or major income criterion. Nevertheless, the responses are reliable due to the fact that most women regarded work under the Mahatma Gandhi National Rural Employment

Table 3.7 *List of FAS study villages with number of households surveyed, male and female composition, and persons aged 15 years and above, West Bengal, 2010 and 2015*

(A) Number of households surveyed

Village	2010	2015
Amarsinghi	127	55
Kalmandasguri	147	52
Panahar	248	107
All	522	214

(B) Persons surveyed

	2010		2015	
	Male	Female	Male	Female
All	1,710	1,631	515	468

(C) Sample persons aged 15 years and above

	2010		2015	
	Male	Female	Male	Female
Total	361	317	372	371
(not surveyed in 2010)	11	54		

Source: FAS village survey data.

[4] There were 317 women in 2010 and 54 women who were added to the panel through marriage.

Guarantee Act (MGNREGA) (because of limited number of work days) and animal husbandry (because of limited time spent in animal husbandry) as their secondary or tertiary activity status. From these data, women who reported themselves as being engaged in economic activity are categorised as workers irrespective of the number of work days. The estimates of workers here are thus an upper limit of female WPR in these villages of West Bengal.

Employment opportunities for women were more or less limited to agriculture-related activities in these three villages. Appendix Table 3.1 shows male and female activities in 2015. Panel (A) indicates the primary and secondary status activities of males in 2015. (We assume that primary and secondary status activities are sufficient to approximate the employment situation in the villages.) On combining the primary and secondary status (PS and SS) activities, we find that about one-half (180) of all men were engaged in non-agricultural employment, most of which was provided outside the village.

Panel (B) in Appendix Table 3.1 shows the primary and secondary status activities of women. Employment opportunities for women were limited in non-agricultural sectors. Only 18 women reported non-farm employment as either primary or secondary status activity. Employment opportunities for women in the village in manufacturing, trade, transport, and government and other service sectors were negligible. The most important activity for women was housework. Thus, 239 women and 51 women reported housework as primary and secondary status activity, respectively. Self-employment in agriculture was next in importance. Adding primary status and secondary status activities, 74 women (19.9 per cent) were self-employed in agriculture. Similarly, 58 women (15.6 per cent) reported agricultural labour as primary or secondary activity. Animal husbandry (AH) was the most important economic activity in terms of the number of women: 4 women reported it as primary status activity and 109 women reported it as secondary status activity.

Table 3.8 shows a cross-tabulation of primary and secondary activities among women in 2010. The key findings are as follows.

(1) The principal activity for a majority of women in the villages was "housework." Out of 371 women, 239 women reported housework as their primary activity. Only 65 women reported economic activities as their primary status activity.

(2) Employment opportunities within the village were limited to agriculture – in the form of self-employment in agriculture, agricultural labour, and animal husbandry.

(3) MGNREGA work was not regarded as an important economic activity, as most participants reported it as tertiary or fourth (or even lower)

Table 3.8 *Women's activities in the FAS study villages, by type of activity, 2010*

Primary activity	No secondary activity	Self-employment in agriculture	Agricultural labour	Animal husbandry	Trade	Government service	Self-employment in service	Other service	Housework	Student	All
Self-employment in agriculture			8	6					7		21
Agricultural labour		5		5			1		20		31
Animal husbandry		2	1						1		4
Manufacturing									2		2
Government service					1		1		3		5
Other service			1	1							2
Housework	82	42	14	96		1	1	2		1	239
Student	26	4	3	1		1	1		16		52
Non-worker	13								2		15
All	121	53	27	109	1	2	4	2	51	1	371

Source: FAS village survey data.

status activity. There were 61 participants in 2010, but the number of MGNREGA work participants fell to six in 2015.

(4) Animal husbandry was one of the most important economic activities in the three villages in terms of the number of women engaged: 178 and 169 women in 2010 and 2015, respectively.

Using this information, we calculated female WPR in two ways: the first includes AH and the second excludes it. Table 3.9 shows WPRs at the all-India level and in West Bengal using NSS and Labour Bureau data, as well as WPR from the FAS village surveys. According to the EUS report of NSSO, female WPR in West Bengal was low. The rural female WPR at the all-India level was 48.5 per cent in 2004–05, while it was only 25.9 per cent in West Bengal. It is assumed that social restrictions and limited employment opportunities were the main reasons for the lower WPR in West Bengal. During recent decades, female WPR has declined significantly in many States, but has remained at almost the same level in West Bengal. It is likely that poverty compelled women from poor families to work outside the homestead. While wage rates

Table 3.9 *Changes in female work participation rate (WPR), 2004–05 and 2015–16* in per cent

			UPS	USS	UPS+USS	SA0104	UPSS+ SA0104
All-India	NSS	2004–05	35.9	12.6	48.5	20.1	68.6
		2009–10	29	8.2	37.2	26.5	63.7
		2011–12	25	10.3	35.2	26.7	61.9
	Labour Bureau	2015–16	24.6	5.6	30.2	NA	NA
West Bengal	NSS	2004–05	14.9	11	25.9	46.1	71.9
		2009–10	12.2	8	20.1	48.1	68.2
		2011–12	14.5	11.3	25.8	44.6	70.4
	Labour Bureau	2015–16	18.1	5	23.1	NA	NA

Changes in female work participation rate (WPR), in per cent

FAS village data			Primary occupation	Secondary/ tertiary occupation	All	Animal husbandry	Worker + AH
AH included		2009–10	10.4	59	69.4		
		2014–15	17.5	45.8	63.3		
AH separate		2009–10	9.8	30.9	40.7	28.7	69.4
		2014–15	16.4	18.9	35.3	28	63.3

Notes: UPS = usual principal status; USS = usual subsidiary status; SA = specified activity; NSS = National Sample Survey; FAS = Foundation for Agrarian Studies; AH = animal husbandry.

rose substantially in the last decade, it is likely that employment did not see a corresponding rise.

Village survey results (the lowest panel) show that the WPRs using primary status was 10.4 per cent in 2010 and 17.5 per cent in 2015, broadly comparable to the NSSO and Labour Bureau estimates, at 14.5 per cent and 18.1 per cent respectively. A large difference, on the other hand, emerges when we use secondary activity status. The village survey results are now much higher: in 2014–15 it was 18.9 per cent excluding AH and 45.8 per cent when AH was included. According to the NSSO's estimates, the female WPR (USS) varied from 8 to 11 per cent.[5]

Even excluding animal husbandry, the WPR of USS workers in the FAS

---

[5] Note that the USS WPR of the Labour Bureau is under-reported, as anticipated.

village survey was 30.9 per cent in 2010 and 18.9 per cent in 2015, while it was 11.3 per cent in 2011–12 for all of West Bengal according to the NSSO. What is the reason for this large difference? We argue that it is most likely on account of self-employment in agriculture.

If we apply the 30-day criterion of the NSSO for usual subsidiary workers, only 9.6 per cent of women who reported cultivation as their activity would be counted as workers (Table 3.10). Further, only about one-half of agricultural labourers reported working for 30 days and more. One reason for this could be our standardisation of days into eight-hour days; for example, five hours spent by women on weeding would not get counted as one work day. It is not clear if the EUS of the NSSO applies standardisation. The concept and definition of the NSSO EUS states that while nominal work is excluded, one hour of work is regarded as half a day for current daily status. Table 3.10 thus shows the difficulties in capturing the number of days of work and categorising a person as a worker or a non-worker in the case of self-employment, or when working as family help in farming or other household industries.

There could be many persons with apparently nominal work or a limited

Table 3.10 *Proportion of women workers in crop cultivation and agricultural labour, by days of work, 2015* in number and per cent

(A) Crop cultivation work status

Days of work	Primary status	Secondary status	Tertiary status	All	Percentage
Less than 10	5	23	28	56	50
10–20	4	17	11	32	28.6
20–30	5	3	4	12	10.7
More than 30	6	4	2	12	10.7
Total	20	47	45	112	100

(B) Agricultural labour work status

Days of work	Primary status	Secondary status	Tertiary status	All	Percentage
Less than 10	1	4	2	7	11.1
10–20	6	7	1	14	22.2
20–30	5	3	2	10	15.9
More than 30	18	12	2	32	50.8
Total	30	26	7	63	100

Note: Standardised to eight working hours per day.
Source: FAS village survey data.

number of work days that would be categorised as non-workers in the NSSO's EUS. The EUS also under-reports unemployment among women. Let us suppose that a woman intends to work or is available for work, but due to lack of employment opportunities she cannot meet the cut-off of 30 days per year to be categorised as a worker. She should then be classified as "unemployed" in usual subsidiary status, but no such category exists in the EUS. Instead, she may be classified as a non-worker with SA01–04 participation. If this is the case, the female WPR should include SA01–04 in defining usual status WPR; that is, we should calculate an augmented WPR as suggested by Kapsos *et al.* (2014), Olsen and Mehta (2006), and others. The augmented WPR from the FAS village survey data were 68.2 per cent in 2009–10 and 70.4 per cent in 2011–12. Female WPR including animal husbandry was 69.4 per cent.

The village survey data provide valuable information on animal husbandry, an important element of women's work participation. Women from the villages participated extensively in animal husbandry. More than 80 per cent of households in all three villages were engaged in animal husbandry, with 81.7 per cent in dairy and 85.2 per cent in goat-keeping. Though some households had two to three female workers, in most cases there was only one female worker in a household. Except for a large dairy, the size of dairying or goat-keeping did not relate to the extent of female participation. Women in rich families were unlikely to commit time to animal husbandry as they were able to hire long-term workers.

Table 3.12 shows the change in the number of women engaged in animal husbandry by activity status: 178 women (56.1 per cent) and 169 women (45.5 per cent) were engaged in animal husbandry in 2010 and 2015, respectively. Two interesting points emerge. The first relates to the activity

Table 3.11 *Female participation in animal husbandry in the study villages, West Bengal* in numbers

Number of cows/ buffaloes	All house-holds	Households with female workers	Number of female workers	Number of goats	All house-holds	Households with female workers	Number of female workers
1	56	46	55	1	19	14	15
2	40	34	43	2	25	21	23
3–5	26	21	28	3–5	33	29	39
6–14	4	2	4	6–12	11	11	12
All	126	103	130	All	88	75	89

Source: FAS village survey data.

Table 3.12 *Change in the number of workers in animal husbandry by activity status, West Bengal villages, 2010 and 2015* in numbers

Activity status (2015)	Activity status (2010)						
	No data	Primary	Secondary	Tertiary	Fourth	Sub-total	New
Primary		1			2	3	1
Secondary	11		39	25	8	72	26
Tertiary	1	1	19	10	12	42	9
Fourth				1	1	2	2
Sub-total		2	58	36	23	119	38
Exited animal husbandry	42		35	12	12	59	101
All	54	2	93	48	35		139

Source: FAS village survey data.

status of animal husbandry. Most women did not regard animal husbandry as an "important" activity. Thus, in 2010, only 2 women reported it as their primary status activity, while 93 women reported it as their secondary activity and 48 women as their tertiary activity. The situation did not change in 2015 with only 4 women reporting animal husbandry as primary status activity, but 109 women and 92 women reporting it as a secondary or tertiary activity respectively.

The second point is that participation in animal husbandry is not stable. Out of 178 women engaged in animal husbandry in 2010, 59 women quit the activity and 38 women newly entered it in 2015. Of the 59 women who stopped working in animal husbandry, a majority (55.9 per cent) were engaged in housework. Of the remaining, 12 were agricultural labourers, 5 were self-employed in agriculture, and 2 reported other employment.

Table 3.13 tabulates the answers to the following question: what was the primary activity of women who reported participation in either animal-rearing or MGNREGA as secondary or tertiary activity? There is an interesting contrast between workers in animal husbandry and in MGNREGA. The main activity of women who were engaged in animal husbandry was "housework" in 84.4 per cent of the responses, whereas that of MGNREGA participants was "self-employed in agriculture" (22 per cent) and "agricultural labour" (45.8 per cent). In short, an overwhelming majority of animal husbandry workers reported their main activity as housework. Engagement in animal husbandry appears to be an "extension of housework" for a woman. Does this mean that there is only nominal participation in animal husbandry?

Table 3.13 *Primary activity of women engaged in animal husbandry and MGNREGA in number and per cent*

Activity	Animal husbandry		MGNREGA	
	Number	Percentage	Number	Percentage
Self-employed in agriculture	8	5.7	13	22
Agricultural labour	6	4.3	27	45.8
Animal husbandry	NA	NA	9	15.3
MGNREGA	2	1.4	NA	NA
Other	2	1.4	2	3.4
Student	4	2.8		0
Housework	119	84.4	8	13.6
All	141	100	59	100

Notes: NA = not applicable. Women engaged in animal husbandry and MGNREGA as their primary status and fourth status activities are excluded.
Source: FAS village survey data.

Table 3.14 *Distribution of households by size of animal husbandry, study villages, 2015* in numbers

Number of cows/buffaloes						Number of goats					
0	1	2	3–5	6–14	All	0	1	2	3–5	6–12	All
88	56	40	26	4	214	126	19	25	33	11	214

Source: FAS village survey data.

Animal husbandry is one of the most widespread activities in the region. According to the village survey results, 177 out of 214 sample households (82.7 per cent) kept some kind of animal (cows/buffaloes, goats, poultry) in 2015. Table 3.14 shows the distribution of households by size of dairy and goat-keeping in the three villages in 2015.

Out of 214 households, 126 (58.9 per cent) and 88 (41.1 per cent) households kept cows/buffaloes and goats, respectively. The scale of animal husbandry was small: out of 126 milch animal owners, 56 (44.4 per cent) households kept one cow/buffalo, and 40 (31.7 per cent) households kept two cows/buffaloes. Similarly, one-half of all households kept one or two goats.

Another important aspect of animal husbandry in the villages was that small and marginal farmers, and landless manual labour households accounted for a majority of those engaged in animal husbandry. Among households keeping milch animals, the shares of poor peasant and manual labour households were 45.2 per cent and 26.2 per cent respectively, and together they accounted for

76 per cent of all milch animals. Their shares in goat-keeping were slightly higher, with manual labour households at 44.1 per cent and poor peasant households at 35.2 per cent.[6]

At this scale, production was mostly for home consumption. In 2015, out of 126 households, 86 households had output of milk but only 19 households (22.1 per cent) sold milk. Average production of milk per year was 438.9 litres per household, and average sale was 430.3 litres per milk-selling household. Of 88 goat-keeping households, 16 households (18.2 per cent) sold goats in 2015. Thus, excluding one big dairy farm with 14 cows/buffaloes, animal husbandry in the three villages in West Bengal was very small in size and mainly for home consumption.

Employment opportunities for women are limited, and there are social and cultural restrictions on females working outside the village. Under such circumstances and given its limited resource requirements, animal husbandry is regarded as a suitable household undertaking. Cows/buffaloes are kept in the compound of the household with or without a cowshed, and they are fed paddy straw and grass collected by women. Most of the work is done by female members of the household. Thus, animal husbandry in the village is seen as one of the survival strategies for a poor family. Production is very small, at about 430 litres of milk per household, which is valued at around Rs 10,000 per year. Milk or eggs are sold if there is a surplus over home consumption. However small the value of production from animal husbandry is, it is an economic activity that requires careful evaluation. Time-use surveys clearly show that taking care of animals is not nominal work (Swaminathan *et al.* 2018). Categorising work in animal husbandry (AH) as a specified activity and female participants in AH as non-workers involves a serious error of underassessment of women's participation in economic activity.

CONCLUSION

Although the National Sample Survey Organisation (NSSO) includes a category of specified activities – namely, maintaining a kitchen garden, animal-rearing, free collection of fodder and firewood – as economic activities, this category is not included in the estimation of usual principal and subsidiary status workers. This is mainly because the work is nominal or the number of work days is less than 30 in a year. When we examine the relationship between the proportion of usual subsidiary status workers and specified activity participants (SA02 animal husbandry), issues of measurement cannot

---

[6] Tables are available on request.

be excluded. From the point of view of conceptual validity and to prevent possible measurement errors, it is preferable instead to calculate an augmented worker population ratio or work participation rate by including the category of specified activities (i).

The methodologies followed by the NSSO's Employment and Unemployment Survey and by the Labour Bureau appear similar, and a comparison may be possible, at least at an all-India level, which allows us to extend the trend of female worker–population ratios in rural India to 2015–16 despite an underestimation of USS workers in the Labour Bureau data of 2015–16. The decline of female worker–population ratios from 2004–05 has continued up to 2015–16.

Village survey data from the Foundation for Agrarian Studies show that female employment opportunities outside the village are few, with most opportunities limited only to agriculture. This is the background for the very low level of female worker–population ratio in West Bengal. Animal husbandry is an important activity in terms of the participation of women in the villages. The survey data clearly show that a majority of, if not all, female workers engaged in animal husbandry are participants in the survival strategies of poor marginal and landless households. We argue that worker–population ratio (WPR) including animal husbandry or WPR (usual principal and subsidiary status + specified activity participation rate) in the NSSO's Employment and Unemployment Survey is more appropriate for measuring women's participation in economic activities than WPR (usual principal and subsidiary status) alone.[7]

BIBLIOGRAPHY

Andres, Luis A., Dasgupta, Basab, Joseph, George, Abraham, Vinoj, and Correia, Maria (2017), "Precarious Drop: Reassessing Patterns of Female Labour Force Participation in India," Policy Research Working Paper 8024, World Bank Group, Washington D. C., April.

Das, Sonali, Jain-Chandra, Sonali, Kochhar, Kalpana, and Kumar, Naresh (2015), "Women Workers in India: Why So Few Among So Many?" IMF Working Paper WP/15/55, International Monetary Fund.

Datta, Amrita, and Rustagi, Preet (2012), *Status of Women in Bihar: Exploring Transformation in Work and Gender Relations*, Institute for Human Development, New Delhi.

Hirway, Indira (2002), "Employment and Unemployment Situation in 1990s: How Good Are NSS Data?" *Economic and Political Weekly*, vol. 37, no. 21, 25 May.

---

[7] A question for future study could be whether the pursuit of small-scale animal husbandry for home consumption can be regarded as "labour market participation."

Hirway, Indira (2012), "Missing Labour Force: An Explanation," *Economic and Political Weekly*, vol. 47 no. 37, 15 September.

Kannan, K. P., and Raveendran, G. (2012), "Counting and Profiling the Missing Labour Force," *Economic and Political Weekly*, vol. 47, no. 6, 11 February.

Kapsos, Steven, Silberman, Andrea, and Bourmpoula, Evangelia (2014), "Why is Female Labour Force Participation Declining So Sharply in India?" ILO Research Paper No. 10, International Labour Office, Geneva, August.

Klasen, Stephan, and Pieters, Janneke (2013), "What Explains the Stagnation of Female Labour Force Participation in Urban India?" IZA Discussion Paper No. 7597, Institute for the Study of Labour (IZA), Bonn.

Kumari, Reena, and Pandey, Aviral (2012), "Women's Work Participation in Labour Market in Contemporary India," *Journal of Community Positive Practices*, Catalactica NGO, no. 1, pp. 18–35.

Mammen, Kristin, and Paxson, Christina (2000), "Women's Work and Economic Development," *The Journal of Economic Perspectives*, vol. 14, no. 4, Autumn, pp. 141–64.

Mathew, Shalina Susan (2015), "Falling Female Labour Force Participation in Kerala: Empirical Evidence of Discouragement?" *International Labour Review*, vol. 154, no. 4, 19 January.

Mehrotra, Santosh, and Parida, Jajati K. (2017a), "Why is the Labour Force Participation of Women Declining in India?" *World Development*, vol. 98, issue C, pp. 360–80.

Mehrotra, Santosh, and Sinha, Sharmistha (2017b), "Explaining Falling Female Employment During a High Growth Period," *Economic and Political Weekly*, vol. 52, no. 39, 30 September.

Naidu, Sirisha C. (2016), "Domestic Labour and Female Labour Force Participation: Adding a Piece to the Puzzle," *Economic and Political Weekly*, vol. 51, nos. 44 and 45, 5 November.

National Sample Survey Organisation (NSSO) (1997a), "Employment and Unemployment Situation in India, 1993-94," National Sample Survey 50th Round, Report No. 409, Ministry of Statistics and Programme Implementation, Government of India, New Delhi.

National Sample Survey Organisation (NSSO) (1997b), "Participation of Indian Women in Household Work and Other Specified Activities, 1993–94," National Sample Survey 50th Round, Report No. 416, Ministry of Statistics and Programme Implementation, Government of India, New Delhi.

National Sample Survey Organisation (NSSO) (2000), "Employment and Unemployment in India, 1999–2000," National Sample Survey 55th Round, Report No. 455, Ministry of Statistics and Programme Implementation, Government of India, New Delhi.

National Sample Survey Organisation (NSSO) (2001a), "Employment and Unemployment Situation in India, 1999-2000," National Sample Survey 55th Round, Report No. 458, Ministry of Statistics and Programme Implementation, Government of India, New Delhi.

National Sample Survey Organisation (NSSO) (2001b), "Participation of Indian Women in Household Work and Specified Activities, 1999–2000," National Sample Survey 55th Round, NSS Report No. 465, Ministry of Statistics and Programme Implementation, Government of India, New Delhi.

National Sample Survey Organisation (NSSO) (2006), "Employment and Unemployment Situation in India, 2004–05," National Sample Survey 61st Round, NSS Report No. 515, Ministry of Statistics and Programme Implementation, Government of India, New Delhi.

National Sample Survey Organisation (NSSO) (2007), "Participation of Women in Specified Activities along with Domestic Duties, 2004–2005," National Sample Survey 61st Round, NSS Report No.518, Ministry of Statistics and Programme Implementation, Government of India, New Delhi.

National Sample Survey Organisation (NSSO) (2011), "Employment and Unemployment Situation in India, 2009–10," National Sample Survey 66th Round, NSS Report No. 537, Ministry of Statistics and Programme Implementation, Government of India, New Delhi.

National Sample Survey Organisation (NSSO) (2013), "Participation of Women in Specified Activities along with Domestic Duties, 2009–10," National Sample Survey 66th Round, NSS Report No. 550, Ministry of Statistics and Programme Implementation, Government of India, New Delhi.

National Sample Survey Organisation (NSSO) (2014a), "Employment and Unemployment Situation in India, 2011–12," National Sample Survey 68th Round, NSS Report No. 554, Ministry of Statistics and Programme Implementation, Government of India, New Delhi.

National Sample Survey Organisation (NSSO) (2014b), "Participation of Women in Specified Activities along with Domestic Duties, 2011–12," National Sample Survey 68th Round, Report No. 559, Ministry of Statistics and Programme Implementation, Government of India, New Delhi.

Neetha, N. (2014), "Crisis in Female Employment: Analysis Across Social Groups," *Economic and Political Weekly*, vol. 49, no. 47, 22 November.

Olsen, Wendy, and Mehta, Smita (2006), *A Pluralist Account of Labour Participation in India*, Global Poverty Research Group Working Paper 042.

Rangarajan, C., Kaul, Padma Iyer, and Seema (2011), "Where is the Missing Labour Force?" *Economic and Political Weekly*, vol. 46, no. 39, 24 September.

Raveendran, Govindan (2016), "The Indian Labour Market: A Gender Perspective," UN Women Discussion Paper Series, UN Women.

Rawal, Vikas, and Saha, Partha (2015), *Women's Employment in India: What Do Recent NSS Surveys of Employment and Unemployment Show?* SSER Monograph 15/1, Society for Social and Economic Research, New Delhi, available at: http: //archive.indianstatistics. org/sserwp/sserwp1501.pdf, viewed on 28 December 2018.

Rustagi, Preet (2010), "Employment Trends for Women in India," ILO Asia-Pacific Working Paper, International Labour Office, Geneva.

Sanghi, Sunita, Srija, A., and Vijay, S. S. (2015), "Decline in Rural Female Labour Force Participation in India: A Relook into the Causes," *Vikalpa: The Journal for Decision Makers*, vol. 40, no. 3, July–September, pp. 255–68.

Sanhita, Sucharita (2013), "Factors Affecting Female Labour Force Participation in India," *Romanian Economic Journal*, vol. 16, no. 48, Department of International Business and Economics, Academy of Economic Studies, Bucharest, June.

Siddiqui, Mohammed Zakaria, Lahiri-Dutt, Kuntala, Lockie, Stewart, and Pritchard, Bill (2017), "Reconsidering Women's Work in Rural India: Analysis of NSSO Data, 2004–05 and 2011–12," *Economic and Political Weekly*, vol. 52, no. 1, 7 January.

Sorsa, Piritta, Mares, Jan, Didier, Mathilde, Guimaraes, Caio, Rabate, Marie, Tang, Gen, and Tuske, Annamaria (2015), "Determinants of the Low Female Labour Force Participation in India," OECD Economics Department Working Papers, No. 1207, OECD, Paris.

Srivastava, Nisha, and Srivastava, Ravi (2009), "Women, Work, and Employment Outcomes in Rural India," Paper presented at the FAO–IFAD–ILO Workshop on Gaps, Trends, and Current Research in Gender Dimensions of Agricultural and Rural Employment: Differentiated Pathways Out of Poverty, Rome, 31 March–2 April.

Sudarshan, Ratna M., and Bhattacharya, Shrayana (2008), "Through the Magnifying Glass: Women's Work and Labour Force Participation in Urban Delhi," ILO Asia-Pacific Working Paper Series, International Labour Organisation, New Delhi.

Swaminathan, Madhura, Chakraborty, Sanjukta, and Vijaykumar, L. (2018), "Women's Work: Evidence from a Pilot Time-Use Study in Karnataka," paper presented at the Conference on Women's Work in Rural Economies, Vayalar, 30 November–2 December.

Tiwari, Rashmi, and Tiwari, Shivani (2016), "Women Employment in Unorganised Sector in India: An Empirical Analysis," *Journal of Rural Development*, vol. 35, no. 4, pp. 645–64.

Appendix Table 3.1 *Employment structure in the three villages of West Bengal, by primary and secondary status activity and gender, 2015*

(A) Primary and secondary status activities, males, 2015

Primary activity	Secondary activity															
	No secondary activity	Self-employment in agriculture	Self-employment in fishery	Agricultural labour	Animal husbandry	Manufacturing	Construction	MGNREGA	Trade	Transport	Self-employment in service	Other service	House work	Student	Non-worker	All
Self-employment (agriculture)	21			40	28	4	3	4	17	2	3	3				125
Self-employment (fishery)		5														5
Agricultural labour	13	16		1	8		11	1	4	1		1	1			57
Animal husbandry	3	1		1												5
Manufacturing	8	3								1				1		13
Construction	11	8	1								1	1				22
MGNREGA													1			1
Trade	17	13		3	3				1		1					38
Transport	2	2														4
Government service	10	2													1	13
Self-employment (service)	4	2														6
Other service	6	3		1		1			5					1		17
Unemployed	2															2
Housework	1															1
Student	19	17		3	3				1	1		1				45
Non-worker	13				1										1	15
No data	3															3
All	133	72	1	49	43	5	14	5	28	5	5	6	2	2	2	372

(*continued*)

(B) Primary and secondary status activities, females, 2015

Primary activity	No secondary activity	Self-employment in Agriculture	Agricultural labour	Animal husbandry	Trade	Government service	Self-employment in service	Other service	Housework	Student	All
Self-employment (agriculture)			8	6					7		21
Agricultural labour		5		5			1		20		31
Animal husbandry		2	1						1		4
Manufacturing									2		2
Government service					1		1		3		5
Other service			1	1							2
Housework	82	42	14	96		1	1	2		1	239
Student	26	4	3	1	1	1			16		52
Non-worker	13								2		15
All	121	53	27	109	1	2	4	2	51	1	371

(C) Secondary and tertiary status activities, females, 2015

Secondary activity	No tertiary activity	Self-emp in agriculture	Agricultural labour	Animal husbandry	MGNREGA	Other service	Housework	All
No secondary activity	121							121
Self-employment (agriculture)	22	4	22	2	3			53
Agricultural labour	2	4	14	1	6			27
Animal husbandry	60	41	1	1	6			109
Trade	1							1
Government service	2							2
Self-employment (service)	3	1						4
Other service	1	1						2
Housework	29	4	2	15	1			51
Student	1							1
All	241	49	8	52	4	1	16	371

4

Proletarianisation and Women's Work
Notes on Rural India

V. K. Ramachandran

Differentiation and accompanying proletarianisation of the peasantry are prominent features of agrarian relations in India today. Most studies of differentiation are of peasant *households* that are not disaggregated by gender.[1] In this chapter, I attempt to extend our understanding of the process of proletarianisation in India by focusing on women's labour in peasant and manual worker households.[2] More specifically, the chapter deals with women's family labour on the farm, labour power hired in on farms, working out at agricultural tasks, and working out at non-agricultural tasks.[3]

This study has been made possible by the availability of gender-disaggregated data on different forms of labour in the database of the Project on Agrarian Relations in India (PARI) conducted by the Foundation for Agrarian Studies (FAS). The chapter uses PARI data from 16 villages.

Peasant households, whose members work on all or some of the major manual operations on the land, constitute the sector of petty producers that lies between landlords and big capitalist farmers on the one hand, and manual workers on the other. The peasantry is a tenacious, enduring social category, having existed continuously under different historical social formations. The transition from a peasantry essentially engaged in subsistence cultivation, in pre-capitalist and early capitalist epochs, to one whose chief characteristic is its subjugation to the market (and, indeed, both types exist concurrently in different parts of the world) is a process that has spanned centuries and historical epochs.

The Marxist position on the peasantry and proletarianisation has its roots

---

[1] An exception is Deere (1995), who makes a similar point for Latin America.

[2] This chapter draws on, and is a companion piece to, Ramachandran (2019).

[3] We have not used, at this stage, the data on work at tasks connected with household animal resources. For the technical reader, the data used are on work that is classified as work under the System of National Accounts (SNA).

in Marx's own writings. In *The Eighteenth Brumaire of Louis Napoleon*, Marx wrote of the small-holding French peasantry that

> their field of production, the small holding, permits no division of labour in its cultivation, no application of science, and therefore no multifariousness of development, no diversity of talent, no wealth of social relationships. Each individual peasant family is almost self-sufficient, directly produces most of its consumer needs, and *thus acquires its means of life more through an exchange with nature than in intercourse with society.* (Marx 1852; emphasis added)

It is clear that such a definition is not true of the modern peasantry, both with regard to the productive forces (and, in particular, the application of science and technology to agriculture) and the relations of production (in particular, the subjugation of the peasantry to the capitalist market).

As commodity production and the development of capitalism in agriculture proceed, so does differentiation of the peasantry. The most complete definition of differentiation is Lenin's classic formulation at the end of Chapter 2 in *The Development of Capitalism in Russia*: The sum total of all the economic contradictions among the peasantry constitutes what we call the differentiation of the peasantry (Lenin [1899] 1972).

Differentiation of the peasantry is not restricted to squeezing out the middle tiers of the peasantry or the consequent exacerbation of inequality, nor is it restricted to the process by which the peasantry, particularly the poor peasantry, is proletarianised. Rather, it encompasses the whole range of contradictions that

> are inherent in every commodity economy and every order of capitalism: competition, the struggle for economic independence, the grabbing of land (purchasable and rentable), the concentration of production in the hands of a minority, the forcing of the majority into the ranks of the proletariat, their exploitation by a minority through the medium of merchant's capital and the hiring of farm labourers. There is not a single economic phenomenon among the peasantry that does not bear this contradictory form, one specifically peculiar to the capitalist system, i.e., that does not express a struggle and antagonism of interests, that does not imply advantage for some and disadvantage for others. (*Ibid.*)

DATA AND METHODOLOGY

Data in this chapter come from surveys conducted as part of the Project on Agrarian Relations in India (PARI) by the Foundation for Agrarian Studies.

PARI involves detailed census-type household surveys in villages across diverse agro-ecological regions of India. The number of villages surveyed as part of PARI is now 25. A note is necessary on the database of villages used in this chapter. Sixteen villages were covered in the earlier study, that is, in the study of all peasant and worker households (Ramachandran 2019). The study of women in peasant and worker households, however, covers 14 villages. This is because, in all but two villages, we were able to estimate the share of women working in groups of piece-rated wage workers, a distinction necessary for the calculations in the present chapter. Women of the household were present when the data on women's work was entered in the schedules.

A great deal of Marxist effort in the study of agrarian relations in India has focused on formulating criteria for identifying classes in the countryside (Ramachandran 2012a). One of the main historical influences on Indian Marxist work in this regard is the work of P. Sundarayya (1913–1985) (Ramachandran 2012b). The major influences on Sundarayya's work in this regard were the writings of Marx and Engels, Lenin's *The Development of Capitalism in Russia* and *To the Rural Poor*, Mao Zedong's writings on the peasantry (especially *Report on an Investigation of the Peasant Movement in Hunan* and *Analysis of the Classes in Chinese Society*), as well as the documents and formulations of land reform legislation in post-liberation China (including Liu Shaoqi's speech titled "On the Agrarian Reform Law"). The actual classifications attempted by Sundarayya were, of course, specific to the conditions that he encountered in his studies in India (see Ramachandran 2012b).

The PARI database provides a list of households in each village categorised into socio-economic classes. The three main socio-economic class strata engaged in crop production in a village are landlords and big capitalist farmers, agricultural workers, and a differentiated peasantry. There are also classes in the village that are not directly engaged in crop production (though they may be associated with the agrarian economy in different degrees), and these are analysed and classified separately.

The peasantry in each village has been categorised into classes based on three criteria. These are, first, the extent to which members of a household participate in manual operations on the land; secondly, the land and asset holdings of the household; and thirdly, the incomes of the household.[4] I have used the PARI classification, which has been made available to data users.

When classifying households by the labour criterion, a labour ratio was computed for each peasant household. In this labour ratio, the numerator is

---

[4] In the actual classification, however, for certain methodological reasons, the total assets of the household were given some priority in assigning class.

the sum of the number of days of family labour on the farm, and the number of days of work by members of the household at agricultural and non-agricultural tasks as hired workers. The denominator is the number of days of work by hired labourers on the family farm (labour hired in). In each village, the peasantry was classified into three or more socio-economic classes. As may be expected, the labour ratio was low for rich peasant households and high for small or poor peasant households.

The database allowed us to pursue our objective of studying the distinctive features of proletarianisation among women. The villages were drawn from a range of agro-ecological zones. The present exercise allowed us to draw some conclusions with reference to these zones, and to develop a methodology for the study of differentiation and proletarianisation among rural farm and non-farm worker women.

Proletarianisation of the Peasantry

Earlier studies based on PARI data attempted to describe and analyse socio-economic characteristics of different classes in rural society. Four of the main findings of our previous research on proletarianisation of the peasantry are as follows.[5]

First, the data showed that even on farms of small and middle peasants, the share of family labour expended on the farm was, in general, less than the share of hired labour employed on the farm (Table 4.1). Most small and medium peasant households thus hired in more labour than provided by members of their family.

Secondly, if the labour power deployed by a peasant household in a year is divided into three parts – family labour on the farm, farm work for wages, and non-farm work for wages – the share of the first element of the total was low, and, in many villages, less than 50 per cent for small peasant households (Table 4.2).

Thirdly, the market for hired labour has broadened, with more sections of the peasantry than before participating in it (Table 4.3). In many villages, workers from small and middle peasant households contribute as much or more to the total number of days of labouring out for wages than workers from manual worker households.

Fourthly, with regard to rural manual workers, one of the major findings of our research was that it was no longer possible to separate a stratum of agricultural workers from non-agricultural workers in rural India. The

---

[5] See Ramachandran (2019).

typical rural manual worker in India today could be characterised more as a "miscellaneous worker in rural society" than solely as a farm or non-farm worker (discussed in, for instance, Ramachandran 2011 and CPI(M) 2016).

The next section attempts to examine these four findings separately for women workers.

Table 4.1 *Days of family labour on farm as a proportion of days of both types of labour (family and hired) on farm, middle and small peasant households, selected villages* in per cent

State/village	Small peasant households (family labour/ family+hired labour)	Middle peasant households (family labour/ family+hired labour)
Andhra Pradesh		
Ananthavaram	32	21
Bukkacherla	26	27
Kothapalle	27	52
Karnataka		
Alabujanahalli	63	52
Siresandra	56	49
Zhapur	48	48
Madhya Pradesh		
Gharsondi	75	53
Maharashtra		
Nimshirgaon	60	38
Warwat Khanderao	45	23
Rajasthan		
25F Gulabewala	47	24
Rewasi	77	71
Uttar Pradesh		
Harevli	87	56
Mahatwar	94	82
West Bengal		
Amarsinghi	56	15
Kalmandasguri	71	43
Panahar	78	32

Source: Ramachandran (2019).

Table 4.2 *Days of family labour as a proportion of days of all types of labour (family and hired), by small and middle peasants, selected villages* in per cent

State/village	Small peasant households	Middle peasant households
Andhra Pradesh		
Ananthavaram	23.2	45.1
Bukkacherla	47.1	64.3
Kothapalle	37.6	66.2
Karnataka		
Alabujanahalli	70.3	94.5
Siresandra	34.9	76.6
Zhapur	33.3	99.7
Madhya Pradesh		
Gharsondi	33.3	66.4
Maharashtra		
Nimshirgaon	44.1	85.3
Warwat Khanderao	33.8	92.4
Rajasthan		
25F Gulabewala	90.9	100
Rewasi	66.1	72.3
Uttar Pradesh		
Harevli	28.2	96.4
Mahatwar	35.2	58.6
West Bengal		
Amarsinghi	49	44.7
Kalmandasguri	53.5	78.5
Panahar	28.7	79.5

Source: Ramachandran (2019).

Table 4.3 *Share of selected classes in total days of wage employment reported by workers in the village* in per cent

Village	Manual workers	Small and middle peasants	All other classes
Andhra Pradesh			
Ananthavaram	42.5	51.9	5.6
Bukkacherla	55.2	43.4	1.4
Kothapalle	83.7	8	8.3
Karnataka			
Alabujanahalli	82	10.9	7.1
Siresandra	27.7	70.3	2
Zhapur	57.2	37.9	5
Madhya Pradesh			
Gharsondi	73.8	18.2	8
Maharashtra			
Nimshirgaon	83.4	11.2	5.4
Warwat Khanderao	59.4	30.8	9.8
Rajasthan			
25F Gulabewala	94.7	0.7	4.6
Rewasi	53.8	42.5	3.7
Uttar Pradesh			
Harevli	39.3	60.4	0.3
Mahatwar	55.8	34.4	9.8
West Bengal			
Amarsinghi	81.5	9.8	8.7
Kalmandasguri	58.3	34.3	7.4
Panahar	43.5	55	1.4

Source: Ramachandran (2019).

What Do the Data on Women Workers Show?

Previous Finding 1

Even on the farms of small and middle peasants, the share of family labour expended on the farm was, in many cases, less than the share of hired labour employed on the farm. In any case, all sections employed hired workers. With respect to this finding, our study of *women's work* on family farms (that is, household operational holdings) led to some interesting conclusions.

Extended finding with special reference to women's work
First, in all villages, all sections of the peasantry hired male and female labour power. This varied by agro-ecological region, and, within that, it varied particularly by crop and the historical features of women's participation in agricultural operations. This is well known but worth repeating, as it means that the mere fact of hiring in does not act as a class demarcator, particularly between the poorer sections of the peasantry (Table 4.4).

Secondly, the ratio of family labour to hired labour among women from all peasant classes on household operational holdings was less than one (Table 4.4). In other words, the number of days of women's family labour on their farms was always lower than the number of days of female farm labour hired in

Table 4.4 *Ratio of female family labour days to hired female labour days, by village* in per cent

Village	Male family labour/ hired male labour (on farm)	Female family labour/ hired female labour (on farm)
Andhra Pradesh		
Ananthavaram	0.8	0.11
Kothapalle	1.7	0.06
Bukkacherla	0.9	0.15
Karnataka		
Alabujanahalli	2.4	0.23
Siresandra	6.7	0.48
Zhapur	2.9	0.42
Maharashtra		
Nimshirgaon	4.9	0.9
Warwat Khanderao	1.7	0.51
Uttar Pradesh		
Harevli	10.3	8.98
Mahatwar	39.4	9.56
West Bengal		
Amarsinghi	1.2	0.45
Kalmandasguri	3.5	0.9
Panahar	1.7	0.68
Bihar		
Katkuian	1.7	0.23

Source: PARI data.

by these households. This was true, interestingly, for *all* villages other than two. The exceptions were the Uttar Pradesh villages, one in Bijnor in the west and the other in Ballia in the east. The immediate reasons for these two exceptions were the prevalence of female family labour in rice and wheat cultivation, including harvest and post-harvest operations, and sugarcane cultivation.

Thirdly, in general, where the ratio of total family labour to hired labour is low, as it is among the lower middle and poor sections of the peasantry, it is because the ratio is brought down by low family labour to hired labour ratios among women.[6] The family labour to hired labour ratio among men in these classes is always greater than the corresponding ratio among women, and generally, as expected, greater than one (Table 4.4).

With regard to female family labour in manual worker households with land, the ratio of family labour to hired labour was greater than one in most villages, with the exception of some villages in south India and east India.

Fourthly, in order to better understand the differences between the use of male and female labour on the family farm, we examined whether the following proposition held:

Family labour of men on farms > family labour of women on farms
AND
Hired female labour on farms > hired male labour on farms

We found that this proposition held for most villages. It held everywhere other than in the two villages in the alluvial zone (Gangetic and Vindhyan) of West Bengal and the eastern Uttar Pradesh village (Table 4.5). In each of these three villages, only the first part of the proposition held (the second did not). We have to examine this phenomenon further, but the reason is likely to be associated with historically low levels of female participation in farm activity and the labour market in these villages.

Previous Finding 2

If the labour power deployed by a peasant household in a year is divided into three parts – family labour on the farm, farm work for wages, and non-farm work for wages – the share of the first element in the total was low, and less than 50 per cent in many villages.

---

[6] We, of course, expect the ratio of family labour to hired labour to be low among the upper middle and rich sections of the peasantry.

Table 4.5 *Ratio of male to female family and hired labour, by village* in per cent

Village	Male family labour/ female family labour	Male hired labour/ female hired labour
Andhra Pradesh		
Ananthavaram	3.5	0.5
Kothapalle	1.5	0.1
Bukkacherla	1.8	0.6
Karnataka		
Alabujanahalli	13	0.9
Siresandra	2.4	0.2
Zhapur	1.8	0.2
Maharashtra		
Nimshirgaon	4.7	0.5
Warwat Khanderao	1.3	0.4
Uttar Pradesh		
Harevli	6.3	0.9
Mahatwar	2.1	1.1
West Bengal		
Amarsinghi	3.3	1.4
Kalmandasguri	2.3	0.6
Panahar	5.4	2.2
Bihar		
Katkuian	4	0.5

Source: PARI data.

Extended finding with special reference to women's work
We tested this finding for the poorest section of the peasantry in 14 villages. The data show that among the poor peasantry, both male and female workers labour outside more than they work on their own farms. The data show, in particular, that this is true for all women with the exception of those in the two West Bengal villages in the alluvial zone (Table 4.6, second column). This reflects, once again, the low development of the market for female hired labour in rice-growing villages in West Bengal. For women, this was mainly on account of wage labour in agriculture, as non-agricultural jobs were few in our study villages.

Table 4.6 *Ratio of labour days deployed on own farm to labour days for wage work by gender, by village* in per cent

Village	Own farm/wage work		Own farm/ agricultural wage work	Own farm/ non-agricultural wage work
	Male	Female	Female	Female
Andhra Pradesh				
Ananthavaram	0.1	0.11	0.1	2.6
Kothapalle	0.5	0.29	0.3	4.2
Bukkacherla	0.6	0.3	0.3	NA
Karnataka				
Alabujanahalli	3.1	0.64	0.9	2
Siresandra	0.6	0.19	0.3	0.7
Zhapur	0.5	0.53	0.6	4.2
Maharashtra				
Nimshirgaon	1	0.91	0.1	NA
Warwat Khanderao	0.4	0.62	0.5	9.3
Uttar Pradesh				
Harevli	0.3	0.34	0.3	16
Mahatwar	0.5	0.92	1.9	1.8
West Bengal				
Amarsinghi	0.8	2.41	3.9	6.2
Kalmandasguri	0.6	1.02	1.1	29
Panahar	0.4	0.25	0.5	0.5
Bihar				
Katkuian	1	0.93	0.9	NA

Note: No non-agricultural work was done by females from poor peasant households in Katkuian, Bukkacherla and Nimshirgaon during the survey years.
Source: PARI data.

Previous Finding 3

The market for hired labour has broadened, with more sections of the peasantry and others participating in it than before.

Extended finding with special reference to women's work
In each village, we took the labour days worked by women of all classes for wages at both agricultural and non-agricultural tasks. We then looked at how this aggregate was distributed among manual workers, various peasant classes,

Table 4.7 *Distribution of total days of female wage work among manual workers, peasant classes, and other socio-economic classes, by village* in per cent

Village	All manual workers	All peasants	Others	Total
Andhra Pradesh				
Ananthavaram	40.6	42.4	17	100
Kothapalle	86.6	5.8	7.6	100
Bukkacherla	86.6	6.2	7.3	100
Karnataka				
Alabujanahalli	83	10.7	6.3	100
Siresandra	32.8	65.8	1.4	100
Zhapur	72.5	23.3	4.3	100
Maharashtra				
Nimshirgaon	83.8	12.6	3.6	100
Warwat Khanderao	57.5	27.7	14.8	100
Uttar Pradesh				
Harevli	55	45	0	100
Mahatwar	48.8	45.2	6	100
West Bengal				
Amarsinghi	79.2	6.3	14.5	100
Kalmandasguri	60.3	29.8	9.9	100
Panahar	49.9	49	1.2	100
Bihar				
Katkuian	92.3	4.8	2.8	100

Source: PARI data.

and other classes. The outcome of the exercise was that while the number of days worked by manual workers generally (as expected) predominated in the aggregate, the share of women from peasant households was also very significant. Table 4.7 summarises the results of this exercise.

Among women as much as among men, significant sections of those who work as hired workers for wages come from peasant households and from households whose main income is from sources other than manual work or crop production.

Previous Finding 4

The typical rural manual worker in India today may be characterised more as a "miscellaneous worker in rural society" than solely as a farm or non-farm worker.

Table 4.8 *Share of female manual workers engaged in wage work, by village* in per cent

Village	No. of female manual workers	Share in wage work	Share in only farm work	Share in only non-farm work	Share in farm and non-farm work
Andhra Pradesh					
Ananthavaram	215	63.3	100	0	0
Kothapalle	80	78.8	90.5	0	9.5
Bukkacherla	246	76	87.2	6.4	6.4
Karnataka					
Alabujanahalli	128	67.2	29.1	14	57
Siresandra	21	71.4	20	20	60
Zhapur	93	86	68.8	23.8	7.5
Maharashtra					
Nimshirgaon	472	37.3	97.2	0	2.8
Warwat Khanderao	131	74	78.4	1	20.6
Uttar Pradesh					
Harevli	32	78.1	84	4	12
Mahatwar	66	47	90.3	6.5	3.2
West Bengal					
Amarsinghi	77	76.6	44.1	5.1	50.8
Kalmandasguri	70	72.9	78.4	2	19.6
Panahar	86	62.8	9.3	42.6	48.1
Bihar					
Katkuian	291	55.6	93.8	1.9	4.3

Source: PARI data.

Extended finding with special reference to women's work
This conclusion varies substantially with region and appears to apply more to men than women (Table 4.8). In some villages, the number who work at both agricultural and non-agricultural tasks constitute a relatively high share, and in some villages a low share. This is clearly an area of further study (see Shruti Nagbhushan, chapter 11 in this volume), and, for a richer picture, will have to be complemented by our data on migration, given that many women are likely to be engaged in non-farm work when they migrate from the village.

SUMMING UP

There are noteworthy gender dimensions to the general process of proletarianisation that has occurred among the peasantry as a whole. Although it is an all-India phenomenon, proletarianisation takes very specific forms regionally, by agro-ecological zone, and by crop.

In this chapter, we studied female labour within peasant households separately in order to explore gender-specific features of the process of proletarianisation. We believe that this exercise has not been undertaken previously. Our effort was made possible by the availability of gender-disaggregated data on different forms of labour in the PARI database.

The different types of female labour covered by our analysis are women's family labour on the farm, female labour power hired in on farms, and women's work outside their farms as hired agricultural and non-agricultural workers.[7]

We find that proletarianisation has specific and identifiable gender dimensions. In this chapter and previous work, we find that even the poor peasantry uses substantial hired labour, thus pushing down the ratio of family labour to hired labour on their farms. An important finding of this chapter is that the low ratio is mainly on account of the low ratio among women. The ratio of family labour to hired labour among men in these classes was not only higher than that of women but usually greater than one. A related observation is that among peasant households, male family labour tends to exceed female family labour, whereas the reverse is true when we consider hired labour on their farms.

Another finding is that women find less non-agricultural employment than men, and the part played by non-agricultural hired work in their annual work calendar is less than the shares of family labour on the farm and hired work in agriculture. Women's work is thus less diverse in absolute and relative terms.

Both these observations need to be studied in the context of migration and the changes that migration brings about: first, in the patterns of work when women workers migrate, and secondly, in the patterns of the labour of women who remain in the village when there is male-specific migration out of the village. As the pace of male migration rises, we need to study in much greater detail changes in women's labour within and outside the family farm.

For women and men, proletarianisation encompasses large new sections of the peasantry, as does the market for wage labour. When all sections hire labour, hired labour becomes an important component of the cost of cultivation even for poor peasants. The other side of the coin is that new sections work as wage workers; thus, struggles that result in higher wage rates for women means higher earnings for more and more women in peasant households as well.

---

[7] At different points of this chapter where we have mentioned female family labour, we referred specifically to female family labour on the family farm, that is, economic activity on the farm, and did not include other work such as animal rearing. This lacuna needs to be filled by future research.

From a political point of view, proletarianisation opens up new possibilities for the worker–peasant alliance in the countryside.

Study of gender-disaggregated features of socio-economic classes, especially peasant and worker classes, has important analytical, social, and political implications. Such an analysis can help formulate new demands that ultimately draw more women – that great untapped reservoir of the agrarian movement – into the ranks of the peasants' and rural workers' movement.

This paper began as a presentation by Shruti Nagbhushan, Subhajit Patra and me at the international conference on "Women's Work in Rural Economies" organised by the Foundation for Agrarian Studies and held in Vayalar, Kerala from 30 November to 2 December 2018. Since then Shruti has been my primary source of help with the database, and has commented on different parts of the paper. Gaurav Bansal made useful comments on the paper (I have not been able to incorporate all his suggestions, but shall do so when I work on this further), and Mansi Goyal edited the pre-final text. Parvathi Menon read and recast the paper entirely. Madhura Swaminathan worked extensively on the text. I am very grateful to all of them.

BIBLIOGRAPHY

Communist Party of India (Marxist) (2016), "Report of Study Group on Agrarian Classes," *The Marxist*, vol. 32, no. 2, April–June, available at http://cpim.org/sites/default/files/marxist/201602-marxist-studynotes-agrarian-classes.pdf, viewed on 27 March 2020.

Deere, Carmen Diana (1995), "What Difference Does Gender Make? Rethinking Peasant Studies," *Feminist Economics*, vol. 1, no. 1, pp. 53–72, available at https://doi.org/10.1080/714042214, viewed on 27 March 2020.

Lenin, Vladimir Illyich ([1899] 1972), *Collected Works, Volume 3: The Development of Capitalism in Russia*, Progress Publishers, Moscow.

Lenin, Vladimir Illyich (1910a), "A General Picture of the Economic System of Modern Agriculture," *The Capitalist System of Modern Agriculture*, available at http://www.marxists.org/archive/lenin/works/1910/csma/i.htm#v16pp74-437, viewed on 17 January 2019.

Lenin, Vladimir Illyich (1910b), "Peasant Farms under Capitalism," *The Capitalist System of Modern Agriculture*, available at http://www.marxists.org/archive/lenin/works/1910/csma/iii.htm#v16pp74-434, viewed on 17 January 2019.

Lenin, Vladimir Illyich (1910c), "The Real Nature of the Majority of Modern Agricultural 'Farms' (Proletarian 'Farms')," *The Capitalist System of Modern Agriculture*, available at http://www.marxists.org/archive/lenin/works/1910/csma/ii.htm#v16pp74-434, viewed on 17 January 2019.

Marx, Karl (1852), "Chapter VII (Summary)," *The Eighteenth Brumaire of Louis Bonaparte*, available at http://www.marxists.org/archive/marx/works/1852/18th-brumaire/ch07.htm, viewed on 15 May 2014.

Ramachandran, V. K. (2011), "The State of Agrarian Relations in India Today," *The Marxist*, XXVII, 1–2, January–June, pp. 51–89.

Ramachandran, V. K. (2012a), "Classes and Class Differentiation in India's Countryside," *World Review of Political Economy*, vol. 2, no. 4, pp. 646–70.

Ramachandran, V. K. (2012b), "P. Sundarayya on the Agrarian Question," *The Marxist*, XXVIII, 3, July–September.

Ramachandran, V. K. (2019), "Aspects of the Proletarianisation of the Peasantry in India," in A. Narayanamoorthy, R. V. Bhavani, and R. Sujatha (eds.), *Whither Rural India? Political Economy of Agrarian Transformation in Contemporary India*, Tulika Books, New Delhi, pp. 69–83.

II

Women's Work in Agriculture and Allied Sectors

5

Sectoral Shifts and Declining Labour Participation Rate of Women

Jayan Jose Thomas

The labour participation rate among females is quite low in India. According to the Periodic Labour Force Survey (PLFS) carried out in 2017–18, workers as a proportion of all females (aged 15 years and above) in rural and urban areas were 24.6 per cent and 20.4 per cent, respectively. The corresponding proportions for males were 76.4 per cent (rural) and 74.5 per cent (urban), as shown in Table 5.1.

The labour force participation rate indicates the proportion of the population

Table 5.1 *Distribution of population by activity status, India, 2017–18* in per cent

	Population				Population aged 15 years and above			
	Rural males	Rural females	Urban males	Urban females	Rural males	Rural females	Urban males	Urban females
Labour force	54.9	18.2	57	15.9	76.4	24.6	74.5	20.4
Workers	51.7	17.5	53	14.2	72	23.7	69.3	18.2
Unemployed	3.2	0.7	4	1.7	4.4	0.9	5.2	2.2
Students	29.3	24.5	27.2	24.8	14.7	10.3	14.5	12.9
Attending domestic duties (92+93)	0.8	43.2	0.7	46.7	1	57.8	0.8	59.4
Population	100	100	100	100	100	100	100	100

Note: Population includes those who are part of the labour force as well as those who are not. Persons who are not part of the labour force include those who are too young or too old to work, students, rentiers, recipients of pensions or remittances, the disabled, as well as people attending to "domestic duties." Persons attending domestic duties are categorised under activity statuses 92 and 93. Activity status 92 refers to persons "attending domestic duties only," while activity status 93 refers to people who were engaged in domestic duties as well as in the free collection of goods (such as vegetables, firewood, and cattle feed) or in sewing, tailoring, and weaving for household use.
Source: PLFS (2019).

that is economically active, which includes those who are employed as well as those unemployed but seeking jobs. The proportion of the population that is employed is denoted by work force participation rate or worker–population ratio (WPR). Persons who are not economically active comprise those who are too young or too old to work, students, rentiers, recipients of pensions or remittances, the disabled, as well as people attending to "domestic duties."

There has been a sharp decline in female WPRs in India since the late 2000s, according to the Employment and Unemployment Survey (EUS) conducted in various years by the National Sample Survey Organisation (NSSO). WPRs among rural females (all ages) in India had risen impressively from 29.7 per cent in 1999–2000 to 32.7 per cent in 2004–05, but rural female WPRs fell subsequently to 24.9 per cent in 2011–12 and 17.5 per cent in 2017–18 (the last rate is based on PLFS), as shown in Table 5.2. The other side of the low rate of female labour force participation is a substantially high proportion of females reporting their activity status as attending to domestic duties. The

Table 5.2 *Distribution of female population by activity status, rural India, 1993–94 to 2017–18* in per cent

	Population					Population aged 15 years and above				
	1993–94	1999–2000	2004–05	2011–12	2017–18	1993–94	1999–2000	2004–05	2011–12	2017–18
Labour force	33.1	30	33.3	25.3	18.2	49	45.2	49.4	35.8	24.6
Workers	32.8	29.7	32.7	24.9	17.5	48.6	45.7	48.5	35.2	23.7
Unemployed	0.3	0.3	0.6	0.4	0.7	0.4	0.5	0.9	0.6	0.9
Students	14.8	18.4	21.3	25.1	24.5	3	4.1	4.9	8.5	10.3
Attending domestic duties (92+93)	29.1	29.4	27.3	35.3	43.2	42.4	43.8	39.8	49.9	57.8
Total working-age population	77	77.8	81.9	85.7	85.9	94.4	94.1	94.1	94.2	92.7
Population	100	100	100	100	100	100	100	100	100	100

Note: Population includes those who are part of the labour force as well as those who are not. Persons who are not part of the labour force include those who are too young or too old to work, students, rentiers, recipients of pensions or remittances, the disabled, as well as people attending to "domestic duties." Persons attending domestic duties are categorised under activity statuses 92 and 93. Activity status 92 refers to persons "attending domestic duties only," while activity status 93 refers to people who were engaged in domestic duties as well as in the free collection of goods (such as vegetables, firewood, and cattle feed) or in sewing, tailoring, and weaving for household use.
Source: EUS (various years); PLFS (2019).

proportion among rural females (all ages) who, according to official data, were attending to domestic duties (activity status 92 and 93 combined, which are described below) was 27.3 per cent in 2004–05, which rose to 35.3 per cent in 2011–12 and still further to 43.2 per cent by 2017–18.

Estimates of the number of workers (or of persons in other activity statuses such as unemployed, not in labour force due to old age, and so on) are obtained by multiplying the WPR (or other relevant proportions) from the National Sample Surveys with the relevant population figures available from the Census of India. In 2011–12, out of India's total population of 1,227.4 million, 472.5 million (or 38.5 per cent) were estimated to be workers and 10.8 million (or 0.9 per cent) were unemployed, as shown in Table 5.3. Among the population not part of the labour force, there were 337.5 million students and another 232.4 million who, according to the official statistics, were described as attending to domestic duties. Out of the total rural female population (of all ages) of close to 410 million (in 2011–12) in India, there were 102 million workers, 1.6 million unemployed, another 102 million who were students, and 144 million women attending to domestic duties. These 144 million rural women who were attending to domestic duties comprised 68.9 million who were "attending to domestic duties only" (activity status 92),

Table 5.3 *Distribution of population by activity status, India, 2011–12* in millions

Activity status	Rural male	Rural female	Urban male	Urban female	Total
Labour force	238.7	103.2	112.5	28.9	483.3
Employed	234.4	101.6	109.1	27.4	472.5
Unemployed	4.3	1.6	3.4	1.5	10.8
Students	129.1	102	58.1	48.2	337.5
Attending to domestic duties only (92)	0.4	68.9	0.4	65.9	135.6
Attending to domestic duties and also engaged in other activities for household use (93)	0.9	75.8	0.2	19.9	96.8
Population	431.7	409.8	199.8	186.1	1227.4

Notes: Estimates of population correspond to 1 January 2012, and refer to usual principal and usual subsidiary status (UPSS) of workers. The total population includes those who are outside the working age population. Activity status 92 refers to persons "attending to domestic duties only," while activity status 93 refers to people who were engaged in domestic duties as well as in the free collection of goods (such as vegetables, firewood, and cattle feed) or in sewing, tailoring, and weaving for household use.

Source: NSSO (2013).

and 75.8 million who were also engaged in free collection of goods (such as vegetables, firewood, and cattle feed) or in sewing, tailoring, and weaving for household use (activity status 93).

The objective of this chapter is to understand the factors underlying the low rate of female participation in the labour force in rural India, as seen from the data of official statistical agencies, and also the sharp dip in this rate over the years. There are at least three main arguments for why the female labour participation rate in India has been low and declining since the 2000s. First, as some studies have pointed out, this decline was in fact associated with some positive changes in the Indian countryside, including an increase in the enrolment of females in education and improvement in the incomes of rural families (Rangarajan *et al.* 2011; Chand and Srivastava 2014).

Secondly, departing from the above-mentioned view, other studies have shown that the low rate of female labour participation in India is linked to some of the long-standing problems in the Indian economy and society. These include the slow growth of job opportunities, especially in rural areas and for women, social barriers to women's participation in activities outside the household, and discrimination faced by women at the workplace (Srivastava and Srivastava 2010; Mazumdar and Neetha 2011; Kannan and Raveendran 2012; Eswaran *et al.* 2013; Abraham 2013; Neetha 2014; Rawal and Saha 2015). Thirdly, there are studies that have focused attention on the problems of measuring female employment in India (Hirway and Jose 2011). This chapter, while building on the evidence presented in earlier studies, extends the analysis to a relatively less researched area: the implications of sector-wise and region-wise aspects of India's economic growth for female employment.

It may be noted that the work force participation rate observed in a particular round of NSSO surveys will reflect both the long-term structural changes in the labour market as well as the short-run impacts of specific conditions (such as a drought or flood) that might have emerged at the time of the survey. When the NSSO conducted its employment surveys during 1999–2000 and 2004–05, India's rural economy had been going through a major crisis, precipitated by a decline in public investment and a slowdown in the growth of agricultural incomes and rural wages. Further, rural areas in many parts of the country had been drought-affected in the year 2004–05. At the same time, by 2004–05, India's non-agricultural economy had begun to stage a revival after a period of slowdown beginning in the late 1990s. Finally, when the NSSO conducted its surveys in 2009–10 and 2011–12, India's rural economy was on a path of recovery. While analysing the results from the employment surveys of various years, we have also considered the specific economic circumstances (discussed above) that prevailed in the survey years.

FEMALE WORK FORCE PARTICIPATION AND EMPLOYMENT GROWTH IN THE 2000s

Female work participation rates in India have been found to be on a secular decline according to the NSSO surveys held since 1993–94, except for the 2004–05 survey. WPRs declined between 1993–94 and 1999–2000 but subsequently increased, such that in 2004–05, they were almost at the same levels as they had been in 1993–94. Female WPRs in India have been declining again, according to the employment surveys of 2009–10, 2011–12 and 2017–18 (see Table 5.2).

These changes in female WPRs have important implications for overall employment growth in India. The size of the female work force increased from 124 million in 1999–2000 to 148.7 million in 2004–05, but declined subsequently to 129 million by 2011–12, as shown in Table 5.4a. The size of the total (female and male) work force in India increased from 398.4 million

Table 5.4a *Estimates of workers by categories, India, 1983 to 2011–12* in millions

Years	All workers	All female workers	Agri-cultural workers	Female agri-cultural workers	Non-agri-cultural workers	Female non-agricultural workers
1983	303.3	102.8	207.2	83.1	96.1	19.7
1993–94	374.4	122	239.6	94.6	134.8	27.4
1999–2000	398.4	124	240.4	93.4	158	30.6
2004–05	457.8	148.7	257.8	107.5	200	41.2
2011–12	472.5	129	224.5	79.2	248	49.8

Source: EUS (various years).

Table 5.4b *Net increase in employment for workers, 1993–94 to 2011–12,* in per cent

	All workers	All female workers	Agri-cultural workers	Female agri-cultural workers	Non-agri-cultural workers	Female non-agricultural workers
1993–94 to 1999–2000	24	2	0.8	–1.2	23.2	3.2
1999–2000 to 2004–05	59.4	24.7	17.4	14	41.9	10.7
2004–05 to 2009–10	4.7	–20	–20.4	–21.2	25.1	1.2
2004–05 to 2011–12	14.7	–19.7	–33.3	–28.3	48	8.6

Source: EUS (various years).

in 1999–2000 to 457.8 million in 2004–05 – an increase of 59.4 million over a five-year period. On the other hand, during the seven years after 2004–05, the size of the total work force increased by only 14.7 million, to reach 472.5 million in 2011–12. The slowdown in the growth of overall employment in India during the second half of the 2000s was mainly on account of the decline in absolute numbers of the size of the female work force.

The slow growth of employment in India after 2004–05 despite the fast rates of economic growth achieved in this period has been a subject of much scholarly and general discussion (Thomas 2012). However, as Thomas (2015) argued, an analysis based on the growth of overall employment (that is, the sum of employment in agriculture and in the non-agricultural sector) could be misleading, especially in the context of a developing country like India. It is expected that employment in agriculture will decline with economic development, both in relative terms and in absolute numbers. Arthur Lewis had famously modelled the movement of "surplus labour" from the traditional (also agricultural or informal) to the modern (also industrial or formal) sectors. With the exhaustion of surplus labour reserves and with an absolute fall in the size of the agricultural work force, it was projected that real wages would rise in the economy (Fields 2004).

Shift of the Work Force Away from Agriculture

In India, the share of agriculture and allied activities in the GDP fell from 35.1 per cent in 1983 to 14 per cent in 2011–12. At the same time, the decline in the share of these sectors in total employment was much more gradual, from 68.2 per cent to 47.5 per cent between 1983 and 2011–12. Agriculture and allied activities continue to be a major source of female employment, accounting for 61.4 per cent of the total female work force even in 2011–12 (Thomas 2015). It must be noted that although women participate in agricultural work both as cultivators and hired labourers, such participation has not translated into greater empowerment for women (Rao 2011).

There has been a substantial diversification of the rural male work force away from agriculture especially since the 2000s. On the other hand, in the case of rural females (of all ages), there has been only a marginal improvement over the years in the proportion of those engaged in non-agricultural employment: from 4.5 per cent in 1993–94 to 6.2 per cent in 2011–12, as shown in Table 5.5. Given this context, the withdrawal of women from agricultural employment since 2004–05 resulted in a decline in rural female WPRs in India.

An overwhelming proportion of all persons joining the agricultural labour force in India between 1999–2000 and 2004–05 (15.5 million out of 17.4

Table 5.5 *Work force participation rates by gender, rural India, 1983 to 2011–12* in per cent

	1983	1993–94	1999–2000	2004–05	2011–12
Males					
Workers in agriculture and allied activities	42.4	41	37.9	36.3	32.2
Non-agricultural workers	12.3	14.3	15.2	18.3	22.1
All workers	54.7	55.3	53.1	54.6	54.3
Females					
Workers in agriculture and allied activities	29.8	28.3	25.5	27.2	18.7
Non-agricultural workers	4.3	4.5	4.2	5.5	6.2
All workers	34.1	32.8	29.7	32.7	24.9

Note: The WPR is based on usual principal and usual subsidiary status (UPSS) workers as a proportion of the population (all ages).
Source: EUS (various years).

million) were self-employed rural females. On the contrary, between 2004–05 and 2011–12, the population of females engaged in agriculture and allied activities declined by 28.3 million, which accounted for a good part of the decline in the total agricultural work force (by 33.3 million) during this period, as shown in Table 5.4b.

GDP growth in Indian agriculture had been statistically insignificant during the first half of the 2000s. Therefore, the rise in the size of the agricultural work force between 1999–2000 and 2004–05 was quite puzzling. Equally puzzling was the sharp fall in the size of the agricultural work force between 2004–05 and 2011–12, because agricultural incomes were revived during that period (Thomas 2015). How could agricultural employment have increased during a period when agricultural incomes stagnated, and later decreased when agricultural incomes revived?

One argument has been that the entry of rural women into the agricultural labour force in the first half of the 2000s (between 1999–2000 and 2004–05) was to supplement low household incomes, given the stagnancy in income growth in the countryside during these years (Abraham 2009). There were some indications of distress employment among rural women during the first half of the 2000s, particularly the relatively fast growth of employment among women in older age-cohorts, and also among women belonging to households with marginal landholdings (*ibid.*). Further, as Mazumdar and Neetha (2011) showed, between 2000 and 2005, the share of unpaid family workers within all rural female workers increased while, at the same time, the share of casual workers declined.

In contrast, during the period after the mid-2000s, both push and pull factors appear to have caused the movement of the work force away from agriculture. The Mahatma Gandhi National Rural Employment Guarantee Act (MNREGA) produced a substantial impact on rural employment and rural wages during the late 2000s. In fact, casual employment in public works accounted for 69 per cent (3.7 million out of 5.4 million, according to the UPSS) of the incremental non-agricultural employment generated for rural females during 2004–05 to 2011–12 (Thomas 2014, p. 16). The daily real wages of rural female causal workers (aged 15–59 years) engaged in works other than public works grew at an average annual rate of only 1.4 per cent between 1999–2000 and 2004–05, but wage growth accelerated to 7.2 per cent between 2004–05 and 2011–12 (Thomas 2015). Usami (2012) found that the real wages of agricultural workers in India remained stagnant or even slightly declined between 1999–2000 and 2006–07, but real wages began to rise after 2007–08.

There have been other factors as well that led to the withdrawal of workers, including male workers, from agriculture. Notable among these is the marked acceleration in the growth of male workers in the construction sector in rural India after 2004–05, a significant part of which occurred in less developed and chiefly agrarian states such as Uttar Pradesh, Rajasthan, Bihar, and Madhya Pradesh. Of course, there have been equally strong factors that appear to have pushed workers out of low-productivity agriculture. Farmer suicides continue to be reported from several regions of the country. Surveys conducted by the Foundation for Agrarian Studies (FAS) showed that a significant proportion of cultivator households in selected villages in Maharashtra and Andhra Pradesh had been earning negative incomes from crop production in 2005–06 (Ramachandran and Rawal 2010). Also, there have been increasing instances across the country of farmlands being acquired for commercial and industrial purposes. As Rawal and Saha (2015) showed, a decline in the proportion of households that cultivate land and an increase in the concentration of operational holdings have contributed to a decrease in opportunities for women to be self-employed in agriculture.

Increase in the Population of Students

Another factor that has influenced India's labour market since the 2000s is a sharp rise in the population of students, notably in rural areas and among females. During the seven years after 2004–05, the students-to-population ratio (SPR) among rural males and females belonging to the 15–19 age group increased by 20 percentage points, reaching 64 per cent and 54 per cent, respectively, by 2011–12 (Thomas 2015). A majority of the students aged 15–19 years are likely to be pursuing post-secondary education. Therefore, the above-mentioned numbers are indicative of some progress achieved in India's higher education after the mid-2000s.

The increase in the population of students has had important implications for India's labour market. Between 2004–05 and 2011–12, while India's female population (all ages) increased by 66.9 million, the population of female students increased by 32.9 million; students thus accounted for 49.2 per cent of the country's incremental female population. In fact, students accounted for 69 per cent of the incremental population of rural females (all ages) (22.4 million out of 32.4 million) during this period. A substantial part of the decline in WPR among rural females in India since the mid-2000s is on account of the increase in the population of students.

The Rise in Women Attending to Domestic Duties: How Real Is It?

There are major difficulties in measuring women's work, which comprises large components of informal work and subsistence work, particularly so in rural areas. As Hirway and Jose (2011) pointed out, women's informal work is sometimes scattered, short-term in nature, often home-based, and largely unpaid. A woman in a rural household may have to collect water, clean the animal shed, milk the animals, work in her family farm, and also work as a hired labourer (*ibid.*). Subsistence work, which is the production of goods (including food, fuel, and clothing) for self-consumption, is included in the production boundary of the United Nations System of National Accounts (UNSNA). On the other hand, India's NSSO does not consider all subsistence work (such as processing of agricultural products for own consumption) as economic activity. Women are also involved in unpaid work for the household, including household management, caring for the young and old, and voluntary services, which are considered non-SNA work or "extended economic work" (Hirway and Jose 2011; Mazumdar and Neetha 2011; Rawal and Saha 2015).

It must be noted that a large part of women's work in rural India comprises unpaid family labour that contributes towards economic activities (this does not include domestic work such as cooking, cleaning, and child care). In 2004–05, 63.7 per cent of all rural female workers in India were self-employed, and unpaid workers accounted for 76 per cent of all self-employed rural females (thus, unpaid workers accounted for 48 per cent of all rural female workers) (Mazumdar and Neetha 2011). It may sometimes become difficult to distinguish between women's informal or subsistence work and household labour (such as, for instance, between cooking for hired farm workers and cooking for family members). As a result, "women's production activities are frequently hidden behind their household work" (Hirway and Jose 2011, p. 70). The problems of measuring female work, discussed above, are compounded by the social and cultural biases of both the respondents and investigators (*ibid.*).

Between 1999–2000 and 2004–05, the proportion of all rural women who reported their economic status as "attending to domestic duties" declined by 2.1 percentage points, while the proportion of workers among rural females increased by 3 percentage points (mostly self-employed in agriculture). But this was reversed between 2004–05 and 2011–12. The proportion of rural females who were attending to domestic duties rose by 8 percentage points (from 27.3 per cent to 35.3 per cent), while the proportion of workers among rural females declined by 7.8 percentage points (from 32.7 per cent to 24.9 per cent), mostly due to the decline of those self-employed in agriculture as shown in Table 5.2. As previously discussed, a possible reason for the return of women to work in their own households during the second half of the 2000s is the improvement in availability of income-earning opportunities for males of the family.

At the same time, it needs to be investigated whether part of the above-mentioned changes in women's employment is a result of some of the changes in the way NSSO measured women's activity status (especially self-employed in agriculture and attending to domestic duties). As already noted above, it may be difficult for investigators to distinguish between rural women's work in their own households (activity statuses 92 and 93) and unpaid labour among women categorised as self-employed. In fact, among all rural women, the combined share of workers and those engaged in domestic duties has remained remarkably stable over the years: 59.1 per cent in 1999–2000, 60 per cent in 2004–05, 60.2 per cent in 2011–12, and 60.7 per cent in 2017–18 (Table 5.2). It is also important to note that the proportions of rural and urban females who are engaged in both domestic duties and activities such as tailoring or weaving for household use (activity status 93) increased considerably during the 2000s (Tables 5.1 and 5.2).

In summary, the slow growth of overall employment in the Indian economy during the 2000s is partly due to the structural changes in the country's labour market. The most important of these changes is the absolute fall in the size of the agricultural labour force. The decline in female agricultural employment during the second half of the 2000s is possibly due to an improvement, even if marginal, and not a worsening of economic conditions in rural India.

Slow Growth of Non-Agricultural Employment Opportunities for Women

The most severe obstacle to female labour participation in India is likely to be the sheer absence of suitable employment opportunities. Females accounted for around 20 per cent of the incremental non-agricultural employment generated in India during the 1980s (7.7 million out of 38.7 million total workers) and 1990s (13.8 million out of 65.2 million), but an even smaller 18 per cent share between 2004 and 2012 (8.6 million out of 48 million) (see Thomas 2015).

With improvement in household incomes and in their own educational achievements, women will have higher expectations for jobs (Andres *et al.* 2017). However, the share of females in better-paid jobs has been particularly small. Between 2004–05 and 2011–12, the share of females in incremental employment was only 21 per cent in financing, real estate, and business services; 18 per cent in computer and related activities; and a meagre 3 per cent in trade, repair, hotels, transport, and communication combined. In 2011–12, women workers formed only 15 per cent or even less of the total employment in financing, real estate, and business services; computer and related activities; and public administration and defence (Thomas 2015). Lahoti and Swaminathan (2016) pointed out that India's recent economic growth led by the services sector might have been particularly slow in creating employment opportunities for women.

In manufacturing, women increasingly found employment as temporary or contract workers. There is some evidence that female workers were hit more acutely than male workers during periods of economic crisis such as in 2008–09 (Thomas 2015). It appears that given the inadequacy in gainful employment opportunities, women tend to withdraw from the labour force, especially so in households whose male members have some income-earning opportunities. The share of females attending to domestic duties rises with household consumption expenditures, particularly in urban areas (*ibid.*).

The slow overall growth of job opportunities in India has hit women more because of socio-cultural factors. In families belonging to the socially dominant castes, women feel pressurised to withdraw from the labour force rather than work in low-paid jobs. In this way, they contribute to the social status of their families, although at the cost of their individual autonomy (Abraham 2013; Eswaran *et al.* 2013). In addition, as Neetha (2014) showed, the decline in opportunities for casual employment since the 2000s has affected livelihood opportunities for women belonging to the Scheduled Castes and Scheduled Tribes.

The above discussion clearly indicates that a number of factors are responsible for the declining female labour force participation in India: improvement in educational achievements and household incomes, social barriers to female participation in the economy, the slow growth of overall employment opportunities, and problems in measuring female work. In fact, Kapsos *et al.* (2014) showed that of the total decline in rural female labour force participation in India between 2005 and 2010, 18 per cent was due to the effects of increased education and household incomes, 42 per cent was due to the general lack of employment opportunities for women, and the remaining 40 per cent was on account of changes in measurement methodology between the various survey rounds.

Female Work Force Participation Across States

In 2011–12, the WPRs of females in rural areas ranged from only 5.3 per cent in Bihar to 52.4 per cent in Himachal Pradesh. Female WPRs are less in urban areas than in rural areas across all Indian States. Urban female WPRs were 4.5 per cent and 21.2 per cent respectively in Bihar and Himachal Pradesh in 2011–12, as shown in Table 5.6.

WPRs in both rural and urban areas have been higher than the corresponding national averages in most of the southern and western States. WPRs of females in rural areas were significantly higher than the Indian average in Tamil Nadu, Andhra Pradesh, and Maharashtra in 2011–12. At the same time, however, female WPRs were lower than the corresponding national averages in rural Kerala, rural Goa, and urban Gujarat. Female WPRs were below the corresponding Indian average also in the case of most of the northern, eastern, and central States. The exceptions were Himachal Pradesh, Chhattisgarh, rural Rajasthan, rural Uttarakhand, and urban areas of West Bengal (Table 5.6).

There is no clear association between female WPRs, on the one hand, and per capita income and indicators of female empowerment (such as female literacy or sex ratio), on the other. Female WPR was only 10.4 per cent in Delhi (urban areas), which has one of the highest levels of per capita income in the country. Female WPR was also quite low in the urban areas of Haryana, which is another relatively rich State. Kerala and Tripura are two of the leading States in India with respect to female literacy rate and sex ratio, in addition to many other aspects of female empowerment. However, women in these States have not managed to achieve a significant degree of participation in the labour market and the economy in general (Table 5.6).

The North Eastern States are known to have more egalitarian gender relations as compared to the rest of India. WPRs of rural women in six out of the eight North Eastern States – namely, Meghalaya, Nagaland, Mizoram,

Table 5.6 *Workers as a proportion of population and selected indicators of social and economic development by State, 2011–12* in per cent

State	WPR in 2011–12				Female literacy rate, 2011	Index of per capita income, 2011–12	Sex ratio, 2011
	Rural male	Rural female	Urban male	Urban female			
Andhra Pradesh	60.2	44.5	55.4	17	59.7	110.8	992
Tamil Nadu	59.5	37.8	58.7	20.1	73.9	146.5	995
Karnataka	61.2	28.7	57.9	16.3	68.1	142.2	968
Kerala	56.5	22.1	55.2	19.1	92	154.3	1084
Maharashtra	57.6	38.8	54.9	16.6	75.5	156.9	925
Gujarat	59.9	27.8	60.3	13.3	70.7	137.8	918
Goa	54.7	21	51.1	15.7	81.8	408.8	973
Uttar Pradesh	49.1	17.7	51.1	10.2	59.3	50.4	908
Rajasthan	49.5	34.7	49	14.1	52.7	90.1	926
Punjab	56.6	23.4	57	13.6	71.3	134.8	893
Haryana	51.8	16.2	51.4	9.7	66.8	167.2	877
Jammu & Kashmir	54.7	25.5	53.9	11.7	58	83.8	883
Uttarakhand	45.2	30.8	50.6	8.6	70.7	158.1	963
Himachal Pradesh	54.1	52.4	60	21.2	76.6	138.2	974
Bihar	47.3	5.3	42.1	4.5	53.3	34.3	916
West Bengal	58.6	18.9	60.2	17.4	71.2	86.5	947
Jharkhand	53.3	19.8	48	6.6	56.2	65	947
Madhya Pradesh	56.1	23.9	52	11.5	60	60.7	930
Odisha	59.2	24.6	57.9	15.5	64.4	76.2	978
Chhattisgarh	55.7	41.5	49.6	24	60.6	86.9	991
Assam	54	12.2	54.2	9	67.3	64.8	954
Tripura	56.2	22.8	52.5	11.3	83.2	74.2	960
Meghalaya	52.7	39.1	50.3	20.2	73.8	94.6	989
Manipur	51	26.2	45.6	18.2	73.2	62.7	985
Nagaland	50.4	31.2	41.2	14.4	76.9	83.5	931
Arunachal Pradesh	48.3	27.8	45.7	12.7	59.6	115.1	938
Mizoram	59.1	39.4	48.7	24.9	89.4	90.8	976
Sikkim	58	48.7	60.9	27.3	76.4	250	890
Delhi	49.3	14.6	53	10.4	80.9	292.1	868
India	54.3	24.8	54.6	14.7	65.5	100	943

Sources: NSSO (2013); Thomas and Satheesha (2018).

Table 5.7 *Workers in agriculture and allied activities by State, 2011* in per cent

States	Based on NSSO 2011–12		Based on Census 2011			
	Workers in agriculture and allied activities as shares of:		Cultivators as shares of:		Agricultural workers as shares of:	
	all workers	female workers	all workers	female workers	all workers	female workers
Andhra Pradesh	52.5	65.5	16.5	14	43	58
Tamil Nadu	33.5	38.4	12.9	13.2	29.2	41.6
Karnataka	48.5	60.5	23.6	19	25.7	40.3
Kerala	20.4	25.5	5.8	3.9	11.4	14.7
Maharashtra	49.1	68.4	25.4	29.6	27.3	39.9
Gujarat	46.9	65.8	22	17.8	27.6	47.1
Goa	3.7	4.3	5.4	7.9	4.6	7.6
Uttar Pradesh	52	72.9	29	22.2	30.3	38.4
Rajasthan	49.9	70.4	45.6	52.6	16.5	24.2
Punjab	35.8	59	19.5	9.9	16	19.1
Haryana	40.9	68	27.8	32.8	17.1	23.1
Jammu & Kashmir	40.2	76.6	28.8	42.5	12.7	11.8
Uttarakhand	46.6	81.7	40.8	64	10.4	8.8
Himachal Pradesh	58.4	84.2	57.9	76.2	4.9	4.7
Bihar	61.6	71.5	20.7	15.3	52.8	60.8
West Bengal	36.8	29.5	14.7	7.7	29.3	34
Jharkhand	49.5	77.3	29.1	32.6	33.9	44.8
Madhya Pradesh	57.7	70.3	31.2	28.5	38.6	51.5
Odisha	54.9	64.2	23.4	12.9	38.4	57.8
Chhattisgarh	71.8	80.1	32.9	31.3	41.8	54.4
Assam	54.3	71.3	33.9	28.1	15.4	20.9
Tripura	24.4	16.8	20.1	15.8	24.1	32.9
Meghalaya	56.3	65.9	41.7	45.1	16.7	19.1
Manipur	38	20.9	39.5	37.9	9.6	13.6
Nagaland	63.2	80.7	55.2	65.2	6.5	7.3
Arunachal Pradesh	65.9	83.6	51.5	63.1	6.2	7.5
Mizoram	53.7	58.5	47.2	51.1	8.6	9.8
Sikkim	55.7	71.3	38.1	47.5	8.4	11.5
Delhi	0.1	0	0.6	0.7	0.7	1
India	47.5	61.4	24.6	24	30	41.1

Sources: EUS (various years); Census of India (2011).

Sikkim, Arunachal Pradesh, and Manipur – are higher than the national average. On the other hand, however, female WPRs in rural and urban areas in Assam and Tripura are significantly less than the corresponding Indian averages (Table 5.6).

Female WPRs seem to be associated with the proportion of the work force engaged in agriculture and allied activities, and also with the proportion of cultivators within the agricultural work force, as shown in Table 5.7. The proportion of the female work force engaged in agriculture and allied activities is quite low in Kerala (25.5 per cent), Goa (4.3 per cent), Tripura (16.8 per cent), and West Bengal (29.5 per cent). It appears that the relatively low female WPRs in the rural areas of these States are linked to the withdrawal of women from agricultural activities. On the other hand, agriculture and allied activities account for 80 per cent or more of the total female work force in Himachal Pradesh, Uttarakhand, and Chhattisgarh, as well as in Nagaland and Arunachal Pradesh; these are States with relatively high rates of female WPRs in rural areas (Tables 5.6 and 5.7).

The Census of India provides data on cultivators and agricultural workers separately. According to the 2011 data, the proportion of cultivators in both the total work force and the female work force were quite high in Himachal Pradesh, Uttarakhand, and Rajasthan, as well as in Meghalaya, Manipur, Nagaland, Arunachal Pradesh, Mizoram, and Sikkim. These are all States with relatively high rural female WPRs (Tables 5.6 and 5.7).

There are a few States in which rural male WPRs are relatively low but rural female WPRs are relatively high. These include Uttaranchal, Himachal Pradesh, and Rajasthan, as well as Meghalaya, Manipur, and Arunachal Pradesh. In Chhattisgarh, too, the rural female WPR is relatively high despite a somewhat high rural male WPR (Table 5.6). It needs to be further explored whether migration of male members of the family from States such as Uttarakhand, Himachal Pradesh, and Rajasthan over the years has resulted in a greater role for women in cultivation.

Changes during the 1990s: 1993–94 to 2004–05

In a number of States, rural female WPR declined sharply between 1993–94 and 1999–2000, and later, increased equally sharply between 1999–2000 and 2004–05, as shown in Table 5.8. It is difficult to attribute these changes in the labour market to what had been happening in the agricultural sector during that period. This is because almost the entire period, particularly between 1995–96 and 2004–05, was one in which India's agricultural growth had been slow. In five out of these ten years (between 1995–96 and 2004–05), the growth of either agricultural incomes or food production in the country had been negative or at very low levels. At the same time, within this period (1995–96 to 2004–05), 1999–2000 was a relatively good year for both agricultural incomes and food production, whereas 2004–05 was a particularly bad year with respect to rural incomes.

Rural female WPRs fluctuated widely over the years in a few States – Karnataka, Haryana, and Manipur. In Karnataka, for instance, rural female WPR declined from 43 per cent to 38.3 per cent between 1993–94 and

Table 5.8 *Female work force participation rates, rural India, 1983 to 2011–12* in per cent

State	1983	1993–94	1999–2000	2004–05	2011–12
Andhra Pradesh	47.1	52.1	47.9	48.3	44.5
Tamil Nadu	45.5	47.8	42	46.1	37.8
Karnataka	38.6	43	38.3	45.9	28.7
Kerala	31.4	23.8	23.8	25.6	22.1
Maharashtra	47.3	47.7	42.8	47.4	38.8
Gujarat	41.1	39.6	40.7	42.7	27.9
Goa	–	26.9	19.6	18.8	21
Uttar Pradesh	25.7	21.9	20.4	24	17.7
Rajasthan	46.6	45.7	38.1	40.7	34.7
Punjab	31.9	22	28	32.2	23.4
Haryana	23.2	27.1	19.7	31.7	16.2
Jammu & Kashmir	28.4	39.1	29.4	27.4	25.5
Uttarakhand	–	–	–	42.7	30.9
Himachal Pradesh	47.6	52	47.7	50.6	52.4
Bihar	24.8	17.2	17.2	13.8	5.3
Bengal	19.3	18.5	14.7	17.8	18.9
Jharkhand	–	–	–	31.3	19.8
Madhya Pradesh	43.2	41	38	36.6	23.9
Odisha	29.4	31.7	29.4	32.2	24.6
Chhattisgarh	–	–	–	45.4	41.6
Assam	12.6	15.9	15.7	21.1	12.2
Tripura	5.9	12.8	6.8	8.5	22.8
Meghalaya	42.8	49.3	42.4	47.8	39.1
Manipur	31.1	30.8	25.6	35.1	26.2
Nagaland	–	21.6	44.2	50.4	31.2
India	34	32.8	29.7	32.7	24.9

Source: EUS (various years).

1999–2000, then increased to 45.9 per cent in 2004–05, only to decline again to 28.7 per cent in 2011–12 (Table 5.8).

The decline in rural female WPRs in a few States appears to be part of the process of the structural shift of the labour force away from agriculture. In Tamil Nadu, Andhra Pradesh, Kerala, Goa, West Bengal, Tripura, and Meghalaya, the proportion of agricultural workers in the population (of rural females) declined and the proportion of non-agricultural workers in the population increased, though at a slower rate as compared to the decline in the agricultural work force in these States. By 2011–12, the proportion of non-agricultural workers in the population of rural females (all ages) was 10 per cent or more in each of the above-mentioned States and also in Manipur, as shown in Table 5.9.

Changes after the Mid-2000s: 2004–05 to 2011–12

As already noted, the growth of agricultural and rural incomes revived in India between 2004–05 and 2011–12. At the same time, however, agricultural employment declined in many States during this period. The decline in agricultural employment among rural females between 2004–05 and 2011–12 was severe in a number of States including Tamil Nadu, Karnataka, Maharashtra, Gujarat, Punjab, Haryana, Uttar Pradesh, Rajasthan, Uttarakhand, Bihar, Jharkhand, Madhya Pradesh, and Odisha. In most of these States, the growth of agricultural incomes and wages between 2004 and 2012 had been faster than in the rest of the country (slower only in Punjab, Uttar Pradesh, and Uttarakhand), as shown in Table 5.10. Therefore, it is unlikely that the sharp decline in agricultural employment between 2004–05 and 2011–12 was due to a "push" from stagnating agriculture.

There appear to be many reasons for the structural shift of the labour market away from agriculture, which is relatively greater in economically fast-growing States. The emergence of opportunities in the non-agricultural sector may have been an important factor in some States, mainly Tamil Nadu, Goa, West Bengal, Tripura, and Manipur. Between 2004–05 and 2011–12, the proportion of the rural female population engaged in non-agricultural work rose from 12.1 per cent to 18.7 per cent in Tamil Nadu, 7.3 per cent to 11 per cent in West Bengal, 4.4 per cent to 18.5 per cent in Tripura, and from 10.9 per cent to 19.9 per cent in Manipur (Table 5.9).

Between 2004–05 and 2011–12, there was an increase in the proportion of students among the population of rural females in a number of States. These include Bihar (with the highest increase of 10.5 percentage points), Jharkhand, Madhya Pradesh, Chhattisgarh, Uttar Pradesh, Rajasthan, Jammu & Kashmir,

WOMEN AND WORK IN RURAL INDIA

Table 5.9 *Workers, students, and those attending to domestic duties as proportions of females, rural India, 1999–2000 to 2011–12* in per cent

State	Workers in agriculture and allied activities			Non-agricultural workers			Students			Attending to domestic duties		
	1999–2000	2004–05	2011–12	1999–2000	2004–05	2011–12	1999–2000	2004–05	2011–12	1999–2000	2004–05	2011–12
Andhra Pradesh	40.3	37.9	34.1	7.6	10.4	10.4	16.9	19.3	20.6	17.7	17.7	21.8
Tamil Nadu	32.1	34.1	19.1	10	12.1	18.7	18.7	20.3	23.3	25.5	20.4	27.2
Karnataka	33.8	39.2	22.8	4.4	6.6	5.9	19.8	19.9	22.9	24.2	20.4	35.1
Kerala	14.4	13.1	8.6	9.4	12.5	13.5	22.2	22.1	23	34.9	30.8	37.5
Maharashtra	40.2	43	34.5	2.6	4.4	4.2	21.6	22	22	17.4	16.4	25.3
Gujarat	37	38	23.8	3.7	4.7	4	17.9	18.9	20.2	22.3	21.9	37.2
Goa	9.8	7.3	1.5	9.8	11.5	19.5	19.9	19.5	17.8	43.3	38.9	46
Uttar Pradesh	18	20.8	14.6	2.3	3.2	3.1	18.6	23.5	28.3	35	31.5	37.2
Rajasthan	35.1	36.4	26.9	3	4.3	7.8	15.3	19.9	24.4	21.1	18.9	24.7
Punjab	25.6	28.9	17.7	2.4	3.3	5.8	24.5	24.2	25	31.9	28.7	38.3
Haryana	18.4	28.7	13.9	1.3	3	2.3	23.6	22.7	24.9	34.8	25.3	45.5
Jammu & Kashmir	27.2	24.1	21.7	2.2	3.3	3.8	22.4	26	30.7	30.9	31.7	30.6
Uttarakhand	–	41	27.8	0	1.7	3		26.8	31.9		16	26.2
Himachal Pradesh	45.6	46.1	45.6	2.1	4.5	6.8	26.8	26.5	25.8	13.1	10.5	10.3
Bihar	14.8	11.9	4.1	2.4	1.9	1.2	11.5	17.2	27.7	39.6	41.8	50.4
Bengal	8.6	10.5	7.9	6.1	7.3	11	19.5	23.3	23.4	43.1	42.3	43.2
Jharkhand	–	26.7	16.7	0	4.6	3.1		18.8	27.2		28.2	36.1
Madhya Pradesh	34.7	32.2	19.1	3.2	4.4	4.8	17	20.2	27	20.2	22.5	34.7

Table 5.9 *continued*

State	Workers in agriculture and allied activities			Non-agricultural workers			Students			Attending to domestic duties		
	1999–2000	2004–05	2011–12	1999–2000	2004–05	2011–12	1999–2000	2004–05	2011–12	1999–2000	2004–05	2011–12
Odisha	23.7	24	17	5.7	8.2	7.5	17.8	18.1	22.1	29.8	29.3	39.2
Chhattisgarh	–	42.4	37.5	0	3	4.1		22.2	29.3		12.9	16.6
Assam	12.6	18.6	9.6	3.2	2.4	2.6	24.5	26.6	26.1	38.5	36.8	50
Tripura	3.2	4.1	4.4	3.6	4.4	18.5	27.2	25	25.2	50.9	47.8	37.1
Meghalaya	37.6	40.5	28.8	4.8	7.3	10.3	26.7	28.6	37.2	10.6	8.1	11.8
Manipur	18.4	24.2	6.3	7.3	10.9	19.9	26.7	29.4	31.6	30.7	24.2	30
Nagaland	40.2	45.6	28.1	4	4.8	3.1	30	30.1	35.2	10.7	9.4	24
India	25.5	27.3	18.6	4.2	5.5	6.2	18.4	21.3	25.1	29.4	27.3	35.3

Source: EUS (various years).

Table 5.10 *Female work force participation rates and average annual growth rates of wages and incomes by State, rural India, 2004–05 to 2011–12* in per cent

States	WPR, 2004–05	Net change in WPR, 2004–05 to 2011–12	Average annual rates of growth		
			Per capita income	Agricultural incomes	Agricultural wages
Andhra Pradesh	48.3	–3.8	0.9	1.1	1.5
Tamil Nadu	46.1	–8.3	1.4	1.2	1.4
Karnataka	45.9	–17.1	1	1.4	1.3
Kerala	25.6	–3.5	1.1	–0.3	1
Maharashtra	47.4	–8.6	1.1	1.2	1.1
Gujarat	42.7	–14.8	1.2	1.3	0.6
Goa	18.8	2.2	1	–0.4	0
Uttar Pradesh	24	–6.3	0.7	0.8	0.8
Rajasthan	40.7	–6	1	1.6	0.3
Punjab	32.2	–8.8	0.8	0.5	1
Haryana	31.7	–15.6	1.1	1.1	0.8
Jammu & Kashmir	27.4	–1.9	0.6	0.6	0.5
Uttarakhand	42.7	–11.8	1.7	0.7	0.9
Himachal Pradesh	50.6	1.8	0.8	0.5	0.1
Bihar	13.8	–8.5	1.2	1.2	1.2
West Bengal	17.8	1.1	0.8	0.5	1
Jharkhand	31.3	–11.5	0.8	2	0.6
Madhya Pradesh	36.6	–12.7	0.9	1.3	1.1
Odisha	32.2	–7.6	0.7	0.9	1.3
Chhattisgarh	45.4	–3.8	0.9	1.5	0.9
Assam	21.1	–8.9	0.6	0.8	0.2
Tripura	8.5	14.3	1.1	2.1	1.2
Meghalaya	47.8	–8.7	0.8	0.6	0.9
Manipur	35.1	–8.9	0.4	0.8	1.2
Nagaland	50.4	–19.3			
India	32.7	–7.9	1	1	1

Note: Average annual growth rates of wages and incomes are normalised to all-India values.
Sources: EUS (various years); Thomas and Satheesha (2018).

Uttarakhand, Odisha, and Meghalaya. The increase in the proportion of students was a factor behind the decline in the proportion of workers in these States (see Tables 5.8 and 5.9).

Another important reason behind the sharp fall in rural female WPRs between 2004–05 and 2011–12 could be a possible confusion (for NSS investigators) between two categories: "self-employed in agriculture" and "attending to domestic duties" (especially occupation category 93). There was a large magnitude of decrease in the proportion of workers engaged in agriculture and allied activities as well as increase in the proportion of those attending to domestic duties in a number of States (Table 5.9). These include Maharashtra, Gujarat, Punjab, Haryana, Uttarakhand, Madhya Pradesh, Odisha, and Nagaland. For example, in the case of Maharashtra, workers in agriculture and allied activities as a proportion of all rural females declined by 8.5 percentage points (from 43 per cent in 2004–05 to 34.5 per cent in 2011–12), whereas the proportion of rural females attending domestic duties increased by 8.9 percentage points. There was no change in the proportions of students or of non-agricultural workers (Table 5.9). Similarly, in the case of Haryana, the proportion of workers in agriculture and allied activities declined by 14.8 percentage points while the proportion of those attending to domestic duties increased by 20.2 percentage points.

SUMMARY

The main objective of this chapter was to understand the factors underlying the low and declining rates of female participation in the labour force in rural India (as seen in data from official statistical agencies), especially since the mid-2000s. Previous studies have identified a number of factors responsible for the declining female labour force participation in India, such as improvement in female enrolment in education and in household incomes, socio-cultural barriers to female participation in the economy, the slow growth of overall employment opportunities in the country, and problems in measuring female work. An important feature of this paper is that it analyses trends in female employment across major Indian States using the NSSO's Employment and Unemployment Surveys.

There is no clear association between female WPRs, on the one hand, and per capita incomes and indicators of female empowerment (such as female literacy or sex ratio), on the other. Female WPRs are extremely low in Delhi and Haryana, and relatively low in Kerala (rural) and Tripura, which are two of the leading States in terms of female literacy rate and sex ratio. It appears that rural female WPRs are closely linked to the relative size of the agricultural work force. The relatively low female WPRs in the rural areas of States such as Kerala, Goa, Tripura, and West Bengal are linked to the large-scale withdrawal of women from agricultural activities in these States. On the other hand, agriculture and allied activities account for 80 per cent or more of the total female work force in Himachal Pradesh, Uttarakhand, and Chhattisgarh, and this has contributed to the high rural female WPRs in these States. Whether the migration of male family members from States such as Uttarakhand, Himachal Pradesh, and Rajasthan have resulted, over the years, in a greater role for women in these States for cultivation must be further explored.

The entry of rural females into self-employment in agriculture had contributed almost a third of the net increase in employment in India during the first half of the 2000s. On the other hand, the female population engaged in agriculture declined equally sharply in India during the second half of the 2000s. The reversal in female agricultural employment after the mid-2000s was associated with some degree of revival of the rural economy. This revival was characterised by an improvement in the growth of agricultural incomes and rural wages, and increased spending on public work programmes, importantly the NREGS. It needs to be noted that female agricultural employment declined after the mid-2000s in Tamil Nadu, Karnataka, Maharashtra, Punjab, Rajasthan, and Uttarakhand despite the relatively fast growth of agricultural incomes and wages in these States.

Between 2004–05 and 2011–12, there had been a large increase in the proportion of students among the population of rural females in a number of States, including Bihar, Madhya Pradesh, and Uttar Pradesh. This has been a factor behind the decline in proportion of female workers in these States.

Another factor behind the decline in rural female WPRs after the mid-2000s could be a result of definitional discrepancy between two categories: "self-employed in agriculture" and "attending to domestic duties." Between 1999–2000 and 2004–05, the number of rural women reporting their economic status as "attending to domestic duties only" declined, while the number of rural females self-employed in agriculture grew. But this was reversed between 2004–05 and 2011–12. The number of rural females who were attending to domestic duties rose sharply, while those who were self-employed in agriculture declined. There is an inverse relationship, across States, between the net increase in the proportion of workers and the net increase in the proportion of those attending domestic duties.

The most severe obstacle to female labour participation in India is the sheer absence of suitable employment opportunities. After the mid-2000s, there had been a significant increase in the proportion of rural females engaged in non-agricultural sectors in a few States, mainly Tamil Nadu, Goa, West

Bengal, Tripura, and Manipur. Nevertheless, rural female WPRs declined even in these States, as the increase in non-agricultural employment opportunities did not sufficiently absorb the agricultural work force. It is clear, therefore, that a range of economic factors has been responsible for the low rates of rural female labour participation in India.

REFERENCES

Abraham, Vinoj (2009), "Employment Growth in Rural India: Distress Driven?," *Economic and Political Weekly*, vol. 44, no. 16, 18 April, pp. 97–104.

Abraham, Vinoj (2013), "Missing Labour or Consistent 'De-Feminisation'?," *Economic and Political Weekly*, vol. 48, no. 31, 3 August, pp. 99–80.

Andres, Luis A., Dasgupta, Basab, Joseph, George, Abraham, Vinoj, and Correia, Maria (2017), "Precarious Drop: Reassessing Patterns of Female Labour Force Participation in India," Policy Research Working Paper 8024, World Bank Group, South Asia Region, Social Development Unit, April.

Chand, Ramesh and Srivastava, S.K. (2014), "Changes in the Rural Labour Market and Their Implications for Agriculture," *Economic and Political Weekly*, vol. 49, no. 10, 8 March, pp. 47–54.

Eswaran, Mukesh, Ramaswami, Bharat, and Wadhwa, Wiliama (2013), "Status, Caste, and the Time Allocation of Women in Rural India," *Economic Development and Cultural Change*, vol. 61, no. 2, pp. 311–33.

Fields, Gary S. (2004), "Dualism in the Labour Market: A Perspective on the Lewis Model after Half a Century," *The Manchester School*, vol. 72, no. 6, pp. 724–35.

Hirway, Indira and Jose, Sunny (2011), "Understanding Women's Work Using Time-Use Statistics: The Case of India," *Feminist Economics*, vol. 17, no. 4, October, pp. 67–92.

Kannan, K. P., and Raveendran, G. (2012), "Counting and Profiling the Missing Labour Force," *Economic and Political Weekly*, vol. 47, no. 6, 11 February, pp. 77–80.

Kapsos, Steven, Silberman, Andrea, and Bourmpoula, Evangelina (2014), "Why is Female Labour Force Participation Declining so Sharply in India?" ILO Research Paper no. 10, International Labour Office, Geneva, August.

Lahoti, Rahul, and Swaminathan, Hema (2016), "Economic Development and Women's Labour Force Participation in India," *Feminist Economics*, vol. 22, no. 2, April, pp. 168–95.

Mazumdar, Indrani, and Neetha N. (2011), "Gender Dimensions: Employment Trends in India, 1993–94 to 2009–10," *Economic and Political Weekly*, vol. 46, no. 43, 22 October, pp. 118–26.

National Sample Survey Organisation (NSSO) (2013), "Key Indicators of Employment and Unemployment in India 2011–12," National Sample Survey 68th Round, Ministry of Statistics and Programme Implementation (MoSPI), Government of India, New Delhi.

National Statistical Office (2019), "Annual Report: Periodic Labour Force Survey (PLFS) (July 2017–June 2018)," Ministry of Statistics and Programme Implementation (MoSPI), Government of India, New Delhi.

Neetha, N. (2014), "Crisis in Female Employment: Analysis across Social Groups," *Economic and Political Weekly*, vol. 49, no. 47, 22 November, pp. 50–59.

Ramachandran, V. K., and Rawal, Vikas (2010), "The Impact of Liberalisation and Globalisation on India's Agrarian Economy," *Global Labour Journal*, vol. 1, no. 1, pp. 56–91.

Rangarajan, C., Kaul, Padma Iyer, and Seema (2011), "Where is the Missing Labour Force," *Economic and Political Weekly*, vol. 46, no. 39, 24 September, pp. 68–72.

Rao, Smriti (2011), "Work and Empowerment: Women and Agriculture in South India," *The Journal of Development Studies*, vol. 47, no. 2, February, pp. 294–315.

Rawal, Vikas, and Saha, Partha (2015), "Women's Employment in India: What do Recent NSS Surveys of Employment and Unemployment Show?," SSER Monograph 15/1, Society for Social and Economic Research, New Delhi, available at http://archive.indianstatistics.org/sserwp/sserwp1501.pdf., viewed on 15 November 2018.

Srivastava, Nisha, and Srivastava, Ravi (2010), "Women, Work, and Employment Outcomes in Rural India," *Economic and Political Weekly*, vol. 45, no. 28, 10 July, pp. 49–63.

Thomas, Jayan Jose (2012), "India's Labour Market during the 2000s: Surveying the Changes," *Economic and Political Weekly*, vol. 48, no. 51, 22 December, pp. 39–51.

Thomas, Jayan Jose (2014), "The Demographic Challenge and Employment Growth in India," *Economic and Political Weekly*, vol. 49, no. 6, 8 February, pp. 15–17.

Thomas, Jayan Jose (2015), "India's Labour Market during the 2000s: An Overview," in K. V. Ramaswamy (ed.), *Labour, Employment and Economic Growth in India*, Cambridge University Press, New Delhi, pp. 21–56.

Thomas, Jayan Jose, and Jayesh, M. P. (2016), "Changes in India's Rural Labour Market in the 2000s: Evidence from the Census of India and the National Sample Survey," *Review of Agrarian Studies*, vol. 6, no. 1, January–June, pp. 81–115.

Thomas, Jayan Jose and Satheesha (2018) 'Wages, Internal Migration and the Labour Markets: An Analysis of Indian States', Unpublished Paper, Indian Institute of Technology Delhi.

Usami, Yoshifumi (2012), "Recent Trends in Wage Rates in Rural India: An Update," *Review of Agrarian Studies*, vol. 2, no. 1, January–June, pp. 171–81.

6

Women in the Rice Economy of India
Evidence from Village Studies

S. Niyati

This chapter examines features of female labour use in rice cultivation, based on data from seven villages located in five predominantly rice-producing States in India. The objectives here are to analyse village-wise variations in the magnitude of labour absorption in rice cultivation, explain village-level differences in the gender division of work in crop operations, and describe forms of labour and wage contracts in the cultivation process.[1]

Historically, rice cultivation has provided enormous employment opportunities to rural women in rice-growing regions in India (Bardhan 1978; Bray 1986). The labour-absorptive capacity of rice was a matter of much discussion and policy interest during the 1980s. Research undertaken in that period showed that women contributed as much as 50 per cent of the total labour input in rice cultivation (Mencher and Saradamoni 1982; Barker, Herdt, and Rose 1985; Agarwal 1985; IRRI 1985; Ramachandran 1990). They worked mainly in transplanting, weeding, harvesting, and post-harvest operations.

India is the world's second largest producer of rice (DES 2016), and rice production contributes to the food security and livelihood of millions in rural India. Moreover, farming practices in rice have undergone many changes. After the introduction of the Intensive Agriculture Development Programme (IADP) in 1960 and later of high-yielding varieties (HYVs) of rice, new areas came under rice cultivation, and the production and productivity of rice increased. In India, the increase in rice production as a consequence of the "green revolution" was accompanied by an increase in labour absorption per hectare (Jose 1984; IRRI 1985; Barker, Herdt, and Rose 1985; Bray 1986; Basant 1987; Ramachandran 1990; da Corta and Venkateshwarlu 1999). In

---

[1] In this chapter, labour absorption refers to the average labour use per hectare of rice cultivation. Labour absorption, demand for labour, labour requirement, and labour use have been used synonymously.

rice cultivation, mechanisation displaced ploughing and field preparation, irrigation, harvesting, and threshing (Agarwal 1985; IRRI 1985; Basant 1987; Ramachandran 1990; Saradamoni 1991). Weeding and transplanting, operations performed mainly by women, were not mechanised. In East and Southeast Asia, by contrast, there was a decline in female labour use per hectare in rice cultivation (IRRI 1985), and weeding, transplanting, and harvesting were mechanised at an early stage (Smith and Gascon 1979; White 1985).

In the 1990s, there were fewer studies of labour absorption (and female labour absorption) in rice cultivation in India than in the early green revolution period. The main conclusions of the few studies conducted on this subject pointed to a decline in labour absorption, including female labour absorption, in rice cultivation (da Corta and Venkateshwarlu 1999; Ramachandran, Swaminathan, and Rawal 2001; Ramachandran and Swaminathan 2006; Duvvuru and Motkuri 2013).

Agriculture continues to play an important part in the livelihoods of 75 per cent of women in rural India, many of whom are involved in rice cultivation. Despite these numbers, absorption of female labour in contemporary rice cultivation has not been studied adequately. This chapter, which examines the deployment of female labour in rice farming in the contemporary period, attempts to partly fill that gap.

THE STUDY VILLAGES

This chapter relies on household-level data of seven villages collected by the Foundation for Agrarian Studies (FAS) under the Project on Agrarian Relations in India (PARI), which surveyed 25 villages from 11 States of India.[2] I have selected seven rice-cultivating villages located in different agro-ecological zones of India.[3] A detailed description of the villages is given in Table 6.1, and the locations of the villages are presented in the map in Figure 6.1.[4] In-depth surveys were conducted in different years between 2005 and 2011 in these villages. Andhra Pradesh was surveyed in 2005, Uttar Pradesh in 2006, Karnataka in 2009, Punjab in 2011, and West Bengal in 2010. These were census surveys with detailed information on income from crop production, animal resources, agricultural and non-agricultural wage labour, salaries, business and trade, rent, and other sources. They contain gender-disaggregated

---

[2] See http://fas.org.in/category/research/project-on-agrarian-relations-in-india-pari/ for details.
[3] The agro-ecological zones are defined according to the National Agriculture Research Project (NARP) classification.
[4] Village-level details have been summarised from Sivamurugan and Swaminathan (2017).

Table 6.1 *List of study villages, year of survey, gross cropped area (GCA) under rice cultivation, agro-ecological zones, type of irrigation, and status of farm mechanisation in rice cultivation* GCA in hectares, share of rice in per cent, and productivity in kilograms per hectare

Village	State	District	Year of survey	GCA under rice (ha)	Share of rice in total GCA (%)	Average productivity (kg/ha)	Agro-ecological zone	Type of irrigation	Status of farm mechanisation
Group A: High productivity									
Tehang	Punjab	Jalandhar	2011	587	43	5,678	Central Plain	Groundwater	Tractors, weeders, combine harvester, threshers
Ananthavaram	Andhra Pradesh	Guntur	2005	457	50	4,914	Krishna–Godavari	Canal	Tractors, threshers
Group B: Medium productivity									
Amarsinghi	West Bengal	Malda	2010	38	66	4,323	New Alluvial	Groundwater	Tractors
Panahar	West Bengal	Bankura	2010	117	66	4,118	Old Alluvial	Groundwater	Tractors, threshers
Alabujanahalli	Karnataka	Mandya	2009	115	41	4,084	Southern Dry	Canal	Tractors, threshers
Group C: Low productivity									
Kalmandasguri	West Bengal	Koch Bihar	2010	39	48	2,996	Terai	Unirrigated	Tractors
Mahatwar	Uttar Pradesh	Ballia	2006	55	44	1,491	Eastern Plain	Groundwater	Tractors

Note: The villages are listed in descending order of average rice productivity.
Source: PARI survey data.

Figure 6.1 *Location of PARI study villages*

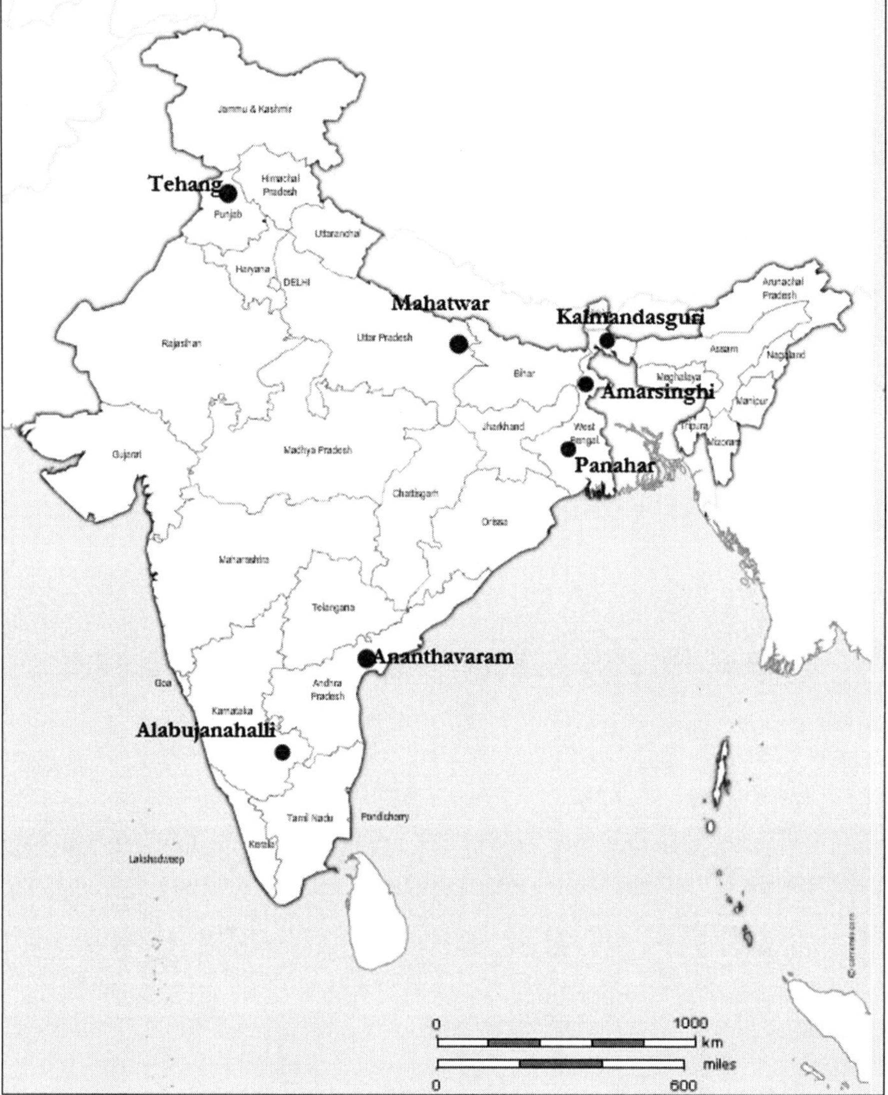

Source: Maps of India (2019).

information on the number of labour days required for cultivation, forms of labour, and wage payments for different farm operations.

The villages are grouped into three categories based on the average productivity of rice (Table 6.1), which was 3,294 kilograms per hectare for India between 2005 and 2011 (DES 2016). Except for the villages Kalmandasguri (West Bengal) and Mahatwar (Uttar Pradesh), the average productivity of rice in all the study villages was higher than the national average. Among the villages, Tehang (Punjab) and Ananthavaram (Andhra Pradesh) had an average productivity of 5 tonnes per hectare and thus were categorised as high area productivity villages, group A. Alabujanahalli (Karnataka) as well as Amarsinghi and Panahar (West Bengal), with medium area productivity, were classified as group B villages.[5] Kalmandasguri (West Bengal) and Mahatwar (Uttar Pradesh) were characterised as low area productivity as their rice productivity was less than the national average. The low productivity of rice in Kalmandasguri was because cultivation happened under unirrigated conditions, whereas Mahatwar was surveyed in a drought year and so the low productivity was because of multiple crop failures.

A Description of the Villages

Ananthavaram, Andhra Pradesh

This village is located in Guntur district of Andhra Pradesh. Around 150 households out of a total of 667 households in the village were surveyed in the year 2005. It lies in the Krishna–Godavari agro-ecological zone and has access to canal water from the Krishna river for irrigation. This region was part of the agricultural development programmes in the 1960s and also experienced technological advancements in the green revolution phase. It was previously studied by Sundarayya (1977).[6] The dominant caste group in the village was Kamma (caste Hindu), which comprised 20 per cent of households in the village and had access to a sizeable share of operational holdings. A total of 65 per cent of households in the village were landless, and mainly belonged to Scheduled Castes and Scheduled Tribes. Women from landless households in the village worked primarily as agricultural workers. The major crops grown were rice, maize, black gram, sesame, sugarcane, and betel-leaf. Rice was the main crop grown in the kharif season, and maize and black gram were grown in the rabi season.[7] A total of 84 households reported cultivation of rice in the kharif season, commonly using the following seed varieties: BPT 5204 (a medium-duration high-yielding

---

[5] The district yield for rice in 2010 was higher for Bankura (3901 kg/ha) than Malda (3752 kg/ha) in West Bengal (DES 2014). However, in Table 1, the average productivity of rice in Panahar was lower than Amarsinghi. This could be because of a large variation in the landholding size under rice cultivation in Panahar, and thus, the lower productivity on smaller plots of land could have pulled down the average productivity for the village.

[6] The district was part of the Intensive Agricultural Area Programme (IAAP), which was aimed to expand area under irrigation.

[7] The kharif season is primarily between the months of June and October.

variety), MTU 2077, and IR 77 (semi-dwarf high-yielding varieties). Around 50 per cent of the total gross cropped area (GCA) (778 hectares) was under rice cultivation, of which more than 90 per cent was under irrigation. Farm mechanisation was limited to ploughing operations and threshing of rice.

Tehang, Punjab

This village is located in Jalandhar district of Punjab. A census survey of 681 households was conducted in the year 2011. It falls under the Central Plain agro-ecological zone, and has tubewells and canals as primary sources of irrigation. This village had directly experienced the effects of Partition in 1947, and several scholars studied it in the twentieth century. The village had no history of rice cultivation until 1970 (The Board of Economic Enquiry, 1962), after the spread of the green revolution in Punjab. Farming was done mostly by migrant workers from Bihar and West Bengal. Migration to other regions and emigration to Canada, the United Kingdom, and other countries were prevalent, shaping the conditions of the village economy. The dominant social group was Jat Sikhs, comprising 20 per cent of all households. Land inequality was very high, and the landless households belonged to the Scheduled Castes. There was meagre participation of women in agricultural operations. Women belonging to peasant households engaged in livestock work, whereas those from manual worker households worked in construction and factories (hosiery) in neighbouring towns and cities. The major crops grown in the village were rice (in the kharif season), and wheat (in the rabi season). Medium-duration varieties (HKR 47 and HKR 127) as well as high-yielding varieties of seed – PR 114 and Pusa 44 (a semi-dwarf HYV that is a cross of two rice varieties, IR 8 and IARI 5901-2) – were used for cultivation of rice. Around 43 per cent of the total GCA (587 hectares) was under rice cultivation, of which almost 98 per cent was under irrigation. Farm operations were mostly mechanised, and the prevalence of combine harvesters was noted.

Alabujanahalli, Karnataka

This village is located in Mandya district of Karnataka. A census survey of 248 households was conducted in 2009. It falls under the Southern Dry agro-ecological zone. Canal water from the Krishnaraja Sagara dam was the primary source of irrigation in the village. Seventy per cent of households in the village belonged to the Vokkaliga caste (classified under Other Backward Classes), and the rest were Scheduled Caste households that had a concentration of manual workers and poor peasants. Women from Vokkaliga households participated in agricultural and livestock work, whereas those from Scheduled Caste households engaged in agricultural wage work. The principal crops grown in the village were rice, ragi (finger millet), and sugarcane. In addition to rice, sugarcane, which is a very labour-intensive crop, generated employment for women. Rice was grown in the kharif and pre-kharif seasons,[8] and occupied 41 per cent of the total GCA; Jaya or IET 723 (medium duration) and MTU 1001 (semi-dwarf) were the prominent rice varieties. A total of 68 per cent of the households reported rice cultivation in the kharif season, of which almost 90 per cent was under irrigated conditions. The presence of tractors and machine threshers was noted in the village.

Amarsinghi, West Bengal

Amarsinghi is a small village located in Malda district of West Bengal. It had 127 households in 2010 when it was surveyed. It falls under the fertile New Alluvial agro-ecological zone. River lift and wells were the primary sources of irrigation, and the average landholding size in the village was 1.2 acres. This village did not have any large landlord or rich capitalist farmer households, but there was a significant presence of small farmer and manual worker households. Women worked as agricultural workers and participated as family labour in their fields. Rice and jute were the major crops with rice cultivation in the kharif (*aman* paddy) and rabi (*boro* paddy) seasons, occupying 66 per cent of the total GCA in the village.[9] Around 71 per cent of the crop grown in kharif and 88 per cent of the rice grown in rabi were under irrigated conditions. MTU 1010, a hybrid seed variety between Krishnaveni and IR 64, and B.B 11 (also known as BR 11 – a medium-duration HYV seed) were prominent in the kharif season, whereas medium-duration (IET 4094 and Jaya) and semi-dwarf (IET 1444) varieties were used in the rabi season. Only a few households reported the use of tractors for land preparation; otherwise, mechanisation was at a nascent stage and the presence of animal labour was noted in different farming operations.

Panahar, West Bengal

This is a village located in Bankura district, in the Old Alluvial zone of West Bengal. The village had 248 households in 2010, when it was surveyed. The primary source of irrigation was tubewells. Bankura district was a part of the IADP programme when it was extended to other districts in India in 1963– 64. It had a few landlord families belonging to caste Hindu social groups, and though Scheduled Castes comprised 60 per cent of the population, they were

---

[8] The pre-kharif season is between the months March and June.
[9] The rabi season is between the months of October and March.

effectively landless. Women in this village engaged in housework and livestock rearing, and very few women from Scheduled Caste households were involved in agricultural work. Rice was cultivated in the kharif (*aman* paddy and *aus* paddy) and pre-kharif seasons (*boro* paddy), and accounted for 66 per cent of the total GCA. For rice cultivation in the kharif and pre-kharif seasons, around 85 and 95 per cent of the land under rice had access to irrigation, respectively, and MTU 7029 (a semi-dwarf hybrid also known as Swarna variety) and IR 36 (semi-dwarf), respectively, were the commonly used varieties. The other major crops cultivated were sesame and a winter crop of potato. Use of tractors and threshers was noted in the village.

Kalmandasguri, West Bengal
Kalmandasguri is a small village located in Koch Bihar district of West Bengal. A total of 147 households were surveyed in 2010. It falls in the Terai agro-ecological zone with poor access to irrigation facilities; rice was cultivated under rainfed conditions. With an average landholding size of 1.8 acres, this village benefited from land reforms under the Left Front government of West Bengal. Muslims and Scheduled Castes were the two main social groups in the village. Whereas non-agricultural employment in construction was noted, women primarily worked as agricultural workers. The major crops in the village were rice and jute. Rice was cultivated in the kharif season on 48 per cent of the total GCA, of which less than 30 per cent was under irrigation. The commonly used rice variety was Swarna Sub-1 (a semi-dwarf hybrid), a long-duration variety used in areas with unassured irrigation. Farm mechanisation was limited to the use of tractors for land preparation, and the presence of animal labour was noted in different crop operations.

Mahatwar, Uttar Pradesh
Mahatwar is a small village located in Ballia district of eastern Uttar Pradesh, falling in the Eastern Plain agro-ecological zone. A census survey of 156 households was done in 2006. More than 60 per cent of households belonged to the Scheduled Castes, and a sizeable section of all households belonged to the landless, manual worker class. The average size of landholdings was less than 2 acres. The year of the survey, 2006, was one of water shortage; hence, many cultivators reported crop failure that year. Men here migrated to nearby towns for non-farm work during the lean season, whereas women worked as agricultural and home-based workers in rolling and packing *bidis*. The major crops cultivated were rice, wheat, and maize. Rice was grown in the kharif season on 44 per cent of the total GCA, of which 90 per cent was under irrigation. The prominent varieties of rice were BPT 5204 (also known

as Mansoori or Sona Masoori) and Sarjoo-52 and MTU 7029 (semi-dwarf varieties known as Natti Mansuri). Very few cultivators reported the use of tractors for land preparation operations.

THE GENDER DIMENSION IN RICE CULTIVATION

A distinct gender division of labour characterises farming operations in rice cultivation. Earlier studies by Moore (1973), Bardhan (1978), Miller (1981), Agarwal (1981), and Saradamoni (1991) have highlighted the critical role played by women in rice cultivation, where their contribution has usually been 50 per cent of the total labour requirement. The participation of women is generally high in transplanting, weeding and harvesting, which are extremely labour-intensive operations. A few villages in this study conformed to this pattern; however, stark variations were also observed.

The Magnitude of Labour Absorption in Rice Cultivation

Several studies point to the more substantial requirement of labour for wet rice cultivation (Miller 1981; Ramachandran 1990). Thus, earlier studies note the higher labour demand in the southern States – Tamil Nadu, southern Karnataka, Kerala, and Andhra Pradesh – as compared to the State of West Bengal. In contrast, village-level analysis showed low labour requirements in Ananthavaram (Andhra Pradesh) and the lowest labour deployment in Tehang (Punjab) (Table 6.2).[10] These two villages required less than 100 eight-hour labour days for cultivating rice on 1 hectare of land. The replacement of human labour by mechanisation of different farm operations explained the change in the scenario. Excluding these two villages, which also had high average area productivity of rice, the average labour use per hectare was around 150 days, with the highest deployment in Amarsinghi (West Bengal), followed by Alabujanahalli (Karnataka). It can be seen from Table 6.2 that as the productivity of rice increased, the total labour use for rice cultivation decreased in the study villages.

The gender-disaggregated estimates of labour requirement are presented in Table 6.2.[11] Excluding Panahar (West Bengal), the female labour deployment

[10] Sidhu (2005) showed a declining trend in the total labour absorption in rice cultivation in Punjab as it fell from 120 to 56 eight-hour labour days per hectare between 1974–75 and 1998–99. From village surveys in three districts of Amritsar, Jalandhar, and Moga districts of Punjab, he noted a significant increase in farm mechanisation in rice cultivation that explained the declining labour demand.

[11] Since total labour includes labour hired on piece-rate contracts, I have used the following method

Table 6.2 *Average labour use per hectare in rice cultivation by sex* in eight-hour labour days per hectare

Village	State	Group	Year of survey	Male labour use	Female labour use	Total labour use
Amarsinghi	West Bengal	B	2010	99	71	170
Alabujanahalli	Karnataka	B	2009	99	69	168
Mahatwar	Uttar Pradesh	C	2006	77	66	143
Kalmandasguri	West Bengal	C	2010	69	52	121
Ananthavaram	Andhra Pradesh	A	2005	42	44	86
Panahar	West Bengal	B	2010	114	34	148
Tehang	Punjab	A	2011	30	1	31

Note: The table is arranged in descending order of the average female labour use per hectare in rice cultivation. Groups are defined in Table 6.1.
Source: PARI survey data.

was lesser in group A villages than in group B and group C villages. Among group A villages, Tehang (Punjab) had very low female labour deployment. Farm mechanisation and use of male migrant labour explained the very low female labour requirement in Tehang. In Panahar, there was a Muslim landlord household that cultivated rice on more than 4 hectares, and a few other Muslim households that cultivated rice on more than 2.5 hectares of operational land. The social-cultural norms prevailing in the households barred women from contributing their labour to farm activities. Women belonging to non-Dalit rice-cultivating households in this village participated in household work. This could explain the lower participation of women in rice cultivation in Panahar.

Ananthavaram (Andhra Pradesh) had the highest share of female labour in the total labour deployed in rice cultivation (Table 6.3).[12] Reasons for the high female share in Ananthavaram could be male out-migration to non-farm sector employment and mechanisation of male-specific tasks in rice cultivation. Excluding Panahar (West Bengal) and Tehang (Punjab), the relative share of female labour to total labour used in rice cultivation was more or less same in all the villages.

---

for disaggregating it into male and female labour. Piece-rate contract groups have a village-specific ratio for crop operations. These contracts are observed in transplanting (the ratio for female to male in a group of 10 is 8:2) and harvesting (the same ratio is 6:4). Such ratios were used for disaggregating the labour hired on these contracts into female and male labour.

[12] Similar findings by da Corta and Venkateshwarlu (1999) were shown in Chittoor district, in the Rayalaseema region. They showed an increase in the relative contribution of female labour in rice cultivation because of male out-migration for non-farm work opportunities.

Table 6.3 *Average share of male and female labour in total labour use per hectare in rice cultivation* in per cent

Village	State	Group	Year of survey	Male labour use	Female labour use	Total labour use
Ananthavaram	Andhra Pradesh	A	2005	49	51	100
Mahatwar	Uttar Pradesh	C	2006	53	47	100
Kalmandasguri	West Bengal	C	2010	57	43	100
Amarsinghi	West Bengal	B	2010	58	42	100
Alabujanahalli	Karnataka	B	2009	59	41	100
Panahar	West Bengal	B	2010	77	23	100
Tehang	Punjab	A	2011	97	3	100

Note: The table is arranged in descending order of the relative share of female labour in total labour used in rice cultivation.
Source: PARI survey data.

Gender Division of Labour

Table 6.4 indicates the share of female labour in the total labour deployed for a specific crop operation. It can be noted that except for Tehang and Panahar, this share was relatively high for transplanting, weeding, and harvesting of rice in the other villages. Land preparation, irrigation, and application of fertilizers were male-specific operations in rice cultivation.

Table 6.4 *Share of female labour in different agricultural operations of rice* in per cent

Village	State	Group	Survey year	Land preparation and other operations*	Sowing and trans-planting	Weeding	Harvest+
Ananthavaram	Andhra Pradesh	A	2005	6	62	91	60
Mahatwar	Uttar Pradesh	C	2006	6	62	46	50
Kalmandasguri	West Bengal	C	2010	1	52	54	47
Amarsinghi	West Bengal	B	2010	3	54	54	53
Alabujanahalli	Karnataka	B	2009	2	68	86	51
Panahar	West Bengal	B	2010	2	35	24	29
Tehang	Punjab	A	2011	0	0	0	0

Notes: * refers to land preparation operations along with the application of fertilizers and irrigation operations, and + refers to harvest and post-harvest operations. The table is arranged in descending order of the relative share of female labour in the total labour used in rice cultivation (refer to Table 6.3).
Source: PARI survey data.

However, there were stark differences in the gender division of labour in farming operations across the villages. In the villages of the southern States – Ananthavaram (Andhra Pradesh) and Alabujanahalli (Karnataka) – transplanting and weeding were performed exclusively by women, and the relative shares of female labour were high in harvesting and threshing operations. In the Punjab village, Tehang, all activities were male-specific; the participation of male migrant workers explained the meagre presence of female labour in transplanting and harvesting operations. There were no female-exclusive crop operations in the West Bengal villages; either the operations were done entirely by men (land preparation, application of fertilizers, and irrigation) or jointly by men and women (transplanting, weeding, and harvesting).

The literature suggests that these regional differences can arise because of differences in the method of cultivation as well as economic and cultural factors (Miller 1981; Mencher and Saradamoni 1982). Among the villages, a higher incidence of direct sowing was noted in the villages of West Bengal and Mahatwar (Uttar Pradesh) in comparison to the southern villages and Tehang (Punjab), which can explain the more substantial participation of male labour in sowing operations and thus in agriculture. Even in the villages that transplanted rice, men participated in this operation. In the Punjab village, sowing was done by female labour whereas transplanting was done by migrant male workers from Bihar.

Cultivation practices have changed over time with rapid farm mechanisation in the regions of Punjab and Andhra Pradesh, which explains the lower absolute requirement of human labour. Apart from transplanting, which is entirely manual, other operations were mechanised in the Punjab village. The use of herbicides reduced the number of weedings and affected the labour demand for weeding in Tehang. In Ananthavaram, mechanised threshing reduced female labour demand in rice cultivation.

Economic and cultural factors also explained the stark differences noted in the village-level analysis. Miller (1981) cites Davis (1975) to argue for the economic value attached to growing rice in West Bengal villages, which explained the higher presence of male labour. A similar pattern continues to exist with a more significant proportion of men working in crop production. In our study villages in West Bengal, female wage workers participated more in non-agricultural work – in household industries or domestic work. In contrast, in Ananthavaram (Andhra Pradesh), the relative contribution of women in agricultural work was greater than that of men, as the latter diversified into non-farm employment.

As mentioned in the literature, there is undoubtedly nothing intrinsic to farm operations that demands the use of female labour (Miller 1981; Saradamoni

1991; Kapadia 1996). Rather, cultural aspects determine the gender division of labour and influence the demand for female labour in crop production. These cultural factors – such as restricting women from participating in field operations, excluding them from using machines, and limiting their work opportunities in the non-farm sector – played a predominant role in the difference in work participation of women across the villages. In addition, the caste structure in rural society also shaped these differences. Labouring in fields is associated with a lower social status. Thus, the participation of women from Scheduled Caste households was higher than of those from other caste households in the villages. In particular, I would like to highlight the case of Panahar (West Bengal) where the work participation of women was low and women belonging to the dominant caste of the village did not participate in agricultural field operations, though some reported engagement in post-harvest operations such as winnowing, threshing, and drying. In Tehang (Punjab), dominant caste women engaged in household work.

In contrast, women in Mahatwar (Uttar Pradesh) participated intensively in farm operations. This village is mostly composed of Scheduled Caste households, most of which were effectively landless or held meagre plots of land. Therefore, women depended on rice cultivation for their livelihood either as cultivators or wage workers.

FORMS OF LABOUR

An understanding of forms of labour is an integral part of studying labour processes in a production system (Ramachandran 1990). Forms of labour are determined by the underlying production relations that exist in a rural economy, and therefore, varied considerably across the study villages. The two primary forms of labour that existed in crop production were family labour and hired labour. The presence of exchange labour was negligible, contributing less than 3 per cent of the total labour involved in rice cultivation: it was absent in Amarsinghi (West Bengal), Ananthavaram (Andhra Pradesh), and Tehang (Punjab) in rice operations, whereas other villages saw its limited presence, mainly in land preparation and weeding. For example, in Panahar (West Bengal), Mahatwar (Uttar Pradesh), and Kalmandasguri (West Bengal), male labour was exchanged for sowing, weeding, and land preparation tasks, whereas in Alabujanahalli (Karnataka), female labour was exchanged for weeding and harvesting tasks. The analysis in this section will focus on the family and hired forms of labour in rice cultivation.

In Table 6.5, the ratio of share of hired labour to share of family labour deployed in total labour used in rice cultivation is computed. The value of this ratio indicates the dominant form of labour used in rice cultivation. Thus, if hired labour is higher than family labour, the ratio will be greater than or equal to one. If it is less than family labour, the ratio will be less than one.

The literature states that the hired form of labour was the predominant way in which labour was organised in an intensive rice cultivation process (IRRI 1985; Ramachandran 1990; Paris 1998), and a similar pattern prevailed in the villages. An exception to this was Mahatwar (eastern Uttar Pradesh), where family labour use was more substantial. The following two reasons could explain this anomaly. First, because of the smaller size of operational holdings, farm operations were done by family members. Secondly, the village was surveyed in a period of water shortage when it had witnessed several cases of crop failure. Thus, crop harvesting, which generally involved a significant share of hired labour, could not happen that particular year. Table 6.5 also shows that the ratio of hired labour to family labour increased as the average productivity of rice increased in the study villages.

Farm operations in rice cultivation involving more hired labour were transplanting, weeding, and harvesting. In Tehang, Ananthavaram, and Alabujanahalli, land preparation using tractors was done by hired workers, whereas irrigation and other crop care activities were performed solely by family labour or long-term workers.

A unique observation can be made concerning the gender dimension of forms of labour. For tasks that involved hired labour, the contribution of female workers was more than that of their male counterparts (Dhar 2017) (Table 6.5). For example, for transplanting rice, which demanded hired workers, the contribution of women workers was greater than that of men workers. Exceptions to this would be Panahar and Tehang, where the share of male labour was higher than female labour in the total labour hired for rice cultivation.

Two important factors that influenced the forms of labour were the average size of operational landholdings (reflecting the scale of production) and the socio-economic status of the households (particularly in relation to women's work participation). Clearly, in Ananthavaram (Andhra Pradesh) and Tehang (Punjab), where the average size of landholdings was relatively large, rice cultivation was done by using hired workers. However, in the other villages, family labour contributed equally to the hired form of labour as the average size of landholdings was small. The pair-wise correlation coefficients between the size of operational landholding under rice cultivation and the ratio of hired labour to family labour in total female labour deployed in rice cultivation is presented in Table 6.6. For Ananthavaram (Andhra Pradesh) and Alabujanahalli (Karnataka), the relative share of hired labour increased with an increase in the size of operational holding under rice cultivation. Even

Table 6.5 *Share of hired labour in total labour deployed in rice cultivation, ratio of shares of hired labour to family labour, and ratio of female to male hired labour*

Village	State	Group	Year of survey	Share of hired labour in total labour (in %)	Ratio of hired labour to family labour	Ratio of female to male hired labour
Tehang	Punjab	A	2011	87	5	0
Ananthavaram	Andhra Pradesh	A	2005	81	4	2
Panahar	West Bengal	B	2010	62	2	0
Alabujanahalli	West Bengal	B	2009	61	2	1
Amarsinghi	West Bengal	B	2010	60	1	1
Kalmandasguri	West Bengal	C	2010	48	1	1
Mahatwar	Uttar Pradesh	C	2006	25	0	0

Note: The table is arranged in descending order of the share of hired labour in total labour used in rice cultivation.
Source: PARI survey data.

Table 6.6 *Pair-wise correlation coefficients between the size of operational area under rice and ratio of hired labour to family labour in the total female labour deployed in rice cultivation*

Village	State	Group	Year of survey	Coefficient
Ananthavaram	Andhra Pradesh	A	2005	0.40*
Alabujanahalli	Karnataka	B	2009	0.10*
Amarsinghi	West Bengal	B	2010	0.05
Kalmandasguri	West Bengal	C	2010	0.03
Panahar	West Bengal	B	2010	0.02
Mahatwar	Uttar Pradesh	C	2006	0.01
Tehang	Punjab	A	2011	0.00

Note: * refers to coefficients significant at the 5 per cent level.
Source: PARI survey data.

though correlation estimates were positive for the other villages, a statistically significant relationship could not be established.

The other factor that determined the use of hired or family labour was the socio-economic status of the cultivating household. Two variables that define this status are the caste and class of the household.[13] Caste played a pivotal

[13] The PARI classification of cultivator households into socio-economic classes is drawn from Ramachandran (2011). It is based on three criteria: the means of production, relative use of family and hired labour, and the household surplus generated in that particular year. The broad

Table 6.7 *Average female labour use disaggregated by forms of labour for Scheduled Caste (SC) and non-Scheduled Caste (SC) rice-cultivating households* female labour use in eight-hour labour days per hectare

Village	State	Group	Year of survey	No. of SC rice-cultivating households	Average hired labour	Average family labour	No. of non-SC rice-cultivating households	Average hired labour	Average family labour
Alabujanahalli	Karnataka	B	2009	35	52	17	134	64	5
Amarsinghi	West Bengal	B	2010	25	43	28	55	55	26
Ananthavaram	Andhra Pradesh	A	2005	25	35	8	59	42	2
Kalmandasguri	West Bengal	C	2010	43	27	25	56	32	20
Panahar	West Bengal	B	2010	91	26	18	74	32	2
Mahatwar	Uttar Pradesh	C	2006	70	22	42	52	26	39
Tehang	Punjab	A	2011	2	0	0	95	1	0

Note: The table is arranged in descending order of the number of hired female labour days per hectare used by Scheduled Caste households cultivating rice in the village.
Source: PARI survey data.

Table 6.8 *Average family and hired female labour use for manual worker and other households* female labour use in eight-hour labour days per hectare

Village	State	Group	Year of survey	Manual workers			Others		
				No. of rice-cultivating households	Average hired labour	Average family labour	No. of rice-cultivating households	Average hired labour	Average family labour
Alabujanahalli	Karnataka	B	2010	26	55	14	143	62	7
Amarsinghi	West Bengal	B	2009	18	43	28	68	46	22
Ananthavaram	Andhra Pradesh	A	2010	4	35	9	80	41	3
Mahatwar	Uttar Pradesh	C	2011	21	31	35	101	32	34
Kalmandasguri	West Bengal	C	2005	29	29	23	78	30	22
Panahar	West Bengal	B	2010	19	22	12	161	27	7
Tehang	Punjab	A	2006	2	0	0	95	1	0

Note: The table is arranged in descending order of the number of hired female labour days per hectare used by manual worker households cultivating rice in the village.
Source: PARI survey data.

role in determining the participation of women in the fields, whether as family or hired labour. The data from the study villages showed that average female family labour use per hectare was relatively higher for households belonging to the Scheduled Caste than for those from other caste households. However, even for Scheduled Caste households, average hired female labour use exceeded family labour use, except in Mahatwar (Uttar Pradesh), where family labour was the predominant form of labour in rice cultivation.

The average female family labour days per hectare was higher for manual worker households than for households of other classes. Manual workers depend on wage work for their livelihood and have smaller operational holdings than other classes. This does not imply that the family form of labour was the predominant form for manual worker households as, even for them, the average hired labour days were much greater than family labour days (Table 6.8).

Type of Wage Contract

The hired form of work was also characterised by different types of wage contracts, namely, time-rates and piece-rates. The time duration of the work determines the time-rate (daily wage rate and long-term contract), whereas the piece-rate is measured by the amount of work done by the workers. It is calculated either in terms of the quantum of output or by the area of land on which the task is performed.

In agriculture, the time spent on a particular operation and the quality of the work explains the choice of the institution of hiring labour. For instance, for tasks like irrigation, agriculture produce processing, transport, and marketing, cultivators hired mostly male farm workers on long-term contracts. At the same time, operations that require timeliness and for which the output can be determined by the quality of work, piece-rate contracts were dominant (Ramachandran 1990). Thus, hired workers for harvesting and transplanting were taken on piece-rate contracts.[14]

---

classes were: landlords, capitalist farmers, peasants, manual workers, and households dependent on business, salaries, remittances, and other sources of income. Landlords held a large part of the land in the village and belonged to traditionally dominant social groups. Capitalist farmers were similar to the landlords, but did not belong to the traditional land-owning castes. Peasants participated in some agricultural operations on the land, as did hired workers. Manual workers were at the bottom of the class ladder, depending on wage incomes, and had less access to land in the village.

[14] Piece-rate contract labour days are calculated as the total cost incurred for a specific operation divided by the standardised village daily-wage rate (eight hours) for that particular crop operation. For instance, if a household spends Rs 2,000 for harvesting 1 acre of land, and if the wage for harvesting is Rs 200, then I deduce that ten eight-hour labour days were used for that operation (2000/200 = 10).

Table 6.9 *Share of hired workers employed on piece-rate contracts among total hired workers in rice cultivation* in per cent

Village	State	Group	Year of survey	Share of piece-rated contracts among total hired labour
Tehang	Punjab	A	2011	88.3
Ananthavaram	Andhra Pradesh	A	2005	70.2
Kalmandasguri	West Bengal	C	2010	61.8
Mahatwar	Uttar Pradesh	C	2006	60.9
Amarsinghi	West Bengal	B	2010	43.5
Panahar	West Bengal	B	2010	40.1
Alabujanahalli	Karnataka	B	2009	28.7

Note: The table is arranged in the descending order of the relative share of piece-rated contracts in total hired labour used in rice cultivation.
Source: PARI survey data.

Table 6.10 *Share of hired workers employed on piece-rate contracts among total hired workers for specific agricultural operations of rice cultivation* in per cent

Village	State	Survey year	Group	Land preparation	Sowing and transplanting	Weeding	Harvest and post-harvest
Ananthavaram	Andhra Pradesh	2005	A	0	98	0	97
Mahatwar	Uttar Pradesh	2006	C	60	75	14	95
Tehang	Punjab	2011	A	37	99	7	89
Amarsinghi	West Bengal	2010	B	60	12	8	87
Kalmandasguri	West Bengal	2010	C	76	79	51	47
Panahar	West Bengal	2010	B	27	57	27	38
Alabujanahalli	Karnataka	2009	B	4	79	4	8

Note: The table is arranged in descending order of share of piece-rated contracts among total hired labour used in harvesting of rice.
Source: PARI survey data.

In Tehang (Punjab) and Ananthavaram (Andhra Pradesh), more than 70 per cent of the workers were hired on piece-rate contracts (Table 6.9). More than 75 per cent of the hired form of labour involved in transplanting and harvesting was under these contracts (Table 6.10). In a group of ten workers, the average female to male labour ratio in these operations, for transplanting, was 8:2. For harvesting, the corresponding ratio was 6:4.

The implications of piece-rate contracts were manifold. First, they raised methodological difficulties in identifying the contribution of female labour, as the gender composition of the piece-rate work groups was not uniform. The gender composition changed with the type of crop and scale of operation. Secondly, the gender division of labour in particular operations was blurred. The timeliness to complete a task demanded the participation of male labour in female-specific tasks as well. Also, the higher remuneration in these contracts attracted the participation of male workers, especially when non-farm employment opportunities were scarce.

SUMMARY

The data from the study villages showed considerable variations in the levels of labour absorption. The magnitude of labour absorption was much lower in Ananthavaram in coastal Andhra Pradesh and Tehang in Punjab relative to the other villages. These villages required less than 100 labour days per hectare for the cultivation of rice. In comparison to the study by Sundarayya (1977) conducted in Ananthavaram, it could be seen that the labour requirement reduced from 180 labour days per hectare in 1973–74 to 86 days in 2005. Ananthavaram and Tehang had average rice productivity of 5 tonnes per hectare, which was much higher than the all-India average of 3.2 tonnes. The lower labour requirement along with the high area productivity of rice resulted in higher labour productivity in these two villages. Excluding Panahar (West Bengal), there was an association between productivity of rice and female labour absorption, where the absolute female labour requirement in group A villages was less than in group B and group C villages. However, the relative contribution of female labour to total labour was more or less the same, excluding Panahar (West Bengal) and Tehang (Punjab). This could be because farm mechanisation was limited to land preparation and some tasks of harvesting that displaced more male labour than the female labour. Among the villages, female labour absorption in an absolute as well as relative sense was low in Panahar and Tehang. Whereas it has been historically low in Tehang, socio-cultural factors may have been a deterrent to women's participation in crop production in Panahar. In Ananthavaram (Andhra Pradesh), the relative share of female labour in total labour used for rice cultivation was the highest among the study villages. The feminisation of labour in rice cultivation here was because of the movement of male labour into non-farm work.

Crop operations can be gender-specific or neutral. In rice cultivation, operations such as irrigation, land preparation, and application of fertilizers and chemicals were exclusively performed by male labour. Among the villages, there were variations in the tasks that were female-specific. Exclusively female operations of transplanting and weeding were noted only in Ananthavaram (Andhra Pradesh) and Alabujanahalli (Karnataka), whereas there was no such female labour-specific operations in the other villages. This variation could be because of the differences in the availability of remunerative non-farm opportunities for male labour, the gender gap in wage rates, and types of labour contracts.

The share of hired labour exceeded the share of family labour in total labour required for rice cultivation in all the villages except Mahatwar (Uttar Pradesh).[15] Furthermore, there were notable dimensions to the forms of labour. First, the share of female labour was higher than that of male labour in total hired labour for rice cultivation, except in Tehang (Punjab) and Panahar (West Bengal). Secondly, the predominance of hired labour was noted in female labour-intensive crop operations such as sowing and transplanting, weeding, and harvesting of rice. Thirdly, there was a shift to piece-rate contracts from daily-wage contracts for labourers hired for cultivating rice. These contracts were more prevalent in female labour-intensive operations (transplanting, weeding, and harvesting) and blurred the gender division of labour, as they raised methodological difficulties in understanding the contribution of female labour.

The total number of hired female labour days per hectare was lower for Scheduled Caste cultivator households than for other caste cultivator households. However, that does not imply that these households predominantly relied on family labour. A similar observation was made for manual worker households wherein the absolute number of hired labour days were fewer than that for other classes. However, there were very few households belonging to the manual worker class that engaged in rice cultivation. In rice cultivation, even the cultivators belonging to manual worker households with small farm size hired labour on piece-rate contracts for labour-intensive operations such as transplanting and harvesting.

A few hypotheses have emerged from this analysis that require further study. First, the penetration of labour-displacing technologies is still limited to male-specific operations, and thus, it displaced more male than female labour. In such crop operations, absolute male labour days were reduced without altering the relative shares between male and female labour. However, in contrast, when female-specific tasks such as threshing or harvesting were mechanised, absolute female labour days were reduced and the relative share of male labour increased for the particular crop operation. This could be

---

[15] The case of Mahatwar could be treated as an anomaly because of crop failure in the survey year, because of which labour for harvesting operation was almost nil.

because of gender-differentiated access to machinery. Secondly, differential access to non-farm productive work has deep implications for the feminisation of rice production. In regions where the availability of remunerative non-farm opportunities existed, the share of female labour in jointly completed crop operations increased. Thirdly, the replacement of daily-wage contracts with piece-rate contracts has reduced gender exclusivity of labour in rice cultivation. This could be explained by a rise in the share of male labour in female-specific tasks because of the higher remuneration associated with piece-rates.

Conclusions

This chapter has examined the characteristics of female labour use in seven rice-cultivating villages in India. The villages belong to different agro-ecological zones of the States of Andhra Pradesh, Karnataka, Punjab, Uttar Pradesh, and West Bengal. The villages were categorised into three groups based on their average rice area productivity. While the results cannot be generalised to district- or State-level narratives, a few interesting findings were deduced from the analysis.

A clear association between area productivity and total labour deployment in rice cultivation was noted. Villages with higher average rice productivity had lower total labour use per hectare. Excluding Panahar (West Bengal), the villages in group A had lower female labour deployment than the villages in group B and group C. Farm operations were relatively more mechanised in group A villages compared to other villages. Among the villages in group A, female labour use was very low in Tehang (Punjab). This could be because the farm operations were done by male migrant workers from Bihar. Low female participation in rice cultivation in Panahar (West Bengal), which was an exception, could be explained by the socio-cultural restrictions against women being engaged in paid work.

Women contributed their labour mostly to transplanting, weeding, and harvesting operations. A distinct gender division of labour in rice farming was noted in Alabujanahalli (Karnataka) and Ananthavaram (Andhra Pradesh), both of which had the most female-specific operations of all villages. In the other villages, men and women participated almost equally in weeding and harvesting operations. Exceptions were Tehang (Punjab) and Panahar (West Bengal), where there was more participation of male labour in all farm operations.

An evaluation of the forms of labour showed a predominance of hired labour in rice cultivation across all villages except Mahatwar (eastern Uttar Pradesh). The share of hired labour in total labour was higher for group A villages than for other villages. An association between higher area productivity and the use of hired labour was noted among the villages. Tasks like transplanting and weeding, which used hired workers, were dominated by women hired workers; this, again, would not apply to Panahar (West Bengal) and Tehang (Punjab).

A significant finding that emerges from this chapter is the proliferation of piece-rate contracts in crop operations, specifically in transplanting and harvesting operations. The share of these contracts was particularly high in Ananthavaram (Andhra Pradesh) and Tehang (Punjab). These contracts blurred the gender division of labour in crop operations and raised methodological difficulties in estimating the contribution of female labour.

The study identified a few features of contemporary rice farming in villages from different agro-ecological regions. In all the villages, the improvement in productive forces was gender-differentiated; there was not even a single case that showed women's access to farm machinery. The fact that women are increasingly getting displaced from productive employment in agriculture, coupled with low access to non-farm work, poses a significant challenge.

Bibliography

Agarwal, Bina (1981), "Agricultural Modernisation and Third World Women: Pointers from the Literature and an Empirical Analysis," World Employment Programme Research Working Paper Series, No. WEP10/WP21, ILO, Geneva.

Agarwal, Bina (1985), "Rural Women and High Yielding Rice Technology in India," in *Women in Rice Farming*, International Rice Research Institute, Gower Publishing Company, England, pp. 307–35.

Bardhan, Pranab Kumar (1978), "On Labour Absorption in South Asian Rice Agriculture with Special Reference to India", in Pranab Kumar Bardhan, A. Vaidyanathan, Y. Alagh, G. S. Bhalla, and Amit Bhaduri, *Labour Absorption in Indian Agriculture: Some Exploratory Investigations*, ILO, Bangkok, November, pp. 1–32.

Barker, Randolph, Herdt, Robert W., and Rose, Beth (1985), *The Rice Economy of Asia*, Resources for the Future, Washington D. C.

Basant, Rakesh (1987), "Agricultural Technology and Employment in India: A Survey of Recent Research," *Economic and Political Weekly*, vol. 22, no. 31, 8 August, pp. 1348–64.

Bray, Francesca (1986), *The Rice Economies: Technology and Development in Asian Societies*, Basil Blackwell, Oxford.

Chand, Ramesh, Srivastava, S. K., and Singh, Jaspal (2017), "Changes in Rural Economy of India, 1971 to 2012," *Economic and Political Weekly*, vol. 52, no. 52, 30 December, pp. 64–71.

da Corta, Lucia, and Venkateshwarlu, Davuluri (1999), "Unfree Relations and the Feminisation of Agricultural Labour in Andhra Pradesh, 1970–95," *The Journal of Peasant Studies*, vol. 26, nos. 2–3, pp. 71–139.

Davis, Marvin G. (1975), "Rank and Rivalry in Rural West Bengal," unpublished doctoral dissertation, University of Chicago.

Dhar, Niladri Sekhar (2017), "Labour in Small Farms," in Madhura Swaminathan and Sandipan Baksi (eds.), *How Do Small Farmers Fare?*, Tulika Books, New Delhi.

Directorate of Economics and Statistics (DES) (2014), *District Wise Crop Production Statistics*, Crop Production Statistics Information System, Ministry of Agriculture and Farmers' Welfare, Government of India, New Delhi.

Directorate of Economics and Statistics (DES) (2016), *Agricultural Statistics at a Glance 2016*, Ministry of Agriculture and Farmers' Welfare, Government of India, New Delhi.

Duvvuru, Narasimha Reddy, and Motkuri, Venkatanarayana (2013), "Declining Labour Use in Agriculture: A Case of Rice Cultivation in Andhra Pradesh," Munich Personal RePEc Archive (MPRA), Paper No. 49024, available at https://mpra.ub.uni-muenchen.de/49204/, viewed on 5 June 2019.

International Rice Research Institute (IRRI) (1985), *Women in Rice Farming*, IRRI and Gower Publishing Company, Aldershot.

Ishikawa, Shigeru (1981), *Labour Absorption in Asian Agriculture: An Issues Paper*, ILO, Bangkok.

Jose, A. V. (1984), "Farm Mechanisation in Asian Countries: Some Perspectives," *Economic and Political Weekly*, vol. 19, no. 26, 30 June, pp. A97–A103.

Kapadia, Karin (1996), *Siva and Her Sisters: Gender, Caste, and Class in Rural South India*, Oxford University Press, Delhi.

Maps of India (2019), "India Outline Map," *Maps of India*, available at https://www.mapsofindia.com/maps/india/outlinemapofindia.htm, viewed on 12 December 2019.

Mencher, Joan P., and Saradamoni, K. (1982), "Muddy Feet, Dirty Hands: Rice Production and Female Agricultural Labour," *Economic and Political Weekly*, vol. 17, no. 52, 25 December, pp. A149–53 and A155–67.

Miller, Barbara D. (1981), *The Endangered Sex*, Cornell University Press, Ithaca, New York.

Moore, Mick (1973), "Cross-Cultural Surveys of Peasant Family Structures: Some Comments," *American Anthropologist*, vol. 75, no. 3, June, pp. 911–15.

Paris, T. R. (1998), "The Impact of Technologies on Women in Asian Rice Farming," in Prabhu. L. Pingali and Mahabub Hossain (eds.), *Impact of Rice Research*, International Rice Research Institute, Philippines, pp. 241–62.

Ramachandran, V. K. (1990), *Wage Labour and Unfreedom in Agriculture: An Indian Case Study*, Clarendon Press, Oxford.

Ramachandran, V. K. (2011), "The State of Agrarian Relations in India Today," *The Marxist*, vol. 27, nos. 1–2, January–June, pp. 51–89.

Ramachandran, V. K., and Swaminathan, Madhura (2006), "Prospects for Rural Employment in Contemporary India," in Mary E. John, Praveen Kumar Jha, and Surinder S. Jodhka (eds.), *Contested Transformations: Changing Economies and Identities in Contemporary India*, Tulika Books, New Delhi.

Ramachandran, V. K., Swaminathan, Madhura, and Rawal, Vikas (2001), "How Have Hired Workers Fared? A Case Study of Women Workers from an Indian Village, 1977 to 1999," CDS Working Paper No. 323, Centre for Development Studies, Thiruvananthapuram.

Rao, Smriti (2011), "Work and Empowerment: Women and Agriculture in South India," *Journal of Development Studies*, vol. 47, no. 2, 27 January, pp. 294–315.

Saradamoni, K. (1991), *Filling the Rice Bowl: Women in Paddy Cultivation*, Sangam Books, Hyderabad.

Sidhu, H. S. (2005), "Production Conditions in Contemporary Punjab Agriculture," *Journal of Punjab Studies*, vol. 12, no. 3, Fall, pp. 197–218.

Sivamurugan, T., and Swaminathan, Madhura (2017), "PARI Villages: An Introduction," in Madhura Swaminathan and Sandipan Baksi (eds.), *How Do Small Farmers Fare?*, Tulika Books, New Delhi.

Smith, Joyotee, and Gascon, F. E. (1979), "The Effect of the New Rice Technology on Family Labour Utilisation in Laguna," IRRI Research Paper Series, No. 42, IRRI, Manila.

Sundarayya, P. (1977), "Class Differentiation of the Peasantry: Results of Rural Surveys in Andhra Pradesh," *Social Scientist*, vol. 5, no. 8, March, pp 51–83.

The Board of Economic Enquiry (1962), "An Economic Survey of Tehang: A Village in Jullundur District," Punjab Village Survey Series, The Board of Economic Enquiry, Punjab.

White, Benjamin (1985), "Women and the Modernisation of Rice Agriculture: Some General Issues and a Javanese Case Study," in *Women in Rice Farming*, International Rice Research Institute, Gower Publishing Company, England, pp. 119 –48.

7

Forms of Wages in the Assam–Dooar Plantations

A Historical Perspective

Jeta Sankrityayana[1]

Jeta Sankrityayana[1]

INDIA IN THE GLOBAL TEA ENTERPRISE

Tea entered the global economy during the period of mercantile rivalry between the Dutch Verenigde Oost-Indische Compagnie (VOC, chartered 1602) and the British East India Company (EIC, chartered 1600). Nevertheless, for more than 200 years, the sources of tea were confined to the traditional growing countries of China and Japan. In 1833, the renewal of the EIC Charter ended the EIC monopoly on tea trade across Britain and the colonies, and a Tea Committee was appointed in 1834 that recommended experimentation with planting tea in the newly annexed territories of Assam and the Himalayas. When the experiment proved successful, the first shipment of 47 chests of Assam tea was auctioned for a promising price at the London Auction in 1839. Exports of Chinese black tea were outcompeted by Indian black tea in terms of average costs and quality within a period of 30 years. From that success onwards, as tea became an item of mass consumption in complementarity with cheap sugar, a strong role was established for Indian tea plantations in the global tea enterprise.

Although China remained the largest global producer of tea on the strength of its large domestic tea market, the British colonies of India, Sri Lanka, and later Kenya became the dominant exporters of tea to British tea blenders, enabling the British beverage industry to rule global markets. Today, the situation has changed appreciably. Together, nearly 80 per cent of global tea exports are sourced from the four countries just mentioned, with Indian tea exports in 2014 being valued at USD 746 million (IBEF 2016). With China resurgent in global tea exports, a considerable squeeze has been applied on

---

[1] This article was first published in *Review of Agrarian Studies*, vol. 8, no. 2, July–December 2018.

Table 7.1 *Recent trends in global tea production and tea exports, 2012 –16* in million kg

Country	2012	2013	2014	2015	2016 (P)
World tea production					
China	1,789.8	1,924.5	2,095.7	2,249	2,350
India	1,126.3	1,200.4	1,207.3	1,208.7	1,239.2
Kenya	369.6	432.5	445.1	399.2	474.8
Sri Lanka	328.4	340	338	329	292.4
Vietnam	174	180.3	175	170	165
Indonesia	137.8	136.9	135.7	129.3	125.5
Others	769.5	781.3	802.7	796.4	815.9
Total	4,695.4	4,995.9	5,199.5	5,281.6	5,462.8
World tea exports					
China	321.8	332.4	301.5	325	328.7
India	208.3	219.1	207.4	228.7	216.8
Kenya	430.2	494.4	499.4	443.5	480.3
Sri Lanka	306	309.2	317.9	301.3	280.9
Vietnam	144	140.3	132	133.5	127
Indonesia	70.1	70.8	66.4	61.9	50
Others	295.1	294.6	301.7	305.6	293.9
Total	1,775.5	1,860.8	1,826.3	1,799.5	1,777.6

Note: (P) stands for provisional.
Source: Adapted from International Tea Committee (ITC) data.

Indian tea exports despite a major expansion in Indian tea production over the last 50 years. In the absence of increasing tea exports, the mass of Indian tea is now domestically consumed. By contrast, India's major competitors in tea exports, Sri Lanka and Kenya, export nearly all the tea they produce. Kenyan and Sri Lankan tea are therefore more sensitive to global tea preferences, while Indian tea in large part caters to a less discerning domestic market. In terms of overall proportion, quality tea produced in India is a smaller share of the total than in Sri Lanka and Kenya.

Recent figures also show that Kenya exports more tea than it produces. This points to Kenya's gradual emergence as the global centre for tea trade after the closure of the 300-year Mincing Lane Tea Auctions in London in 1998 (Talbot 2002). With the major international tea blenders all active in the Kenyan auctions, third-party teas are now increasingly dealt with at these auctions, pushing the tea auctions at Kolkata, Colombo, and elsewhere into subsidiary trading positions.

India now consumes domestically more than four-fifths of its annual tea crop, making the demand for tea highly sensitive to domestic tea prices. While tea exports remain a large foreign exchange earner for India, the rise of tea competition from other countries and the sluggishness of tea earnings as a result of a long-term decline in global tea prices have played increasing havoc with the Indian tea plantation industry over at least 20 years, disrupting production patterns and production relations. Tea workers, still the most powerless of all organised sector workers, must bear the brunt of commercial adjustments.

As women have traditionally constituted more than half the work force in tea, working in plucking operations as field workers, the brunt of labour adjustments has been borne by income-poor plantation women who have seen an erosion in their status, social power, and earnings. The largest segment of the Indian tea labour force is deployed in the tea-growing regions of Assam and West Bengal, and the two States have seen dismal conditions in the tea sector. There has been worker distress and starvation deaths over two decades, without adequate measures for restitution of worker rights.

The contexts prevailing in the Assam and West Bengal tea industry, their manifestations, and proximate causes and reasons are outlined in reference to global and Indian tea trends in this study.

The Advent of Tea in Eastern and North Eastern India

Colonial annexations of territory in North East India, of Assam from Burma (1826), the Darjeeling Hills from Sikkim (1835), and Bengal and the Assam Dooars from Bhutan (1865), opened the way for planter capital. Plantations needed a large permanent labour force to plant new territories. Just as the Indian indenture system transported Indian coolie labour to colonial sugar colonies in the Caribbean and the Indian Ocean, internal indenture brought Adivasi families from central India to Assam. In a later phase, labouring families from the Nepal Hills were brought to the Darjeeling Hills after being recruited by labour *sardars*, while Adivasi labour for the Bengal and Assam Dooars was recruited from Jharkhand and Chhattisgarh through free labour agents or *arkatis*, Lutheran and Catholic missions, and Tea District Labour Boards.

The scale of labour migration into new tea territories during this period was immense. At the same time, it also encouraged voluntary migration and methods to resolve the inequities of enslaved plantation labour markets in the past era. The tea labour system tied entire families for several generations into a reproducible work force for plantation work.

Reorganisation of plantations in India over a century and a half has been gradual and obscure. Changes have nevertheless occurred in the dominant modes of ownership and control of plantations, in the national and international markets supplied by plantation products and their marketing chains, and in the dominant scale of operation of plantations.

Women have always played a pivotal role as field workers in plantation production. Gradual changes in the plantation industry in Assam and North Eastern India have brought about changes in forms of plantation labour deployment and organisation. The impact of recent changes on the engagement of women in the tea industry in the major growing regions of Assam and West Bengal is described and explored below.

Tea History and Tea Competition

The tea plantation boom in the nineteenth century that followed the successful marketing of Indian tea at the London Auctions has been characterised as "tea mania." During this period, easy land grants for plantation development under various Wasteland Acts brought in planters and planter capital on a large scale. Tea plantations rapidly spread from the Upper Assam region (1840–60) to Darjeeling (1860–60) and the Dooars (1860–80), and through southern India and Ceylon, i.e. Sri Lanka (1880–90). The chief attractions of planter enterprise were the negligible costs of acquiring and running land estates, and the low capital component in the process of manufacturing vis-à-vis high expected profits. The principal constraint was the recruitment of a large plantation labour force, which was overcome in different regions by different means. In Assam, where early recruitments were done in the Company period, the chief instrument was internal labour indenture – a system also used with success in recruiting Indian "coolie" labour for plantations in the Caribbean, the Indian Ocean, and Fiji. Recruitment of free labour for the Darjeeling and Dooars tea territories was made by labour agents and *sardars* using inducements of land availability for cultivation. The *kangany* system used in south India to recruit Tamil workers for plantations in south India, Sri Lanka, and Malaysia was similar in nature, while plantations in the Cardamom Hills offered seasonal employment to labour drawn from the hill tribes (Wenzlhuemer 2007). This period of labour recruitment, during which some of the worst excesses occurred, has remained largely undocumented.

The "tea mania" lasted till the 1890s, following which a tea glut emanating from the advent of new tea plantations in southern India, Sri Lanka, and Java led to market saturation and inevitable price fall. In replacement of the old labour-intensive system of hand-manufacture of tea, which had required a huge complement of tea labourers, the first steps towards technical change and mechanisation were seen in the gradual introduction of rolling machines and roll-breaking machines for manufacturing orthodox tea, starting from Assam. While meagre capital investment has made mechanical innovation in the tea industry rather slow, the alternative approach applied for raising tea profitability and productivity has been through organisational change. Thus, after the first tea crisis, a number of pioneer planters who had developed the original leases sold out to large corporate tea companies. The large tea estate and the multi-estate tea company were thus born.

Regulation of Tea Enterprise

The first tea regulation emerged in 1903 through the Indian Tea Cess Bill, which provided for a levy on Indian tea exports to be used for the promotion of Indian tea within the country. The Tea Cess Committee was redesignated in 1937 as the Indian Tea Market Expansion Board. Meanwhile, in the wake of worldwide crises in commodity markets during the Great Depression, India, Ceylon, and Java signed an International Tea Agreement in 1933, and effective regulation of the tea industry in India began under the Indian Tea Control Act of 1938, which established the Indian Tea Licensing Committee in order to limit the extent of land areas hitherto available for tea expansion. Succeeding this, a Central Tea Board was established after Independence under provisions of the Central Tea Board Act of 1949, and the Tea Board of India came into existence with the passing of the Tea Act in 1953 (Mukherjee 1978).

While the legislation under which the Indian Tea Board is constituted and the various regulations under Tea Marketing Control are the province of the Union government in India, implementation of the Plantation Labour Act, 1951, and the plantation rules made thereunder lie within the province of respective State governments in the tea-growing States. Besides exercising powers relating to grants of land made to plantations and the lease terms for the same, the States also regulate tea plantations through the monitoring of labour standards.

Because of the isolation of plantation populations in arduous conditions of work, the Plantations Labour Act (PLA) has mandated that decent welfare benefits including drinking water and conservancy be provided by employers to all resident plantation workers compelled by work exigencies to reside within the plantation tea estates. Provision of health care with adequately staffed hospitals and dispensaries, sickness and maternity benefits to workers, and provision of decent housing, worker canteens, and child crèches to working mothers with minor children, along with adequate educational and recreational facilities, is also mandated. While these so-called "fringe" or "non-wage" benefits are often cited by planters as part of the obligatory "social costs" that have expanded investment outlays on plantation labour, making Indian tea plantations uncompetitive, their quantum is included notionally in the computation of tea workers' wages, thus reducing wag payments made in cash. In the large tea-growing States of Assam and West Bengal, realisation of PLA benefits has been a major focus for plantation labour movements, while in Tamil Nadu and Kerala, which have different state-mandated plantation labour rules, this has been less of an issue.

Several provisions of the PLA have direct implications for women workers. The hours of regular *haziri* (daily wage) work are limited to 48 hours per week for adults and 27 hours for non-adults. Beyond these duty hours, *thika* or double wages are to be paid. Rest intervals of half an hour are mandated after every continuous five-hour work stretch, while women workers with infant children are entitled to two nursing breaks a day till the child has attained the age of 15 months. In addition to statutory holidays, earned leave with full pay is to be provided to workers at the rate of one day of earned leave for 20 days of work, and all workers suffering illness are entitled to sickness allowance. Women workers were entitled to maternity allowances and benefits under the Maternity Benefit Act of 1961. Besides the statutory provisions of PLA 1951, tea-worker families in Assam and West Bengal under bipartite or tripartite agreement with labour unions receive subsidised rations, free fuel, and dry tea, as a consequence of which they draw lower money wages compared to their counterparts in southern India (GoI 1951).

Welfare benefits under PLA are accessible to permanent resident workers and their bonafide dependents. Subsidised rations are admissible to children of tea-worker families up to the age of 16, provided they depend fully on their parents and are not employed elsewhere. In a subtle gender distinction between dependants of male and female workers, ration benefits extend to the spouses and minor children of employed male workers, but are limited to the immediate family of women workers when their spouses are not permanent tea workers. PLA medical benefits admissible for women workers are similarly restricted to women workers and their dependent children.

Progress in the implementation of PLA has been tardy both in Assam and West Bengal, because of major weaknesses in the infrastructure for plantation inspections, as well as non-compliance of planters in filing mandatory PLA returns because of the very minor cash penalties for PLA violations. Shortfalls in decent work conditions as well as in the provision of statutory labour benefits continue to persist.

Gender Roles in the Assam–Dooars Plantations

The estate work force engaged on large tea plantations in Assam and West Bengal is categorised into standard groups of field workers engaged for upkeep of tea bushes and plucking of tea leaves, and factory workers engaged for processing and manufacture of tea produced by the estate factory. By tradition, the factory work force has been overwhelmingly male and the field work force has been dominated by women workers engaged in large numbers for the manual plucking of tea. Although promotional literature extols this as a hallmark of the gender equality prevalent on plantations, the truth is quite different.

Women tea workers have been characterised paternalistically in the literature (Griffiths 1967) as "nimble-fingered," more disciplined, and compliant, but through much of plantation history were paid much less as compared to male workers. The modes of wage payment, by which men receive time-rated wages while women receive piece-rated wages upon fulfilling assigned plucking tasks, also create substantive gender discrepancies between male and female tea workers. Male tea workers can expect to progress into supervisory tasks offering higher wages in the course of their careers. Because of piece-rate payment for their work, women cannot expect to progress to higher wage levels, and remain pluckers drawing standard piece-rated wages for the duration of their engagement as workers.

A large number of women are engaged as field workers on labour-intensive tea estates. The attempted cost-cutting by plantation managements through reduced engagement of permanent workers and progressive casualisation of field work has inordinately hit women tea workers, who have faced significant reductions in their overall earnings.

GLOBAL RESTRUCTURING OF TEA

Since the era of colonial plantations, the three major plantation crops in India have been tea, coffee, and rubber. There has been a dramatic transformation in the ownership of plantations over the last five decades, particularly affecting coffee and rubber plantations, with a dynamic trend towards an increase in smallholder units and a decline of large plantations. The smallholder sector has now emerged as the major stakeholder in coffee and rubber. Tea plantations have not undergone the same scale of transformation favouring smallholders, and large integrated tea estates continue to dominate the area under tea (72 per cent) and tea production (80 per cent) in India.

In 2008–09, tea accounted for 0.6 million hectares (36 per cent) of the total plantation area of 1.6 million hectares under these three plantation crops

(Viswanathan and Shah 2016), with 82 per cent of the total tea produced being consumed domestically. In contrast, 63 per cent of the coffee produced in India was exported. The share of smallholders in total area and production under tea stood at around 26–28 per cent, while smallholder share in total area and production under coffee was appreciably higher, between 70 to 75 per cent (*ibid.*). Assam and West Bengal, respectively, accounted for 56 per cent and 20 per cent of the area under tea in India, and 51 per cent and 24 per cent of the tea produced in India. The three other major tea-growing States in the country were Tamil Nadu (14 per cent area, 16 per cent production), Kerala (6 per cent area, 7 per cent production), and Karnataka (0.4 per cent area, 0.5 per cent production), all in southern India. Collectively, these five major tea-growing States accounted for more than 96 per cent of the area under tea and 98 per cent of tea production in India (*ibid.*).

Restructuring Global Tea Markets

Restructuring within the Indian tea industry has inevitably been spurred by changes occurring in global tea markets, where global tea prices have declined in real terms since the 1970s. Since earliest times, the tea market had been dominated by large sterling tea companies that had secured their economies of scale by operating multiple estates in several tea territories. In close coordination with tea merchants, the large companies were able to protect tea prices by controlling the volume of tea entering the international market, through the consolidated agency of planters' associations that set out plantation and marketing quotas for their members. This generally helped maintain international tea prices at reasonably high levels by tightly matching the quantity of tea produced to existing market demand. As long as major tea corporates ruled the roost, tea estates occupied the dominant rung of market organisation in the global tea industry, and many international tea corporates had combined business interests in plantation ownership and in global tea marketing. In India, all this began to change after Independence, bringing the tea-marketing chains of global beverage companies to the fore.

As noted earlier, promulgation of various State legislations for acquiring excess estate lands, such as the West Bengal Estates Acquisition Act, 1953 and enforcement of the Foreign Exchange Regulation Act (FERA), 1973, triggered the decline of sterling tea companies in India from the 1970s, followed by their mass exodus to Kenya and eastern Africa, where the new tea industry emerged as a dominant global player. Both Sri Lanka and India reacted variously to this change. Nationalisation of large tea estates in Sri Lanka by the Sri Lanka Freedom Party (SLFP) government under the land reform laws of 1972 and 1975 was reversed in 1992 by re-privatisation under the United National Party (UNP) government, following which the smallholder sector took off, emulating the success of small tea plantations in Kenya (Ganewatta and Edwards 2000).

Smallholder tea operations in India, long in existence in the Nilgiris, initially proliferated through the grant of small land leases to Indian Tamil tea workers repatriated from Sri Lanka under the Shastri–Sirimavo pact, followed by adoption of the small tea garden–bought leaf factory (STG–BLF) model that has since been replicated across many tea-growing areas in India. However, in a peculiarity that separates it from smallholder tea cultivation elsewhere, the Indian STG–BLF model has expanded on non-tea lands culled from crop-farming operations and replanted with tea, while the traditional estate mode of manufacture continues to coexist. Based on the principle that "many hands make light work," the STG model has been instrumental in expanding virtual tea productivity because of the invisibility of the many hands engaged in tea-plucking. However, its emphasis on maximising quantity of green leaf production does not translate immediately into tea quality, where estate production continues to hold its own.

The price impetus for such changes has been provided by restructuring within international tea markets, caused by the declining importance of estate companies in favour of tea corporates and international tea blenders. Along with changes in international tea marketing, these have changed the hierarchical importance of different tea-producing countries, and placed Kenya at the fore.

Figure 7.1 *Long-term fluctuations and deviations from the long-term average in international tea auction prices* in USD per kg

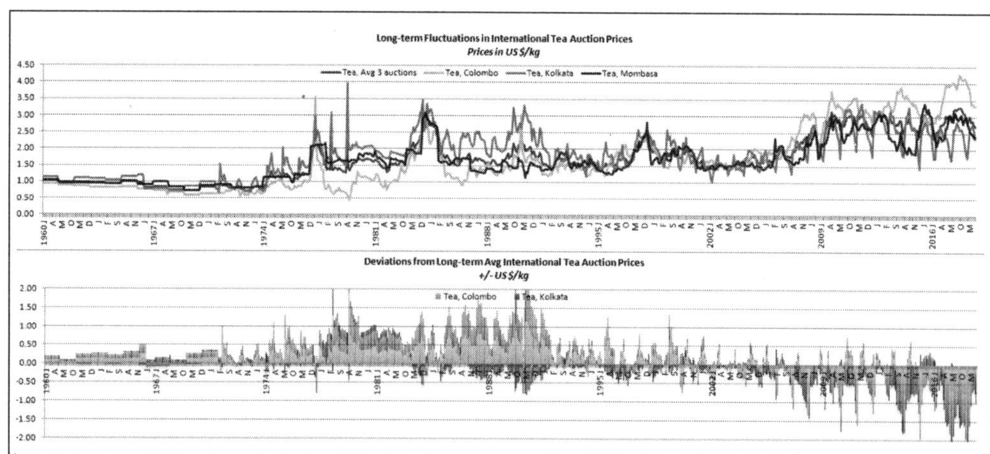

Source: Data drawn from Commodity Price Data, *The Pink Sheet* (World Bank 2018).

Commodity trade trends in global tea from the World Bank commodity database are illustrated in Figure 7.1, which compares prices in the Mombasa, Colombo, and Kolkata tea auctions. From 1706 to 1998, global price trends for tea were set at the London Tea Auction, with quick price responses from the Calcutta Tea Auction, followed by the auctions at Colombo and Mombasa. Mombasa was a relatively late addition to the global tea auction system, with Kenya Tea Auctions initially established in 1956 at Nairobi and shifted to the port-city of Mombasa in 1969 (EATTA 2018). From 1992, the Mombasa Tea Auction became dollar-denominated with full convertibility, driving it into a position of price leadership over global tea prices. Sensitivity analysis thereafter indicates that Mombasa tea auction prices were followed in suit by the Colombo Auction, while the Calcutta Tea Auction followed at a distant third.

Restructuring of Plantations and the Plantation Work Force

Tea grants and attached wasteland grants during the colonial era were held under extremely favourable long-lease terms. In Darjeeling district in West Bengal, nearly half the tea estates in 1951 were held under freehold or revenue-free terms. Attachment of additional land grants to tea estates were made to provide homesteads and marginal farmlands to migrating tea labour communities. In 1953, along with rationalisation of land rents, the West Bengal Estates Acquisition Act sought to replace these varying land dispensations with a uniform renewable lease of 30 years, besides resuming such lands within the grant that were being used for purposes other than growing tea. The intention was to prevent tea estates from functioning as "mini zamindaris" (Ghosh 1987, p. 84). This was vigorously contested by the sterling estates, as this stripped them of residual power as landlords, turning them into tenants of the government.

Based on a survey of tea-estate lands executed by the Settlement Directorate in the 331 tea estates in existence in the 1950s, the original Tea Garden Advisory Committee constituted under the West Bengal Estates Acquisition Act, 1955 had recommended the resumption of surplus lands in the case of 225 tea estates (*ibid.*, p. 81). Implementation of this recommendation was delayed by 16 years, till the Calcutta High Court judgment on the Malhati Tea Syndicate case cleared the way in 1970. Combined with regulations under the Foreign Exchange Regulation Act (FERA), which diluted foreign equity in the tea industry to 40 per cent, the period following the mid-1970s saw the departure of the London-incorporated sterling companies that had dominated the Indian tea sector for over 100 years, as well as the advent of new Indian tea-group companies.

After the removal of legal encumbrances and resumption of surplus tea-estate lands during the mid-1970s, the tea industry in West Bengal and Assam often sought additional land grants from the government for expanding tea cultivation. Following the tea boom from the mid-1980s onwards, the tea industry again sought releases of additional government land for expanding plantations. In acknowledging the difficulty of securing forest lands for plantation purposes after the Forest Conservation Act, 1980 (ITA 1986, p. 2), the industry noted in reference to Assam that estate lands allotted to local farming populations in the State were unsuited to paddy cultivation. To circumvent legal problems that would arise if these lands were given over to tea estates, the idea of parcelling out such lands to small growers for tea cultivation was conceived.

In the old tea-growing regions of Assam and northern West Bengal where large tea estates were concentrated, the presence of small tea growers (STG) is relatively new. Progressive assignment of ceiling-surplus homestead lands to landless farmers under the land redistribution policy of West Bengal from the late 1970s left little land in non-traditional areas to be granted for new tea leases. In the traditional growing areas of the Darjeeling Hills, the Terai and the Dooars, conversion of forests into revenue lands had reached a standstill after Independence. All large tea estates had been established well before the 1930s.

Three-fourths of the 49,397 hectares of vested lands transferred for homesteads and cultivation to 0.2 million landless beneficiaries in Darjeeling and Jalpaiguri were located in Jalpaiguri district. While the unit sizes of the redistributed lands were small (less than 0.3 hectare), the land units transferred in Jalpaiguri were twice as large as the average land transfer under land reforms across the State, providing an impetus to rural migration to Darjeeling and Jalpaiguri districts. By 1996, nearly 70 per cent of the farmers in the two tea-growing districts were marginal farmers cultivating an average plot of 0.5 hectare. Nearly 56 per cent of land transfers in the two tea-growing districts were made in the later phase of land reforms between 1980 and 1990 (Chakraborti *et al.* 2003). During this period of aggressive land reforms after 1977, assignment of government-held vested land for other non-agricultural and commercial purposes was not an alternative.

ISSUES OF TEA-WORKER DEPLOYMENT AND WAGES

Plantation wages in Assam and West Bengal are determined by bipartite wage agreements between employers' associations and labour unions, or tripartite agreements with additional government arbitrage according to the Plantation Labour Rules made by the respective State, under provisions of the Plantation

Labour Act, 1951. Even though tea wages are a State subject, the Minimum Wages Act, 1948 had provided for fixing minimum wages for tea labour. Not until 2006 were minimum wages for tea workers actually fixed by the State governments of Tamil Nadu, Karnataka, and Kerala, which now stand at Rs 310, Rs 263, and Rs 241, respectively. Meanwhile, the respective State governments of the large tea-growing States of Assam and West Bengal, where tea wages are the lowest, are in the process of negotiating minimum wages for tea workers.

The modes of formulation for wages have been subject to longstanding debate, from the Royal Commission on Labour, 1931 to the First and Second National Commission of Labour (1969 and 2002). Since, by definition, minimum wages are applicable to unskilled casual labour, two alternative wage concepts that have received some attention are *fair* wages and *living* wages (National Commission on Rural Labour 1991).

While a *fair wage* would provide for a modicum of education, health care, and amenities over and above the statutory minimum wage, a *living wage* would be at a level that provides standards of comfort over and above necessities like food, shelter, and clothing to workers (*ibid.*, section 1.8). Attached to this is the concept of a *family wage*, in which a typical worker family is taken to comprise three consumption units of the adult wage-earner, his spouse, and two minor children. Thus, an adult male earning a living wage would be able to provide adequately for a family of three consumption units.

In tea plantations where family labour has been the prevalent practice since inception, the standard mode of wage fixation by the agreements has been to fix the joint earnings of two working spouses within a family at a level that will collectively provide for a family of four. Each earning spouse has thus been paid enough support for one and one-half consumption units per family. Wage stresses emerge, particularly in labour households headed by widowed or single women whose wage earnings prove inadequate to support their family. Non-wage benefits such as subsidised food rations are also given to dependent children, but are unavailable to male spouses who do not work on the plantation. Other members from tea-labour households engaged temporarily for seasonal plucking as casual or *bigha/bustee* labour are also not entitled to non-wage benefits.

Prior to the Equal Remuneration Act, 1976 and the Child Labour (Abolition and Regulation) Act, 1986, women, adolescents, and child workers from Indian plantation labour families constituted a cheap labour pool available to estate managements for engagement as field workers, in direct continuity with the family mode of labour common on tea plantations. While daily-rated permanent or *hazira* workers were available for work around the year, other casual workers were engaged during seasons of peak labour demand. By securing statutory non-wage benefits for worker families residing in labour lines within the plantation, the Plantation Labour Act, 1951 gave rise to a new work category of "outside" workers. These outside workers only drew wages and no non-wage benefits, and so quickly became a low-cost option for tea plantations. As temporary *bigha* workers engaged from outside the plantation were engaged at prevailing wages only during peak plucking seasons, and did not draw PLA non-wage benefits for themselves or their dependents, they became a low-cost labour option for plantations. Creation of labour categories of different descriptions among plantation workers encouraged the development of a highly segmented labour market. Performing the same tasks as resident workers, the increased employment of casual labour in increasing numbers significantly reduced wage costs on tea plantations. Temporary workers drawn from outside the plantation are not entitled to regular work engagement, and have thus become a floating labour reserve that can be engaged and laid-off at will.

The tea industry in India has been comprehensively documented between 1955 and 2004, when the Tea Board of India regularly published its twin compendia, *Tea Statistics* and *Tea Digest*. From 1998 onwards, the Tea Board began to include production data for small STG tea gardens below 25 acres (10.2 hectares), and as the tea databases grew in size, regular publication of the data compendia soon ceased. In 2004, the last year for which the Tea Board's *Tea Statistics* are available, the total field work force on Indian tea plantations numbered around 1.3 million, with a 9.3 per cent increase over the work force strength in 1996. Of the total tea work force, 71 per cent was engaged on plantations in northern India, primarily Assam and West Bengal, while 39 per cent was engaged on plantations in southern India. However, in comparative terms, absolute attrition in the tea work force in northern India was led by a 12 per cent decline in the tea work force in West Bengal. The eight-year decline was most marked in the case of resident tea workers, which declined by 35 per cent over the period even as the all-India figure increased by 3.3 per cent, with most of the accretion occurring in southern India. This was followed by increases of over 90 per cent in the deployment of outside permanent workers throughout India, with the accretion in West Bengal alone amounting to over 95 per cent.

In sum, the casual work force engaged on tea plantations in India increased by over 0.8 million workers between 1996 and 2004, with the bulk of labour casualisation occurring in southern India (0.2 million) and West Bengal (0.2 million). On account of an overall decline in resident permanent workers in plantations in northern India, the number of bonafide dependants also fell

Table 7.2 *Changes in the deployment of the work force in tea plantations, by region and type of employment, 1996–2004 in numbers*

Region	1996	1997	1998	1999	2000	2001	2002	2003	2004
All workers in tea estates									
Assam	590,968	591,036	598,825	596,943	602,531	611,063	619,663	619,322	617,518
West Bengal	293,093	282,806	286,967	251,012	253,459	255,569	259,182	260,336	262,672
Northern India	903,204	892,556	904,654	864,916	873,058	883,450	895,900	896,272	896,717
Tamil Nadu	132,703	143,378	145,183	245,379	255,790	267,665	275,723	268,351	266,027
Karnataka	5,885	4,642	281	3,680	3,789	3,837	3,953	4,403	4,508
Kerala	99,235	97,592	96,465	74,496	77,086	77,198	79,524	87,184	90,358
Southern India	237,827	245,612	241,929	323,555	336,665	348,700	359,200	359,938	360,893
All India	1,141,031	1,138,163	1,146,583	1,188,471	1,209,723	1,232,150	1,255,100	1,256,210	1,257,610
Resident workers in tea estates									
Assam	449,981	446,288	451,896	423,473	423,437	426,807	432,839	457,942	464,755
West Bengal	255,140	243,887	247,289	198,724	198,849	199,757	202,579	216,090	220,332
Northern India	716,123	700,467	709,352	632,929	633,036	637,049	646,052	684,914	696,119
Tamil Nadu	109,331	119,200	120,532	131,157	132,212	133,114	137,122	154,012	160,406
Karnataka	5,602	4,366	4,345	3,440	3,464	3,485	3,591	3,980	4,123
Kerala	81,753	79,333	78,400	67,093	67,515	67,541	69,576	79,411	83,102
Southern India	196,685	202,899	203,277	201,690	203,191	204,140	210,289	237,403	247,631
All India	912,809	903,366	912,629	834,619	836,227	841,189	856,341	922,317	943,750

Table 7.2 *continued*

Region	1996	1997	1998	1999	2000	2001	2002	2003	2004
Outside workers in tea estates									
Assam	140,987	144,748	146,929	173,470	179,094	184,256	487,670	512,790	519,635
West Bengal	37,989	38,919	39,678	52,288	54,610	55,812	214,715	228,317	232,532
Northern India	187,081	192,089	195,302	231,987	240,022	85,701	714,138	753,098	764,305
Tamil Nadu	23,372	24,178	24,651	114,222	123,578	134,551	149,446	166,362	172,782
Karnataka	283	276	0	240	325	352	3,591	3,980	4,123
Kerala	17,386	18,259	18,065	7,403	9,571	9,657	75,498	138,662	89,032
Southern India	41,141	43,613	42,716	121,865	133,474	144,560	228,535	255,678	265,937
All India	228,222	234,802	238,018	353,852	373,496	390,961	942,673	1,008,776	1,030,242
Outside permanent workers in tea estates									
Assam	48,750	50,519	51,261	54,187	54,463	54,568	432,839	457,942	464,755
West Bengal	10,756	10,808	10,980	12,036	12,083	12,110	202,579	216,090	220,332
Northern India	61,686	63,017	63,951	67,298	67,674	67,804	646,052	684,914	696,119
Tamil Nadu	9,256	10900	11,108	12,066	12,215	12,292	137,122	154,012	160,406
Karnataka	–	–	–	–	–	–	3,591	3,980	4,123
Kerala	8,835	9242	9,130	5,655	5,948	5,928	69,576	79,411	83,102
Southern India	18,091	21042	20,238	17,721	18,163	18,220	210,289	237,403	247,631
All India	79,777	83,159	84,189	85,019	85,837	86,024	856,341	922,317	943,750

Table 7.2 *continued*

Region	1996	1997	1998	1999	2000	2001	2002	2003	2004
Outside temporary workers in tea estates									
Assam	92,237	94,229	95,668	119,283	124,631	129,688	54,831	54,848	54,880
West Bengal	27,233	28,111	28,698	40,252	42,527	43,702	12,136	12,227	12,200
Northern India	125,395	129,072	131,351	164,689	172,348	17,897	68,086	68,184	68,186
Tamil Nadu	14,116	13,278	13,543	102,156	111,363	122,259	12,324	12,350	12,376
Karnataka	283	276	–	240	325	352	–	–	–
Kerala	8,551	9,017	8,935	1,748	3,623	3,729	5,922	59,251	5,930
Southern India	23,050	22,571	22,478	104,144	115,311	126,340	18,246	18,275	18,306
All India	148,445	151,643	153,829	268,833	287,659	304,937	86,332	86,459	86,492
Bonafide dependents of resident workers									
Assam	651,014	658,660	668,629	652,562	652,393	653,175	131,993	106,532	97,883
West Bengal	361,265	346,528	351,376	326,214	325,814	326,054	44,467	32,019	30,140
Northern India	1,023,399	1,016,251	1,031,141	989,351	988,777	989,788	181,762	143,174	132,412
Tamil Nadu	188,203	157,833	161,189	162,427	163,173	163,422	126,277	101,989	93,245
Karnataka	589	666	672	680	682	684	362	423	385
Kerala	62,636	65,606	65,035	65,993	65,873	65,930	4,026	1,848	1,326
Southern India	251,428	224,105	226,896	229,100	229,728	230,036	130,665	104,260	94,956
All India	1,275,827	1,240,356	1,258,037	1,218,451	1,218,505	1,219,824	312,427	247,434	227,368

Table 7.2 *continued*

Region	1996	1997	1998	1999	2000	2001	2002	2003	2004
Resident workers and dependants									
Assam	1,241,982	1,249,696	1,267,454	1,249,505	1,254,924	1,264,238	751,656	725,854	715,401
West Bengal	654,358	629,334	638,343	577,226	579,273	581,623	303,649	292,355	292,812
Northern India	1,926,603	1,908,807	1,935,795	1,854,267	1,861,835	1,873,238	1,077,662	1,039,446	1,029,129
Tamil Nadu	320,906	301,211	306,372	407,806	418,963	431,087	402,000	370,340	359,272
Karnataka	6,474	5,308	953	4,360	4,471	4,521	4,315	4,826	4,893
Kerala	161,871	163,198	161,500	140,489	142,959	143,128	83,550	89,032	91,684
Southern India	489,255	469,717	468,825	552,655	566,393	578,736	489,865	464,198	455,849
All India	2,416,858	2,378,519	2,404,620	2,406,922	2,428,228	2,451,974	1,567,527	1,503,644	1,484,978
Dependency ratio among resident workers									
Assam	1.102	1.114	1.117	1.093	1.083	1.069	0.213	0.172	0.159
West Bengal	1.233	1.225	1.224	1.300	1.285	1.276	0.172	0.123	0.115
Northern India	1.133	1.139	1.140	1.144	1.133	1.120	0.203	0.160	0.148
Tamil Nadu	1.418	1.101	1.110	0.662	0.638	0.611	0.458	0.380	0.351
Karnataka	0.100	0.143	2.391	0.185	0.180	0.178	0.092	0.096	0.085
Kerala	0.631	0.672	0.674	0.886	0.855	0.854	0.051	0.021	0.015
Southern India	1.057	0.912	0.938	0.708	0.682	0.660	0.364	0.290	0.263
All India	1.118	1.090	1.097	1.025	1.007	0.990	0.249	0.197	0.181

Source: Computed from *Tea Statistics*, Tea Board of India, various years.

from 1 million in 1996 to 0.1 million. Thus, at an all-India level, the number of resident workers and bonafide dependants entitled to receive PLA non-wage benefits was curtailed in absolute terms from 2.4 million to 1.5 million between 1996 and 2004, while in Assam and West Bengal alone, the number of PLA non-wage beneficiaries was slashed by nearly 0.9 million consumption units.

In the late 1980s, before the advent of globalisation, resident workers comprised over 80 per cent of the total tea labour force. By 2004, their overall proportion within the aggregate labour force had come down to half through 75 per cent attrition in resident labour positions, while the remainder of the aggregate tea work force comprised outside workers, of whom 90,000 were enagaged on casual contracts. Thus, although the aggregate tea labour force in India grew by more than 0.27 million in the 15-year period between 1985 and 2000, the increase in resident tea workers amounted to only around 59,000, indicating the massive scale of labour casualisation that occurred in the tea sector after liberalisation.

In tea plantations in Assam and West Bengal, which are generally located at a distance from urban settlements and dominated by the large-scale tea-estates sector, the impact of labour casualisation on the tea work force has been particularly marked. The proportion of outside *bigha* workers engaged has risen from 12 per cent to nearly 89 per cent on tea estates in West Bengal, and from 22 per cent to 84 per cent on plantations in Assam, between 1985 and 2004. Keeping in mind that tea estates in northern India are very large and located on forest peripheries at immense distances from the sites of general habitation, workers engaged in casual employment on tea plantations do not have other local sources of alternative work. Meanwhile, although money wages in the Assam and West Bengal tea plantations are negotiated by bipartite or tripartite agreements, their levels continue to be much lower than wages paid to tea workers in southern India. Tea workers in Assam and West Bengal are entitled instead to non-wage benefits under PLA 1951, such as subsidised fuel and rations. On the other hand, tea workers on plantations in southern Indian are paid a scalable dearness allowance in lieu of non-wage benefits in addition to the basic worker wage, that is, the allowance is scaled upwards periodically to compensate for increases in the cost of living.

Plantation workers recruited from outside the tea estates and their dependants are not entitled to these non-wage benefits. Hence, attrition of the permanent tea work force through reorganisational devices such as mass casualisation has drastically brought down social costs previously borne by the tea industry, unmatched by any long-term increase in average tea prices. In a classic characterisation of the Prebisch–Singer hypothesis, the estate owners secure profits by cutting down on the wage bill, rather than through aggressive marketing and better price realisation. The inability of tea labour to resist attrition in numbers and real wages has even led, in times of great financial stringency, to starvation deaths.

Reorganisations in the Indian Tea Sector

Evolution of Plantations in India

Large-scale changes in ownership in the India tea industry occurred after the enactment of legislations such as the Plantation Labour Act in 1951 and the Foreign Exchange Regulation Act (FERA) in 1973. Many sterling tea companies had already departed Indian shores for greener pastures in East Africa (Wickizer 1957), while persuading others to find Indian partners to buy out a part of their equity. While growing tea might technically be described as a monocultural tree-farming operation, the estate sector also represents a mode of commercial organisation for large-scale cultivation of tea. Not designed specifically for commercial tea plantations, the organisational system was borrowed from the nineteenth-century sugar and cotton plantations of the New World. The estate system underwent a process of continuous evolution on the large tea plantations of Assam and the Dooars, before settling into a model of rigorous supervision of tea labour on plantations, coupled with a tightly controlled agronomy. Once this was set, the new estate model was rapidly replicated in many other tea areas in India and abroad. Essentially, the estate model worked splendidly in minimising labour costs, fostering a highly exploitative labour system over which early planters exercised coercion through quasi-legal powers. On account of the sheer size of the tea tracts, remnants of this coercive planter power survive on large tea plantations today, with little civil restitution available.

During its most regressive period, tea production was undertaken on an industrial scale through internal indenture in Assam, to supply the needs of distant colonial metropoles. Eventually, the early pioneer tea plantations evolved into a large corporatised model, in which the relative positions of the estate owners versus plantation labourers were highly uneven. Rather than being "paternalistic," as colonial writers have pointed out (Griffiths 1967), planters were ruthless in coercing labour in their pursuit of profit. Labour regulation through legislations enacted after Independence failed to achieve the desired results, because of huge disparities between the powers of planters versus labour unions. Instead of achieving minimum wages as provided for under the Minimum Wages Act of 1948, tea workers had to settle for vastly inferior wage agreements where social welfare components were priced notionally as wages in kind, considerably reducing the money wage to be paid. Tea-estate workers thus received the lowest organised sector wages compared to other plantation crops as well as the mining sector, which was subsequently nationalised.

Compared to the small tea grants made to pioneer planters in Assam and the Dooars, tea grants became progressively larger as investor interest increased, prompting planters who had pooled their resources to form registered tea associations (GoWB 2000). This is particularly visible in the Dooars, where a large land tract annexed from Bhutan was specifically dedicated to tea grants. As the capital of tea companies expanded and estate areas also grew, some of them began to buy out individual planters in order to consolidate their lease, particularly during tea slumps. Cross-holding of tea estates in multiple tea regions was first found when the consolidated Assam Dooars Tea Company acquired several tea leases in the Dooars. New leases thereafter were generally taken out by tea corporates.

Consolidation of tea holdings in the early phase allowed the achievement of production economies of scale, and expanded marketing economies by limiting transaction costs of the tea trade. Similar size and scale dynamics, which are also noticed in several plantation commodities produced in other parts of the world, including cotton and sugarcane (Shlomowitz 1984), represented the ability of the producing industry to meet the changing demands of world trade. For tea plantations in India, this process was so successful that by the late 1880s, Indian-made tea had supplanted Chinese tea from the London market. By producing tea at a low cost, the large-scale estate system in India also standardised the quality of Indian tea, enabling tea to become a commodity for mass consumption.

Besides organisational innovations in the scale of ownership and production, the process of tea manufacture essentially remained the same. Beyond mechanisation of processing at tea factories, tea production remained labour-intensive. This allowed the use of artisanal processes of plucking that maximised product quality. Such processing and production methods remain substantially untransformed in the Assam and West Bengal tea estates even today, even though corporate ownership of the estates has grown substantially after Independence.

During the departure of sterling tea companies, several diversified Indian corporate houses made their forays into tea, expanding their interests by setting up semi-independent tea divisions and affiliates. Even so, most Indian tea corporates are closely held and even those with market-listed shares see little trading in those shares. An overwhelmingly large number of tea companies in northern India are closely-held private limited operations, indicating that their corporate status is more a business convenience than a device for mobilising additional capital. With more capital being deployed for corporate mergers and acquisition, very little planter capital today is applied to improve agronomic conditions in the Indian tea industry.

Intra-Industry Innovation: Tea Estates versus Small Tea Growers (STGs)

While organised tea corporates in India may hold periodic increases in tea wage and non-wage benefits as responsible for falling profits in the tea sector (Tharian 1984), this is a largely circular argument. As plantation production has been highly labour-intensive from its inception, the plantation work force is necessarily large, while capital outlays are traditionally low. Although tea companies invariably declared high dividends regardless of price buoyancy, they failed to build adequate cash reserves out of profits, relying excessively instead on bank finance (Mukherjee 1978). Financial situations are even more stringent on estates in Assam and the Dooars, where tea production reaches a standstill for four months in the winter. To tide the estate over during the lean season, tea companies hypothecate their expected first flush tea crop to commercial banks in lieu of bridge credit. Whenever financial expectations fail to materialise because of inclement weather or low price realisation, tea corporates point out that Indian tea has progressively become uncompetitive because of "social burdens" placed on planters in the form of non-wage payouts to workers.

Large tea estates in Assam and the Dooars form contiguous fiefdoms, with tea cultivated over huge land tracts. Open labour markets have not developed as a result. With tea workers bound to servitude on tea estates, even rudimentary health care, housing, and education depend on the whims of the estate management. By the 1980s, when the sterling tea companies that were part-controlled by big international tea blenders had departed from India, global tea prices began to drift downwards in real terms. Unlike in the past when corporate dividends and their forward linkage with the global beverage industry had continuously buoyed tea companies, the bottom-lines of tea started slipping. With their new corporate owners more occupied in skimming tea profits for business investment elsewhere, perceptions grew that the archetypal integrated tea estate was beginning to outlive its utility.

The changes that followed were of an organisational kind. While the tea boom during the 1980s had centred around the provision of additional plantation lands, the focus was now on revenue lands that had previously been resumed from the estates. The idea of parcelling out these lands for smallholder tea cultivation, preferably by ex-tea workers living on the estate fringe, hence took shape. By organising "project gardens" in close vicinity through transfers of technology and supply of planting materials, large estates were able to secure outside sources of green leaf on buy-back terms for processing at their factories, without having to increase social payouts to their own workers. Thus the small tea growers (STGs) coopted by the estate sector became yet another low-cost segment for increasing tea production in India.

A major cause of the commercial crisis in the Indian tea sector has been the inability of tea exports to increase in tandem with tea production. Over seven decades since 1948–49, tea production in India has multiplied manifold, but Indian tea exports have stagnated at about 200 million kg per annum. The creation of the Tea Board of India under the Tea Act in 1953 for tea promotion has achieved very little in terms of augmenting tea exports. With stagnant tea exports, the bulk of Indian tea is absorbed by the domestic market that has grown phenomenally over the same period.

Sluggishness in Indian tea exports has been mistakenly attributed to the inability of Indian tea production to keep up with the needs of the domestic market, thus limiting the quantity of tea available for export. Other limiting factors, such as tea quality, chemical constituents of processing, market imperfections, and emergence of new international tea competition are ignored. Unlike the era of sterling tea companies when competitive international pricing was preserved through careful regulation of annual tea output, the Tea Board has ascribed the sluggishness of tea exports to the crisis of underproduction. Constant efforts have been made to raise tea output in the country (Bhowmik 1991). In 1983, for instance, the Tea Development Plan formulated by the Tea Board projected a minimum production target of 950 million kg to be realised in 15 years, based on a projected 28 per cent share for India in the global tea trade, with per capita domestic tea consumption projected at 0.6 kg per annum (ITA 1983). Provisional tea export figures of 216.8 million kg in 2016 would put India's share in global tea exports much lower, at 12.2 per cent. The size of the domestic tea market that year would thus be estimated at 1,022.4 million kg.

Appropriate questions might be asked about whether shortfalls in Indian tea exports can be legitimately attributed to the aggressive growth of domestic tea demand, or whether the growth of the domestic tea market is actually the *fait accompli* through which non-exportable tea output is absorbed. With low realisation of export earnings, and because domestic tea consumers are more price-conscious and less quality-conscious, the quality of tea produced in India has undergone a commensurate decline in a bid to keep production costs at a minimum in order to preserve levels of corporate profits.

The STG model therefore emerged as a solution to persisting problems of the tea industry. By outsourcing green tea from independent tea farming operations located outside the plantations, tea producers were able to delink tea production from the tea work force. Engagement with STG growers enabled tea producers to generate profits on a new bottom line, in which "social costs" were considerably low. The fall-outs of this new "profitability" were passed down to the working class, with tea workers across India experiencing a major fall in real wages. The engagement with STGs offered another strategy for tea manufacturers to expand profits by delinking wages from work and working around PLA provisions. Under the terms of the Plantation Labour Act (PLA), 1951, smallholder tea gardens below 25 acres (10.2 hectares) in size, which employ less than 15 workers, are not classified as plantations. The STGs therefore operate beyond the pale of PLA provisioning for housing, health care, education, and other non-wage benefits to plantation workers. Further, STG operations have very low production costs as they fall under the category of farming operations outside the organised sector. Many are small-sized family farming enterprises, with minimal engagement of wage workers from outside. By operating within the traditional ambit of family labour where all family members jointly contribute to work, the STG model reinforced the use of family-based labour for tea production while lowering attendant costs. Even gross rights violations such as labour exploitation and use of child labour go unnoticed on smallholder tea gardens.

Restructuring the tea sector in India on the lines of the STG model thus brought the misery of plantation labour into conflict with the misery of the poor peasantry. Because of the adverse impact on real earnings of workers, one of the most pressing demands of the labour movement, that is, the fulfilment of PLA provisions, was accorded low priority on corporate plantations. With more than half the estimated 2-million-strong tea work force in India comprising women tea pluckers, it is this section of plantation women that has been particularly hard hit.

Fallouts for Plantation Women

The high level of female work participation in tea plantations is a historical relic of the plantation system based on employment of the family labour unit. The switch to the smallholder mode of tea production invisibly drew the family labour unit into the tea production chain without formally engaging its labour. Family-based application of labour had traditionally served to tie plantation families to the plantation. As women plantation workers legally drew a lower wage than their male counterparts until 1976, use of plantation women for field labour indicated labour substitution through the employment of cheaper women's labour. The practice also helped the estate management in bidding down wage demands made by workers.

In view of the Tea Board's projections for augmented tea production in India, there was a pressing need to raise tea productivity on the large plantations of Assam and the Dooars. However, because of the high labour intensity of plucking operations, wage costs on the estates would expand commensurately with their need for women pluckers. Two modes of manual plucking have usually been resorted to on the Assam and Dooars tea estates. *Fine-plucking* by skilled hands had traditionally ensured better tea quality and higher price realisations for the orthodox tea produced on large plantations. For the more price-conscious market segment, *coarse-plucking* was undertaken, which took in more of the stem and leaves. While tea produced though the coarse-plucking process was of lower quality and would fetch lower prices, estate managements could maximise green leaf output without engaging the same number of pluckers. Alternatively, since the hiring of outside workers not on the permanent estate payroll reduced wage costs, permanent women workers who retired were not replaced. As a new generation of temporary and casual pluckers stepped into their place, women's work on the tea estates became marginalised.

Another important factor that has marginalised economic rewards to plantation women is the practice of paying piece-rated wages to women pluckers as against time-rated wages paid to male workers. Each estate plucker has to fulfil an assigned plucking task each working day, without receiving any benefits for the length of her experience. While male tea workers can expect to progress through the ranks to the level of sub-staff, no seniority dividends accrue to plantation women. Once recruited as a plucker, the woman remains a plucker, performing the same task and earning the same wage. through the duration of her working life.

Figure 7.2 *Growth of smallholder tea gardens in India, by type of holding and aggregate land-size, 2000–06* in numbers and thousand hectares

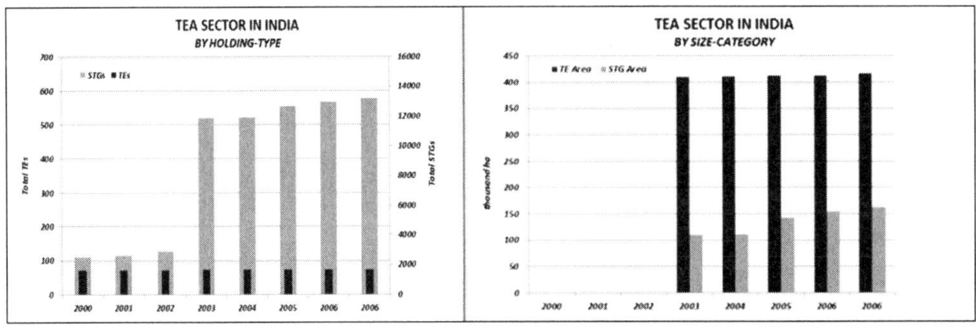

Notes: TE stands for tea estate; STG stands for smallholder tea garden.
Source: Tea Board of India (2008).

Takahashi and Mani (2004, p. 4) estimate that a woman tea plucker has to complete 900 plucking movements with her hands in order to assemble 1 kg of green tea leaf. This varies according to the quality of plucking demanded: fine plucking requires many more hand movements. Women pluckers also have to traverse uneven terrain carrying loads of 24–26 kg per day. The wages paid to women plantation workers do not reflect the arduousness of their work.

With identical piece-rates applying to women pluckers irrespective of whether they are *hazira* (permanent) or *bigha* (temporary) workers, wages on the Assam and Dooars plantations have been designed to extract the maximum time contribution per women worker, automatically translating into higher plantation productivity, without meaningfully compensating her for the additional work-time she contributes. Meanwhile, since the number of women pluckers deployed varies according to season, it is meaningless to speak of worker productivity as a universal attribute of efficiency for all plantations.

Information on the growth of smallholder tea plantations across various tea regions of India remained opaque till the Tea Board began to include data on the STG sector from 1998. Nevertheless, establishment of the first smallholder plantations supplying green tea to estate factories in the Nilgiris district of Tamil Nadu has been recorded from the 1920s. After the repatriation of Indian Tamil tea workers from Sri Lanka in the 1960s, a new round of tea expansion occurred in traditional non-tea areas in Tamil Nadu, with processing support from independent bought leaf factories (BLFs). Following the tea boom of the 1980s and the resulting Tea Development Plan, the STG–BLF cluster model began to spread to other tea-growing States, albeit slowly at first. In the large tea tracts of Assam and the Dooars where the alternative "project garden" approach had evolved by centering around existing estate factories, the expansion of BLFs was slow until the post-liberalisation policies of the 1990s. Thereafter, the growth of the STG sector increased rapidly, particularly in Assam.

Changes in the tea work force over the post-liberalisation period from 1996 to 2004 – the last year for which Tea Board data are publicly available – are documented in Table 7.3. The aggregate tea work force in Assam has grown in marked opposition to the downscaling of the work force in West Bengal. Similar opposite trends are seen in the expanded tea work force in Tamil Nadu versus the marked downscaling in Kerala and Karnataka. However, as the growth of the tea work force in southern India was strong enough to counteract the decline in northern India, the overall tea work force in India grew over this period. Significantly, the growth of *hazira* workers in Assam was more than offset by their decline in West Bengal. In southern India, despite the steep decline in Kerala, the permanent tea work force as a whole grew because of marked growth in the Nilgiris in Tamil Nadu.

Table 7.3 *Changes in tea work force on plantations in India, by type of worker and region, 1996–2004* in numbers

Tea regions	1996	1997	1998	1999	2000	2001	2002	2003	2004	1996–2004
All tea workers										*Change*
Northern India										
Assam	590,968	591,036	598,825	596,943	602,531	611,063	619,663	619,322	617,518	26,550
West Bengal	293,093	282,806	286,967	251,012	253,459	255,569	259,182	260,336	262,672	–30,421
Others	19,143	18,714	18,862	–	–	–	17,055	16,614	16,527	–2,616
Northern India	903,204	892,556	904,654	864,916	873,058	883,450	895,900	896,272	896,717	–6,487
Southern India										
Tamil Nadu	132,703	14,337	145,183	245,379	255,790	267,665	275,723	268,351	266,027	133,324
Karnataka	5,885	4,642	281	1,945	1,958	1,952	2,011	2,381	2,464	–3,421
Kerala	99,235	97,592	96,465	3,680	3,789	3,837	3,953	4,403	4,508	–94,727
Southern India	237,827	245,612	241,929	323,555	336,665	348,700	359,200	359,938	360,893	123,066
All India	1,141,031	1,138,163	1,146,583	1,188,471	1,209,723	1,232,150	1,255,100	1,256,210	1,257,610	116,579
Permanent workers										*Change*
Northern India										
Assam	498,731	496,807	503,157	477,660	477,900	481,375	487,670	512,790	519,635	20,904
West Bengal	265,860	254,695	258,269	210,760	210,932	211,867	214,715	228,317	232,532	–33,328
Others	13,218	11,982	11,877	–	–	–	11,753	11,991	12,255	–963
Northern India	777,809	763,484	773,303	700,227	700,710	865,553	714,138	753,098	764,305	–13,504

Table 7.3 *continued*

Tea regions	1996	1997	1998	1999	2000	2001	2002	2003	2004	1996–2004
Southern India										
Tamil Nadu	118,587	1,059	131,640	143,223	144,427	145,406	149,446	166,362	172,782	54,195
Karnataka	5,602	4,366	281	1,933	1,926	1,921	1,975	2,234	2,335	–3,267
Kerala	90,684	88,575	87,530	3,440	3,464	3,485	3,591	3,980	4,123	–86,561
Southern India	214,777	223,041	219,451	219,411	221,354	222,360	228,535	255,678	265,937	51,160
All India	992,586	986,520	992,754	919,638	922,064	927,213	942,673	1,008,776	1,030,242	37,656
Temporary workers										*Change*
Northern India										
Assam	92,237	94,229	95,668	119,283	124,631	129,688	131,993	106,532	97,883	5,646
West Bengal	27,233	28,111	28,698	40252	42,527	43,702	44,467	32,019	30,140	2,907
Others	5,925	6,732	6,985	–	–	–	5302	4,623	4,272	–1,653
Northern India	125,395	129,072	131,351	164,689	172,348	17,897	181,762	143,174	132,412	7,017
Southern India										
Tamil Nadu	14,116	13,278	13,543	102,156	111,363	122,259	126,277	101,989	93,245	79,129
Karnataka	283	276	–	12	32	31	36	147	129	–154
Kerala	8,551	9,017	8,935	240	325	352	362	423	385	–8,166
Southern India	23,050	22,571	22,478	104,144	115,311	126,340	130,665	104,260	94,956	71,906
All India	148,445	151,643	153,829	268,833	287,659	304,937	312,427	247,434	227,368	78,923

Source: Compiled from *Tea Statistics*, Tea Board of India, various years.

Overall engagement of temporary tea workers on plantations in India, however, grew much more strongly, driven by sharp growth in Tamil Nadu and positive increases in Assam and West Bengal, particularly in tea areas in Darrang district in Assam. In West Bengal, growth in the temporary tea work force was greatest in the Terai and the Dooars regions. Attrition of the permanent work force and resulting casualisation of plantation labour has been most severe on the Dooars estates: nearly 22,000 permanent worker positions have been lost over the reference period.

Changes in the deployment of male and female tea workers in India between 1995 and 2004, as depicted in Tables 7.4 and 7.5, show opposing trends between tea plantations in north India and south India. The figures in the tables represent the rise or decline in the number of workers in each category. While the aggregate tea work force grew in Assam and West Bengal for both male and female tea workers, the male and female tea work force in the southern Indian States of Kerala and Karnataka experienced a very sharp decline. The tea work force in India is characteristically categorised into resident and outside workers. As mentioned above, plantation workers who reside within the tea estate with their bonafide dependants are entitled to receive PLA non-wage benefits. Conversely, tea workers who reside outside the estate receive only wages. The category of outside workers comprise both outside permanent workers who are entitled to *haziri* employment round the

Table 7.4 *Change in the number of tea workers, by sex and region, 1995–2004* in numbers

Tea region	Male workers	Female workers	Total workers
Northern India			
Assam	30,897	29,491	50,120
West Bengal	3,057	5,751	4,493
Others	1,310	–434	335
Northern India	35,264	34,808	54,948
Southern India			
Tamil Nadu	72,452	82,854	155,278
Karnataka	–29,307	–37,557	–67,774
Kerala	–48,009	–47,650	–96,660
Southern India	–327,023	–286,675	–667,894
All India	597,835	620,750	1,257,610

Source: Computed from *Tea Statistics*, Tea Board of India, various years.

Table 7.5 *Changes in field work force, by type of worker and sex, 1995–2004* in numbers

States	Resident males	Resident females	Resident field workers	Outside males	Outside females	Outside field workers
Northern India						
Assam	12,039	41,280	47,668	5,130	−14,093	−12,317
West Bengal	1,503	17,243	18,344	258	−12,589	−16,122
Others	948	333	1,034	159	−400	−530
Northern India	14,490	58,856	67,046	5,547	−27,082	−28,969
Southern India						
Tamil Nadu	24,993	35,735	60,592	46,351	46,255	92,711
Karnataka	−294	714	414	122	39	137
Kerala	1,974	14,564	15,791	1,726	126	1,977
Southern India	26,673	51,013	76,797	48,199	46,420	94,825
All India	41,163	109,869	143,843	53,742	19,338	65,856

Source: Computed from *Tea Statistics*, Tea Board of India, various years.

year and outside temporary (*bigha*) workers who are recruited as casual labour for short durations during plucking cycles. The tea work force also comprises *field workers* who are engaged for plucking and plantation maintenance, and *factory workers* who perform various processing tasks at the estate factories. Table 7.5 only shows the figures for resident and outside field workers.

Between 1995 and 2004 there was a substantial decline in the field work force engaged from outside for plantations in Assam and West Bengal. The decline has been sufficiently marked for outside female field workers, although the numbers of outside male field workers has grown. Conversely, in plantations in southern India, where non-wage benefits are generally not paid out, the outside male and female work force has grown.

The Indian retail tea market has been dominated by Hindustan Lever Limited (HLL) and Tata Tea, both of which had a strong vertically integrated presence in tea blending and in running their own tea plantations. After the commercial crisis in the 1990s, both corporates divested their ownership of tea plantations to concentrate on the retail end of the tea value chain, where profits were secure. While the erstwhile HLL estates were sold *en masse* to other tea majors such as McLeod Russell, the Tata-owned plantations (formerly Tata–Finlay) were restructured into two new entities comprising the Kanan Devan Hills Plantation Company in south India and the Amalgamated Plantations Private Limited (APPL) in Assam and the Dooars (CULS 2014). Both new entities were created to run the tea plantations on principles of worker ownership, by which means the risks of running plantation operations could be transferred to plantation workers while the profits from the retail segment were secured firmly with the blending companies. Two comprehensive studies document the fall-out of labour distress among estate workers (CULS 2014; FIAN 2016), along with evidence of widespread gender inequality and discrimination.

Although disaggregated data after 2004 have not been published by the Tea Board, growth of small tea garden (STG) plantations burgeoned in Assam and the Dooars over the subsequent 14-year period. However, this did not represent the conversion of existing plantation estates into smallholder tea plantations. The area brought under STG plantations has thus been a sizeable addition to the large area under tea cultivation that already existed on the Assam and Dooars tea estates. This was achieved through the conversion of farmlands where agricultural cropping was abandoned for perennial tea cultivation. The incentive to convert revenue lands to tea plantations was provided by high buyback prices for green tea that prevailed for a short time. Subsequently, when green leaf prices drastically fell, the profitability of STG operations saw extreme fluctuations.

This problem principally arose because of the lack of stable pricing for green leaf sales by STG producers to bought leaf factories (BLFs). As smallholder tea plantations are essentially farming operations with no fixity in wage payments, STG growers depended exclusively on BLF tea producers for their earnings. Whenever green tea prices crashed, they resorted to even greater volumes of tea plucking to make up for shortfalls in earnings. This had the effect of magnifying price volatility in the STG sector. Secondly, as green leaf prices were paid after the realisation of market prices by the BLFs, the latter were able to transfer their market risks entirely to STG growers.

Over the last 14 years, a cloak of invisibility has been thrown over the working conditions of women workers on STG plantations. Women pluckers who were field workers and wage earners in their own right on the large estate plantations were now only able to add an informal helping hand to family labour applications on smallholder plantations. While it appears that the ills of the estate system disappeared from oversight in the STG segment, gender inequality and discrimination became far more embedded. Women on STG plantations once again substituted male family labour by unremunerated women's work.

In the wake of deepening distress caused by juxtaposing two categories of poor tea workers against one other, competitiveness has weakened in labour markets. Tea corporates are able to cite the low productivity of their workers to further casualise the work force, reduce wage costs, and increase the magnitude of plucking tasks assigned to women workers. Since, under the prevailing system of productivity-linked wages, overtime wage pay-outs are only made after completion of daily plucking tasks, worker productivity can be raised without incurring additional labour costs.

The rates of casualisation displayed in the above tables have grave implications. Women workers are marginalised on the Assam and West Bengal tea plantations, where their expanded presence indicates they are increasingly substituting for male work. The growth of casual plantation work opportunities for women comes at the cost of reduction of permanent earning opportunities for other family members. Meanwhile, the growth of smallholder tea operations outside the estate periphery is transforming small peasant holdings into new plantations. STG tea plantations have invisibly captured the labour that farm women and children had previously devoted to food production. This has been accomplished without arbitration by a formal labour market or a formal labour wage. Restructuring of the tea sector in Assam and West Bengal has worked in favour of sustaining the development and growth of Indian tea through innovations in labour reorganisation. However, this has not liquidated the large estates, but has further bolstered their market power.

IMPORTANCE OF PLANTATION RESTRUCTURING

The plantation economy in India, since its inception, has retained its early attributes of low levels of capital, high labour absorption, and labour unfreedom perpetuated through family wage determination and piece-rated work in Assam and the Dooars. High absorption of women's labour on tea plantations persists as a means for tying tea labour to plantations and lowering labour costs, rather than as a progressive indicator of gender equity in plantation work. Despite multiple legislations to alleviate the exploitation of plantation workers after Independence, labour conditions on tea plantations have not changed fundamentally. Phenomenal growth in the domestic market for tea has not resulted in increased prices and profitability of the Indian tea industry, which still remains a passive player in the global tea value chain where the bulk of profits accrue at the upper end to international tea blenders and the beverage industry. While the large tea estates of Assam and the Dooars have sought to preserve competitiveness by seeking dilution of plantation labour benefits, the burgeoning small tea-grower sector in India has been used to play off one section of poor plantation workers against another. In the absence of comprehensive policy initiatives to understand and engage with the changing character of global tea marketing, the long-term prognosis for the Indian tea industry remains poor.

GLOSSARY

bigha workers — literally, casual tea workers engaged for limited periods/tasks on the Assam plantations, also known as *faltu* workers.

hazira workers — literally, daily-rated permanent tea workers entitled to payment of the *haziri* wage-rate when daily work is assigned to them.

haziri — literally, the daily wage payable to a permanent tea worker when s/he shows up for work.

kangany — overseer-cum-labour contractor.

mini-*zamindari* — a system of notional sub-infeudation whereby the leaseholder of an estate leases out unutilised estate lands to tenant farmers on consideration of cash rental payment.

thika — literally, the minimum daily plantation task to be fulfilled by daily-rated tea workers to earn the task wage. For women pluckers, the plucking *thika* is tasked at the given daily wage. Under the system of productivity-linked wages, any surplus of leaves plucked after the completion of the *thika* task is remunerated at the higher extra-task rate.

REFERENCES

Bhowmik, Sharit (1991), "Small Growers to Prop Up Large Plantations," *Economic and Political Weekly*, vol. 26, no. 30, pp. 1789–90.

Chakraborti, Anil K., Mukhopadhyay, Apurba K., and Roy, Debesh (2003), *Beneficiaries of Land Reforms: The West Bengal Scenario*, State Institute of Panchayats and Rural Development (SIPRD) and Spandan, Kolkata.

Columbia University Law School (CULS) (2014), *The More Things Change: The World Bank, Tata and Enduring Abuses on India's Tea Plantations*, Human Rights Institute, Columbia University Law School, New York.

East Africa Tea Trade Association (EATTA) (2018), *Mombasa Tea Auction Process*, East Africa Tea Trade Association, available at https://www.eatta.com/the-mombasa-tea-auction/, viewed on 11 December 2018.

FIAN International (2016), *A Life without Dignity – The Price of Your Cup of Tea: Abuses and Violations of Human Rights in Tea Plantations in India*, Fact Finding Mission Report, Global Network for the Right to Food and Nutrition.

Ganewatta, Gaminda, and Edwards, G. W. (2000), "The Sri Lanka Tea Industry: Economic Issues and Government Policies," paper presented at the 44th Annual Conference of the Australian Agricultural and Resource Economics Society, University of Sydney, 23–25 January.

Ghosh, Tushar Kanti (1987), *Tea Gardens of West Bengal: A Critical Study of Land Management*, B. R. Publishing Corporation, New Delhi.

Government of India (GoI) (1951), "Plantation Labour Act 1951, as amended uptil 1986," available at http://www.teaboard.gov.in, viewed on 9 January 2018.

Government of West Bengal (GoWB) (2000), "Extract from the Lease-holders Register of Jalpaiguri District," *Paschim Banga*, Department of Information and Cultural Affairs, Government of West Bengal, Kolkata, pp. 52–66.

Griffiths, Percival (1967), *The History of the Indian Tea Industry*, Weidenfeld and Nicholson, London.

India Brand Equity Foundation (IBEF) (2016), *Tea Statistics*, India Brand Equity Foundation, available at www.teacoffeespiceofindia.com/tea/tea-statistics, viewed on 11 December 2018.

Indian Tea Association (ITA) (1983), *Tea India*, Newsletter, Indian Tea Association, Calcutta, 1 August.

Indian Tea Association (ITA) (1986), *Tea India*, Newsletter, Indian Tea Association, Calcutta, 4 November.

Mukherjee, Sibsankar (1978), "Changing Control in Some Selected Tea Producing Companies of Jalpaiguri Town," *Social Scientist*, vol. 6, no. 11, pp. 57–69.

National Commission on Rural Labour (1991), *Report of the Wage Study Group*, available at http://www.indialabourarchives.org, viewed on 9 January 2018.

Shlomowitz, Ralph (1984), "Plantations and Smallholdings: Comparative Perspectives from the World Cotton and Sugar Cane Economies, 1865–1939," *Agricultural History*, vol. 58, pp. 1–16.

Takahashi, Baku, and Mani, Devyani (2004), "Mission Report to Tea Estates and Related Institutions in Battaramulla and Nuwara Eliya, Sri Lanka," United Nations Centre for Regional Development, available at http://www.uncrd.or.jp, viewed on 9 January 2019.

Talbot, John M. (2002), "Tropical Commodity Chains, Forward Integration Strategies, and International Inequality: Coffee, Cocoa, and Tea," *Review of International Political Economy*, vol. 9, no. 4, pp. 701–34.

Tea Board of India (2008), *Tea Statistics*, available at http://www.teaboard.gov.in/TEABOARDPAGE/ODA=, viewed on 9 January 2018.

Tharian, George K. (1984), "Historical Roots of the Crisis in the South Indian Tea Industry," *Social Scientist*, vol. 12, no. 4, pp. 34–50.

Viswanathan, P. K., and Shah, Amita (2016), "Gender Impact of Trade Reforms in India: An Analysis of Tea and Rubber Production Sector," in K. J. Joseph and P. K. Vishwanathan (eds.), *Globalisation, Development, and Plantation Labour in India*, Routledge, New Delhi.

Wenzlhuemer, Roland (2007), "Indian Labour Immigration and British Labour Policy in Nineteenth-Century Ceylon," *Modern Asian Studies*, vol. 41, no. 3, pp. 575–602.

Wickizer, Vernon D. (1957), *Coffee, Tea and Cocoa: An Economic and Political Analysis*, Stanford University Press.

World Bank (2018), *World Bank Commodity Price Data, The Pink Sheet*, World Bank, Washington D. C.

8

Women in Livestock-Rearing

R. Vijayamba

The livestock sector has contributed 40 per cent of the global value of agricultural output. It has played an essential role in sustaining the livelihoods of almost 1.3 billion people in various ways (Köhler-Rollefson 2012). Livestock provides many economic benefits to rural households, namely income, employment, savings, as well as nutrition and food security through meat and milk. It helps in maintaining cash and savings, and acts as an asset and insurance. Furthermore, livestock is an essential source of input for agriculture as draught power and manure. For risk management, especially in times of food shortage, rural households can secure resources and food security by selling livestock. There are around 400 million rural women livestock keepers in the world, and they play a significant role in maintaining livestock resources (Njuki and Sanginga 2013; Kristjanson *et al.* 2010).

In India, the livestock sector has been a critical component of the economy and contributed significantly to its growth. The share of gross value added by the livestock sector to the agriculture sector increased from 21 per cent in 2011–12 to 25 per cent in 2015–16 (GoI 2017). According to the Land and Livestock Holdings Survey 2013, 65 per cent of rural households owned livestock. Livestock was concentrated among landless, small, and marginal farmers who owned around 75 per cent of all species of livestock (NSSO 2014). In addition, livestock-rearing has been an essential source of employment for rural women. The latest Periodic Labour Force Survey (PLFS), of 2017–18, showed that 84 per cent of the rural female agricultural work force was engaged in crop production and 9 per cent was engaged in livestock-rearing. Women's participation in dairy cooperatives has been integral to the livestock economy. The initiatives of the National Dairy Development Board aided women's involvement in dairy cooperatives.[1]

Unfortunately, official statistics underestimate rural women workers in

---

[1] The number of all-women dairy cooperative societies increased from 18,954 in 2012 to 32,092 in 2015–16. The share of women-run dairy cooperatives out of all dairy cooperatives rose from 12 per cent in 2012 to 18 per cent in 2016 (NDDB 2015).

general and women workers in the livestock economy in particular. The nature of women's work in livestock-rearing makes it challenging to estimate the number of women engaged in it. It is scattered and sporadic, not taking place at one point of time but rather spread out throughout the day, and combined with other duties such as household work and cooking. The level of women's engagement in raising animals varies with agricultural season, ownership of animals, and socio-economic features of the household.

The complicated nature of women's work in livestock-rearing makes these women workers invisible, giving rise to survey and definitional problems. The survey problems include respondent and investigator bias. Respondent bias occurs when women respondents engaged in livestock-rearing identify themselves as only attending to domestic duties. Village studies by Usami (see chapter 3 in this volume) and Swaminathan and Usami (2016) show that women who engaged in livestock-rearing reported "household work" as their primary activity. On the other hand, investigator bias occurs, for example, when male investigators collect information from the male head of the household and identify women as engaged in only domestic duties. In addition, definitional problems emerge from the narrow definition of work. The classification of a worker based on only one activity results in a limited understanding of all the other activities performed by that person. The lack of distinction in time spent between economic and non-economic work results in definitional errors. For a woman engaged in livestock-rearing, there is no time differentiation between household work and livestock-rearing activities. The other definitional issues are combining one's individual contribution with that of the family, and the inseparability between production for sale and for self-consumption (Mehta and Pratap 2017). These problems apply to women engaged in other home-based economic activities as well, and result in an underestimation of women workers.

In this chapter, I estimate rural female work participation rates (FWPR) in the livestock sector for India and its States from 1993–94 to 2017–18. I address the underestimation of the FWPR in the livestock sector by calculating an augmented FWPR.

Sources of Data

The chapter uses the National Sample Survey Office's (NSSO) Employment and Unemployment Surveys (EUS), the pilot Time-Use Survey (TUS), and the Periodic Labour Force Survey (PLFS). These sources of data have collected information on women workers in the livestock sector.

Employment and Unemployment Survey (EUS)

These surveys were mainly designed to obtain estimates of the labour force participation rate, worker–population ratio, unemployment rate, and wages of employees. There are nine quinquennial rounds of the EUS, but this chapter uses five rounds, namely, 1993–94 (50th Round), 1999–2000 (55th Round), 2004–05 (61st Round), 2009–10 (66th Round), and 2011–12 (68th Round).

Time-Use Survey (TUS)

India conducted its first pilot Time-Use Survey in six states – Haryana, Madhya Pradesh, Gujarat, Orissa, Tamil Nadu, and Meghalaya – in 1998–99. A TUS was conducted from January to December 2019 for all States and Union Territories except the Andaman and Nicobar Islands.

Periodic Labour Force Survey (PLFS)

PLFS 2017–18 provides annual estimates of employment and unemployment (worker–population ratio, labour force participation rate, and unemployment rate) for both rural and urban areas in usual and current weekly statuses.

Defining Women Workers in Livestock-Rearing

A person involved in the production of goods and services, which adds value to the national output, is a worker. This definition includes market (production for pay) and non-market activities – production of primary commodities for one's own consumption and own-account production of fixed assets (NSSO 2014a). The concept of work was the same for all the rounds of EUS used here, the PLFS, and the pilot TUS.[2]

The EUS categorises a person as belonging to the labour force based on the criterion of major time. The labour force includes those who are working and actively seeking employment, categorised as employed or unemployed. Activity status, industry, and occupation are determined once a person is classified as a worker in usual principal or subsidiary status.[3]

---

[2] From 1993–94 (50th Round), the National Sample Survey Office (NSSO) used the "economic activity approach" to define work, whereas the concept of gainful activity was used earlier. The difference came from the inclusion of own-account production of fixed assets as a work-related activity in the economic activity approach.

[3] Industry and occupation were determined based on National Industrial Classification (NIC) codes and National Classification of Occupations (NCO), respectively.

Table 8.1 *Activity status and corresponding codes used in the EUS*

Labour force		Out of labour force
Employed	Unemployed	
11: worked in household enterprise (self-employed) as an own-account worker	81: seeking or available for work	91: attended educational institutions
12: worked in household enterprise (self-employed) as an employer		92: attended to domestic duties only
31: worked as regular salaried/ wage employee		93: attended to domestic duties and was engaged in free collection of goods
41: worked as casual labourer in public works		94: rentiers, pensioners, remittance recipients
51: worked as casual labourer in other types of works		95: not able to work due to disability
		96: beggars, prostitutes

For example, a woman who spends the majority of her time in livestock-rearing during the reference year is a worker in usual principal activity status (UPS). She is a worker in usual subsidiary status (USS) if she spends less time in livestock-rearing than a UPS worker, but not less than 30 days.

The NSSO asked women usually engaged in domestic duties (codes 92 and 93) if they pursued specific activities for household consumption along with their normal domestic duties. Listed in Table 8.2, these activities relate to agricultural production like maintenance of a kitchen garden, work in household poultry or dairy, free collection of agricultural products (wild fruits, vegetables, cow dung, cattle feed, or firewood for household consumption), processing of primary products (husking paddy, grinding foodgrain, or making baskets), and activities resulting in economic benefits to the households (bringing water from outside household premises). If a person was nominally (less than 30 days) involved in the specified activity of household dairy/poultry, she was considered a non-worker with participation in livestock-rearing as a specified activity.

Field studies have pointed out that if a rural household owned a cow, the woman of the household spent at least an hour per day taking care of it; the time spent could also reach up to seven hours per day (Narayana 2002; Baliyan 2017; Raut 2004). Women were primarily engaged in milking, bathing, feeding, and grazing the animals, cleaning the sheds, preparing the feed, and making cow-dung cakes. If reporting activity status 11, 12, or 31, women

Table 8.2 *Specified activities asked of women who attend domestic duties (code 92) or engage in domestic duties along with other activities for household consumption (code 93) in usual principal activity status*

	Description of activity
01	Maintenance of kitchen garden
02	Working for household dairy/poultry
03	Free collection of eatables
04	Free collection of fuel for household use
05	Paddy husking
06	Grinding foodgrains
07	Preparation of molasses
08	Making baskets and mats
09	Making dung cakes
10	Sewing, tailoring, or weaving
11	Tutoring own or other's children free of charge
12	Bringing water from outside

Source: NSSO (2014a).

engaged in livestock were counted as workers. If women who were engaged in livestock-rearing reported being involved in domestic duties, they were counted as non-workers with participation in specified activities. Given the observations from field studies and the measurement error of women workers in the EUS, scholars have proposed the calculation of augmented work participation rate – that is, the addition of workers in the specified activities to workers in principal and subsidiary status, to get an accurate count of women's participation in economic activities (Kapsos *et al.* 2014; Siddiqui *et al.* 2017; Chakravarty 2015; Mehta and Pratap 2017).

Usami (chapter 3 in this volume) points out that the abnormal fluctuations in the number of workers in livestock-rearing and participants in a specified activity related to animal husbandry may be due to errors in the classification of workers and non-workers. The study compares augmented FWPR with estimates from the Foundation for Agrarian Studies village data for West Bengal from 2004–05 to 2011–12 by taking the first four specified activities, and thus argues that the usual principal and subsidiary status (UPSS) plus the specified activity participated in (SA01–04) may be more relevant for estimating women's participation in economic activities in rural areas than the UPSS alone.[4]

---

[4] A few other studies have calculated the augmented definition for rural FWPR, and considered different age groups and years. Different criteria have been used for the estimation. Siddiqui *et*

AUGMENTED FEMALE WORK PARTICIPATION RATE IN THE LIVESTOCK SECTOR

To estimate the augmented FWPR in livestock-rearing for all-India and States, I have calculated WPR based on usual principal status (UPS), subsidiary status (USS), and those in specified activities (SA02) for women reported in codes 92 and 93. I calculated the rural FWPR in the livestock sector in UPSS and augmented definition as a ratio of women workers in livestock-rearing to the total rural female population, for persons above 15 years of age.

UPSS is the sum of women workers in livestock in usual principal and subsidiary status, and SA02 is the number of women non-workers who are principally engaged in domestic duties and also engaged in the specified activity of household dairy/poultry. The augmented FWPR in livestock is UPSS+SA02 of codes 92 and 93. To identify women workers in livestock, I used the National Industrial Classification (NIC) codes.[5]

The calculation of augmented WPR (UPSS+SA02) resulted in a higher estimate of women workers in livestock in all the years. In 1993–94, the

Table 8.3 *Rural female work participation rates in the livestock sector, 1993–94 to 2011–12, India* in per cent

Years	UPS	USS	UPSS	SA02	UPSS+ SA02
1993–94	1.3	5.6	7	12.8	19.8
1999–2000	1.2	3	4.2	10.8	15
2004–05	2.1	5.8	7.9	9.9	17.9
2009–10	1.3	3	4.3	10.5	14.8
2011–12	0.9	2.4	3.4	9.1	12.2

Note: Calculations are done for the rural female population aged 15 years and above. SA02 of codes 92 and 93 refer to women who were principally engaged in domestic duties and performing household dairy/poultry work, but were not workers in subsidiary status.
Source: Author's estimation from NSSO's EUS rounds and PLFS.[6]

---

al. (2017) included women who performed any three of all the specified activities, and Mehta and Pratap (2017) added all women in specified activities to the estimates of augmented work participation rate (AWPR). In 2011–12, the augmented definition estimation was higher by 20 percentage points in both the studies. Chakravarty (2015) included all women in specified activities when estimating AWPR and the estimation in 2011–12 was higher by 18 percentage points.

[5] For 1993–94 (50th Round), I used the NIC code (1987) 02 for rearing of livestock. I used the NIC code (1998) for 1999–2000 (55th Round) and 2004–05 (61st Round). The code 012 was for animal farming. In 2009–10 (66th Round), the NIC code (2004) was 012. In 2011–12 (68th Round) and 2017–18 (PLFS), the NIC code (2008) for animal production was 014.

[6] In 2017–18, rural female work participation in the livestock sector in UPS was 0.9 per cent, USS was 0.7 per cent, and UPSS 1.6 per cent. PLFS 2017–18 has not collected data on the specified activities.

augmented definition was higher than WPR in UPSS by 12.8 percentage points. The augmented WPR was higher than WPR in UPSS by around 10 percentage points in 1999–2000, 2004–05 and 2009–10, and in 2011–12, it was higher by 8.8 percentage points.[7]

The trend of women's participation in livestock-rearing shows that there was a continuous decline in women's participation in all the years except for a slight increase in 2004–05. FWPR in livestock in UPSS declined by 2.8 percentage points from 1993–94 to 1999–2000. It increased by 3.7 percentage points in 2004–05 and decreased by 3.6 percentage points in 2009–10, 0.9 percentage points in 2011–12 and 1.8 percentage points in 2017–18.[8]

Women in SA02 declined by 2.9 percentage points from 1993–94 to 2004–05, increased by 0.6 percentage points in 2009–10, and decreased by 1.4 percentage points in 2011–12. Augmented WPR of women in livestock declined by 4.8 percentage points from 1993–94 to 1999–2000. It increased by 2.9 percentage points in 2004–05, and steadily declined by 3.1 percentage points in 2009–10 and 2.6 percentage points in 2011–12.[9]

Mapping State-level Trends

In this section, I map the FWPR (UPSS) and augmented FWPR (UPSS+SA02) in the livestock sector for all States in 1993–94 (Maps 8.1 and 8.2) and 2011–12 (Maps 8.3 and 8.4). The legend is uniform for all the maps, and assigns States into ten classes with intervals of 5 percentage points (0–5, 5–10, etc.).

Firstly, the augmented female work participation rates were higher than the female work participation rates (UPSS) in livestock for all States in both years. Secondly, the change in levels of female participation in livestock-rearing through the estimation of the augmented definition varied. For example, Haryana had high female participation in livestock-rearing while Andhra Pradesh had low participation. Map 8.1 shows that Haryana stayed on the interval of 20–25 per cent for FWPR in livestock (UPSS) and shifted to the 45–50 per cent interval in Map 8.2 after estimation of the augmented FWPR in livestock in 1993–94. Female work participation through the estimation of the augmented definition

[7] The augmented FWPR in livestock was higher by 182 per cent in 1993–94, by 257 per cent in 1999–2000, by 126 per cent in 2004–05, by 244 per cent in 2009–10, and 258 per cent in 2011–12.
[8] FWPR in livestock in UPSS declined by 40 per cent from 1993–94 to 1999–2000, increased by 88 per cent from 1999–2000 to 2004–05, decreased by 45 per cent in 2009–10, by 20 per cent in 2011–12, and by 52 per cent in 2017–18.
[9] Women in SA02 declined by 22 per cent from 1993–94 to 2004–05, increased by 6 per cent in 2009–10, and declined by 13 per cent in 2011–12. AWPR (UPSS+SA02) of women in livestock declined by 24 per cent from 1993–94 to 1999–2000, increased by 19 per cent in 2004–05, and steadily declined by 17 per cent in 2009–10 and in 2011–12.

Map 8.1 *Female work participation rate in livestock (UPSS), 1993–94* in per cent

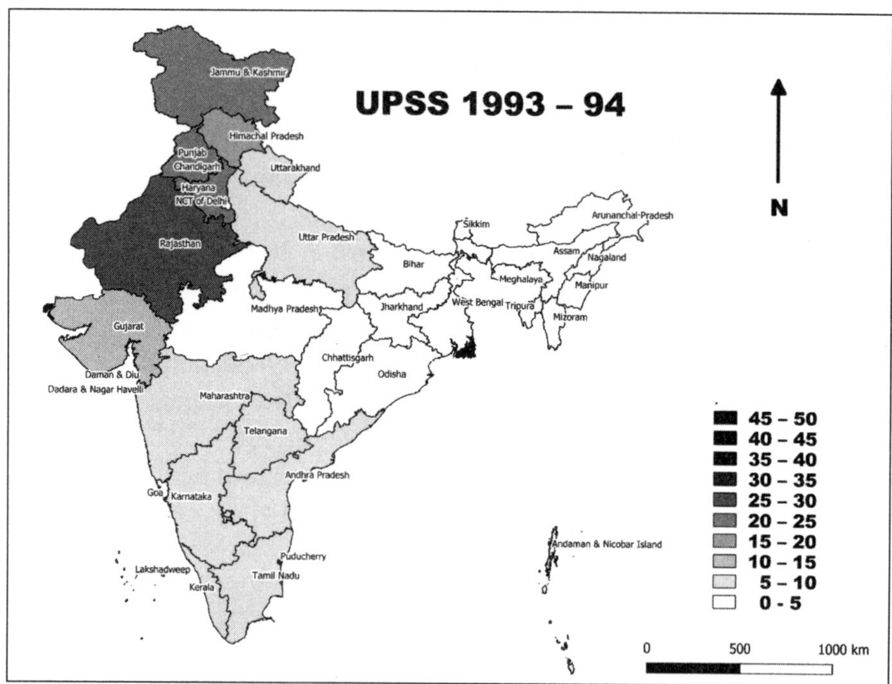

Source: Author's estimation from NSSO's EUS.

was higher by 26 percentage points. On the other hand, for Andhra Pradesh, FWPR (UPSS) in livestock was 6 per cent and augmented FWPR (UPSS+SA02) was 9 per cent in 1993–94. Thus, the addition of the specified activity (SA02) brought about an increase of only 3 percentage points in augmented FWPR. In Maps 8.1 and 8.2, Andhra Pradesh remained in the same interval of 5–10 per cent. Similarly, Jammu and Kashmir's FWPR in livestock (UPSS) was 14.2 per cent, and the augmented estimation was 34 per cent in 2011–12. It moved from the 10–15 per cent interval in Map 8.3 to the 30–35 per cent interval in Map 8.4. But in the case of Tamil Nadu, the augmented estimation made no difference (only an increase of 1 percentage point in 2011–12), so it remained in the 0–5 per cent interval in Maps 8.3 and 8.4.

Thirdly, by both definitions there was a decline in FWPR in livestock for most of the States from 1993–94 to 2011–12.[10] For example, Rajasthan's

---

[10] Appendix Table 8.3 shows that for many States, the increase in the FWPR (UPSS) and augmented FWPR in livestock in 2004–05 was followed by a decline in 2011–12. However, the decline was not pronounced for FWPR in livestock (UPSS) for Bihar, Meghalaya, Mizoram, Odisha, and Sikkim. No decline was noted in augmented FWPR in livestock for Arunachal Pradesh, Assam, Madhya Pradesh, Manipur, and Odisha.

Map 8.2 *Augmented female work participation rate (UPSS + SA02) in livestock, 1993–94* in per cent

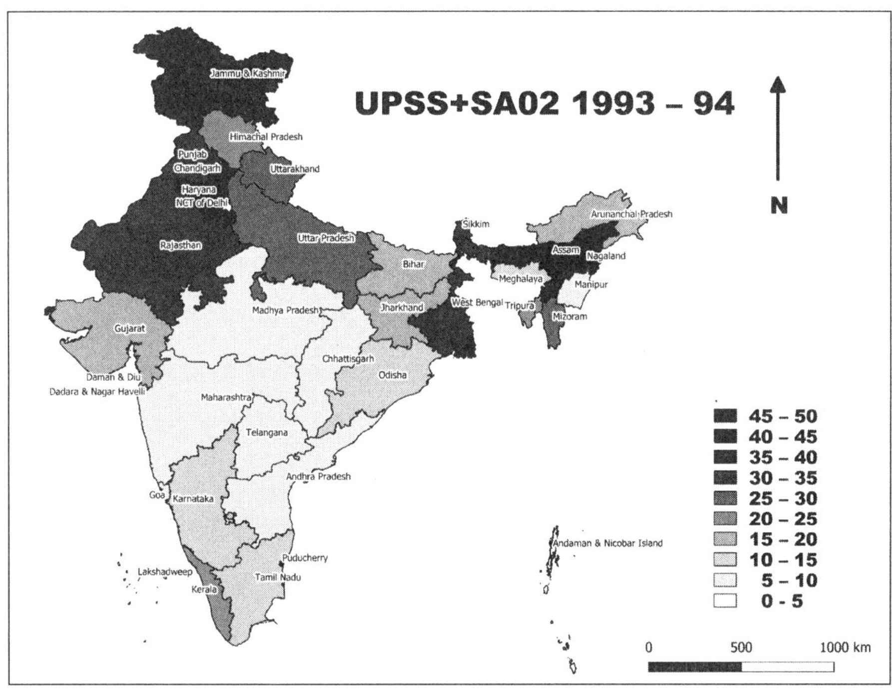

Source: Author's estimation from NSSO's EUS.

FWPR (UPSS) in livestock was 25 per cent in 1993–94 and declined to 6 per cent in 2011–12. A decline of 19 percentage points was noted. Thus the State moved from the 20–25 per cent interval in Map 8.1 to the 5–10 per cent interval in Map 8.3. For West Bengal, augmented FWPR in livestock was 33 per cent in 1993–94 and declined to 17 per cent in 2011–12. This decline of 16 percentage points shifted the State from the 30–35 per cent interval in Map 8.2 to the 15–20 per cent interval in Map 8.4. For Haryana, the augmented FWPR in livestock was 46 per cent, remaining in the 45–50 per cent in 1993–94 in Map 8.2. The augmented estimate for 2011–12 was 28 per cent, thus moving the State to the 25–30 per cent interval in Map 8.4.

Maps 8.5 and 8.6 show the position of all States in relation to the all-India FWPR, and augmented FWPR in livestock for 1993–94 and 2011–12. There is a regional pattern here: a rise in augmented FWPR was higher for the northern and North Eastern States than for the central and southern States. Haryana, Punjab, Rajasthan, Uttar Pradesh, and Jammu and Kashmir had FWPR (UPSS) and augmented FWPR (UPSS+SA02) in the livestock sector that were higher than the all-India values for both years. The North Eastern

Map 8.3 *Female work participation rate in livestock (UPSS), 2011–12* in per cent

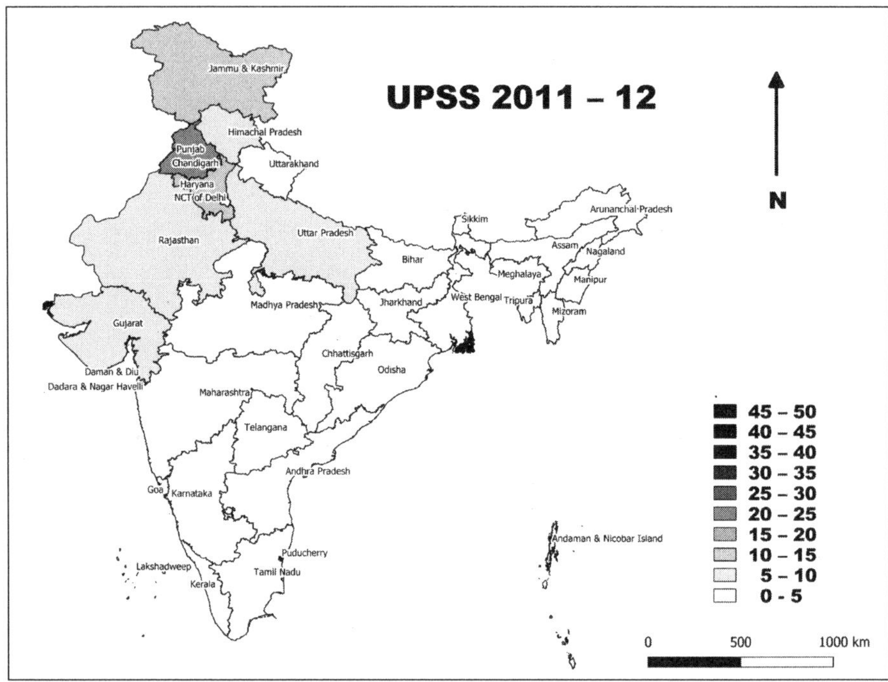

Source: Author's estimation from NSSO's EUS.

States – Nagaland, Mizoram, Tripura, Assam, and West Bengal – had lower female work participation (UPSS) in livestock than the all-India value, and augmented FWPRs in livestock greater than the all-India value in both the years. In general, rural female work participation was lower in the northern States. Women who did not participate in the labour market within or outside villages engaged in domestic duties and also raised livestock – taking care of animals was regarded as a part of their domestic duty. Therefore, the increase seen in augmented work participation in livestock was higher in the northern and North Eastern States.

Some States – Madhya Pradesh, Maharashtra, Andhra Pradesh, Bihar, and Meghalaya – had lower female work participation in livestock and augmented estimates than all-India in both the years. Among the States mentioned, Andhra Pradesh and Meghalaya had relatively high rural female work participation.

NUMBER OF WOMEN WORKERS IN LIVESTOCK-REARING

Table 8.4 shows the number of female workers in livestock from 1994 to 2012 in absolute terms. The number of female workers in livestock in 1994 was 19

Map 8.4 *Augmented female work participation rate (UPSS+SA02) in livestock, 2011–12* in per cent

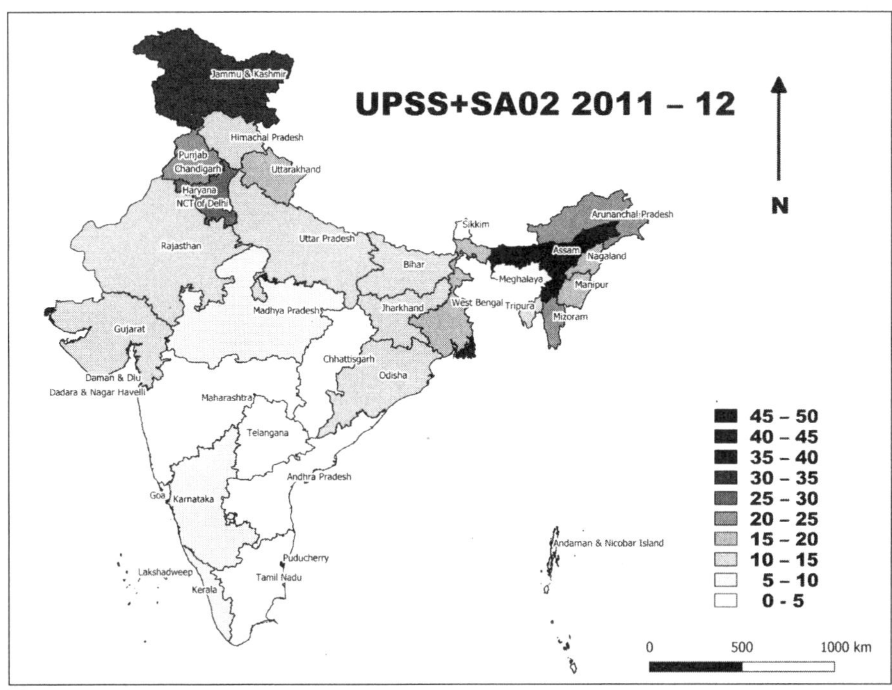

Source: Author's estimation from NSSO's EUS.

million and the augmented estimate was 52 million; the augmented estimate was higher by 33 million. Likewise, in 2012, the number of female workers in livestock was 12 million and the augmented estimate was 49 million; the augmented definition was higher by 36 million. In short, I estimate that 50 million rural women are livestock workers.

The number of female workers in livestock obtained from the Time-Use Survey (1998–99) was higher than the augmented estimate from the EUS (1999–2000) for all the States.[11] For example, in Gujarat, the number of women workers from the augmented definition and Time-Use Survey was 2.1 million and 5.7 million, respectively; for Haryana, the same figures were 2.4 million and 3.4 million, respectively.

Employment and Unemployment Surveys do not capture all women involved in the livestock sector due to the above-mentioned survey and definitional problems. Time-Use Surveys (TUS) are better suited to address

---

[11] Refer to Appendix Table 8.1. In the Time-Use Survey, women spending at least an hour during a week in livestock-rearing are defined as workers.

Map 8.5 *States in relation to all-India female work participation rate (UPSS) and augmented female work participation rate (UPSS+SA02) in livestock, 1993–94*

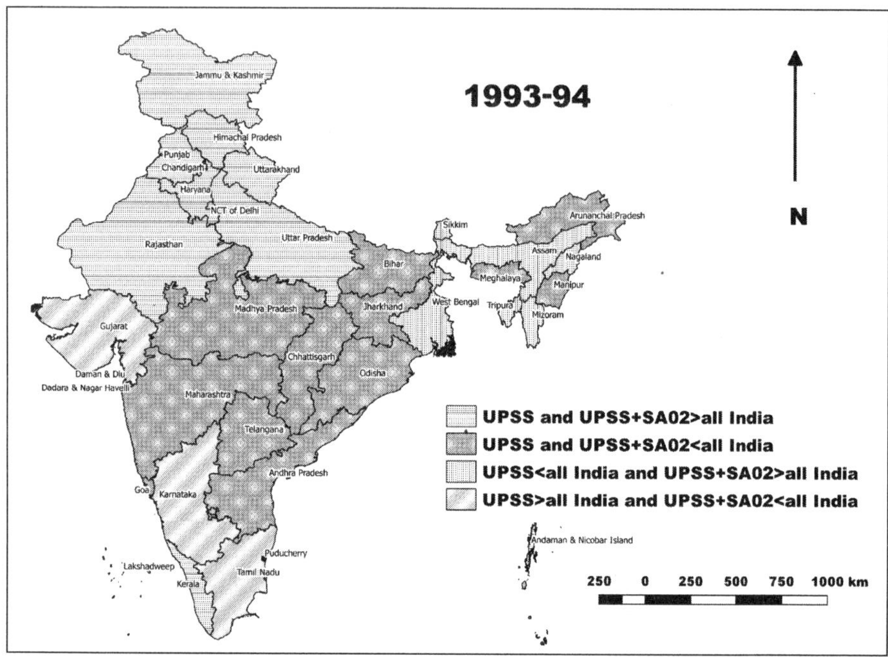

Note: The all-India FWPR (UPSS) and augmented FWPR (UPSS+SA02) in livestock for 1993–94 were 7 and 19 per cent, respectively.
Source: Author's estimation from NSSO's EUS.

Table 8.4 *Estimated rural female population and workers in livestock from EUS, 1994 to 2012, in millions*

		Female workers in livestock	
Year	Rural female population	UPSS	Augmented definition
1994	274	19	52
2000	306	12	45
2005	378	26	64
2010	400	16	56
2012	409	12	49

Notes: Census population as on March 2011 and percentage decadal change in population between 2001 and 2011 are from Primary Census Abstracts. Projected rural female population as of January 2012 has been derived using the formula A = [A1 * (1+R/100)^10]/120, where A1 is the rural female population as per the census on 1 March 2011; R is the percentage decadal change in rural female population between Census 2001 and Census 2011; and A is the projected rural female population as of 1 January 2012.
Source: Author's estimation from NSSO's EUS (figures adjusted to the Census population).

Map 8.6 *States in relation to all-India female work participation rate (UPSS) and augmented female work participation rate (UPSS+SA02) in livestock, 2011–12*

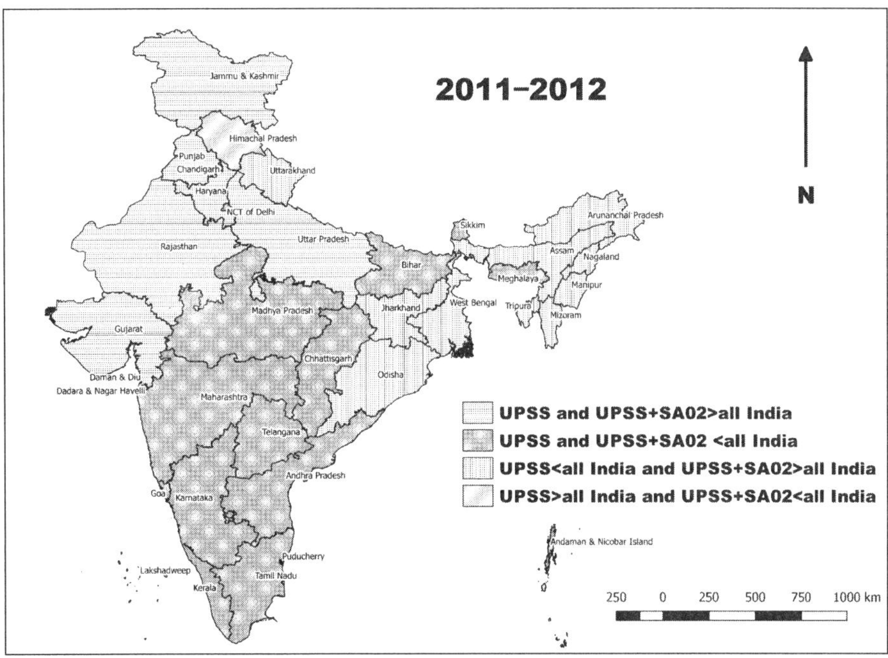

Note: The all- India FWPRs (UPSS) and augmented FWPRs (UPSS+SA02) in livestock for 2011–12 were 3 and 12 per cent, respectively.
Source: Author's estimation from NSSO's EUS.

these biases (Hirway 2017; Hirway and Roy 1999; Hirway and Jose 2011; Zaman 1995). They record all activities performed by respondents in the reference period (usually a week). In the TUS, there is an existing activity classification list that consists of the System of National Accounts (SNA) activities and non-SNA activities.[12] The activities are then coded and classified under the categories of SNA, extended SNA, and non-SNA activities.

DISCUSSION

Estimation of women workers in livestock-rearing is challenging due to the nature of women's work in livestock, as well as the survey and definitional problems in labour force participation surveys. Definitional issues arise from

---

[12] The activities are broadly grouped as SNA, extended SNA, and non-SNA activities. SNA includes market activities, and non-market SNA activities like collection of water, fuel, and fodder and production of goods for self-consumption. Extended SNA includes household maintenance, child care, and community service. Non-SNA is personal care that cannot be delegated to others.

the way "work" is defined. For example, classification of a woman worker based on only one activity results in a limited understanding of all the other activities that she performs. The lack of distinction in time spent between SNA work and extended SNA work results in definitional errors. For a woman engaged in livestock-rearing, there is no time differentiation between household work and livestock-rearing activities. The other definitional issues are combining women's contribution in livestock with that of the family, and inseparability between production for sale and for self-consumption.

Time-use studies have shown that if a household owned a cow, then women spent at least an hour daily on livestock-rearing work. Thus, their participation in livestock-rearing is not nominal (<30 days). If a woman principally engaged in livestock-rearing reports herself as being involved in domestic duty, NSSO counts her as a non-worker with participation in the specified activity (SA02) of livestock-rearing.

Usami (chapter 3 in this volume) shows that there may be errors in the classification of workers and non-workers in the Employment and Unemployment Surveys (EUS). One way of addressing the incorrect estimation of women workers in the livestock sector is to include the women in the specified activity to the existing female work participation rates in livestock-rearing – that is, by calculating an augmented WPR.

In this chapter, the augmented work participation rate in livestock has been calculated for India from 1993–94 to 2011–12, and for all States in 1993–94, 2004–05, and 2011–12. The augmented WPR was higher than the UPSS work participation rate in livestock by 12 percentage points in 1993–94; by 10 percentage points in 1999–2000, 2004–05, and 2009–10; and by 8.8 percentage points in 2011–12. The augmented WPR tended to be higher in the northern States because a large number of women engaged in domestic duty wherein livestock-rearing is considered as an extension of domestic duty.

There was a declining trend of women workers in livestock-rearing from 1993–94 to 2017–18, and it was more pronounced after 2004–05. The decline in the number of working cattle, dairy cattle, and buffaloes was consistent with the decline of rural female workers in livestock-rearing. The decline in the number of working cattle owned by rural households could be explained by mechanisation in Indian agriculture (NSSO 2006b).[13] A few studies have argued that it is an ongoing crisis, especially in the context of surplus milk production and small farmers being forced to sell their animals (Ramdas 2018; Das 2015; Ramdas 2015). This could result in a gradual shift towards large-scale, commercial animal farms.

---

[13] Refer to Appendix Table 8.2.

Estimates of women livestock workers from the TUS (1998–99) are higher than even the augmented estimates from the EUS (1999–2000). No Time-Use Survey has been conducted after the pilot round till 2019. In its place, the calculation of augmented work participation of women workers in livestock is a suitable measure. In absolute terms, the augmented estimate of female workers in livestock is higher than the UPSS estimate by 30 to 40 million workers.

Augmented FWPR is still an underestimate because the NSSO does not ask all respondents if they participated in specified activities; this is asked only to women whose principal status is domestic duty. The latest PLFS survey has not collected data on specified activities. Participation in specified economic activities along with time spent on them should be asked of all women workers. Time spent in specified activities can be added to the time spent in other economic activities to determine whether women are usual principal or subsidiary status workers.

I acknowledge the support of my colleague Niyati S. in data extraction from PLFS 2017–18.

BIBLIOGRAPHY

Baliyan, Kavita (2017), "Unequal Sharing of Domestic Work: A Time Use Study of Farm Households in Western Uttar Pradesh," *Indian Journal of Gender Studies*, vol. 24, no. 3, 8 October, pp. 341–59.

Chakravarty, Debabani (2015), "Capturing Female Work Patterns in Rural Bihar through NSS and TUS: A Methodological Note," *Indian Journal of Human Development*, vol. 9, no. 2, 17 July, pp. 269–84.

Das, Sohini (2015), "Amul's Not So Marginal Farmers," *Business Standard News*, 23 October, available at https://www.business-standard.com/article/companies/amul-s-not-so-marginal-farmers-115102300023_1.html, viewed on 20 December 2018.

Desai, Sonalde, Dubey, Amaresh, Joshi, Brij Lal, Sen, Mitali, Sharif, Abusaleh, and Vanneman, Reeve (2010), *Human Development in India: Challenges for a Society in Transition*, New Delhi: Oxford University Press.

Government of India (GoI) (2017), "Basic Animal Husbandry and Fisheries Statistics 2017: Tables," Department of Animal Husbandry, Dairying and Fisheries, Ministry of Agriculture and Farmers Welfare, New Delhi.

Hirway, Indira (2017), "Challenges to Measuring Workforce/Labour Force in Global South," in Indira Hirway (ed.), *Mainstreaming Unpaid Work: Time-Use Data in Developing Policies*, Oxford University Press, New Delhi, pp. 199–230.

Hirway, Indira, and Jose, Sunny (2011), "Understanding Women's Work using Time Use Statistics: The Case of India," *Feminist Economics*, vol. 67, no. 92, 3 November, pp. 67–92.

Hirway, Indira, and Roy, Anil Kumar (1999), "Women in Rural Economy: The Case of India," *Indian Journal of Agricultural Economics*, vol. 54, no. 3, July–September, pp. 251–71.

Kapsos, Steven, Silberman, Andrea, and Bourmpoula, Evangelina (2014), "Why is Female Labour Force Participation Declining so Sharply in India?," ILO Research Paper no. 10, International Labour Office, Geneva, August.

Köhler-Rollefson, Ilse (2012), "Invisible Guardians: Women Manage Livestock Diversity," FAO Animal Production and Health Paper No. 174, Food and Agriculture Organisation, Rome.

Kristjanson, Patti, Waters-Bayer, Ann, Johnson, Nancy, Tipilda, Anna, Njuki, Jemimah, Baltenweck, Isabelle, Grace, Delia, and MacMillan, Susan (2010), "Livestock and Women's Livelihoods: A Review of the Recent Evidence," Discussion Paper No. 20, International Livestock Research Institute, Nairobi.

Mehta, Aasha Kapur, and Pratap, Sanjay (2017), "Exploring the Possibility of Estimating the Monetary Value of Women's Contribution to GDP," Indian Institute of Public Administration, New Delhi.

Narayana, D. (2002), "Dairying in Malabar: A Venture of the Landowning Based on Women's Work?" *Indian Journal of Agricultural Economics*, vol. 57, no. 4, October–December, pp. 698–713.

National Dairy Development Board (NDDB) (2015), "Dairying in Karnataka: A Statistical Profile 2015," Anand, February.

Njuki, Jemimah, and Sanginga, Pascal C. (2013), "Gender and Livestock: Key Issues, Challenges and Opportunities," in Jemimah Njuki and Pascal C. Sanginga (eds.), *Women, Livestock Ownership and Markets: Bridging the Gender Gap in Eastern and Southern Africa*, Routledge, Abingdon, pp. 1–8.

National Sample Survey Organisation (NSSO) (1997a), "Employment and Unemployment Situation in India, 1993–94," National Sample Survey 50th Round, Report No. 409, Ministry of Statistics and Programme Implementation (MoSPI), Government of India, New Delhi.

National Sample Survey Organisation (NSSO) (1997b), "Participation of Indian Women in Household Work and Other Specified Activities, 1993–94," National Sample Survey 50th Round, Report No. 416, Ministry of Statistics and Programme Implementation (MoSPI), Government of India, New Delhi.

National Sample Survey Organisation (NSSO) (1998), "Report of the Time Use Survey," Ministry of Statistics and Programme Implementation (MoSPI), Government of India, New Delhi.

National Sample Survey Organisation (NSSO) (2000), "Employment and Unemployment in India, 1999–2000," National Sample Survey 55th Round, Report No. 455, Ministry of Statistics and Programme Implementation (MoSPI), Government of India, New Delhi.

National Sample Survey Organisation (NSSO) (2001a), "Employment and Unemployment Situation in India, 1999–2000," National Sample Survey 55th Round, Report No. 458, Ministry of Statistics and Programme Implementation (MoSPI), Government of India, New Delhi.

National Sample Survey Organisation (NSSO) (2001b), "Participation of Indian Women in Household Work and Specified Activities, 1999–2000," National Sample Survey

55th Round, Report No. 465, Ministry of Statistics and Programme Implementation (MoSPI), Government of India, New Delhi.

National Sample Survey Organisation (NSSO) (2006a), "Employment and Unemployment Situation in India, 2004–05," National Sample Survey 61st Round, Report No. 515, Ministry of Statistics and Programme Implementation (MoSPI), Government of India, New Delhi.

National Sample Survey Organisation (NSSO) (2006b), "Livestock Ownership Across Operational Land Holding Classes in India," National Sample Survey 59th Round, Report No. 493, Ministry of Statistics and Programme Implementation (MoSPI), Government of India, New Delhi.

National Sample Survey Organisation (NSSO) (2007), "Participation of Women in Specified Activities along with Domestic Duties, 2004–2005," National Sample Survey 61st Round, Report No. 518, Ministry of Statistics and Programme Implementation (MoSPI), Government of India, New Delhi.

National Sample Survey Organisation (NSSO) (2009), "Report of the NSC Committee on Periodic Labour Force Survey," Ministry of Statistics and Programme Implementation (MoSPI), Government of India, New Delhi.

National Sample Survey Organisation (NSSO) (2011), "Employment and Unemployment Situation in India, 2009–10," National Sample Survey 66th Round, Report No. 537, Ministry of Statistics and Programme Implementation (MoSPI), Government of India, New Delhi.

National Sample Survey Organisation (NSSO) (2013), "Participation of Women in Specified Activities along with Domestic Duties, 2009–10," National Sample Survey 66th Round, Report No. 550, Ministry of Statistics and Programme Implementation (MoSPI), Government of India, New Delhi.

National Sample Survey Organisation (NSSO) (2014), "Key Indicators of Land and Livestock Holdings in India 2013," National Sample Survey 70th Round, Report No. 70/18.1, Ministry of Statistics and Programme Implementation (MoSPI), Government of India, New Delhi.

National Sample Survey Organisation (NSSO) (2014a), "Employment and Unemployment Situation in India, 2011–12," National Sample Survey 68th Round, Report No. 554, Ministry of Statistics and Programme Implementation (MoSPI), Government of India, New Delhi.

National Sample Survey Organisation (NSSO) (2014b), "Participation of Women in Specified Activities along with Domestic Duties, 2011–12," National Sample Survey 68th Round, Report No. 559, Ministry of Statistics and Programme Implementation (MoSPI), Government of India, New Delhi.

National Sample Survey Organisation (NSSO) (2016), "Periodic Labour Force Survey Instructions to Field Staff," Ministry of Statistics and Programme Implementation (MoSPI), Government of India, New Delhi.

Ramdas, Sagari R. (2015), "Death of Small Farmer Dairies amidst India's Dairy Boom," *Economic and Political Weekly*, vol. 50, no. 19, 9 May, pp. 21–23.

Ramdas, Sagari R. (2018), "Bovine Politics and Climate Justice," *Economic and Political Weekly*, vol. 53, no. 41, 13 Oct ober, pp. 92–98.

Raut, K. C. (2004), "Estimation of Woman Labour in Animal Husbandry Activities," *Journal of Indian Society of Agricultural Statistics,* vol. 57, pp. 171–77.

Rawal, Vikas, and Saha, Partha (2015), "Women's Employment in India: What Do Recent NSS Surveys of Employment and Unemployment Show?," SSER Monograph 15/1, Society for Social and Economic Research, New Delhi, available at http://archive.indianstatistics.org/ sserwp/sserwp1501.pdf, viewed on 15 January 2017.

Siddiqui, Mohammed Zakaria, Lahiri-Dutt, Kuntala, Lockie, Stewart, and Pritchard, Bill (2017), "Reconsidering Women's Work in Rural India: Analysis of NSSO Data, 2004–05 and 2011–12," *Economic and Political Weekly*, vol. 52, no. 1, 7 January, pp. 45–52.

Swaminathan, Madhura, and Usami, Yoshifumi (2016), "Women's Role in the Livestock Economy," *Review of Agrarian Studies*, vol. 6, no. 2, July–December, pp. 123–34.

Zaman, Habiba (1995), "Patterns of Activity and Use of Time in Rural Bangladesh: Class, Gender and Seasonal Variations," *The Journal of Developing Areas*, vol. 29, no. 3, April, pp. 371–88.

APPENDIX

Appendix Table 8.1 *Estimated rural female population and workers in livestock from TUS 1998–99 and EUS 1999–00,* in millions

State*	Rural female population	Female workers in livestock	
		Time-Use Survey	Augmented definition
Haryana	6.7	3.4	2.4
Madhya Pradesh	22	5.5	1.3
Gujarat	15	5.7	2.1
Orissa	15.2	3.5	1.8
Tamil Nadu	17.6	2.5	1.2
Meghalaya	0.9	0.1	0.1

Notes: * States are arranged in ascending order based on their rural FWPR. Women's participation in livestock-rearing was higher in States where a large number of women were principally engaged in domestic duties. States with the lowest FWPR were Haryana and Gujarat, and those with the highest FWPR were Tamil Nadu and Meghalaya.

Census population as of March 1999 and percentage decadal change in population between censuses are from Primary Census Abstracts. For example, for any category of people, the projected population as of March 1999 has been derived using the formula A = P1991 + (P1991*R/10*8), where R is the percentage decadal change in population between Census 1991 and Census 2001, and A is the projected population as of March 1999.
Source: Author's estimation from NSSO's EUS (1999–2000) and Time-Use Survey (1998); figures have been adjusted to the census population.

Appendix Table 8.2 *Number of livestock owned by rural households, India,* in millions

	1991–92	2002–03	2012–13
Working cattle	68	51	–
In milk cattle	30	28	–
Others	71	75	–
Total cattle	169	154	135
Buffaloes	69	76	69
Sheep and goat	99	95	99
Pig	5	5	6
Poultry	193	182	255

Note: Information on working cattle, dairy cattle, and buffaloes were separately collected in the Land and Livestock Holdings Survey's 48th (1991–92) and 59th (2002–03) Rounds. There was no such classification in the 70th (2012–13) Round.
Sources: NSSO (2006b, 2014).

Appendix Table 8.3 *Female work participation rates (UPSS) and augmented (UPSS+SA02) female work participation rates in livestock for all states, 1993–94, 2004–05, and 2011–12* in per cent

States	UPSS			UPSS+SA02		
	1993–94	2004–05	2011–12	1993–94	2004–05	2011–12
Andhra Pradesh	6.9	6.5	1.6	9.7	7.8	2.5
Arunachal Pradesh	0	0	0	16.6	10.1	23.7
Assam	0.4	0.4	0.1	38.3	38.5	49.9
Bihar	0.1	1.8	0.8	16.1	20.3	11.9
Chandigarh	5.9	2.3	0.9	9.7	11.5	0.9
Chhattisgarh	0.7	0.3	0.0	8.1	4.4	3.6
Delhi	1.9	3.8	0	11.3	3.8	1.7
Goa	4.9	0.2	0	6.9	0.7	2.7
Gujarat	12.6	17.3	7.1	17.6	20.9	13.4
Haryana	20.8	33.6	11.3	46.6	40.8	28.3
Himachal Pradesh	16.8	17.1	9.5	22.5	21.8	12.2
Jammu & Kashmir	21.9	9.4	14.2	37.7	41.1	34.3
Jharkhand	0.1	0.6	0	16.1	14.4	14.3
Karnataka	8.3	5.1	2.4	13.2	7.6	7
Kerala	8	6.4	3.2	21.5	12.4	8.6
Madhya Pradesh	0.7	0.5	0.4	8.1	10.7	9.9
Maharashtra	5.7	4.1	1.1	8.6	4.6	2.8
Manipur	0.1	0.2	0	8.4	11	17.6
Meghalaya	0.1	1.4	0.4	11.9	6.9	8.5
Mizoram	0.2	0.2	0.8	25.2	16.6	22.5
Nagaland	0.2	7.9	1.1	35.2	14.8	18.6
Odisha	1.1	0.8	2.5	13.1	13.3	14.6
Pondicherry	13.3	9.5	2.2	34.4	11.2	2.4
Punjab	23	38.2	20.6	32.1	40.2	22.9
Rajasthan	25.1	18.5	6.9	34	26.2	12.7
Sikkim	0	2.3	0.4	31.3	11.6	2.7
Tamil Nadu	9.1	9.5	2.2	12.2	11.4	3.5
Tripura	0	0.3	0	20.2	23.8	13.2
Uttar Pradesh	7.2	11.5	5.2	26.8	22.6	14.3
Uttarakhand	7.2	19.2	2.3	26.8	24.8	15.2
West Bengal	3.7	1.8	2.3	33.7	26.1	17.8
All India	7	8	3.3	19.8	18	12.5

Source: Author's estimation from NSSO's EUS rounds.

III

Caste and Class Issues

9

Scheduled Caste Women in India's Periodic Labour Force Survey

Khalid Khan and Sukhadeo Thorat

Workers can be categorised by occupation and by income group, but the division of labour based on caste is a specific feature of the Indian labour market. Existing prejudices and restrictions on occupations of rural Scheduled Caste (SC) workers result in their exclusion from and discrimination in economic spheres. During the post-Independence period, there was some improvement in the conditions of SC workers in the rural labour market in terms of self-employment. There was also an increase in land ownership, albeit marginal, among SCs due to legal provisions relating to property rights. However, customary restrictions and, hence, discrimination against SCs in both farm and non-farm activities continues in a modified form (Thorat, Mahamallik, and Sadana 2012). There are very few studies specifically focusing on SC women in rural areas.[1] Rural SC women are an extremely vulnerable social group, and are subjected to inhumane living conditions and human rights violations. They are denied opportunities, choices, and freedoms in all spheres of life.

In addition to SCs, the exclusion of Scheduled Tribes (STs) and of Muslims reveals various forms of discrimination. Social and geographical isolation is the main reason for the low participation of STs in employment. Studies have documented economic discrimination against Muslims in India, such as unfavourable access to the labour market and religious discrimination in employment (Thorat and Newman 2012). A study on urban housing settlements in Delhi shows denial of work and lower payment as important forms of discrimination (Naik, Khan, and Verma 2018). Thorat and Attewell (2012) studied caste and religious discrimination in access to jobs in the urban

---

[1] Related studies on discrimination in accessing water have documented the hostile environment for SC women in rural areas. The issue of water is important because it symbolises the struggle for power in a village wherein SC women regularly face challenges while fetching water. They face verbal and physical abuse from dominant caste members and remain under constant threat while collecting water from common sources (Dutta, Sinha, and Prashar 2018).

private sector, and concluded that applicants with SC and Muslim names were significantly less likely to be hired than equally qualified applicants with Hindu higher caste (HHC) names. Comparative studies analysing identity-based discrimination against women in rural areas are rare, but the limited available evidence shows that SC women in rural areas are more vulnerable on account of untouchability, verbal and physical abuse, and violence. The division of occupations based on ascribed status, particularly in rural areas, creates watertight compartments for different castes, denying upward mobility to marginalised groups such as SCs. The vulnerability of SC women intensifies due to their caste and economic background in addition to their gender.

Madheswaran and Attewell (2012) found that returning to education was considerably less among SC/ST dropouts than among other social groups at all levels of education over the last two decades. Among rural women, income is another important factor responsible for reduction in work force participation. With rising household incomes, the household's reliance on women's incomes may fall, and women may invest their time in domestic activities and child care (Neff, Sen, and Kling 2012). However, women from marginalised groups, particularly SCs and STs, are less likely to be inactive as compared to women belonging to higher castes (Olsen and Mehta 2006). The conventional negative relationship of income and education to participation in the labour market may not hold for women belonging to marginalised groups such as SCs, STs, and Muslims due to their already weak economic background and subjection to identity-based discrimination. In fact, reduced work force participation among rural women from marginalised groups with increased incomes may hold only if the household crosses a minimum threshold level of income (*ibid.*).

Thus, women belonging to marginalised groups such as SCs, STs, and religious minorities face double discrimination: gender discrimination reinforced by vulnerabilities due to the social group they belong to. This chapter focuses on the access of SC women to the rural labour market. Social background is important not only in terms of obtaining a job but also in the nature of employment. Besides, compulsory and forced work governed by caste-based obligations, and exclusion of some groups from certain jobs due to the notion of purity and pollution, are other forms of discrimination in the rural labour market (Thorat 2008a). Thus, it is important to analyse the work participation of SC women by type of employment.

The analysis in this chapter is based on the unit-level Periodic Labour Force Survey (PLFS), 2017 conducted by the National Sample Survey Organisation (NSSO). It discusses employment patterns among rural women aged 15 and above of different socio-religious groups, as well as type of employment, unemployment, and the effect of education and income on employment. We have compared the status of women with men as well as the status of SC women with women belonging to HHCs.

EMPLOYMENT PATTERN

Gender

The work force participation rate (WPR) is defined based on the usual principal and subsidiary status (UPSS). In 2017, the overall WPR at the all-India level in rural areas was 35 per cent, whereas the WPR among males was nearly three times that of females (52 per cent versus 18 per cent). This gender disparity is evident from the composition of workers by sector (Table 9.1b). Rural women workers in general were under-represented in every sector. Across all sectors, women's share in the total work force was 24 per cent, or about one-third that of men.

Among all sectors, agriculture employs the largest share of rural workers, both male and female. The share of agriculture among female workers (71 per cent) is higher than the corresponding share among male workers (55 per cent) (Table 9.1a). Furthermore, the industrial sector absorbs more than four times as many male workers as female workers (Table 9.1b). In general, the agricultural

Table 9.1a *Workers by gender, by sector, rural India, 2017* in per cent

Sector	Male	Female	Total
Agriculture	55.2	70.8	59
Industry	23.7	16.3	21.9
Service	21.2	12.8	19.2
Total	100	100	100

Source: PLFS (2017).

Table 9.1b *Workers by sector, by gender, rural India, 2017* in per cent

Sector	Male	Female	Total
Agriculture	70.7	29.3	100
Industry	81.8	18.2	100
Service	83.6	16.3	100
Total	75.6	24.4	100

Source: PLFS (2017).

sector is highly feminised as compared to other industrial and service sectors, but this is probably due to family-based agricultural activities or casual labour in agriculture which involve more of women's labour (Appendix Table 9.1).

Socio-Religious Groups

To understand the status of women in the rural labour market, it is important to analyse the labour market scenario by socio-religious group. Our analysis is based on five groups, namely, Scheduled Tribes (STs), Scheduled Castes (SCs), Hindu OBCs (HOBCs), Hindu higher castes (HHCs), and Muslims.

It must be noted at the very outset that the general pattern of gender disparity persists in each socio-religious group. The work participation rate is lower for females than for males overall (24 per cent versus 72 per cent), but varies notably across socio-religious groups. The overall rate ranges between 48–58 per cent among STs, SCs, and OBCs, as compared to 42–45 per cent among HHCs and Muslims (Table 9.2). Gender disparity in WPR is the highest among Muslims, followed by HHCs, HOBCs, SCs, and STs.

High gender disparity in WPR may be attributed to both cultural and economic factors. Weak economic conditions often push SC women to join the labour market, wherein they are largely confined to informal work. The high concentration of SC women in landless rural labour households provides evidence of a push factor determining their employment. On the other hand, the employment rate is low among HHC and Muslim women. Between 2011 and 2018, there was a reduction in jobs among women from every socio-religious group, with a notable reduction of 4.7 million jobs among SC women. The corresponding job loss was 2.5 million among STs, 9.6 million among OBCs, 3.2 million among Muslims, and 1.8 million among others (Kannan and Raveendran 2019).

Table 9.2 *Work force participation rate by socio-religious group, by gender, rural India, 2017* in per cent

Socio-religious group	Male	Female	Total
SC	72.6	24.2	48.9
ST	77.6	38.4	58.2
HOBC	71.7	24.2	48.1
HHC	69.7	19.7	45
Muslim	71.4	14.2	42.3
Total	72	23.7	48.1

Source: PLFS (2017).

Table 9.3 *Female work force participation rate by socio-religious group, by age, rural India, 2017* in per cent

Socio-religious group	0–14	15–29	30–59	≥60
SC	0.3	12.1	35.5	15.1
ST	0.2	27.9	51.4	19
HOBC	0.1	12.8	35.6	11.6
HHC	0.1	10.8	28.6	8.5
Muslim	0.3	10.3	19.2	6.8
Total	0.2	13.8	34	11.7

Source: PLFS (2017).

Table 9.4a *Workers by socio-religious group, by gender, rural India, persons aged 15 and above, 2017* in per cent

Socio-religious group	Male	Female	Total
SC	75.8	24.2	100
ST	68	31.9	100
HOBC	75.8	24.2	100
HHC	79.3	20.7	100
Muslim	84.6	15.4	100
Total	76.7	23.3	100

Source: PLFS (2017).

Table 9.4b *Workers by gender, by socio-religious group, by share of socio-religious group in the total population, rural India, persons aged 15 and above, 2017* in per cent

Socio-religious group	Male	Female	Total	Population Share
SC	19.3	20.3	19.5	21.4
ST	8.6	13.3	9.7	10.5
HOBC	35.2	37.1	35.6	36.6
HHC	21.3	18.3	20.6	16.5
Muslim	11.7	7	10.6	11.4
Total	100	100	100	100

Source: PLFS (2017).

Table 9.3 shows employment rates of rural women by socio-religious and age groups. Among SC women, the WPR was highest for non-working age groups, that is, below 15 years and above 59 years. This indicates that the working population among rural SC women extends across a wider age range to include children and the elderly.

The distribution of workers by gender (see Table 9.4a) shows a slight disparity across socio-religious groups, with women constituting a quarter or more of workers among SCs, STs, and HOBCs. Table 9.4b shows the distribution of rural workers across socio-religious groups by gender. Among all rural women workers, SCs constitute 20.3 per cent (one of the highest shares after HOBCs), corresponding to their population share of 21.4 per cent.

TYPE OF EMPLOYMENT

Sector and Broad Industry Division

In order to analyse the type of employment of women by socio-religious group, we first discuss the distribution of employment by activity and industrial classification. The data show a higher concentration of SC workers in the industrial sector, though the agricultural sector is the major source of employment in rural areas. Table 9.5a shows that across all social groups, agriculture constitutes the largest share of rural workers (71 per cent), followed by industry and the service sector (16 per cent and 13 per cent, respectively). The share of SC women workers in agriculture (68 per cent) is lower than the corresponding share of all women workers (70.8 per cent), whereas their share in industry (20 per cent) is higher than the corresponding share of all women workers (16.3 per cent).

It is to be noted, however, that the concentration of rural SC women is higher in casual labour than any other type of labour, irrespective of the sector considered. Appendix Table 9.1 shows the distribution of SC and HHC women workers across agriculture, industry, and the service sector. The share of SC women workers in the industrial sector (18 per cent) is the highest as compared to all other social groups. The starkest distinction is in the agriculture sector, wherein 39 per cent of SC women workers are casual labourers as opposed to 12 per cent of HHC women workers. This pattern further worsens if we consider SC households headed by women. Nearly 53 per cent of these households are engaged in agricultural casual labour, whereas the corresponding share is only 27 per cent for households headed by HHC women. The distribution of employment by socio-religious group (Table 9.5b) reveals a higher representation of SC women in the industrial sector, whereas their share in the agricultural and service sectors is on par with their aggregate share in total employment. As far as the service sector is concerned, the share is lower for SC women than for HHC women.

The PLFS categorises information relating to the particular industry in which a person is working based on the National Industrial Classification (NIC). All industries are broadly grouped into eight industrial groups and identified based on a one-digit NIC code; in this chapter, these eight groups are referred to as "broad industry divisions" (see Appendix Table 9.2). The data show a high representation of SC women workers in construction, more than 8 per cent, as compared to around 5 per cent of all rural women workers (Table 9.6a). The distribution of employment in construction by socio-religious group shows that SC women constitute 33 per cent of total workers in construction, whereas their overall employment share is only 21 per cent (Table 9.6b). Furthermore, the share of those engaged in agriculture among SC women workers was lower than the corresponding share among all women workers.

Table 9.5a *Women workers by socio-religious group, by sector, rural India, persons aged 15 and above, 2017* in per cent

Socio-religious group	Agriculture	Industry	Service sector	Total
SC	67.5	19.6	12.9	100
ST	82.1	11.8	6.1	100
HOBC	71.8	16.1	12.1	100
HHC	71.8	11.1	17.2	100
Muslim	50.7	32.5	16.8	100
Total	70.8	16.3	12.8	100

Source: PLFS (2017).

Table 9.5b *Women workers by sector, by socio-religious group, rural India, persons aged 15 years and above, 2017* in per cent

Socio-religious group	Agriculture	Industry	Service sector	Total	Population share
SC	20.2	25.5	21.3	21.2	21.4
ST	19.3	12	7.9	16.6	10.5
HOBC	38.1	37	35.4	37.6	36.6
HHC	14.8	9.9	19.6	14.6	16.5
Muslim	4.6	12.8	8.4	6.4	11.4
Total	100	100	100	100	100

Source: PLFS (2017).

Table 9.6a *Women workers by socio-religious group, by broad industry division, rural India, persons aged 15 and above, 2017* in per cent

Industry	SC	ST	HOBC	HHC	Muslim	Total
Agriculture	70.9	85.3	74.3	73.3	50.2	73.2
Mining	0.07	0.09	0.27	0	0.63	0.17
Manufacturing	7.8	2.3	7.7	6.8	29.8	8.1
Construction	8.4	6	5.3	2.1	2.4	5.4
Trade	3.2	0.9	3.4	3	5	3.1
Education	4.1	2.6	4.3	9.6	4.8	5.1
Health	1.6	0.97	1.1	1.4	1.7	1.4
Others	4	1.8	3.7	3.9	5.5	3.7
Total	100	100	100	100	100	100

Source: PLFS (2017).

Table 9.6b *Women workers by broad industry division, by socio-religious group, rural India, persons aged 15 and above, 2017* in per cent

Industry	SC	ST	HOBC	HHC	Muslim	Total
Agriculture	20.5	19.4	38.1	14.7	4.4	100
Mining	9	8.5	57.5	0.1	23.3	100
Manufacturing	20.3	4.7	35.7	12.3	23.7	100
Construction	33.2	18.8	36.9	5.6	2.9	100
Trade	22.4	4.9	41.5	14.3	10.6	100
Education	17.1	8.5	31.9	27.5	6.1	100
Health	25	11.7	29.3	15.2	8.2	100
Others	22.8	8.2	38.3	15.3	9.6	100
Total	21.2	16.6	37.6	14.6	6.4	100

Source: PLFS (2017).

Occupation

Departing from previous employment categories, "occupation" groups cover a wide range of work activities that cut across sectors and broad industry divisions. The distribution of employment by occupation group clearly showed disparities across socio-religious groups. In particular, among SC women workers, those engaged in "elementary occupations" comprised the largest share at 50 per cent, which was higher than the corresponding share (35 per cent) for all rural women workers considered together. On the other hand, 31 per cent of rural SC women workers were engaged as "skilled agricultural and fishery workers," which was lower than the corresponding share for all women workers (45 per cent).

Data confirm the concentration of SC women workers in particular occupation groups. For example, they comprise 30 per cent of all rural women workers in elementary occupations, whereas their share in the rural population is 21 per cent. On the other hand, there is a high concentration of HHC women workers in occupations such as legislators, professionals, and technicians. The high concentration of SC women in elementary occupations indicates their dependence on manual labour.

Given that rural SC women workers are predominantly engaged in elementary occupations or as skilled agricultural and fishery workers, it is worth describing the sub-occupations within both these occupations. First, a disaggregation of skilled agricultural and fishery workers reveals that the overall share of rural women workers engaged as market-oriented gardeners and crop growers was the highest among all sub-occupations, although this share was low for SC women as compared to HHC women (Appendix Table 9.3). Similarly, the share of market-oriented animal producers and related workers – which includes dairy and livestock, poultry, apiarists, sericulturists, and animal producers – was lower among SC women (13 per cent) as compared to HHC women (19 per cent). However, a much higher share of SC women workers were engaged in subsistence agricultural and fishery work (9 per cent), as compared to HHC women (2 per cent). The two main sub-occupations where SC women comprised a much higher share as compared to HHC women workers were "fishery workers, hunters, and trappers," and "subsistence agricultural and fishery workers" (Appendix Table 9.3). This concentration can in part be explained by the high incidence of landlessness among SCs, and rural SC women in particular.

Secondly, given that rural SC women workers were concentrated in elementary occupations, it is not surprising that their share was higher than that of HHC women in all of its sub-occupations. A disaggregation of elementary occupations by socio-religious group clearly indicates the caste-based nature of work within this occupation group. SC women workers constituted more than half of the total women workers in cleaning and waste-related jobs, whereas the share of HHCs was just 7 per cent. SCs comprised over half of all rural women workers engaged in garbage collecting, shoe cleaning, mining, and construction, implying that caste still played an important role in rural women's occupations. Also, among women workers engaged in elementary occupations, a major section was engaged in agriculture and fishery-related wage labour, but this share was relatively higher among HHC women workers than SC women (80 per cent versus 74 per cent) (Appendix Table 9.4).

Table 9.7a *Women workers by socio-religious group, by occupation, rural India, persons aged 15 and above, 2017* in per cent

Occupation	SC	ST	HOBC	HHC	Muslim	Total
Legislators, officials, managers	2.5	0.7	2.8	3.8	7.7	2.9
Professionals	1.3	0.8	1.6	3.1	2.2	1.9
Technicians	3.3	2.1	3.4	7.3	4.3	3.9
Clerks	0.2	0.1	0.6	0.2	0.3	0.4
Service workers	4.4	1.7	4.1	4	4.5	3.8
Skilled agricultural and fishery workers	31.1	50.7	48.2	55.8	35.4	44.9
Craft and trade workers	6.8	1.8	6.3	5.9	24.4	6.8
Plant and machine operators	0.7	0.1	0.5	0.4	0.4	0.4
Elementary occupations	49.7	42	32.6	19.4	20.7	35
Total	100	100	100	100	100	100

Source: PLFS (2017).

Table 9.7b *Women workers by occupation, by socio-religious group, rural India, persons aged 15 and above, 2017* in per cent

Occupation	SC	ST	HOBC	HHC	Muslim	Total
Legislators, officials, managers	18.7	3.9	36.5	19.7	17.3	100
Professionals	15.2	7.4	31.1	24.6	7.4	100
Technicians	18.1	8.8	32.3	27.2	7.1	100
Clerks	10.8	4	58.8	8	6	100
Service workers	24.5	7.6	40.9	15.3	7.6	100
Skilled agricultural and fisheries workers	14.7	18.8	40.3	18.2	5.1	100
Craft and trade workers	21.4	4.4	34.9	12.9	23.3	100
Plant and machine operators	30.6	4.1	43.9	12.7	6.1	100
Elementary occupations	30.1	20	35	8.1	3.8	100
Total	21.2	16.6	37.6	14.6	6.4	100
Population share	21.4	10.5	36.6	16.5	11.4	100

Source: PLFS (2017).

EDUCATION AND EMPLOYMENT

Next, we turn to the distribution of employment by level of education among socio-religious groups. As seen in Table 9.8a, the share of workers with higher education was very low, constituting only 4 per cent of the total rural female work force. There is also a disparity in the education of rural women workers based on socio-religious group: the share of illiterate workers was highest among SC women with the exception of ST women. The share of women workers with school education (middle, secondary, and higher secondary) and higher education was lowest among SCs than all other socio-religious groups except STs. On the other hand, among HHCs, the share of illiterate women workers was lowest at 33 per cent and the share of those with higher education was the highest at 8 per cent.

Scheduled Caste women workers comprised 21 per cent of the total rural female work force, as against 15 per cent of HHC women. Further, the share of SC women workers was higher than that of HHCs among illiterate women workers (23 per cent versus 9 per cent). This pattern, however, was reversed

Table 9.8a *Women workers by socio-religious group, by education, rural India, persons aged 15 and above, 2017* in per cent

Socio-religious group	Illiterate	Up to primary school	Middle school	Secondary school	Higher secondary school	Diploma	Graduate and above	Total
SC	56.2	19.9	11.7	5.5	2.9	0.74	3.1	100
ST	64.1	16.8	11.6	3.7	2.5	0.23	1.2	100
HOBC	52.3	18.8	13.8	6.9	4	0.61	3.5	100
HHC	33.2	22.2	18	11.5	6.3	0.83	8	100
Muslim	50.3	20.8	14.1	6.2	5	0.44	3.2	100
Total	51.3	19.5	13.8	6.8	4	0.65	3.9	100

Source: PLFS (2017).

Table 9.8b *Women workers by education, by socio-religious group, rural India, persons aged 15 and above, 2017* in per cent

Socio-religious group	Illiterate	Up to primary school	Middle school	Secondary school	Higher secondary school	Diploma	Graduate and above	Total
SC	23.2	21.7	17.9	17.1	15.7	24.2	16.9	21.2
ST	20.8	14.4	13.9	8.9	10.3	6	5.2	16.6
HOBC	38.3	36.3	37.6	38.1	38	35.6	33.6	37.6
HHC	9.4	16.7	19.1	24.7	23	18.9	30	14.6
Muslim	6.3	6.9	6.6	5.8	8.1	4.4	5.3	6.4
Total	100	100	100	100	100	100	100	100

Source: PLFS (2017).

in the case of women workers with school education (middle, secondary, and higher secondary) and higher education – 30 per cent of women workers with higher education belonged to HHCs while this share was 17 per cent for SC women. Thus, in addition to the direct relationship of occupation with socio-religious group, it is important to explore if the disparity in education levels across socio-religious groups has linkages with the occupations of rural women.

Appendix Table 9.5 shows the distribution of SC women workers by occupation and level of education. As mentioned earlier, these workers were concentrated in two occupational groups, "skilled agriculture and fishery workers," and "elementary occupations." The share of SC women workers in these two occupations was higher for those who were not literate (90 per cent). However, this share reduced at higher levels of education. Also, the share of workers in professional and formal occupations was lowest for SC women who were illiterate and highest for those with higher education. The distribution of workers by education shows that nearly 56 per cent of SC women workers were not literate, and that merely 3.9 per cent of them had completed their higher education. Thus, given the link between the education of SC women and their occupation, it is clear that low levels of education are an important factor contributing to their vulnerable condition in the rural labour market.

INCOME AND EMPLOYMENT

The distribution of rural women workers by income and socio-religious group is examined in Tables 9.9a and 9.9b.[2] These show a clear contrast in the representation of SC and ST women workers across expenditure quintiles; together, they constituted nearly 54 per cent of total employment in the bottom income group and only 25 per cent in the top income group. On the other hand, the share of HOBC and HHC women workers gradually increased from the bottom to the top quintile. The distribution confirms the over-representation of SC women workers in lower income groups and their under-representation in higher income groups (Table 9.9a).

Almost 23 per cent of SC women workers belonged to the bottom income group, whereas the corresponding figure for HHC women workers was 11 per cent; the pattern is reversed for the top income group. Thus, SC women workers largely belong to the economically poorer sections, whereas HHC women workers belong to the relatively higher income groups.

In order to explore the link between income and employment, the share of

[2] As there is no data on income, we have used monthly per capita expenditure (MPCE) as a proxy, and used income and expenditure interchangeably.

Table 9.9a *Women workers by income quintiles, by socio-religious group, rural India, persons aged 15 and above, 2017* in per cent

Socio-religious group	0–20	20–40	40–60	60–80	80–100	Total	Population share
SC	22.8	23	21.1	20.6	18.8	21.2	21.4
ST	30.9	21.1	14	11.4	6	16.6	10.5
HOBC	31	37.6	38.3	39.9	41.3	37.6	36.6
HHC	7.6	10.8	15.5	18.5	20.6	14.6	16.5
Muslim	5.8	5.6	7.6	6.9	6.1	6.4	11.4
Total	100	100	100	100	100	100	100

Note: Monthly per capita consumption is used as a proxy for income.
Source: PLFS (2017).

Table 9.9b *Women workers by socio-religious group, by income quintile, rural India, persons aged 15 and above, 2017* in per cent

Socio-religious group	0–20	20–40	40–60	60–80	80–100	Total
SC	21.7	19.7	22.2	19.1	17.3	100
ST	37.7	23	18.8	13.5	7	100
HOBC	16.7	18.2	22.8	20.9	21.5	100
HHC	10.5	13.5	23.6	24.9	27.5	100
Muslim	18.3	15.8	26.4	21	18.5	100
Total	20.2	18.2	22.4	19.7	19.5	100

Note: Monthly per capita consumption is used as a proxy for income.
Source: PLFS (2017).

SC and HHC women workers by income group and occupation is shown in Appendix Table 9.6. From the preceding sections, we know that elementary occupations predominated among rural SC women workers (50 per cent). However, these workers mostly belong to the bottom four income quintiles (42 per cent), and their share in elementary occupations fell to 15 per cent in the top income quintile. It must, however, be noted that the share of SC women workers in elementary occupations was higher than that of HHC women for every income group. In fact, elementary occupations constituted the highest share of SC women workers in every income group. Furthermore, the share of professional and formal sector workers, which may be considered "better quality" occupations as compared to elementary occupations, was lower among rural SC women workers than among HHC women for all income groups. This disparity widened further for the top income quintile.

SUMMARY AND CONCLUSION

To understand the status of employment among rural SC women, this chapter analysed data from PLFS (2017) based on sector, broad industrial division, and occupation. The overall employment rate was lower for women compared to men regardless of socio-religious group, and there was a relatively higher percentage of SC women among youth and elders in the rural work force. High work participation of younger and elderly women in the work force indicated distress employment and economic vulnerability, as their domestic responsibilities prevented them from otherwise participating in the labour market (Rangarajan, Kaul, and Seema 2011; Kannan and Raveendran 2012). The high concentration of SC women workers in the agricultural sector was primarily due to their high share in casual labour in agriculture.

Employment rates were higher among SC women workers than among HHC women. Poor economic conditions and low levels of education often pushed SC women to join the rural labour market, wherein they were largely confined to informal work. For instance, there was high representation of SC women in the construction sector. Furthermore, occupational segregation among SC women is itself a manifestation of the features of the caste system wherein they lack choice in occupation. SC women workers constituted more than half of the total women workers in cleaning and waste-related jobs, whereas the share of HHCs in the same was only 7 per cent. SCs comprised over half of all rural women workers engaged in garbage collection, shoe cleaning, mining, and construction, implying that caste played an important role in rural women's occupations.

Though the employment rate among SC and HOBC women workers was similar overall, upon disaggregation by broad industrial division, it could be seen that dependence on agriculture was lower among SC women. This was possibly due to low ownership of land among SCs. On the other hand, the share of rural SC women workers in the construction sector was higher than that of OBC women.

The data also revealed better conditions in terms of education and income for HOBC and HHC women workers, as compared to SC women workers. The share of illiterate workers was higher among SC women than among HOBC and HHC women. Unlike SCs, the representation of HOBCs and HHCs in the top income groups was higher than their population share. Thus, given the link between the education levels of SC women and their occupation, it is clear that low levels of education are an important factor contributing to their vulnerable condition in the rural labour market. The data also confirmed the over-representation of SC women workers in lower income groups and their under-representation in higher income groups.

To sum up, low employment rates among rural women indicated the existence of gender disparities in rural areas among all socio-religious groups. In general, agriculture is a major source of employment for women in rural areas. The employment rate among rural SC women workers was higher than that of all other socio-religious groups, but these workers were largely confined to elementary occupations; this in particular reveals the traditional caste–occupation nexus. Even those engaged in skilled agricultural and related occupations largely belonged to economically poor groups and had low levels of education. Households with lower levels of landholdings and education were likely to rely on unskilled labour (Micevska and Rahut 2008; Tao Yang 1997). The conventional hierarchy among social groups persists in the rural labour market, which keeps SC women in precarious conditions compounded by identity-based discrimination (Thorat and Attewell 2007). The issue of discrimination cannot be remedied with the self-correcting mechanism of the free market and requires government intervention.

References

Das, Maitreyi Bordia, and Desai, Sonalde (2003), "Why are Educated Women Less Likely to be Employed in India? Testing Competing Hypotheses," Social Protection Discussion Paper, No. 313, May, The World Bank, Washington D. C.

Dutta, Swarup, Sinha, Ishita, and Prashar, Adya (2018), "Dalit Women and Water: Availability, Access and Discrimination in Rural India," *Journal of Social Inclusion Studies,* vol. 4, no. 1, 18 June, pp. 62–79.

Kannan, K. P., and Raveendran, G. (2012), "Counting and Profiling the Missing Labour Force," *Economic and Political Weekly*, vol. 47, no. 6, February, pp. 77–80.

Kannan, K. P. and Raveendran, G. (2019), "From Jobless to Job-Loss Growth: Gainers and Losers During 2012–2018," *Economic and Political Weekly*, vol. 54, no. 44, November, pp. 38–44.

Madheswaran, S., and Attewell, Paul (2012), "Wage and Job Discrimination in the Indian Urban Labour Market," in Sukhadeo Thorat and Katherine S. Newman (eds.), *Blocked by Caste: Economic Discrimination in Modern India*, Oxford University Press, New Delhi, pp. 123–47.

Micevska, Micevska, and Rahut, Dil Bahadur (2008), "Rural Nonfarm Employment and Incomes in the Himalayas," *Economic Development and Cultural Change*, vol. 57, no. 1, pp. 163–93.

Naik, Ajaya K., Khan, Khalid, and Verma, Ashutosh (2018), "Muslims in Urban Informal Employment: A Scoping Study of Experiences of Discrimination," *Journal of Social Inclusion Studies*, vol. 3, nos. 1–2, 28 December, pp. 47–64.

Neff, Daniel, Sen, Kunal, and Kling, Veronika (2012), "The Puzzling Decline in Rural Women's Labor Force Participation in India: A Reexamination," GIGA Working Papers, No. 196, May, German Institute of Global and Area Studies Research Unit, Institute of Asian Studies, Hamburg, Germany.

Olsen, Wendy, and Mehta, Smita (2006), "A Pluralist Account of Labour Participation in India," GPRG Working Paper Series, No. 042, May, Global Poverty Research Group, University of Manchester, available at http://www.gprg.org/pubs/workingpapers/pdfs/gprg-wps-042.pdf, viewed on 23 January 2020.

Rangarajan, C., Kaul, Padma Iyer, and Seema (2011), "Where is the Missing Labour Force?" *Economic and Political Weekly*, vol. 46, no. 39, September, pp. 68–72.

Tao Yang, Dennis (1997), "Education and Off-Farm Work," *Economic Development and Cultural Change*, vol. 45, no. 3, April, pp. 613–32.

Thorat, Sukhadeo (2008a), "Labour Market Discrimination: Concept, Forms and Remedies in the Indian Situation," *The Indian Journal of Labour Economics*, vol. 51, no. 1, January, pp. 31–52.

Thorat, Sukhadeo (2008b), "Social Exclusion in the Indian Context: Theoretical Basis of Inclusive Policies," *Indian Journal of Human Development*, vol. 2, no. 1, pp. 165–81.

Thorat, Sukhadeo, and Attewell, Paul (2007), "The Legacy of Social Exclusion: A Correspondence Study of Job Discrimination in India," *Economic and Political Weekly*, vol. 42, no. 41, October, pp. 4141–45.

Thorat, Sukhadeo, and Attewell, Paul (2012), "The Legacy of Social Exclusion: A Correspondence Study of Job Discrimination in India's Urban Private Sector," in Sukhadeo Thorat and Katherine S. Newman (eds.), *Blocked by Caste: Economic Discrimination in Modern India*, Oxford University Press, New Delhi.

Thorat, Sukhadeo, Mahamallik, M., and Sadana, Nidhi (2012), "Caste System and Pattern of Discrimination in Rural Markets," in Sukhadeo Thorat and Katherine S. Newman (eds.), *Blocked by Caste: Economic Discrimination in Modern India*, Oxford University Press, New Delhi, pp. 52–87.

Thorat, Sukhadeo, and Newman, Katherine S. (2012), "Introduction: Economic Discrimination Concept, Consequences, and Remedies," in Sukhadeo Thorat and Katherine S. Newman (eds.), *Blocked by Caste: Economic Discrimination in Modern India*, Oxford University Press, New Delhi, pp. 148–78.

APPENDIX

Appendix Table 9.1 *Scheduled Caste and Hindu high caste women workers by sector, by category of employment, rural India, 2017* in per cent

	Sector	SEA	SENA	RW	CLA	CLNA	Others	Total
SC	Agriculture	36	6	6.4	39.1	11.6	0.98	100
	Industry	14	16.8	13.9	18.3	35.5	1.5	100
	Service	13.3	23.1	40.8	7.5	15	0.42	100
HHC	Agriculture	68.3	5.3	9.2	12.5	3.9	0.89	100
	Industry	31.2	19.1	17.1	13.8	17.4	1.5	100
	Service	19	27.9	45.2	0.5	4.1	3.4	100

Notes: SEA = self-employed in agriculture; SENA = self-employed in non-agriculture; RW = regular wage worker; CLA = casual labour in agriculture; CLNA = casual labour in non-agriculture.
Source: PLFS (2017).

Appendix Table 9.2 *Broad industry divisions as defined by the Periodic Labour Force Survey*

	Industry
1	Agriculture, forestry, and fishing
2	Mining and quarrying
3	Manufacturing Electricity, gas, steam, and air conditioning supply Water supply, sewage, waste management, and remediation activities
4	Construction
5	Wholesale and retail trade, repair of motor vehicles and motorcycles Transportation and storage Accommodation and food services activities Information and communication Financial and insurance activities Real estate activities Professional, scientific, and technical activities Administrative and support activities Public administration and defence, compulsory social security
6	Education
7	Human health and social work activities
8	Others

Source: PLFS (2017).

Appendix Table 9.3 *Scheduled Caste and Hindu high caste women workers in skilled agricultural and fishery work by sub-occupation, rural India, persons aged 15 and above, 2017* in per cent

Sub-occupation of skilled agricultural and fishery workers	Row per cent		Column per cent	
	SC	HHC	SC	HHC
Market-oriented gardeners and crop growers	13.9	18.2	69.2	72.8
Market-oriented animal producers and related workers	13.8	24.6	13.1	18.9
Market-oriented crop and animal producers	18.7	16.7	9	6.5
Forestry and related workers	0.62	4.07	0.04	0.22
Fishery workers, hunters, and trappers	45.3	20.6	0.1	0.04
Subsistence agricultural and fishery workers	24.1	5.5	8.5	1.6
All skilled agricultural and fishery workers	14.7	18.2	100	100

Source: PLFS (2017).

Appendix Table 9.4 *SC and HHC women workers in elementary occupations by sub-occupation, rural India, persons aged 15 and above, 2017* in per cent

Sub-occupation of elementary occupations	Row		Column	
	SC	HHC	SC	HHC
Street vendors	29.4	4.6	0.91	0.54
Shoe cleaning, building caretakers and cleaners, messengers, porters, door keepers, garbage collectors, and others	53.3	7	1.8	0.88
Domestic and related helpers	29.3	9.3	3.2	3.7
Agriculture- and fishery-related labourers	30.2	8.7	74.2	79.6
Mining and construction labourers	29.2	5.8	17.4	12.7
Manufacturing labourers	26.1	7.4	2.3	2.4
Transport workers, freight handlers, and others	30.4	3.3	0.16	0.06
All elementary occupations	30.1	8.1	100	100

Source: PLFS (2017).

Appendix Table 9.5 *SC women workers by education, by occupation, rural India, persons aged 15 and above, 2017* in per cent

Occupation	Illiterate	Up to primary school	Secondary and higher secondary school	Diploma and higher education	Total
Legislators, officials, and managers	1.6	4.2	2.7	2.2	2.5
Professionals, technicians, and clerks	0.32	2.1	22.5	56.2	4.9
Service workers	2.5	5.2	9.2	14.8	4.4
Skilled agricultural and fishery workers	34.7	28.6	27.4	5.5	31.1
Craft and trade workers, and plant and machine operators	5.4	10.2	10.1	10.3	7.5
Elementary occupations	55.5	49.8	28.1	11.1	49.7
Column total	100	100	100	100	100
Legislators, officials, and managers	35.5	52.1	9	3.3	100
Professionals, technicians, and clerks	3.7	13.2	38.8	44.3	100
Service workers	32.1	37.2	17.8	13	100
Skilled agricultural and fishery workers	62.8	29.1	7.4	0.68	100
Craft and trade workers, and plant and machine operators	40.4	43	11.3	5.3	100
Elementary occupations	62.7	31.7	4.8	0.86	100
Row total	56.2	31.6	8.4	3.9	100

Note: Due to inadequate sample sizes, several occupations have been combined.
Source: PLFS (2017).

Appendix Table 9.6 *Scheduled Caste and Hindu high caste women workers by MPCE quintile, by occupation, rural India, persons aged 15 and above, 2017* in per cent

Occupations	SC				HHC			
	Bottom 40%	Middle 40%	Top 20%	Total	Bottom 40%	Middle 40%	Top 20%	Total
Legislators, officials, and managers	2.1	2.5	3.6	2.5	2.2	3.4	6.1	3.8
Professionals, technicians, and clerks	2.3	5.4	9.9	4.9	4	8.6	20	10.6
Service workers	3.5	4.2	6.7	4.4	2.7	3.5	5.9	3.9
Skilled agricultural and fishery workers	34.6	29.8	26.7	31.3	60	58	48.2	55.8
Craft and trade workers, and plant and machine operators	7.5	5.9	11.1	7.5	7.8	6.1	5.5	6.3
Elementary occupations	50.1	52.3	42	49.6	23.3	20.5	14.4	19.5
Column total	100	100	100	100	100	100	100	100
Legislators, officials, and managers	34.3	40.7	25	100	13.5	42.4	44.1	100
Professionals, technicians, and clerks	19.4	45.3	35.4	100	9.1	39.1	51.9	100
Service workers	33.8	39.6	26.6	100	16.5	42.5	40.9	100
Skilled agricultural and fishery workers	46	39.2	14.8	100	25.8	50.4	23.8	100
Craft and trade workers, and plant and machine operators	41.6	32.8	25.7	100	29.4	46.5	24.1	100
Elementary occupations	42	43.4	14.6	100	28.7	51	20.3	100
Row total	41.6	41.1	17.3	100	24	48.5	27.6	100

Note: MPCE stands for monthly per capita consumption and is used as a proxy for income since data on incomes is not available.
Source: PLFS (2017).

10

Employment Trends among Scheduled Tribe Women

Athary Janiso

Using data from Employment and Unemployment Surveys (EUS) conducted by the National Sample Survey Office (NSSO), Karat and Rawal (2014) discuss three important points related to the livelihood patterns of rural Scheduled Tribe (ST) women. First, in spite of regional variations, on an average, rural ST women have a higher work participation rate than rural women of other social groups, although their wages are lower.[1] Secondly, this high labour force participation rate (LFPR) of rural ST women exists alongside casualisation of the Adivasi work force, leading to a greater proportion of Adivasi women workers combining cultivation with wage labour as compared to any other social group. Small landholding size, a common feature found across all rural ST households, indicates a higher probability of household members pursuing multiple income-generating activities. Thirdly, there is increasing proletarianisation among significant sections of Adivasis. The proportion of rural ST households working as wage labour has increased, and the proportion of households whose primary occupation is wage labour is higher than the proportion of households whose primary occupation is cultivation. This is likely a result of increasing landlessness among ST households between 1987 and 2011.

This note seeks to build upon the observations in Karat and Rawal (2014) regarding the labour force participation of Adivasi women, and examine the changes that may have occurred since 2011. Using various rounds of the Employment and Unemployment Survey (EUS) of the National Sample Survey (NSS) from 1983 to 2011–12, and the Periodic Labour Force Survey (PLFS) of 2017–18, it presents trends in the worker–population ratio (WPR) of rural ST women aged 15 years and above in India.[2] It provides a comparative study of employment of rural women in two broad categories of States in

---

[1] Worker–population ratio is defined as the number of persons employed among the total persons in the working age group (15–59 years).

[2] All the analysis in this chapter presents estimates for rural women aged 15 years and above.

Table 10.1 *Scheduled Tribe population by State, rural India, 2011*

State	Total population (lakhs)	ST population (lakhs)	Share of State ST population in total State population (%)	Share of State ST population in all-India ST population (%)
Central States under the Fifth Schedule				
Chhattisgarh	255.5	78.2	30.6	7.5
Jharkhand	329.9	86.5	26.2	8.3
Odisha	419.7	95.9	22.8	9.2
Madhya Pradesh	726.3	153.2	21.1	14.7
Other States under the Fifth Schedule				
Gujarat	604.4	89.2	14.8	8.5
Rajasthan	685.5	92.4	13.5	8.8
Maharashtra	1,123.7	105.1	9.4	10.1
Telangana	351.9	32.9	9.3	3.1
Himachal Pradesh	68.7	3.9	5.7	0.4
Andhra Pradesh	493.9	26.3	5.3	2.5
North Eastern States				
Mizoram	11	10.4	94.4	1
Nagaland	19.8	17.1	86.5	1.6
Meghalaya	29.7	25.6	86.1	2.4
Arunachal Pradesh	13.8	9.5	68.8	0.9
Manipur	28.6	11.7	40.9	1.1
Sikkim	6.1	2.1	33.8	0.2
Tripura	36.7	11.7	31.8	1.1
Assam	312.1	38.8	12.4	3.7
Others				
Jammu & Kashmir	125.4	14.9	11.9	1.4
Goa	14.6	1.5	10.2	0.1
Karnataka	611	42.5	7	4.1
West Bengal	912.8	53	5.8	5.1
Uttarakhand	100.9	2.9	2.9	0.3
Kerala	334.1	4.9	1.5	0.5
Bihar	1,041	13.4	1.3	1.3
Tamil Nadu	721.5	8	1.1	0.8
Uttar Pradesh	1,998.1	11.3	0.6	1.1
Haryana	253.5	No ST	NA	NA
Punjab	277.4	No ST	NA	NA

Table 10.1 *continued*

State	Total population (lakhs)	ST population (lakhs)	Share of State ST population in total State population (%)	Share of State ST population in all-India ST population (%)
Union Territories				
Lakshadweep	0.6	0.6	94.8	0.1
Dadra and Nagar Haveli	3.4	1.8	52	0.2
Andaman and Nicobar Islands	3.8	0.3	7.5	0
Daman and Diu (*Goa)	2.4	0.2	6.3	0
Chandigarh	10.6	No ST	NA	NA
National Capital Territory of Delhi	167.9	No ST	NA	NA
Puducherry	12.5	No ST	NA	NA
India	12,108.6	1,045.5		8.6

Source: Census of India (2011).

India, namely States under the Fifth Schedule and the North Eastern States, where the proportion of the ST population is higher than in the other States. Union Territories (UTs) and other States are excluded from the analysis owing to the small proportion of STs living there.

In Table 10.1, the States under the Fifth Schedule are further divided into central Indian States and other States. This was necessary because the four central Indian States account for about 40 per cent of the total ST population in the country. Even though all the North Eastern States have tribal populations, the proportion they contribute to the total tribal population of the country is very small: 94 per cent of the population of Mizoram is comprised of STs, but they make up only 1 per cent of the total ST population in the country. Madhya Pradesh has the highest share of ST population in the country at 14.7 per cent, followed by Maharashtra at 10 per cent and Odisha at 9.2 per cent.

COMPARING THE WPR OF RURAL SCHEDULED TRIBE WOMEN
WITH OTHER SOCIAL GROUPS

Worker–population ratio (WPR) is defined by the NSSO as the share of people engaged in economic activity in the total population. The WPR of rural women is estimated for both Scheduled Tribes and other social groups, which include Scheduled Castes (SCs), Other Backward Classes (OBCs), and

Table 10.2 *Worker–population ratio of women by social group, rural India, 1983 to 2017–18*

Year	ST women (per cent)	Other social groups (per cent)	Difference in WPR between STs and other social groups (percentage points)	All-India rural female WPR (per cent)
1983	71.2	48.6	22.6	50.9
1987–88	67.4	45.4	22	47.7
1993–94	71.7	46	25.7	48.7
1999–2000	67.1	42.3	24.8	44.9
2004–05	69.5	46.1	23.4	48.5
2005–06	67.6	43	24.6	45.6
2007–08	59.2	40.1	19.1	42.2
2009–10	52.5	35.4	17.1	37.2
2011–12	53	33.1	19.9	35.2
2017–18	37.4	21.9	15.5	23.7

Source: Author's calculations from unit-level data of the Employment and Unemployment Survey (EUS) and Periodic Labour Force Survey (PLFS) of various rounds.

other castes, using the usual principal and subsidiary status (UPSS) definition. All rural females aged 15 years and above are considered for the analysis.

Across NSSO rounds, the share of the working population among rural ST women has remained consistently higher than for other social groups. Noticeably, it has remained above the national average of the WPR of women throughout the study period. The WPR of women has steadily declined for both STs and other social groups within the period under study: it has decreased for rural women by 27.2 percentage points between 1983 and 2017–18. The period between 2011–12 and 2017–18 saw the largest decline in percentage points. The analysis shows that ST women are dropping out of work at a higher rate as compared to other social groups.

There was a difference of about 22 percentage points between the WPR of women from other social groups and that of ST women in 1983; the highest gap was seen a decade later, at about 26 percentage points. Since then, the gap between the two groups has declined consistently: between 2011 and 2017, there was a reduction of about 4 percentage points (see Table 10.2).

State-Wise Variations

Table 10.3a shows substantial regional variation in the employment of ST women aged 15 years and above in rural India. This variation is discussed in terms of the levels and trends of WPR by region. The WPR of ST women declined between 2011–12 and 2017–2018 across all States except Madhya Pradesh, which witnessed positive growth of employment in 2017. The largest decline was observed in the North Eastern State of Mizoram. However, during the period 1983 to 2017–18, the largest decline in rural ST women workers was in Gujarat.

Among all States under the Fifth Schedule, the WPR of ST women in Jharkhand was consistently low between 2011–12 and 2017–18. The decline of ST women workers was highest in Odisha among all States under the Fifth

Table 10.3a *Worker–population ratio of ST women by State, rural India, 1983 to 2017–18* in per cent

State	1983	1987–88	1993–94	1999–2000	2004–05	2005–06	2007–08	2009–10	2011–12	2017–18
Central States under the Fifth Schedule										
Chhattisgarh					78.1	78.3	73.2	63.1	66.2	55.4
Jharkhand					63.2	67.4	56.7	35.4	36.6	24
Odisha	66.1	68.5	76.7	71.7	71.3	65.4	61.7	58.2	57	30.3
Madhya Pradesh	77.8	76.3	79.6	75.8	74.8	77.5	60.4	53.9	48.5	54.8
Other States under the Fifth Schedule										
Gujarat	71.5	75.4	71.9	71.1	76.5	72.7	56.4	52.3	52.5	24.4
Rajasthan	87.3	84.3	82.7	75.2	80.7	82.2	69.6	66.1	65.6	43.7
Maharashtra	81.9	74.6	79.9	74.4	75.9	65.9	67.1	66.8	65.1	40.6
Telangana										43.8
Himachal Pradesh	87.1	68.2	84.2	64.7	78.6	65.3	70.7	58.4	84	57.2
Andhra Pradesh	82.6	79.1	85.4	80.7	82	71.5	77.8	73.1	72.2	52.8
North Eastern States										
Mizoram	46.9	47.1	51.2	64.7	62.7	57.8	53.7	57.3	58.3	25.9
Nagaland			36.3	67.2	74.8	81.7	67.2	42.2	39.8	10.6
Meghalaya	71	70.4	74.8	71	76.3	70.7	58.6	56.5	62	55.7
Arunachal Pradesh		52.3	62.3	49.3	68	59.8	52.3	47.4	43.2	11.2
Manipur	63.6	50.2	65.4	40.4	58.7	36.4	41.6	38.2	37.2	15.9
Sikkim	46.3	55.5	33.6	34.9	48.3	55.2	45.4	57.5	71.6	44
Tripura	18.5	36.3	33.9	14.9	14.9	13.5	19.1	22.8	27.9	12.3
Assam	22.1	20.6	23.5	33	37.4	41.7	22.7	26	23.9	5.1
India	71.3	67.5	71.7	67.1	69.5	67.6	59.2	52.5	53	37.4

Source: Author's calculations from unit-level data of the Employment Unemployment Survey (EUS) and Periodic Labour Force Survey (PLFS) of various rounds.

Table 10.3b *Worker–population ratio of women from other social groups by State, rural India, 1983 to 2017–18* in per cent

State	1983	1987–88	1993–94	1999–2000	2004–05	2005–06	2006–07	2009–10	2011–12	2017–18
Central States under the Fifth Schedule										
Chhattisgarh					65.9	68.5	68.5	51.2	58	51.5
Jharkhand	34.5	27.5	24.6	27	43.3	47.7	40.9	20.5	27.2	10.7
Odisha	34.4	31.7	35.4	33.1	36.9	40.9	34.6	26.5	27	15.6
Madhya Pradesh	61.9	59.4	56.1	54.5	51.8	47.9	45.3	38.7	30.8	27.8
Other States under the Fifth Schedule										
Gujarat	59.2	50.4	54.1	55.9	58.4	46.8	49.2	41	33.1	20.7
Rajasthan	63.7	65.7	64.2	55.5	59.4	57.3	53.7	50.9	47.2	27.6
Maharashtra	68.9	66	69.3	60.3	64.2	57.9	58.3	51.1	49.6	36.1
Telangana										36.4
Himachal Pradesh	69.6	71.4	72.5	67.6	69.4	68.3	60.6	63.8	65.6	49.4
Andhra Pradesh	66.8	65.5	71.2	65.2	64.1	60.1	61.8	56.8	56.5	42.7
North Eastern States										
Mizoram	37.4	49.7	25.7	20.6	36.2	18.8	62.6	41.5	58.9	22.7
Nagaland		3.3	43.2	44.7	39.7	21.6	37.3	0	0	
Meghalaya	45.7	38.2	67	54.4	62	50.2	27.4	40.1	60.6	52.9
Arunachal Pradesh	100	20.6	63.7	41	50.4	57.4	47.5	32.3	33.8	30.6
Manipur	36.9	14.7	37.5	33	38.2	26.5	28.3	23.5	37.6	21.8
Sikkim	36.3	49.4	28	37.3	44.6	34.2	41.2	38.8	64.9	47.3
Tripura	7.7	11.2	17	9.5	10.5	7.9	13.6	26.5	32.3	9
Assam	19.8	21.1	24	22.5	30.5	29	21.6	21.8	15.7	11.4
India	48.6	54.6	46	42.3	46.2	43	40.1	35.4	33.1	21.9

Source: Author's calculations from unit-level data of the Employment and Unemployment Survey (EUS) and Periodic Labour Force Survey (PLFS) of various rounds.

Schedule; WPR decreased by 27 percentage points in this period. Among the Central Indian States, Chhattisgarh was the only one whose WPR remained above the national average in both 2011 and 2017. In 2011, the other States under the Fifth Schedule had comparatively higher WPRs than the Central Indian States, even though the WPRs in the former declined considerably from 2011 to 2017. The WPRs in most States under the Fifth Schedule were above the national average of 37 per cent in 2017.

Historically, the employment rate of ST women from the North Eastern States has remained below the national average; this trend continued to hold true between 2011–12 and 2017–18. Meghalaya is an outlier as it has consistently performed well across the years. The percentage of rural ST women in the North Eastern States unable to find employment increased between 2011 and 2017. Meghalaya and Sikkim were two States whose employment rates were higher than the national average in 2017. On the other hand, about 5 per cent of ST women in Assam managed to find gainful employment, the lowest proportion among all States in India.

Table 10.3c *Difference in WPRs between ST and other social groups by State, rural India, 2011–12 and 2017–18*

State	2011–12			2017–18		
	ST WPR (per cent)	Others' WPR (per cent)	Difference (percentage points)	ST WPR (per cent)	Others' WPR (per cent)	Difference (percentage points)
Central Indian States under the Fifth Schedule						
Chhattisgarh	66.2	58	8.3	55.4	51.5	3.9
Jharkhand	36.6	27.2	9.4	24	10.7	13.3
Odisha	57	27	30	30.3	15.6	14.6
Madhya Pradesh	48.5	30.8	17.7	54.8	27.8	27.1
Other States under the Fifth Schedule						
Gujarat	52.5	33.1	19.4	24.4	20.7	3.7
Rajasthan	65.6	47.2	18.4	43.7	27.6	16.2
Maharashtra	65.1	49.6	15.5	40.6	36.1	4.5
Telangana			0	43.8	36.4	7.4
Himachal Pradesh	84	65.6	18.4	57.2	49.4	7.9
Andhra Pradesh	72.2	56.5	15.7	52.8	42.7	10.2
North Eastern States						
Mizoram	58.3	58.9	−0.6	25.9	22.7	3.2
Nagaland	39.8	0	39.8	10.6	0	10.6
Meghalaya	62	60.6	1.4	55.7	52.9	2.8
Arunachal Pradesh	43.2	33.8	9.3	11.2	30.6	−19.4
Manipur	37.2	37.6	−0.4	15.9	21.8	−5.9
Sikkim	71.6	64.9	6.7	44	47.3	−3.3
Tripura	27.9	32.3	−4.4	12.3	9	3.3
Assam	23.9	15.7	8.3	5.1	11.4	−6.3
India	53	33.1	19.9	37.4	21.9	15.6

Source: Author's calculations from unit-level data of the Employment and Unemployment Survey (EUS) and Periodic Labour Force Survey (PLFS) of various rounds.

Disparity in WPR

Between 2011 and 2017, the WPR for women aged 15 years and above declined by 16 and 11 percentage points, respectively, for rural ST women and rural women from other social groups. Despite significant regional variations in terms of women's participation in economic activities in both groups, the employment rate of ST women in 2017 continued to be higher than that of other social groups.

Among the Central Indian States under the Fifth Schedule, the difference in WPR between STs and other social groups in 2011 was the highest in Odisha at 30 percentage points, which declined to 14 percentage points in 2017. On the other hand, in the same year, the gap widened by about 10 percentage points in Madhya Pradesh.

It is interesting to see that Gujarat, which showed the greatest difference between the two groups in 2011, managed to considerably reduce the gap by about 4 percentage points. This was mostly possible because the share of ST women who withdrew from work increased substantially in 2017, whereas the WPR remained unchanged for women from other social groups.

In the North Eastern States of Assam and Manipur, the WPR of women from other social groups was higher than that of ST women in 2017. This was mainly due to a huge decline in the latter's WPR rather than an increase in the WPR of other social groups (see Table 10.3c).

Variations in Type of Work

The NSSO classifies workers into three broad categories on the basis of their autonomy and the nature of work contracts. These are: self-employed, regular salaried/wage employees, and casual wage labourers. The self-employed are defined as workers who operate a farm or non-farm business on their own or with a partner, and have autonomy in decision-making processes. Regular salaried/wage employees and casual wage labourers are differentiated on the basis of the renewal of their work contracts. Regular salaried/wage employees receive payment on a regular basis, while casual wage labourers are paid according to the terms of a periodic work contract.

The shares of the self-employed as well as regular wage employees among ST women have remained lower than that of other social groups over the years (see Table 10.4); however, their participation in casual wage labour has consistently remained higher. The share of self-employed among ST women remained unchanged between 1983 and 2017–18 at 57 per cent, but for the other social groups, this share marginally decreased to 57.7 per cent from 59.5

during the same period. In 2017–18, the share of ST women working as self-employed and casual wage labourers constituted about 92 per cent, whereas it was 88 per cent for other social groups. The share of women working in regular salaried jobs remained abysmally low for most rural women even though regular salaried/wage work increased marginally between 2011–12 and 2017–18 for both groups.

Given that the majority of rural women workers are self-employed, it is important to explore the sectors in which self-employed and other types of women workers may predominate. Table 10.5 shows that in 2017–18, around 86 per cent of ST women workers in rural areas were employed in the agriculture sector, and 81 per cent of ST women employed in agriculture

Table 10.4 *Worker–population ratio among women from STs and other social groups by type of work, rural India, 1983 to 2017–18* in per cent

Year	Scheduled Tribes			Other social groups		
	Self-employed	Regular salaried/ wage	Casual wage labour	Self-employed	Regular salaried/ wage	Casual wage labour
1983	56.9	2.1	40.9	61.9	2.9	35.3
1987–88	55.9	2.8	41.3	60.6	4	35.8
1993–94	54.6	1.6	43.8	59	2.9	38.1
1999–2000	52.2	2.2	45.5	57.9	3.3	38.7
2004–05	57.9	2.5	39.7	64.5	4	31.5
2005–06	58.6	2.1	39.3	62.6	4.4	33.1
2007–08	53.6	2.6	43.8	59	4.4	36.6
2009–10	53	2.6	44.4	55.9	4.8	39.4
2011–12	57.2	3.4	39.5	59.5	6.1	34.4
2017–18	57.5	7.8	34.7	57.7	11.1	31.1

Source: Author's calculations from unit-level data of the Employment and Unemployment Survey (EUS) and Periodic Labour Force Survey (PLFS) of various rounds.

Table 10.5 *Women workers in non-farm and farm sectors by social group, 2017–18* in per cent

	Scheduled Tribes	Other social groups
Farm	86.6	81.5
Non-farm	13.4	18.5

Source: Author's calculations from unit-level data of the Employment and Unemployment Survey (EUS) and Periodic Labour Force Survey (PLFS) of various rounds.

were casual workers. In other words, ST women in rural India find very few opportunities of self-employed work in the non-agriculture sector as compared to women from other social groups.

Comparison by Type of Work and State

This section explores the type of work ST women do and whether it follows a particular pattern that can be generalized across all Indian States. The PLFS, 2017–18 reveals contrasting regional variations by type of work among

Table 10.6 *Worker–population ratio of women by State, type of work, and social group, rural India, 2017–18* in per cent

States	Scheduled Tribes			Other social groups		
	Self-employed	Regular salaried/ wage	Casual Wage	Self-employed	Regular salaried/ wage	Casual Wage
Central Indian States under the Fifth Schedule						
Madhya Pradesh	50.08	1.87	48.05	50.23	5.35	44.42
Chhattisgarh	67.99	1.6	30.4	69.96	2.51	27.53
Odisha	67.9	2.36	29.74	75.41	2.99	21.6
Jharkhand	82.31	3.51	14.18	66.72	4.1	29.18
Other States under the Fifth Schedule						
Andhra Pradesh	40.71	3.82	55.47	43.41	4.07	52.52
Telangana	54.1	5.29	40.62	54.94	5.9	39.16
Gujarat	49.52	6.28	44.21	66.54	4.08	29.38
Himachal Pradesh	56.1	1.77	42.13	49.25	3.58	47.17
Maharashtra	34.29	3.78	61.93	54.33	4.03	41.65
Rajasthan	81.54	1.45	17	82.63	2.69	14.69
North Eastern States						
Arunachal Pradesh	43.19	3.7	53.11	54.39	7.24	38.37
Assam	80.74	5.22	14.04	64.32	15.92	19.76
Manipur	40.25	1.64	58.12	48.73	2.21	49.06
Meghalaya	79.73	8.72	11.55	87.27	3.19	9.53
Mizoram	91.67	4.6	3.73	85.15	5.35	9.5
Nagaland	52.33	2.78	44.89	58.03	1.25	40.72
Sikkim	58.41	2.08	39.51	53.67	2.95	43.38
Tripura	59.59	2.53	37.88	52.71	5.35	41.94
India	55.3	3.5	41.1	59.3	5.2	35.5

Source: Author's calculations from unit-level data of the Employment and Unemployment Survey (EUS) and Periodic Labour Force Survey (PLFS) of various rounds.

rural ST women (Table 10.6). Across all States, more than 90 per cent of ST workers were found to be either self-employed or in casual wage labour. This means that the majority of ST women cannot find regular salaried jobs. ST women in Mizoram had the highest share of self-employed workers at 91 per cent. It is also the only State where the share of women working in regular salaried jobs was higher than that of casual wage labour. The share of women working in regular salaried jobs was highest in Meghalaya. About 80 per cent of total workers were self-employed in States like Rajasthan, Assam, Meghalaya, and Jharkhand. On the contrary, Maharashtra had a majority of ST women working as casual wage labourers.

Among the States under the Fifth Schedule, Maharashtra and Andhra Pradesh had the least number of self-employed rural ST women workers. Excluding Rajasthan, all the remaining States had a higher share of rural ST women working as casual wage labourers than the national average. According to Karat and Rawal (2014), this was partly due to increasing landlessness among ST communities that forced them to work as daily labourers: landlessness among rural ST households increased to 24 per cent in 2011 from 16 per cent in 1987. While Gujarat and Andhra Pradesh had a relatively higher share of women working in regular salaried jobs, Chhattisgarh and Rajasthan had a lower share of ST women working in these kinds of jobs.

The North Eastern States witnessed the highest regional variations related to casual wage employment. Further study is needed to explore the factors causing these variations. The high number of ST women in most North Eastern States working as casual wage labourers is particularly unexpected considering the nature of agriculture in these States, with small holdings and use of family and exchange labour (Karat and Rawal 2014).

CONCLUSION

Three broad points emerge from the NSSO data regarding the work participation of Scheduled Tribe women. First, the worker–population ratio (WPR) of all rural women decreased from 1983 to 2018, but the WPR of ST women remained higher than that of any other social group. While the national female WPR for rural areas according to PLFS (2017–18) data was 23.7 per cent, it was 37.4 per cent for rural ST women. Secondly, more than 90 per cent of rural ST women workers were engaged in the agriculture sector as either self-employed or casual labourers. Lastly, the WPR of rural ST women and their type of work varied substantially over time and across States, especially between the North Eastern States and States under the Fifth Schedule. This needs to be studied further in order to understand the changes in the livelihoods of Adivasis due to the growth of capitalism in Adivasi-inhabited areas.

REFERENCES

Karat, Brinda, and Rawal, Vikas (2014), "Scheduled Tribe Households: A Note on Issues of Livelihood," *Review of Agrarian Studies*, vol. 4, no. 1, pp. 135–58.

National Sample Survey Organisation (NSSO) (1983), *Surveys of Employment and Unemployment, 38th Round (July 1982–June 1983)*, National Sample Survey Organisation, Ministry of Statistics and Programme Implementation, Government of India, New Delhi.

National Sample Survey Organisation (NSSO) (1988), *Surveys of Employment and Unemployment, 43rd Round (July 1987–June 1988)*, National Sample Survey Organisation, Ministry of Statistics and Programme Implementation, Government of India, New Delhi.

National Sample Survey Organisation (NSSO) (1994), *Surveys of Employment and Unemployment, 50th Round (July 1993–June 1994)*, National Sample Survey Organisation, Ministry of Statistics and Programme Implementation, Government of India, New Delhi.

National Sample Survey Organisation (NSSO) (2000), *Surveys of Employment and Unemployment, 55th Round (July 1999–June 2000)*, National Sample Survey Organisation, Ministry of Statistics and Programme Implementation, Government of India, New Delhi.

National Sample Survey Organisation (NSSO) (2005), *Surveys of Employment and Unemployment, 61st Round (July 2004–June 2005)*, National Sample Survey Organisation, Ministry of Statistics and Programme Implementation, Government of India, New Delhi.

National Sample Survey Organisation (NSSO) (2010), *Surveys of Employment and Unemployment, 66th Round (July 2009–June 2010)*, National Sample Survey Organisation, Ministry of Statistics and Programme Implementation, Government of India, New Delhi.

National Sample Survey Organisation (NSSO) (2012), *Surveys of Employment and Unemployment, 68th Round (July 2011–June 2012)*, National Sample Survey Organisation, Ministry of Statistics and Programme Implementation, Government of India, New Delhi.

National Sample Survey Organisation (NSSO) (2018), *Surveys of Employment and Unemployment, Periodic Labour Force Survey (July 2017–June 2018)*, National Sample Survey Organisation, Ministry of Statistics and Programme Implementation, Government of India, New Delhi.

11

Employment and Unemployment in Manual Worker Households

Shruti Nagbhushan

Both official statistics and village data show that there has been feminisation of agriculture. Official statistics reveal that even though women's work participation has been declining, the agriculture sector is still the largest employer of rural women. It engages more than 73 per cent of rural female workers, of whom nearly 34 per cent are casual wage workers (PLFS 2018).[1] Village-level data allow us to examine some aspects of the feminisation of agriculture in greater detail. Specifically, we can identify socio-economic classes and focus solely on women wage workers from the class of hired manual workers.[2]

The literature based on village-level data identifies three features of this feminisation: more women agricultural wage workers than men, a greater share of rural women's labour days in agriculture than in non-agriculture, and a majority of the total wage-labour days in agriculture contributed by women (Ramachandran 2011; Dhar 2013). In this chapter, we have disaggregated the data by social group for each of these features. We have examined data from 21 villages across ten States in different agro-ecological zones of India between 2006 and 2016, based on village surveys conducted under the Project of Agrarian Relations in India (PARI) by the Foundation for Agrarian Studies (FAS). (See Appendix Table 11.1.)

SOME METHODOLOGICAL ASPECTS

In the PARI villages, manual worker households are a socio-economic classification based on whether the majority of household income in

---

[1] The proportion of rural female workers engaged in agriculture in 1977–78 was 88.1 per cent; this proportion has gradually declined over the years to 74.9 per cent in 2011–12 and 73.2 per cent in 2017–18 (PLFS 2018).

[2] In this chapter, the terms "days of employment," "days of wage work," and "days of work" have been used interchangeably. Please note, all employment and work referred to here is only casual wage work.

such households came from members working as hired wage workers and whether a major proportion of their work time was spent as hired labourers (Ramachandran 1990). Most manual workers are casual labourers engaged in agricultural and non-agricultural work on daily-rated and piece-rated contracts. These workers could also be engaged in monthly or annual wage contracts for non-manual work, but these cases have not been included here as the focus is on casual wage employment. In this chapter, we explore the share of women dependent on wage employment among workers, that is, those who received at least one day of paid work in the reference year.[3]

Manual workers form the single largest class in many villages and may be smaller only in relation to the undifferentiated peasant class (Ramachandran *et al.* 2014). In most of the study villages, manual worker households formed around a quarter of all households; in 11 out of 21 villages, they constituted over one-third of all households; and in some cases, they constituted more than 50 per cent of all households (see Table 11.1). Furthermore, in 14 out of 21 villages, more than 50 per cent of manual worker households were landless. The extent of landlessness was 100 per cent in two villages in Tripura, and more than 90 per cent in Zhapur village in Karnataka and 25F Gulabewala village in Rajasthan. The study villages have been grouped based on the share of manual worker households so that we can clearly differentiate villages by the share of households dependent on wage work. For example, three villages

Table 11.1 *Share of manual worker households among total households, by village* in per cent

Manual worker households as a proportion of total households (in per cent)	Villages (survey year)
>50	25F Gulabewala (2007), Nayanagar (2012)
40–50	Katkuian (2012), Kalmandasguri (2010), Kothapalle (2006), Zhapur (2009)
30–40	Warwat Khanderao (2007), Nimshirgaon (2007), Panahar (2010), Amarsinghi (2010), Alabujanahalli (2009)
20–30	Mainama (2016), Muhuripur (2016), Bukkacherla (2006), Mahatwar (2006), Harevli (2006), Ananthavaram (2006), Gharsondi (2008)
<20	Siresandra (2009), Rewasi (2010), Khakchang (2016)

Note: Landlessness among manual worker households is lowest in Rewasi, at 8 per cent, and highest in Muhuripur and Mainama, at 100 per cent.
Source: FAS survey data.

[3] See chapter 4 in this volume for the share of women in each village who received employment.

– Siresandra in Karnataka, Rewasi in Rajasthan, and Khakchang in Tripura – were characterised as peasant economies (see Appendix Table 11.1). This grouping would be helpful in contextualising the observations regarding work participation or days of employment received by women from the manual worker households. Among the study villages, 25F Gulabewala in Rajasthan and Nayanagar in Bihar were two villages where more than 50 per cent of the households were classified as manual worker households.

WOMEN WORKERS FROM MANUAL WORKER HOUSEHOLDS

Women comprised between 35 and 65 per cent of all wage workers from manual worker households in all the study villages (see Figure 11.1). The proportion of women among wage workers was between 40 and 50 per cent in the majority of the villages. Moreover, the proportion of women among all wage workers was more than that of men in five of the villages – Siresandra in Karnataka, Bukkacherla in Andhra Pradesh, Warwat Khanderao in Maharashtra, 25F Gulabewala in Rajasthan, and Kothapalle (almost 65 per cent) in Andhra Pradesh. Thus, the work participation of women from the class of manual worker households in most of the surveyed villages was almost equal to, or greater than, that of men.

Figure 11.1 *Proportion of women workers among total workers from manual worker households, survey villages* in per cent

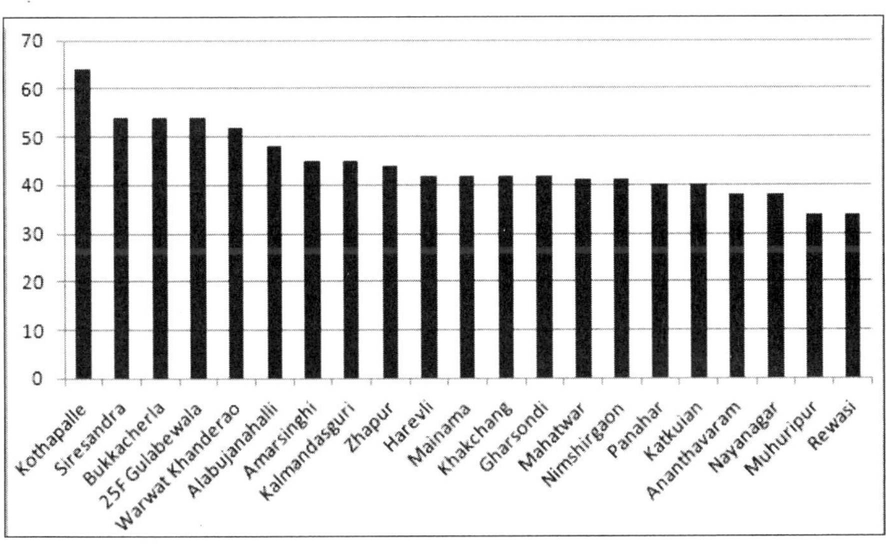

Source: PARI data.

Social Group Composition

In the social composition of manual worker households across most of the study villages, the share of Scheduled Caste (SC) households was higher than their share in the village population (Dhar 2013). In addition, region-specific oppressed castes like Scheduled Tribes (STs) and Nomadic Tribes in the surveyed villages in Maharashtra and Andhra Pradesh, and Other Backward Classes (OBC) in some of the surveyed villages, constituted a significant share of the class of manual workers in those regions. The share of other castes in the class of manual workers was small (less than 15 per cent in all but five villages and absent in eight out of 21 villages). (See Table 11.3.)

In more than half of the villages, the largest share of women workers from manual worker households belonged to SCs, and this share was as high as 98

Table 11.2 *Distribution of women workers from manual worker households by village and social group* in per cent

Village	State	SC	ST	OBC	Other castes	Nomadic Tribes	Total
25F Gulabewala	Rajasthan	98	–	2	–	–	100
Mahatwar	Uttar Pradesh	94	–	6	–	–	100
Amarsinghi	West Bengal	86	2	12	–	–	100
Siresandra	Karnataka	80	–	20	–	–	100
Panahar	West Bengal	80	10	8	2	–	100
Harevli	Uttar Pradesh	76	–	16	8	–	100
Ananthavaram	Andhra Pradesh	65	15	6	14	–	100
Nayanagar	Bihar	58	–	42	–	–	100
Nimshirgaon	Maharashtra	57	–	6	34	3	100
Zhapur	Karnataka	56	20	24	–	–	100
Rewasi	Rajasthan	45	9	14	32	–	100
Bukkacherla	Telangana	38	–	33	29	–	100
Kothapalle	Andhra Pradesh	30	2	61	7	–	100
Muhuripur	Tripura	29		43	28	–	100
Alabujanahalli	Karnataka	28	3	69	–	–	100
Katkuian	Bihar	22	1	74	3	–	100
Kalmandasguri	West Bengal	19	6	69	6	–	100
Warwat Khanderao	Maharashtra	19	–	31	21	29	100
Gharsondi	Madhya Pradesh	13	47	40	–	–	100
Mainama	Tripura	–	70	25	5	–	100
Khakchang	Tripura	–	100	–	–	–	100

Note: Villages are arranged in descending order by share of SC women workers.
Source: FAS survey data.

Table 11.3 *Manual worker households by village and social group* in per cent

Village	SC	ST	OBC	Other castes	Nomadic Tribes	All
25F Gulabewala	98	0	2	0	0	100
Mahatwar	92	0	8	0	0	100
Panahar	82	7	8	3	0	100
Siresandra	75	0	25	0	0	100
Harevli	75	0	13	13	0	100
Amarsinghi	73	2	25	0	0	100
Zhapur	59	14	25	2	0	100
Ananthavaram	59	19	7	14	0	100
Nimshirgaon	58	0	5	36	2	100
Nayanagar	54	0	45	0	0	100
Bukkacherla	45	0	25	30	0	100
Kothapalle	34	3	55	8	0	100
Alabujanahalli	31	1	68	0	0	100
Rewasi	27	8	22	43	0	100
Kalmandasguri	27	4	60	9	0	100
Muhuripur	22	0	34	44	0	100
Warwat Khanderao	21	0	33	24	22	100
Katkuian	19	1	77	3	0	100
Gharsondi	16	40	43	0	0	100
Mainama	5	62	26	7	0	100
Khakchang	0	100	0	0	0	100

Note: Villages are arranged in descending order by share of SC households.
Source: FAS survey data.

per cent in one village in Rajasthan. On the other hand, in the two villages in Tripura, namely Mainama and Khakchang, women workers belonged almost entirely to STs (there were no SCs in these villages). Among the other villages the participation of women from OBC manual worker households was high in Alabujanahalli in Karnataka, Kothapalle in Andhra Pradesh, Kalmandasguri in West Bengal, Muhuripur in Tripura, and Katkuian in Bihar; in one village in Maharashtra, Nomadic Tribes formed a high share of women workers (Table 11.2). Women who belonged to the others category, which includes the socially dominant castes in a village, constituted a relatively small share (less than ten per cent of all women workers) compared to other social groups in 15 out of 21 villages. Exceptions to this were the two villages in Maharashtra, Rewasi in Rajasthan, Bukkacherla in Telangana, and Muhuripur in Tripura; here, other caste households also comprised around 50 per cent of the total households.[4]

---

[4] In Nimshirgaon and Warwat Khanderao villages, women workers from the "other castes" category are predominantly Muslim.

The caste composition of women workers is an important deflection from the findings when all rural manual workers from the class of hired manual workers are considered together. Ramachandran (2011) has stated from evidence in villages in India that rural manual workers tend to be the most caste-heterogeneous class in a village, given that they are considered to engage in occupations of last resort. However, if we look at the social composition of women workers from manual worker households in the study villages, we find that there is scant evidence of caste heterogeneity. It can be seen clearly that there is a high proportion of SCs and other region-specific oppressed castes among women workers from manual worker households across all the villages (see Table 11.2). It was only in six out of the 21 villages that women from manual worker households belonging to the "other castes" group participated in wage work, which can be explained by the poor economic condition of

Table 11.4 *Shares of SC households in manual worker households, and SC manual worker households with women workers, by village* in per cent

Village	Share of SC households in manual worker households	Share of SC manual worker households with women workers
Amarsinghi	73	94
Warwat Khanderao	21	94
25F Gulabewala	98	92
Siresandra	75	89
Bukkacherla	45	89
Alabujanahalli	31	86
Kothapalle	34	85
Zhapur	59	81
Rewasi	27	80
Katkuian	19	79
Gharsondi	16	73
Panahar	82	71
Ananthavaram	59	71
Nimshirgaon	58	67
Mahatwar	92	64
Nayanagar	54	64
Muhuripur	22	64
Harevli	75	56
Kalmandasguri	27	53
Mainama	5	0

Source: FAS survey data.

these households. Also, among SC manual worker households, the share of households with at least one women worker in the house was more than 60 per cent in the majority of villages (see Table 11.4).

So, in terms of participation in work, we find that women participated almost equally in wage work as compared to men. Further, women who engaged in paid manual work primarily belonged to SCs and other region-specific oppressed castes.

Gender Disparity in Employment

The second feature we examine is the degree of unemployment or underemployment based on the average number of days of wage employment received.[5] Three major observations can be made regarding the days of wage employment received by women from manual worker households. First, the average days of employment per woman wage worker were very low – less than three months in most of the study villages. Secondly, in the majority of villages, the proportion of women wage workers who received more than 100 days of employment was less than 20 per cent. Thirdly, there exists a stark gender disparity within a village in terms of the days of employment received.

The average number of days of employment received by women wage workers was very low, as mentioned above – between 35 and 140 days per worker (see Figure 11.3). In Amarsinghi and Kalmandasguri villages of West Bengal, and particularly in Nayanagar village of Bihar, the average number of days of work per female worker was less than two months in a year. Incidentally, these were also the villages where participation of women from manual worker households in wage work was low. In most of the villages, women wage workers received less than three months or 90 days of wage employment. The only exceptions to this were the two villages in Maharashtra and three villages in Karnataka, wherein women wage workers were primarily engaged in agriculture. However, in Zhapur (Karnataka), stone quarrying work provided women wage workers an average of 200 days of employment per worker.

In addition to the average number of days of wage work received by women workers, it is also worthwhile to explore the upper limit of the range of days of wage work received and the proportion of the population that received this. In the majority of surveyed villages, the proportion of women from manual worker households who received more than 100 days of wage work was less than 20 per cent (see Figure 11.2), and nowhere was that proportion greater than 70 per cent. Also, there were only three villages – Harevli, Zhapur, and

---

[5] Eight-hour work days have been used as the standard work day.

Siresandra – where more than 50 per cent of the women from manual worker households got more than 100 days of work. In Harevli, this employment was provided primarily by sugarcane harvesting, whereas in Zhapur, it was stone quarrying. In Siresandra, very few women received more than 100 days of work (mostly for agricultural work such as tomato picking and finger millet harvesting), but the high proportion is explained by the overall small number of women workers from manual worker households.

Furthermore, the proportion of workers who received more than 100 days of employment was generally higher for men than for women (see Figure 11.2). There were also villages, however, where the proportion of women who received more than 100 days of employment was higher than that of men, although the differentiation was not very stark. Khakchang was one such village where the high proportion of women could be explained by National Rural Employment Guarantee Scheme (NREGS) work. In Kothapalle, where agricultural work (maize harvesting, cotton picking, paddy transplanting) as well as non-agricultural work (like *bidi* rolling and construction work) were available for women, a larger share of women workers as compared to men were employed for more days on average. Also, in Harevli, where the average days of employment per woman were high due to sugarcane harvesting, the proportion of women who received more than 100 days work was higher than men.

The second observation was that men from manual worker households received more days of employment per worker than women across all villages, with the exception of Kothapalle in Andhra Pradesh and Warwat Khanderao

Figure 11.2 *Shares of male and female workers from manual worker households with more than 100 days of wage employment in a year* in per cent

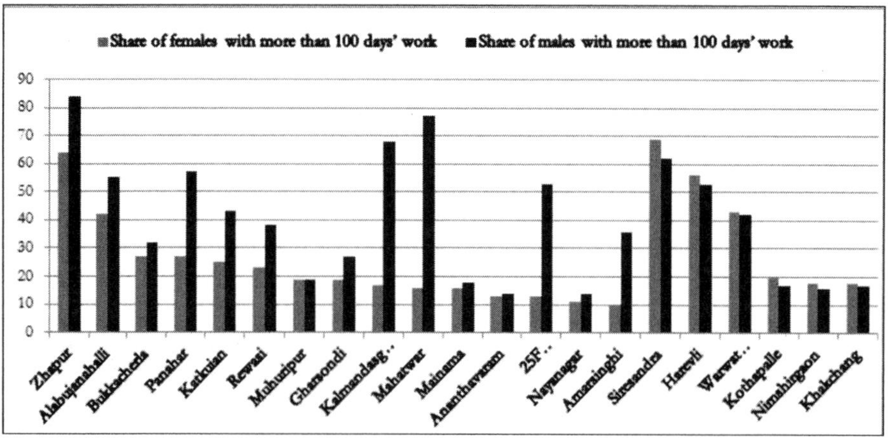

Source: FAS survey data.

Figure 11.3 *Average days of wage employment per worker received by men and women from manual worker households, by village* in number

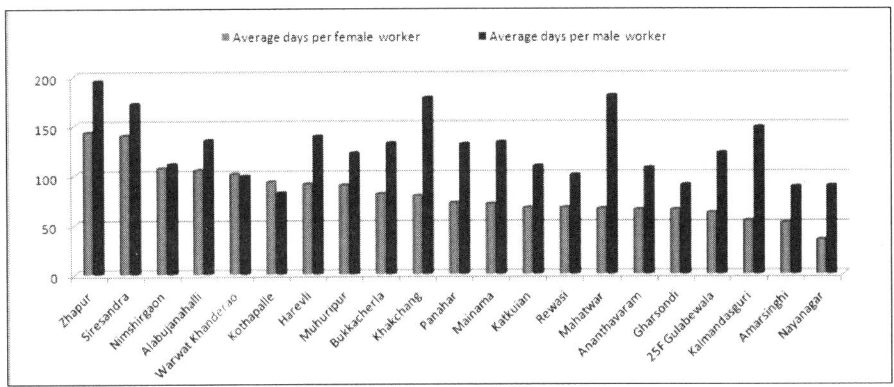

Source: FAS survey data.

in Maharashtra (see Figure 11.3). The fact that the gender difference in average days of employment per worker was not very stark in both these villages can be attributed to the average days of employment for men being among the lowest in the two villages, particularly in Kothapalle. This observation about gender disparity in days of employment is corroborated by various primary studies conducted in different States which show that women receive significantly fewer days of employment as compared to men (Ramakumar 2004; Rawal 2006; Dhar 2013; Ramachandran *et al.* 2014).

Type of Wage Work

It is not possible to distinguish workers as strictly agricultural or non-agricultural in any of the villages as agricultural workers also engaged in non-agricultural tasks, depending on work availability. One measure of understanding whether agriculture dominates women's work is to explore the actual number of days they worked in agricultural and non-agricultural tasks. Some recent studies based on primary data on rural employment of women show a gender disparity in the type of employment: women are relegated to low-paying agricultural wage work that is mostly within the village (Ramachandran 2011; Dhar 2013).

The pattern across the 21 study villages shows that of the total days worked by women from manual worker households, the share of agricultural work was significantly higher than of non-agricultural work (see Table 11.5). Exceptions to this pattern where the share of agriculture in days worked by women was less than 50 per cent were seen in six villages – Khakchang, Mainama, and Muhuripur in Tripura; Rewasi in Rajasthan; Panahar in West Bengal; and Zhapur in

Table 11.5 *Share of agricultural and non-agricultural days of employment, by village and sex in per cent*

Village	State	Female		Male	
		Days worked in agriculture	Days worked in non-agriculture	Days worked in agriculture	Days worked in non-agriculture
Ananthavaram	Andhra Pradesh	100	0	62	38
Harevli	Uttar Pradesh	99	1	61	39
Nimshirgaon	Maharashtra	97	3	63	37
Katkuian	Bihar	91	9	51	49
Bukkacherla	Telangana	90	10	56	44
25F Gulabewala	Rajasthan	81	19	71	29
Kalmandasguri	West Bengal	80	20	46	54
Warwat Khanderao	Maharashtra	79	21	55	45
Kothapalle	Andhra Pradesh	78	22	32	68
Mahatwar	Uttar Pradesh	61	39	23	77
Amarsinghi	West Bengal	59	41	46	54
Gharsondi	Madhya Pradesh	59	41	52	48
Nayanagar	Bihar	57	43	39	61
Alabujanahalli	Karnataka	54	46	61	39
Siresandra	Karnataka	51	49	69	31
Zhapur	Karnataka	46	54	17	83
Panahar	West Bengal	46	54	46	54
Mainama	Tripura	45	55	30	70
Rewasi	Rajasthan	42	58	36	64
Muhuripur	Tripura	38	62	13	87
Khakchang	Tripura	31	69	29	71

Note: Villages are arranged in descending order by share of female days worked in agriculture.
Source: FAS survey data.

Karnataka. In the three Tripura villages, the high share of non-agricultural work for women could be attributed to relatively large-scale implementation of the National Rural Employment Guarantee Act (NREGA).[6] Similarly, in Rewasi and Panahar, women actively participated in NREGA work, and received around 76 days and 21 days of work on average per worker, respectively.[7] In Zhapur, women were mainly engaged in quarrying (stone cutting and loading). Thus, except for the six villages where non-agricultural work was available in

[6] More than 90 per cent of households enrolled in NREGA received employment in the three villages of Tripura (Swaminathan and Basu, eds. 2019).
[7] However, it is important to note that the survey year was a drought year in Rewasi, and thus employment in agriculture was very low that year.

the village and thus predominated women's wage employment, the remaining 15 villages saw women primarily engaged in agriculture.

The dependence of women workers on agriculture was even more apparent among Scheduled Caste manual worker households. With the exception of Zhapur, Rewasi, and Muhuripur, for reasons described previously, the share of days worked by SC women in agriculture in all the other villages was at least 56 per cent of the total days worked. In eight of the 21 villages, more than 90 per cent of the total days worked by SC women were in agriculture. Data from 21 villages support the finding that agriculture dominated the wage work done by Dalit women workers in manual worker households (see Ramachandran *et al.* 2014). Thus, the pattern of actual deployment of labour time by women workers from different social groups shows how caste, in addition to gender, intervenes in the social division of labour.

In general, in many of the villages, agriculture did not provide sufficient employment (see Table 11.5). Thus we find that availability of specific non-agricultural work within a village, particularly ones that had low agricultural employment or bad agricultural years, facilitated women's participation in wage work. This is important as we did not find many instances of women commuting or migrating for work outside the villages.

SUMMING UP

The PARI database is unique as it allows us to understand employment patterns in the study villages in detail, with particular focus on the class of hired manual workers who form the core of the rural labour force. From the patterns of wage employment of women from manual worker households, three major points can be observed across the 21 study villages (barring a few exceptions). First, in the majority of the villages, between 40 and 50 per cent of all workers from manual worker households were women. In fact, in five of the villages, the share of women among all wage workers was more than 50 per cent. This shows that women were as much a part of the work force in manual worker households as men. Though the class of manual workers is said to be the most caste-heterogeneous among all classes in a village, women workers from this class generally belonged to SCs or other region-specific oppressed castes.

Secondly, despite participating equally in the wage labour market, women workers from manual worker households generally received few days of employment (less than three months per worker in most villages), and much less than men, on average. Women received between 60 and 100 days of employment per worker, whereas men received between 80 and 150 days of employment on average, and even more than 170 days in some villages. The extent of underemployment among women workers from manual worker households has also been shown for a village in Kerala by Ramakumar (2004); for two villages in Haryana by Rawal (2006); and for nine villages across Andhra Pradesh, Uttar Pradesh, Maharashtra, and Rajasthan by Dhar (2013).

Thirdly, the share of agricultural work was significantly higher than that of non-agricultural work in the total days worked by women from manual worker households. This makes women in these villages more vulnerable to changes in agricultural production and growth, as well as structural changes due to the development of capitalist forces in agriculture, given that they do not have the mobility to find work outside the village.

I would like to thank Madhura Swaminathan and Aparajita Bakshi for their comments on previous drafts.

References

Dhar, Niladri Sekhar (2012), "On Days of Employment of Rural Labour Households," *Review of Agrarian Studies*, vol. 2, no. 2, July–December, pp. 106–15, available at http://www.ras.org.in/on_days_of_employment_of_rural_labour_households, viewed on 25 July 2019.

Dhar, Niladri Sekhar, with Kaur, Navpreet (2013), "Features of Rural Underemployment in India: Evidence from Nine Villages," *Review of Agrarian Studies*, vol. 3, no. 1, January–June, pp. 14–54, available at http://ras.org.in/index.php?Article=features_of_rural_underemployment_in_india&q=niladri&keys=niladri#fn3, viewed on 25 July 2019.

National Statistical Office (2019), "Annual Report: Periodic Labour Force Survey (PLFS) (July 2017–June 2018)," Ministry of Statistics and Programme Implementation (MoSPI), Government of India, New Delhi.

Ramachandran, V. K. (1990), *Wage Labour and Unfreedom in Agriculture: An Indian Case Study*, Clarendon Press, Oxford.

Ramachandran, V. K. (2011), "The State of Agrarian Relations in India Today," *The Marxist*, vol. 27, nos. 1–2, January–June, pp. 51–89.

Ramachandran, V. K., Dhar, Niladri Sekhar, and Kaur, Navpreet (2014), "Hired Manual Workers: A Note," in V. K. Ramachandran and Madhura Swaminathan (eds.), *Dalit Households in Village Economies*, Tulika Books, New Delhi, pp. 294–304.

Ramakumar, R. (2004), "Socio-Economic Characteristics of Agricultural Workers: A Case Study of a Village in the Malabar Region of Kerala," PhD thesis, Indian Statistical Institute, Kolkata.

Rawal, Vikas (2006), "The Labour Process in Rural Haryana (India): A Field Report from Two Villages," *Journal of Agrarian Change*, vol. 6, no. 4, 7 September, pp. 538–83.

Swaminathan, Madhura, and Basu, Ranjini (eds.) (2019), *Socio-Economic Surveys of Three Villages in Tripura*, Tulika Books, New Delhi.

APPENDIX

Appendix Table 11.1 *List of PARI villages by sub-district, district, State, and agro-ecological zone*

Village	Sub-district	District	States	Agro-ecological Zone
Ananthavaram	Kollur	Guntur	Andhra Pradesh	Krishna–Godavari Zone
Bukkacherla	Raptadu	Anantapur	Andhra Pradesh	Scarce Rainfall Zone of Rayalaseema
Kothapalle	Thimmapur	Karimnagar	Telangana	North Telangana Zone
Harevli	Najibabad	Bijnor	Uttar Pradesh	Bhabar and Tarai Zone
Mahatwar	Rasra	Ballia	Uttar Pradesh	Eastern Plain Zone
25F Gulabewala	Karanpur	Sri Ganganagar	Rajasthan	Irrigated North-Western Plain Zone
Rewasi	Sikar	Sikar	Rajasthan	Transitional Plain Zone of Inland Drainage
Nimshirgaon	Shirol	Kolhapur	Maharashtra	South Konkan Coastal Zone
Warwat Khanderao	Sangrampur	Buldhana	Maharashtra	Western Maharashtra Plain Zone
Gharsondi	Bhitarwar	Gwalior	Madhya Pradesh	Gird Zone
Alabujanahalli	Maddur	Mandya	Karnataka	Southern Dry Zone
Siresandra	Kolar	Kolar	Karnataka	Eastern Dry Zone
Zhapur	Gulbarga	Kalaburagi	Karnataka	North East Dry Zone
Kalmandasguri	Cooch Behar-II	Cooch Behar	West Bengal	Terai Zone
Amarsinghi	Ratua-I	Malda	West Bengal	New Alluvial Zone
Panahar	Kotulpur	Bankura	West Bengal	Old Alluvial Zone
Katkuian	Bagaha	West Champaran	Bihar	North-West Alluvial Gangetic Region
Nayanagar	Rosera	Samastipur	Bihar	North-West Alluvial Gangetic Region
Khakchang	Dasda	North District	Tripura	North Eastern Hill
Mainama	Manu	Dhalai	Tripura	North Eastern Hill
Muhuripur	Julaibari	South District	Tripura	North Eastern Hill

Source: FAS survey data.

IV

Women in Non-Agricultural Work

12

Conditions of Work among "Scheme Workers"

K. Hemalata

CONTEXT

From 1991 onwards, with the onset of liberalisation policies in India, social sector spending has come under attack. While no unidirectional change has occurred over the last 28 years, the tendency, especially over the last four to five years, has been of a decline in social sector spending – on health and education, in particular.

The Union government's budgeted expenditure on education as a share of GDP increased from 0.5 per cent in 1999–2000 to barely 0.9 per cent in 2010–11, but decreased to 0.45 per cent in 2019–20. As a share of the Union budget, spending on education fell from 4.7 per cent in 2012–13 to 3.7 per cent in 2017–18 (CBGA 2019). State governments account for nearly three-fourths of total public spending on education. Taking the total budgeted expenditure on education of State and Central governments as a share of GDP, the ratio increased gradually between 2004–05 and 2013–14 from 2.1 to 3.3 per cent, but declined to 2.6 per cent in 2015–16 (CBGA 2016). Similarly, public expenditure on health by State and Central governments as a share of GDP stagnated for almost three decades, from 0.99 per cent in 1980–81 to 1.04 per cent in 2010–11 (CBGA 2011). The goal of public health expenditure as 2.5 per cent of GDP is unlikely to be met by 2025.

Not only is the budgeted expenditure on health, education, nutrition, and other social sectors low, but the utilisation of funds in these sectors is also poor. In 2017–18, the Department of School Education utilised only 65 per cent of the allocated funds due to improper absorption of funds by the States. In the same year, the Ministry of Health and Family Welfare surrendered funds amounting to Rs 10,490 million due to their non-utilisation. Increasing contractualisation and poor remuneration of the health work force were identified as possible causes for this underspending (CBGA 2019).

A second feature of liberalisation relevant to this paper is the informalisation of employment in public services by means of a rise in contractual employment and the use of "volunteer workers." In the health sector, for example, recruitment of regular health workers was halted to make way for flexible labour and informal employment contracts. This resulted in the creation of new categories of health workers, with their specific tasks being shifted from those of qualified health workers to minimally trained, low-skilled, and voluntary health workers (Som 2016). Similarly, in the education sector, the Sarva Shiksha Abhiyan, India's flagship programme to provide universal primary education, launched in 2001, depends on part-time or para-teachers, not regular teachers, to achieve its goals.

The workers most affected by this trend of informalisation of public employment in the social sector are women. The only major "regular" employment for women in rural areas, as Ghosh (2006) found, was "volunteer" work in public programmes. Contractual and volunteer workers are mainly concentrated in tasks that are seen as "women's tasks," such as care work. As Palriwala and Neetha (2010) argues, low-paid care services are increasingly getting feminised, even though women's overall work participation has been low and declining. Since these tasks are considered women's tasks, these women workers are also underpaid (Razavi 2007).

Given this context of (i) falling public expenditure on health, education, nutrition, and other social sectors; (ii) growing informalisation of employment; and (iii) women's labour in low-paid, "volunteer" work linked to their contribution to care work, this paper provides a unique perspective from the trade union movement.

– Editors

This chapter examines wages and working conditions of rural India's "scheme workers." While not an official designation or classification of work established by the government, this term was coined and popularised by trade unions in the country to refer to a category of workers engaged to implement, at the ground level, the various schemes and programmes of the Government of India. The overwhelming majority of scheme workers live in rural India, and around 60 to 70 per cent of all scheme workers in the country are women. Furthermore, a large number of them belong to the socially oppressed sections of society, that is, the Scheduled Castes (SCs), Scheduled Tribes (STs), and Other Backward Classes (OBC). Single women form a significant section of women scheme workers.

There is evidence now, as seen from the All India Rural Financial Inclusion Survey (NAFIS), released in 2018 by NABARD, which dispels the general impression that rural India is mainly agricultural. The NAFIS estimated the average monthly net income of rural households at Rs 8,059; of this, only Rs 1,832 came from cultivation and livestock rearing, while Rs 5,410 came from agricultural and non-agricultural wage labour (Rs 3,504) and government or private service jobs (Rs 1,906). It is notable that around 57 per cent of the income of "agricultural households" came from non-agricultural sources. The earnings of scheme workers comprise an important part of this non-agricultural income of both agricultural and non-agricultural rural households.

Who Are Scheme Workers?

In the process of organising anganwadi workers (AWWs) and anganwadi helpers (AWHs) employed in the Integrated Child Development Services (ICDS) scheme under the Ministry of Women and Child Development, Government of India, cadres of the Centre of Indian Trade Unions (CITU) discovered several workers, many of whom were women, working under similar conditions as part of different government schemes. Besides ICDS, other such schemes run by the Government of India include: the National Rural Health Mission (NRHM), which later became the National Health Mission (NHM); the National Rural Livelihood Mission (NRLM); Mid-Day Meal Scheme (MDM); Sarva Shiksha Abhiyan (SSA); Kasturba Gandhi Balika Vidyalaya (KGBV); Saakshar Bharat Mission; National Child Labour Project (NCLP); Agriculture Technology Management Agency (ATMA); and Yashoda/Mamta schemes under the Norway India Partnership Initiative (NIPI). It was during a campaign organised by CITU that the term "scheme worker" was coined to refer to all of these workers who more or less faced similar working conditions.[1]

Number of Scheme Workers

According to CITU's estimates, as of 2019, more than 8 million scheme workers are employed in the various schemes sponsored by the Government of India and implemented by State governments. This figure does not include the schemes independently run by different State governments. Women constitute a significant proportion of these scheme workers, and this can be more clearly understood when workers are disaggregated by scheme. The ICDS engages over 2.6 million anganwadi workers and helpers, all of whom

---

[1] CITU organised a two-day movement or *mahapadav* of scheme workers, on 26–27 November 2012 in Delhi, to highlight the common problems of all workers employed under different schemes and programmes of the Government of India.

are women. The NHM has a total of 1 million women working as Accredited Social Health Activists (ASHAs) and Urban Social Health Activists (USHAs). In addition, there are several million women employed as Second Auxiliary Nurse cum Midwives (Second ANMs), laboratory assistants, technicians, etc., in the health Sub-Centres (SCs), Primary Health Centres (PHCs), and Community Health Centres (CHCs). The Mid-Day Meal Scheme has over 2.7 million cooks and helpers, 90 per cent of whom are women. The Sarva Shiksha Abhiyan employs around 1 million para-teachers, *shiksha mitras* (teaching buddies), *shiksha karmis* (teaching helpers), and guest teachers, and around 60 per cent of them are women. NRLM employs around 0.15 million Village Assistant Officers (VAOs), Community Resource Persons (CRPs), bookkeepers, *grama deepikas* (village illuminators), etc., with different names in different States, of whom around 80 per cent are women (Press Information Bureau 2017). Thousands of women work under the Yashoda/Mamata scheme and under the Agriculture Technology Management Agency as extension workers. Further, NCLP employs around 50,000 teaching and non-teaching staff in special schools, of whom over 40 per cent are women. In addition to the above-mentioned figures of women engaged in government schemes, there are various other schemes that employ around 1.7 million persons in total.[2]

Contracts and Conditions of Work

None of the above-mentioned 8 million workers are recognised as workers or "employees." They are called "social workers," "volunteers," "activists," "guests," "friends," and some of them are even called "Yashodas" and "Mamtas."[3] The government decides their recruitment criteria, job responsibilities, working conditions and payment, and government officers supervise their work and take disciplinary action such as deduction in remuneration and removal from service for any alleged violation. Nonetheless, the government stubbornly refuses to recognise these scheme workers as workers.

The remuneration paid to scheme workers for their work is not called a wage or salary; it is called an "honorarium," which can be as low as Rs 1,000 per month for ten months a year, as in the case of Mid-Day Meal workers.

---

[2] While totals are provided by Ministry websites, the data are not disaggregated by scheme and numbers change every year. The disaggregated figures reported here are from the latest data collected during activities organised by CITU. We estimate that the number of other scheme workers, including *grama deepikas*, *shakti sahayikas*, community resource persons, and record keepers in the villages would total at least 1.7 million people.

[3] Yashoda is the foster mother of Krishna, a deity in Hindu mythology, and *mamta* can be translated as motherly affection.

Being denied the status of workers, those engaged in schemes are deprived of all statutory benefits applicable to workers such as minimum wages and basic labour rights including the right to collective bargaining.

Some scheme workers often perform the duties of regular employees but are not compensated accordingly. For example, Second ANMs under the NHM are only paid an honorarium of Rs 3,000 per month even though they perform the same job as regular ANMs in the health department. Similarly, para-teachers under the SSA are employed on contract and paid a consolidated amount between Rs 6,000 and Rs 10,000, while their responsibilities are on par with those of permanent teachers in the education department. The government pays only a fraction of permanent employees' salaries to these scheme workers as an honorarium; this, despite a Supreme Court judgement stating that the same wages and benefits should be paid to contract workers doing the same or similar work as permanent workers.[4]

Scheme workers fall outside the ambit of benefits received by other workers, and thus are not covered by social security benefits such as the Employees' Provident Fund or the Employees' State Insurance (ESI). Furthermore, these "social workers" are compelled to "retire" upon reaching a certain age (which is not uniform across schemes), but are not paid any retirement benefits such as gratuity and pension. Only anganwadi workers and helpers are now eligible for paid maternity leave, a benefit they obtained after lengthy struggles.[5] No maternity benefits or paid maternity leave are available to other scheme workers.

Under the National Rural Livelihood Mission, women workers are given attractive names such as *sakti sahayika* (energy assistant) and *grama deepika* (village illuminator), but their conditions of work are no different than that of other scheme workers. Similar are the conditions of several million guests, friends, and volunteers employed under the Sarva Shiksha Abhiyan.

Scheme workers may not be directly involved in primary production in the rural areas, but – as can be seen from the list of schemes and implementing departments – they provide basic and essential services, particularly to women, children, and the poor in rural areas. These services relate to health, education, nutrition, food, and livelihood security, and are of immense value for those

[4] A bench of the Supreme Court comprising Justices J. S. Khehar and S. A. Bobde, in a judgement dated 26 October 2016, ordered that the principle of "equal pay for equal work" be made applicable to those engaged as daily wage workers as well as casual and contractual employees who perform the same duties as regular workers (Supreme Court of India 2016).

[5] In July 2006, around 20,000 anganwadi workers and helpers from 22 States participated in a ten-day hunger strike organised by the All India Federation of Anganwadi Workers and Helpers. The following year a rally and march to Parliament by anganwadi workers, and an all-India strike by nearly 8,00,000 anganwadi workers and helpers were observed. More information about these struggles is available at http://aifawh.org/struggles-and-experiences/centre.

employed in primary sector jobs, particularly poor working people, both in rural and urban areas.

By denying these more than 8 million working people the status of workers, the government has been extracting billions of rupees' worth of unpaid labour every year from these poor, mostly women workers in the rural areas. Thus, scheme workers have been subsidising the government, which in turn has handed over huge amounts of money by way of "incentives" to large domestic and foreign corporations.

Any government committed to the welfare of its citizens should provide social services as basic entitlements to all, but in India, they are provided through "schemes" that have no statutory guarantee of being continued. Their continuation depends on the whims and fancies of the government of the day, which can freely manipulate them by cutting down budgetary allocations, changing the norms, privatising them, or withdrawing them altogether. All of these actions have been tried with regard to schemes such as ICDS, NHM, and MDM over the last two decades.

The government's treatment of these workers and the schemes they implement reflects its attitude towards the marginalised and poorer sections of society. The necessity of the poor, particularly of women, to support their families is exploited by the government, which compels them to work for pathetic wages. The workers, as well as the high-level bureaucrats who formulate these schemes, know quite well that their work in these schemes does not arise out of a desire to serve society without any monetary returns; they must earn a living. Given the low income of rural households, particularly agricultural households, even the meagre amount earned by working in government schemes becomes significant for household sustenance. In addition to the more or less regular and guaranteed income, though low, there is also a lingering hope that working in a government scheme might one day open up a chance to become a regularised government employee with job security and social security benefits; this hope continues to drive these millions of workers to continue working and fighting for their rights.

The general attitude prevailing in society is that taking care of the family, providing food, and looking after children, the sick, and the elderly, is the responsibility of women. By utilising their services in various schemes related to health, education of children, providing food, and so on, the government seeks to extend these jobs which women perform for their own families, in the name of "social service." The scheme workers are expected to provide their services for free, as they do for their own families. Whatever meagre payment they receive is made to appear as a favour, as an "honorarium" for which the women scheme workers are expected to be grateful. The few men who are also employed in these schemes are also paid a low honorarium. Furthermore, poor women with no support or family obligations can be coerced into spending their entire time and energy on this scheme-based "social service."

To elaborate on these issues, we examine the scheme-wise working conditions in the following sections.

Anganwadi Workers

Integrated Child Development Services (ICDS) is the oldest of all existing Government of India schemes. All its predecessors were terminated within a few years of their launch, some even before they could take off. Started in 1975, ICDS has been proclaimed by the government to be the largest and most comprehensive scheme for child development in the world.

Under ICDS, one anganwadi centre (AWC) is established for a population of around 1,000; this population criterion is lower for tribal and hilly areas. One anganwadi worker and one anganwadi helper run an anganwadi centre, which provides six basic services: supplementary nutrition, preschool education, health checks, immunisation, referral services, and health and nutrition education to women in the reproductive age group.

Despite the fact the ICDS is a holistic programme for child development, it took the government more than 35 years to universalise it, at least on paper. This was done only after a strong demand from anganwadi employees' unions and the interventions of several child rights groups, including prolonged legal battles in the Supreme Court, which ultimately ordered firm directives.[6]

The educational qualification required for an anganwadi worker is completion of Class 10. However, today, large numbers of graduates and postgraduates are working as anganwadi workers, and there are large numbers of graduates even among the anganwadi helpers. This reflects the lack of appropriate employment opportunities for educated women in rural areas, particularly those who cannot afford to leave their families and travel for work.

The current monthly remuneration paid by the Government of India for anganwadi workers and helpers is Rs 4,500 and Rs 2,250, respectively. Initially, ICDS was totally funded by the Government of India except for the supplementary nutrition component, but the government has gradually reduced its share to 60 per cent. Accordingly, the Union government now pays only Rs 2,700 and Rs 1,350, respectively, of the workers' and helpers'

---

[6] The Supreme Court, in its interim orders of November 2001, April 2004, October 2004, and December 2006, directed the Government of India to universalise coverage of the ICDS scheme (Ministry of Women and Child Development, 2012).

honorarium; the balance has to be borne by State governments. Under pressure from organised movements led by CITU and other central trade unions, several State governments have raised the remuneration amount. Thus, different State governments pay different amounts, depending on the bargaining power of the unions in the States.[7]

What is appalling is the extent of unpaid labour sought to be extracted from anganwadi workers by the government. Many tasks totally unrelated to their ICDS work are thrust upon them under threat of termination of services. These include conducting different types of surveys related to ration cards, hand pumps, toilets in the village, disease prevalence, disabilities, beggars, and stray dogs; taking photographs of people resorting to open defecation and shaming those individuals as part of the Swachh Bharat Abhiyan ("Clean India Mission"); and working as booth-level officers during elections, and as census workers during the decennial Census of India.

Most of these additional tasks are not paid for; and even if they are, it is a meagre amount given after much delay. More important than non-payment or delayed payment is the impact of these additional tasks on the implementation of ICDS, for which these workers were hired in the first place. The anganwadi worker and helper have to keep the anganwadi centre open for six hours, and the AWW must spend an hour on home visits every day in addition to maintaining different records and registers, which takes at least one hour. Since running an anganwadi centre is a full-time job, forcing AWWs to do other non-ICDS jobs means that the services provided by the anganwadi centre suffers, thus defeating the very purpose of ICDS.

After the issues of anganwadi employees were raised in Parliament and by representations to successive Prime Ministers, the Parliamentary Committee on Empowerment of Women examined the issue and placed its report before the Lok Sabha in August 2011. Asserting that there was a need to assess the workload of anganwadi workers, it stated:

> The Committee note with concern that every rural based programme in the country today is put on the fragile shoulders of the AWWs/AWHs. To make matters worse, some States take work from them even without paying extra or with very nominal payment. The Committee, therefore, desire that Ministry of Women and Child Development should take up the matter with the States and

---

[7] For example, the total amount paid to anganwadi workers in Andhra Pradesh is Rs 11,500 out of which only Rs 2,700 is paid by the Union government and the rest by the State government. Similarly, in Telangana an anganwadi worker is paid Rs 10,500, of which only Rs 2,700 is paid by the Union government. This is the situation is many States including Tamil Nadu, Kerala, Puducherry, Karnataka, Maharashtra, Punjab, and Madhya Pradesh.

direct them not to assign non-ICDS work to Anganwadi Workers. (Committee on Empowerment of Women 2011, p. 34)

The situation remains unchanged even after eight years. The Committee made another important recommendation:

The Committee are happy to note that the Government of India has doubled their honoraria . . . to Rs 3,000/- and Rs 1,500/- . . . for AWWs/AWHs respectively. However, the Committee note that it took 36 years and seven revisions for the honoraria to reach the current figures. This has happened because of not having a definite procedure/methodology for effecting the revisions. The Committee are of the strong view that the valuable services rendered by AWWs/AWHs to the children in this country need to be recognised and their motivation levels need to be boosted continually. The Committee, therefore, recommend that a mechanism should be evolved for periodic review/revision of their honoraria and benefits like yearly increments and dearness allowance linked with consumer price index should be worked out. (Committee on Empowerment of Women 2011, p. 37)

The Report of the Parliamentary Committee was placed before the Lok Sabha in 2011, a few months after the remuneration given to anganwadi workers and helpers was revised by the government. Though the next revision was made in 2018, on the eve of the seventeenth Lok Sabha elections, no mechanism has since been evolved for periodic review or revision of these "wages." Even now, neither anganwadi workers and helpers nor any of the scheme workers are paid a dearness allowance linked to the consumer price index.

Emphasising the need for pensions and other benefits to anganwadi workers and helpers, the Parliamentary Committee said:

. . . the Committee regret to note the indifference of the Central Government towards extending any type of retirement benefits to AWWs/AWHs, be it in the form of pension or in the form of lump sum. As these workers are the backbone of a sustainable support system in the care of children and women belonging to under-privileged sections, the Committee recommend that the Ministry of Women and Child Development should either provide a lump sum as parting gift to AWWs/AWHs when they retire or should work out with Pension Fund Regulatory and Development Authority the modalities of extending pension benefits to the Anganwadi workers and helpers. For this purpose, the Central Government should set up a special national Fund with adequate allocation. (Committee on Empowerment of Women 2011, p. 39)

Currently, this recommendation too remains only on paper.

Mid-Day Meal Workers

The conditions of nearly 2.7 million mid-day meal workers are even worse than that of anganwadi workers. The exception here is Tamil Nadu, where the Nutritious Noon Meal Programme was started well before the national Mid-Day Meal Scheme. Though the workers of this programme are not recognised as government employees, they receive dearness allowance, regular pay revision, and certain other benefits.

The Indian government contends that mid-day meal workers are "part-time workers" engaged only for three to four hours a day to cook and serve meals to schoolchildren. The fact, however, is that it takes at least five to six hours a day to prepare the materials for cooking, to cook and serve the food, wash the utensils, and clean the kitchen and dining spaces. In addition, these workers are often made to clean and sweep the school premises as well. Thus, there is no rationale behind fixing Rs 1,000 a month, i.e. less than Rs 35 a day, as the "honorarium" for five to six hours of work, when the daily minimum wage for unskilled workers is around ten times that amount in many States. Furthermore, this paltry amount is paid for only 10 months in a year. A representative of the Department of School Education and Literacy stated as follows at the 45th session of the Indian Labour Conference (ILC): "The Department is also considering a proposal to enhance the honorarium from Rs 1,000 to Rs 1,500 for the year 2013–14 and 2014–15 and further to Rs 2,000 for the years 2015–16 and 2016–17" (Ministry of Labour and Employment 2013, p. 19). This is probably still under "consideration" after more than six years. Meanwhile, the remuneration paid to mid-day meal workers by the Government of India remains Rs 1,000. Even when an enhancement in the remuneration of anganwadi workers and helpers and Accredited Social Health Activists (ASHAs) was announced in September 2018, mid-day meal workers were ignored altogether.

In most States, the task of cooking is given to women's self-help groups, members of which take turns to cook and serve. While the government provides subsidised rice or wheat through ration shops, the women have to buy other necessities like pulses, vegetables, and oil. In several States, they are also required to provide eggs at least twice a week. The problem is that while the women must invest money to buy these items, the government does not provide them with regular reimbursements. There are many instances of mid-day meal workers not being reimbursed for over six months. They must, however, continue to feed the children – their own children as well as children of the village; whether by begging, borrowing or stealing, they find a way to feed them.

Needless to say, most schools do not have proper infrastructure for cooking, and mid-day meal workers often sustain burns and other injuries.[8] They are not, however, covered by any insurance or medical facilities, and of course, they receive no social security benefits or paid maternity leave.

Health Workers

The conditions of ASHAs (Accredited Social Health Activists) belie the "hope" in the Hindi acronym of their designation. The number of persons serviced by ASHAs is similar to that of anganwadi workers, i.e. one ASHA covers a population of 1,000 (with relaxation for tribal, hilly, and desert areas). In most cases an ASHA is a local woman, with adequate representation from disadvantaged groups; preferably married, but could also be widowed or divorced; and aged between 25 to 45 years. Though the formal educational qualification required is only Class 8, most ASHAs have completed Class 10 and many have graduate degrees (Ministry of Health and Family Welfare, 2011).

According to the government, "ASHA will be the first port of call for any health related demands of deprived sections of the population, especially women and children, who find it difficult to access health services" (National Health Mission). The duties of an ASHA include providing information and creating awareness on health, nutrition, basic sanitation, hygiene, healthy living and working conditions, and health and family welfare services among the deprived sections. ASHAs are also expected to mobilise local people towards health planning and accessing health services, and are required to provide a minimum package of curative care for diarrhoea, fever, tuberculosis, and first aid for minor injuries. Their responsibility with respect to maternal health is primarily to counsel women on birth preparedness, safe delivery, breast-feeding, immunisation, contraception, prevention of common reproductive tract infections, and care of the young. However, they also have to arrange escorts or accompany pregnant women and children requiring treatment to the nearest health facility. In addition to all of the above responsibilities, ASHAs are supposed to be depot holders for essential provisions like oral rehydration therapy (ORT), iron folic acid (IFA) tablets, chloroquine, disposable delivery kits, oral pills, and condoms, as well as to promote household toilet construction. Furthermore, they are required to inform Sub Centres and Primary Health Centres about births and deaths in the village, alongside any unusual health problems and outbreak of diseases. Ideally, all these tasks are fulfilled through continuous training and upgradation of skills, spread over two years or more.

[8] Accidents were reported in the all-India working committee meetings of the Mid-Day Meal Workers' Federation of India (affiliated to CITU).

What is the order of remuneration ASHAs receive? According to the government, the above-mentioned tasks are not time-consuming, and an ASHA, being an "activist," can manage to do them in addition to her own jobs and responsibilities, whether domestic or livelihood-related. She is not paid a fixed remuneration or even an "honorarium," only an "incentive" which is piece-rated and fixed according to tasks. For example, a sum of money is paid for ensuring a pregnant woman gets three prescribed medical checks including immunisation, for accompanying a pregnant woman to the hospital for delivery and ensuring that she gives birth in the hospital, for ensuring a child gets immunised and is breast-fed, and so on. These tasks may also have accompanying technicalities: for example, if the ASHA is not present in the room when a woman has a hospital birth, she will not receive her incentive even if she had accompanied the woman to the hospital. Altogether, these incentives may total to around Rs 2,000 in a month.

After long and arduous struggles by unions of ASHAs in different States, several State governments have agreed to pay a fixed remuneration in addition to the incentives, or adjust the incentives in such a way that ASHAs would receive a guaranteed monthly income. Despite working for the health of the community, ASHAs themselves do not have paid maternity leave or holidays, social security benefits, or even a physical space where they can wait in hospitals.

Other Scheme Workers

The relatively new Yashoda or Mamta scheme was implemented under the National Health Mission through the Norway India Partnership Initiative in Bihar, Madhya Pradesh, Odisha, and Rajasthan (Norway India Partnership Initiative 2010). The scheme has detailed guidelines that pertain to work allotment, remuneration, incentives, punishments, and duties, as well as describe the required feedback and assessment to test the technical knowledge and counselling skills of the Yashodas (see Appendix 12.1).

The guidelines list the responsibilities of these workers in detail. Yashodas are a crucial part of the maternity ward, responsible for the quality of maternal and newborn care. They primarily provide counselling to mothers on self-care, post-natal care, breast-feeding techniques, and immunisation schedules. Yashodas are also expected to help mothers get registered as Janani Suraksha Yojana (JSY) beneficiaries.

Similar guidelines relating to recruitment criteria and process, training, assessment, supervision, monitoring, rewards and punishments, honorarium, etc., are prescribed for all scheme workers including anganwadi workers and helpers and ASHAs, and can be found on the websites of the concerned ministries. While there are detailed and specific guidelines for all aspects pertaining to the work of scheme workers, the government does not recognise them as workers. Rather, the government refers to them as "volunteers" or "social workers" to avoid paying minimum wages and providing benefits such as pensions and leave. The government considered the demands of the organised struggles of anganwadi workers and helpers and ASHAs for better remuneration and other benefits while formulating the guidelines for the Yashoda scheme. To thwart any attempt at raising grievances, the government has prescribed that 20 per cent of Yashodas should be replaced every third year to ensure that the threat of losing income discourages the formation of unions.

Trade Union Demands

In 2013, the 45th session of the Indian Labour Conference (ILC) held a discussion on "Service Conditions, Wages, and Social Security for Various Categories of Workers Employed in Different Central Government and State Government Schemes (Anganwadi, Mid-Day Meal, ASHA, Sarva Shiksha Abhiyan, and other schemes under various ministries of Central Government)," on the initiative of the central trade unions. The ILC, which is the highest tripartite body in the country comprising Central and State government representatives, employers' organisations, and central trade unions, made several important recommendations related to scheme workers. The most important of these recommendations was for scheme workers to be recognised as workers, and not as volunteers or honorary workers. Further, the ILC put forth that scheme workers should be paid minimum wages, and receive social security benefits like pension, maternity benefit, and a one-time gratuity or a lump sum payment even for those already retired (particularly anganwadi workers and helpers). It also proposed that workers have the right to organise and bargain collectively. To regularise the employment of scheme workers, the ILC recommended that the respective departments under which these schemes operate should formulate "Employment Standing Orders" wherever they do not exist.

These recommendations were reiterated at the 46th session of the ILC held in 2015, but no initiative has yet been undertaken by the Government of India to implement them. Furthermore, no ILC has been held under the present Bharatiya Janata Party-led regime.

Conclusion

Proper provision of basic necessities, presently extended in an ad-hoc manner, as entitlements to all citizens, as well as decent and dignified working conditions to the workers who provide these services, will greatly improve parameters related to education, health, wages, income, and gender equality in our country. A government committed to neoliberalism, however, cannot be expected to do this. Over the last two decades, attempts have been made to hand over the responsibility of implementing these basic services to private players including large NGOs. For example, the Mid-Day Meal Scheme is sought to be handed over to NGOs like ISKCON, Akshaya Patra, Naandi Foundation, etc. Similarly, anganwadi centres are sought to be "adopted" by corporates, freshly cooked food is slated to be replaced by packed and ready-to-eat food against the advice of nutrition experts, Primary Health Centres are being handed over to private hospitals, and direct benefit transfers (DBT) or cash transfers are being proposed and implemented in some cases. Budgetary allocations in the social sector are being drastically diminished. These measures have not only put livelihoods and incomes of scheme workers in jeopardy, but billions of poor women and children, particularly in the rural areas, will be deprived of the small benefits these programmes and schemes have provided. The idea appears to be to ultimately dismantle these schemes and hand over these basic services to market forces.

Any demand from workers for higher remuneration is denied and, ironically, explained away by lack of funds. This, even as wealth is created by the working people in rural and urban areas, by men and women, by workers and peasants. In every year of the past decade, according to budget records, the government has provided over Rs 5,000 billion in tax concessions to large corporations and businesses, and every year, tax evasion by the very wealthy amounts to over Rs 7,000 billion.

In February 2019, a meeting of a group of intellectuals and experts from different fields in New Delhi indicated how resources could be mobilised to meet peoples' basic aspirations and necessities.[9] According to them, levying a 20 per cent inheritance tax, a progressive wealth tax for wealth above Rs 100 million, a corporate social tax linked to turnover rather than profit, green taxes to encourage lower carbon emissions, and a pollution tax would enable the government to resolve the lack of funds, which in turn could help expand

---

[9] In a meeting held at the Press Club of India (New Delhi), "Reclaiming the Republic," a group of concerned citizens including Justice A. P. Shah, Prashant Bhushan, Prabhat Patnaik, Jayati Ghosh, Srinath Reddy, Sujatha Rao, and Harsh Mander, released a "Manifesto for Change" (Bhushan and Bharadwaj 2019).

good-quality public education for all, provide health and other essential public services, and fill up employment vacancies wherever they exist. These additional resources, the group suggested, would allow the government to treat all workers (anganwadi workers and helpers, ASHAs, mid-day meal workers, etc.) as essential service workers and as regular government employees, and would provide the workers with employee benefits like maternity leave, universal pension, gratuity, etc. Further, the group estimated that increasing government expenditure on health care to 3 per cent of the GDP would enable the government to strengthen primary, preventive, and promotive health care, and improve health infrastructure by providing the necessary health staff and medical supplies as well as by employing two ASHAs, instead of one, with salaries and benefits at par with current government staff.

Around 8 million scheme workers, most of them women, have been discharging very important responsibilities in providing basic essential services to the masses, particularly women and children, in rural areas. On the one hand, they form an important section of rural non-agricultural workers contributing to the incomes of rural households. On the other hand, they have been enabling other rural workers, particularly women directly engaged in primary sector work, to perform their jobs by taking care of these workers' children's education and health. Thus, scheme workers have contributed to the human development of millions in our country.

The work done by scheme workers, however, is not properly recognised by the government. Most of them perform tasks like cooking, feeding, taking care of children and their health and education, which are generally perceived as women's jobs and thus undervalued. The government utilises this general perception about care work to exploit these workers and treat them as "volunteers," though it clearly knows that they do not do these jobs in such a capacity; women's unpaid work within the family is thus extended to society and continues to be highly underpaid. The government utilises their situation of unemployment to extract cheap labour from them as they desperately need to earn whatever they can to support their families; it is an atrocious form of government exploitation in a supposedly democratic society.

Scheme workers have been organising and fighting for improved wages and working conditions in almost all the States. Wherever they could unite and fight, they have been able to improve their conditions to some extent, even though their basic demand for recognition as workers remains unfulfilled. Many scheme workers, such as anganwadi workers and helpers and ASHAs, have also been trying to gain the support of the people they serve, the scheme beneficiaries, by campaigning among them. They understand that such support can significantly increase the impact of their struggle. A strong joint movement of scheme workers and the larger public, particularly the beneficiaries of the schemes, demanding increased allocation of funds to ensure the schemes' effective implementation as well as recognition of scheme workers as workers can surely help improve both the scheme workers' working conditions and the schemes themselves for the benefit of the poor, particularly in rural areas. Our country has the human and financial resources, but requires the political will to pursue "people-first policies" by taking bold decisions to reverse the neoliberal policies that only benefit a few.

References

Bhushan, P., and Bharadwaj, A. (2019), "Manifesto for Change: 'Reclaiming the Republic: 19 Issues for Elections 2019'," available at https://scroll.in/article/912101/manifesto-for-change-reclaiming-the-republic-19-issues-for-elections-2019, viewed on 7 May 2019.

Centre for Budget and Governance Accountability (CBGA) (2011), "Budget Track, Volume 8, Track 2, August 2011," available at http://www.cbgaindia.org/wp-content/uploads/2016/03/BT_Vol_8_Track_2.pdf, viewed on 2 October 2019.

Centre for Budget and Governance Accountability (CBGA) (2016), "Public Financing of School Education in India: A Fact Sheet," available at http://www.cbgaindia.org/wp-content/uploads/2016/12/Fact-Sheet-CBGA-and-CRY.pdf, viewed on 2 October 2019.

Centre for Budget and Governance Accountability (CBGA) (2019), "Numbers that Count: An Assessment of the Union Budgets of NDA II," available at https://www.cbgaindia.org/wp-content/uploads/2019/02/Numbers-That-Count-An-Assessment-of-the-Union-Budgets-of-NDA-II.pdf, viewed on 2 October 2019.

Committee on Empowerment of Women (2011), *Working Conditions of Anganwadi Workers*, available at https://eparlib.nic.in/bitstream/123456789/63973/1/15_Empowerment_of_Women_8.pdf, viewed on 30 March 2020.

Comptroller and Auditor General of India (2012), "Universalisation of ICDS Scheme," *Performance Audit of ICDS Scheme*, Report No. 22, Chapter 3, pp. 15–24, available at https://cag.gov.in/sites/default/files/audit_report_files/Union_Performance_Civil_ICDS_Scheme%20_Ministry_Women_Child%20Development_22_2012_Chapter_3.pdf, viewed on 7 May 2019.

National Health Mission (n.d.), "About Accredited Social Health Activist," available at https://nhm.gov.in/index1.php?lang=1&level=1&sublinkid=150&lid=226, viewed on 12 December 2019.

Norway India Partnership Initiative (NIPI) (2010), *Operational Guidelines for Yashodas/Mamta: An Enabling Intervention for Quality Maternal and Newborn Care at the Facility Level*, available at https://www.undp.org/content/dam/india/docs/NIPI/Resources_ManualsAndGuidelines_YashodaOperationalGuidelines_New.pdf, viewed on 12 December 2019.

National Rural Health Mission (2011), *Update on the ASHA Programme*, available at http://nhsrcindia.org/sites/default/files/Update%20on%20ASHA%20Programme%20%20July%202011.pdf, viewed on 12 December 2019.

Ministry of Labour and Employment (2013), "Summary Record of Discussions of the 45th Session of Indian Labour Conference," 17–18 May, available at https://labour.gov.in/lcandilasdivision/list-indian-labour-conferences, viewed on 12 December 2019.

Palriwala, R., and Neetha, N. (2010), "Care Arrangements and Bargains: Anganwadi andPaid Domestic Workers in India," *International Labour Review*, vol. 149, no. 4, 17 March, pp. 511–27.

Press Information Bureau (2017), "DAY-NRLM – Transforming Lives through Livelihood Thrust," 6 April, available at http://pib.nic.in/newsite/PrintRelease.aspx?relid=160572, viewed on 7 May 2019.

Razavi, S. (2007), "The Political and Social Economy of Care in a Development Context: Conceptual Issues, Research Questions and Policy Options," Gender and Development Programme Paper Number 3, June, available at http://www.unrisd.org/80256B3C005BCCF9/(httpAuxPages)/2DBE6A93350A7783C12573240036D5A0/$file/Razavi-paper.pdf, viewed on 12 December 2019.

Som, M. (2016), "Volunteerism to Incentivisation: Changing Priorities of Mitanins Work in Chhattisgarh," *Indian Journal of Gender Studies*, vol. 23, no. 1, 18 January, pp. 26–42, available at doi:10.1177/0971521515612862, viewed on 12 December 2019.

Supreme Court of India (2016), "Civil Appeal No. 213/2013," available at https://indiankanoon.org/doc/106416990/, viewed on 7 May 2019.

APPENDIX *12.1*
OPERATIONAL GUIDELINES FOR YASHODAS/MAMTA

The Norway India Partnership Initiative (NIPI) is a project implemented in Bihar, Madhya Pradesh, Odisha, and Rajasthan, under the National Health Mission. *Operational Guidelines for Yashodas/Mamta: An Enabling Intervention for Quality Maternal and Newborn Care at the Facility Level*, published by NIPI in 2010, describes the duties of a Yashoda:

I am part of Yashoda process, and a new member of the maternity ward team. I have several responsibilities:

I welcome the pregnant woman heartily and make sure that she relaxes, and reassures that she is in a safe place and among people, who care for her.

I help her to get registered as JSY beneficiary.

I get information on her status from accompanying ASHA/family member ANC card and inform the nurse if she needs extra care.

I provide moral support to her in the labour room.

I observe the nurse and learn to weigh the newborn, wrap her well and support mother to initiate breastfeeding.

I ensure the cleanliness including toilets and functionality of the postnatal ward during my shift.

I counsel the mother on basic hygiene practices to avoid infection for the newborn.

I ensure that the baby's bed is clean; no one is sitting or eating near the bed and not crowding around the bed.

I support the mother by showing her the correct positioning for breastfeeding.

I educate her on the importance of exclusive breastfeeding, keeping the baby warm, and seeking help of a nurse when the baby is sick.

I also ensure that BCG and polio dose is given before the baby leaves the hospital; inform mother about the immunisation schedule, when and where she can get it done in her village.

I inform her on birth spacing options and where she can get the services when she goes home.

I maintain records of all the vital information on the baby and the mother.

I ensure that each mother leaves the facility as a satisfied person, with more understanding on basic newborn care and happy about the cleanliness and support in the hospital.

No work is too small or too big for me as long as it can help the mother and newborn. I am proud of the fact that I can empower each mother with information that can build her confidence to take care of her baby. (NIPI 2010, p. 2)

The guidelines include several aspects related to the engagement of Yashodas, their work allotment, payment, etc., and lay out the following procedures:

a. Placing Local Newspaper Advertisement: This will be placed by District Immunisation Officer (DOI) or Chief Medical Officer (CMO)/Civil Surgeon/RCH Nodal Officer/DPM with permission from District Health Society (DHS).

b. Suggested criterion for selection:
   - A local woman living within the municipal limits
   - Has completed 8th grade as a minimum
   - She agrees to work as a volunteer
   - She will receive performance-linked incentives
   - Her engagement as volunteer worker does not entitle her to claim the regular position in the system
   - Free from communicable diseases, subject to clearance by the Medical Officer
   - Willing to work on rotational basis including night shifts.
     Decision on the criteria are to be finalised at the district level by the DHS and/or Rogi Kalyan Samiti (RKS) of the hospital. These agencies must have a process for screening of the applicants within a limited time since large numbers may apply for a few positions.

c. Shortlisted candidates will be invited for interview. (*Ibid.*, p. 18)

On duty allocation, the guidelines state that in the context of all the mothers and newborns receiving the services of a Yashoda, it must be ensured that the duty roster is prepared such that work is distributed among all the Yashodas equitably. All Yashodas will be entitled to receive the same amount of incentives according to the duty roster.

Additionally, Yashoda services must be available in the ward at all times without any break. Currently, the three shift timings are: morning duty (08:00–14:00), afternoon (14:00–22:00), and night (22:00–08:00). The supervisory cadre must ensure that the shift timings are readjusted in such a way that there is no gap in service.

It has been observed that varied standards of duty allotment to Yashodas, including inter-district variation, are adopted by the States. In Rajasthan, the shift is organised so as to give every fourth day off to Yashodas. In Odisha, Yashodas do 10 days' shift duty followed by night duty on a rotation basis. In Madhya Pradesh, Yashodas are given every sixth day off. The facilities, as well as the Yashodas, seem to have adjusted well to this duty allocation pattern in their respective States.

While the districts have their own rationale for fixing rotational duty suited to their contexts, care must be exercised to ensure that all Yashodas have equal work and equal rest. The Rajasthan model offers 27/4 shifts of work and 91 rest days in a year, while in other States, Yashodas work for 313 days and receive 52 rest days. The Rajasthan model seems to facilitate the Yashoda to function optimally (since she gets rest after night duty) without compromising the quality of work and to help her balance her personal life. The other three States may explore the possibility of readjusting the schedule such that Yashodas get an optimal number of off-days as in the case of Rajasthan, especially since they do not have the opportunity to avail any other leave.

The guidelines also include measures for "Periodic Internal Assessment and Feedback." It is essential to assess the technical knowledge and counselling skills of a Yashoda every six months and gauge whether she has acquired the expected standard to function effectively. This will be a useful input for refresher training as well.

There are specific guidelines for human resource management:

> To remain a catalytic process, the Yashoda intervention has to be innovative. In order to have in-built self resurgence and keep Yashodas alert, it is suggested that the HR policy should consider inducting 1/5 of new Yashodas every third year by replacing from the existing pool. This method would ensure continuation of experienced staff but induction of new Yashodas periodically. (*Ibid.*, p. 16)

13

Women's Participation in NREGA
A Review of the Literature

Smita Ramnarain and Smriti Rao

The implementation of the Mahatma Gandhi National Rural Employment Guarantee Act (MGNREGA or NREGA henceforth) in 2006 in 100 of the poorest districts in India, and its expansion to the whole country in 2008, has been globally hailed as a landmark exercise in the provision of social protection and poverty reduction. Between 2015 and 2019, nearly 9.7 billion work-days were generated under this scheme in total, with women accounting for more than half of these work-days.

The NREGA has come to occupy an important space in the literature on public policy and economics as an example of a large-scale employment guarantee programme in a time of global concern about employment growth. Based on a range of studies that point to its positive impact on wages, reducing migration, and welfare for participating households, the general consensus appears to be that the programme has operated largely as intended, despite concerns about inefficiency, corruption, and lack of bureaucratic competence (Basole 2019). There is also the important caveat that the programme currently includes only about 15 per cent of the rural Indian working-age population on average, with considerable variation across States. Its positive effects thus have had a limited impact upon the rural economy as a whole. Indeed, the literature largely concludes that this programme deserves greater administrative attention and funding, and has the potential to expand even to urban India (*ibid.*).

This chapter shares the generally positive view of NREGA in the literature. It has been written with the awareness that any expansion of the programme will have to be fought for, given that the current government in India has not always shared this positive assessment of NREGA.[1] This chapter is also

---

[1] In an address to the Parliament in March 2015, Prime Minister Narendra Modi called NREGA a "living monument" of poverty (https://www.financialexpress.com/india-news/pm-narendra-modi-denounces-communalism-attacks-congress-on-poverty/48577/). More recently, however, the Modi government has praised NREGA and hailed its achievements over the past decade as a cause for "national pride and celebration" (https://www.business-standard.com/article/economy-

written with the awareness that at this point, the majority of the programme's beneficiaries in most States are women, and that any future expansion of the programme will depend upon their ability and willingness to mobilise in its support. Understanding what has drawn women into the programme may be critical to producing such a mobilisation.

The programme's success in including women (as well as marginalised social groups) is quite remarkable, given women's relative exclusion from Indian politics and also from much of the market/paid economy. The relatively high participation of women arguably has been a surprise, at least with respect to the original design of NREGA. The fact that the programme included a 33 per cent quota for women suggests that the planners were sceptical about whether women would be included in the absence of quotas. Yet, as per official data, by 2017–18 all States in India, with the exception of Jammu and Kashmir, reported women's participation rates in excess of the quota (Department of Rural Development 2020). According to official NREGA records, the share of female work-days in total NREGA work-days provided has risen (from 48 per cent in 2009–10 to 53 per cent in 2017–18) even in years when the overall provision of work-days through NREGA fell (*ibid.*). Viewed against the larger history of quotas for women in politics or employment, where the impact of such quotas has been highly variable across contexts, high participation of women is a remarkable achievement (Krook 2006).

The programme has a number of features that distinguish it from previous anti-poverty or public works programmes, many of which have been stymied by corruption, bureaucratic inefficiency, and the exclusion of large numbers of the poor due to targeting practices. First, NREGA is based on a right-to-work principle, making the State government legally accountable for providing at least 100 days of minimum wage employment per year to every rural household that demands work. If the state is unable to provide the applicant with a work assignment under this scheme when it is demanded, it must pay an unemployment allowance after fifteen days of the application. Further, workers must be paid for work performed within fifteen days of work completion. Secondly, there is no explicit targeting or screening of applicants who wish to participate in the programme. As such, the programme is universal, demand-driven, and available to any rural household that has a programme job card and wishes to avail it. The wage employment – provided on public works projects aimed at building community assets such as wells, tanks, canals, and roads –

policy/10-years-on-centre-hails-mgnrega-as-national-pride-116020200037_1.html). At the time of writing, it remains to be seen, however, if these sentiments lead to further concrete support of the programme.

is manually arduous and acts as a self-selecting mechanism. The assumption here is that an applicant would choose this work only after weighing other options and finding the scheme's hard manual labour paid at minimum wage worthwhile. Thirdly, the programme includes explicit gender mainstreaming provisions, discussed in greater detail in the next section, to encourage female participation.

The question of why and how the programme included women is at the heart of this chapter. We argue below that the literature largely points to supply-side features of the NREGA to explain its success in including women. Without denying that these design features are important and deserve to be replicated in other such programmes across the world, we think that the literature misses the connection between NREGA participation and larger macro-structural changes in India. These larger changes, which operate across gender and class, need to be connected to NREGA to give a complete picture of why women have become major beneficiaries of this programme. We argue that a confluence of factors has produced an outcome whereby more women take up NREGA work, but this is a contingent outcome with complex implications for the well-being of the women themselves.

Further, supply-side or proximate factors such as gender mainstreaming and/or effective implementation only partially explain the programme's overall success in employing women. They do not explain why women seek manually arduous work in such large numbers, in the first place. In other words, the so-called demand-side factors are comparatively neglected. In this chapter, we review the existing literature and provide a critical analysis of three such factors driving overall participation and female participation in particular. The first is that due to an unevenly distributed agrarian crisis, rural households have had to adopt a variety of gendered coping strategies to piece together their livelihoods, of which participation in NREGA is one. Secondly, the non-agricultural sector has been largely closed off to women and has provided them with few opportunities to make a living. Finally, we connect women's participation in NREGA to their burdens of reproductive work. In the larger context of recent transformations in the agrarian economy in India, these factors must be studied in greater detail.

A more nuanced analysis of women's participation in NREGA is important for a few different reasons:

(i) In a country with generally low female labour force participation, participation in NREGA may suggest an appetite for employment among women that is thwarted by larger macro-structural factors, not just gender bias or "culture" but the nature and structure of the economy.

(ii) It may also be the case that not all of women's participation in NREGA is cause for celebration, if some of it is driven by dire inequalities of class, gender, and caste.

(iii) These complexities are important to keep in mind for those like us who are interested in seeing the lessons of NREGA applied to other such employment guarantee programmes in other parts of the world, as well as being improved upon/expanded within India.

Participation in NREGA: A Review of the Literature

We begin by discussing existing explanations for participation of the rural poor in NREGA. Marxian studies of NREGA place class at the forefront of the analysis, while in non-Marxian explanations, governance or state commitment and capacity are put forward as the main reasons for variations in NREGA's functioning (Pellisery and Jalan 2011). Notably, Marxian explanations are relatively silent on the ways in which gender and class may *intersect* to shape patterns of participation in NREGA, a gap that we hope to fill in this chapter. In this section, we review the existing literature that discusses the determinants of participation – both overall and that of women – in NREGA. Table 13.1 briefly summarises the main factors emphasised by select literature on NREGA participation.

Overall Participation and Outcomes:
Marxian vs. Non-Marxian Explanations

Non-Marxian studies attribute observed differential outcomes to institutions and governance, and thus to the state's commitment and capacity. For instance, the effective implementation of NREGA in States such as Rajasthan and Andhra Pradesh is attributed to committed leadership and governance structures held accountable by an active civil society in the form of non-governmental and advocacy organisations (Menon 2008; Reddy 2013). In Kerala, the effective delivery of NREGA has been associated with decentralisation of decision-making powers in scheme implementation to panchayats and women's village-level groups (Sudarshan *et al.* 2010; Kannan and Jagajeevan 2013). On the other hand, when it comes to ineffective delivery of the programme in poor-performing States or districts, studies point to a lack of awareness-building on the scheme (Bhatia and Drèze 2006), inefficiencies and corruption in implementation (Ambasta *et al.* 2008), and elite capture (Kumbhar 2013; Bhatia and Drèze 2006).

However, the question to be posed to such non-Marxian explanations then

Table 13.1 *Summary of select literature on factors impacting NREGA effectiveness*

Factors behind effective implementation	State(s)	Reference
Effective bureaucracy, high governance capacity, committed leadership	Rajasthan, Andhra Pradesh, Tripura	Reddy *et al.* (2010), Reddy (2013), Swaminathan (2019)
Presence of prominent civil society and advocacy organisations	Rajasthan	Menon (2008)
Physical proximity of particular villages to urban centres or to formal political institutions	Karnataka	Pattenden (2011a), Pattenden (2015)
Social proximity to state	Andhra Pradesh	Veeraraghavan (2017)
Ruling party connection to implementation villages/districts	Punjab	Gill *et al.* (2013)
Diffusion of power to labouring classes and castes	Tamil Nadu, Andhra Pradesh	Carswell and de Neve (2014), Harriss *et al.* (2010)
Participation of women's self-help groups and panchayats	Kerala	Sudarshan *et al.* (2010), Kannan and Jagajeevan (2013)
Factors behind ineffective implementation	**Study area(s)**	**Reference**
Entrenched income or power inequalities/elite capture	Uttar Pradesh, Jharkhand, Odisha	Bhatia and Drèze (2006), Kumbhar (2013)
State governments having control over productive resources and local institutions	Andhra Pradesh, Karnataka	Reddy (2013), Pattenden (2011b)
Lack of awareness about the programme	Jharkhand, Chhattisgarh, Odisha	Banerjee and Saha (2010)
Corruption and administrative inefficiencies	Bihar, Madhya Pradesh	Reddy *et al.* (2010), Ambasta *et al.* (2008)

Note: The references are illustrative and not comprehensive, as multiple factors would be involved in each State.
Source: Authors' compilation.

is: what causes governance structures to be inadequate in the first place? While mainstream explanations might hint at elite capture, the nature of such capture and its consequences on the functioning of NREGA might be derived using the lens of class politics as done by Marxian analyses. Marxian explanations argue that understanding class and caste coalitions (which may frequently overlap) at the local level is key to understanding how NREGA functions and its outcomes at the State, district, or sub-district levels (Pattenden 2015; Roy 2015; McCartney and Roy 2016; Jakimow 2014). As Chibber (2012, p. 179) remarks, understanding "the degree of power and representation achieved by labouring groups" is critically connected to welfare policies implemented in capitalist contexts. This is more common in developing countries wherein existing policies for economic growth already have a bias towards asset holders as opposed to the asset-poor or landless. Given the powerful entrenched and local nature of rural class and caste relationships, poverty alleviation and social protection policies implemented before the NREGA – the public distribution system (PDS), the Integrated Rural Development Programme (IRDP), and various credit and extension programmes intended for rural farmers – have capitulated to some form of control by dominant class and caste groups (McCartney and Roy 2016). Although NREGA has, despite its size and scale, worked reasonably effectively as a rules-based welfare programme, intra- and inter-class relations have played a significant role in determining the efficacy and equitability of its implementation in different States (Pattenden 2015; Roy 2015; Veeraraghavan 2017).

From a Marxian political economy perspective, precisely due to its emphasis on rural workers' wages and enhancing their bargaining power, dominant rural classes – classes producing agricultural surpluses and hiring labour – remain either vehemently opposed or ambivalent at best to NREGA (see Jakimow 2014). At the State and district level, a process of "colonization, co-option and opposition" exists with respect to the relationship between dominant classes and the state, or between different rural classes (Jeffrey and Lerche 2000, p. 1). Studies therefore find that NREGA's outcomes too depend on the degree of control that these dominant classes are able to exercise over its implementation. More antagonistic forms of control exercised by dominant classes have included militant tactics to dissuade participation, such as delaying wage payments or implementation, or increasing mechanisation (Pattenden 2015; Gill *et al.* 2013; Kumbhar 2013). Less antagonistic forms have involved the use of NREGA opportunities to deter out-migration, timing NREGA works during slack seasons, and using labour for productivity enhancements on the lands of surplus-producing farmers (Pattenden 2015). Thus, where a non-fragmented, active, and dominant class (or caste) is able to function in a unified manner to preserve its own interests, it is able to acquire a greater say in how the programme is run and the extent of their own participation. As a corollary, if rural working classes remain fragmented and are unable to act cohesively to preserve the benefits of the programme, an insufficient counter exists to elite capture at the local level. The distribution of power between rural classes plays a significant role in determining participation and the effectiveness with which NREGA functions as a demand-based programme, with interesting implications for collective action (see Pattenden 2010).

There is a further disjuncture in the political economy literature on NREGA.

Even as the scholarly Marxian literature neglects the intersection of gender and class, the genesis of NREGA reflects a concrete understanding of gender issues on the ground by Left women's organisations. For instance, though detractors argued that quotas would undermine the demand-driven nature of the scheme, or that there was 37 per cent women's participation in such public works schemes nationwide without any quotas, these women's organisations insisted on the quota due to concerns that the payment of minimum wage would lead to the displacement of women by men in NREGA (Gupta 2009; Armstrong 2014). As is clear from the data, however, women's participation far exceeded the quota; the reasons for this phenomenon are less clear from the literature, with the exception of studies that report NREGA to be relatively well-functioning in regions where women's collective action and organisations have played a significant part in labour organising (Sudarshan *et al.* 2010; Pattenden 2010, 2015). We do not fully understand, however, the degree to which women's participation is shaped by class, and the extent to which inequalities along gender and class dimensions determine access to the programme.

Women's Participation: Supply-Side Explanations

Existing studies focusing on explaining women's participation in NREGA point to the gender-sensitive provisions that make it especially attractive to women. While women have always participated in public works programmes – such as the Employment Guarantee Scheme in Maharashtra (a precursor to NREGA) (Dev 1995) – in large numbers in India, the provisions included in NREGA explicitly recognise the special role that public works programmes play in reducing poor rural women's vulnerability and ensuring a basic minimum level of social protection. The empowerment of vulnerable groups including women is an explicit goal of the programme (Department of Rural Development 2013, p. 3). Besides the quota for women of at least one-third of persons to whom work is allocated, the Act emphasises that equal wages be paid to women and men. This provision is significant given that women are frequently paid lower wages than men are for the same tasks. Further, the village panchayat issues a job card to the household listing all adult household members eligible to work, regardless of gender. Since the decision of how work is to be allocated is left to the members of the household, space is created, arguably, for the participation of women (Khera and Nayak 2009; Narayanan and Das 2014).

Gender-mainstreaming provisions are integrated into every level of the NREGA, from recruitment of supervisory staff to work-site amenities and wage payments. The guidelines emphasise that preference be given to women and differently abled persons in the recruitment of staff and supervisors in the programme (Department of Rural Development 2013, p. 28). Given instances of harassment and exploitation reported by women in previous public works programmes, NREGA prohibits the operation of middlemen or contractors, at least in theory,[2] leaving programme implementation to the village panchayat. To address mobility concerns that women in particular may have, the programme stipulates that work be provided within a five-kilometre radius of the applicant's home, and that women be given preference in the allocation of work sites closest to their homes (*ibid.*, p. 22; Narayanan and Das 2014). If five or more young children (below the age of six) accompany women workers to the work site, the programme provides for a crèche, with one woman worker deputed to care for the children at the prevalent wage rate (Department of Rural Development 2013, p. 66). To prevent male control over women's earnings, the programme guidelines specify that wage payments to women must be made into individual or, at the very least, joint bank accounts, rather than to the account of a spouse or male family member.

A wide variety of studies draw on conventional explanations around NREGA's gender-sensitivity in these provisions to explain women's participation. Further, women's participation is attributed to their "preference" for it, given that NREGA wages may be higher and more reliable than market wages and are seen to be provided by the government (Reddy *et al.* 2014; Reddy *et al.* 2010; Pankaj and Tankha 2010; Khera and Nayak 2009; Sudarshan *et al.* 2010). On the other hand, women's non-participation is frequently explained as the consequence of a lack of awareness of the scheme or the unavailability of child-care facilities in addition to the arduousness of the work, or implementation issues such as delayed payments or the presence of contractors (Khera and Nayak 2009; Datta and Singh 2012; Narayanan and Das 2014). The presence of "alternative income sources" or social norms preventing women's work also finds mention (Khera and Nayak 2009; Datta and Singh 2012). Occasionally, studies list certain systematic ways in which women are kept out of NREGA participation, wherein men workers feel that women workers slow them down or there is a preference for male workers who are seen as breadwinners (Khera and Nayak 2009, p. 9; Pellissery and Jalan 2011, p. 290; Pattenden 2015),[3]

---

[2] Contractors were also often accused of inflating muster rolls and harassment in previous public works schemes. While NREGA guidelines ban contractors completely, there have been reports of their continued presence in some areas (Vanaik and Siddhartha 2008). Since, however, payments for work are made directly to workers' accounts in NREGA, it is argued that this step mitigates the undue influence of contractors to a large extent (Drèze 2007).

[3] Khera and Nayak (2009) report instances where women workers are expected to make way for men. Pattenden (2015, p. 13) reports that since NREGA work in Dharwad, Karnataka was channelled through men, women's access to the work was reduced by the insistence that digging work be done in male–female pairs.

although other evidence points to lower rationing rates for female workers overall (Narayanan and Das 2014). The policy prescription emerging from this work is that better implementation and gender mainstreaming will encourage women's participation where it is low.

While the policy provisions outlined above are progressive and desirable, we are concerned that such a perspective is overly sanguine about the processes that increase women's participation in the programme, obscuring the larger macro-structural forces creating demand for NREGA employment in the first place. In other words, what looks like inclusion into the programme is a result of forms of exclusion based on gender and class that operate in the wider economy. Therefore, a more careful analysis of the intersections between class and gender, or what one might more conventionally call demand-side factors, is needed. We hope to briefly theorise some of those interactions here, hoping that they will stimulate further empirical research.

Women's Participation: Demand-Side Explanations

Feminist political economy focuses on the mutually constitutive relationship between gender and class, and the way in which this relationship can shape outcomes such as participation in NREGA. NREGA is, of course, an entitlement at the household level – each rural household is entitled to 100 days of work if so demanded. The question of who participates in the programme thus operates at two levels: the level of the household that receives the job card and demands NREGA work, and the level of the individual from the household who actually takes up the work when made available. To use Deere's (1990) term, "household relations" intersect with class relations to produce high or low levels of women's participation in NREGA. We do not mean to imply, however, that gender relations operate only at the intra-household level, whereas class relations are a household-level factor. Instead, as we argue below, gender and class intersect to shape which households respond as well as which individuals within a household respond to programmes like NREGA.

We looked at official NREGA data for 20 large States (i.e. States with more than 0.5 per cent of the population; we excluded overwhelmingly urban areas such as Delhi and the Union Territories) and computed an overall participation rate by State, defined as "total persons worked" per official NREGA data for 2017–18 as a percentage of the rural working-age population (per NSS 2011–12). We then compared this to the female share of person-days worked in NREGA, based on official 2017–18 data for the same 20 States. First, we found that for the major States, the overall participation rate in NREGA is positively correlated with the female share of NREGA workers, although the correlation is not very large. Secondly, we noted that of the 20 States, 12 now have female shares of total person-days above 45 per cent, and only in five States did the female share of person-days decline in 2017–18 as compared to 2011–12. In the largest States in the country, therefore, NREGA has become an increasingly female-dominated programme (see Table 13.2).

Even as overall participation has not increased, there is a clear pattern of

Table 13.2 *NREGA indicators, major States, rural India, 2011 and 2017* rates and shares in per cent

State	Overall participation rate, 2011	Overall participation rate, 2017	Change in overall participation (percentage points)	Female share of NREGA workers, 2011–12	Female share of NREGA workers, 2017–18	Change in female share (percentage points)
States with greater than 50% female shares						
Kerala	10	10	0	93	91	–2
Tamil Nadu	38	27	–11	74	86	12
Rajasthan	22	23	1	69	65	–4
Punjab	3	7	4	43	63	20
Himachal Pradesh	17	18	1	59	62	3
Andhra Pradesh	14	17	3	56	60	4
Uttaranchal	13	15	2	45	54	9
Chhattisgarh	51	37	–14	46	50	4
States with less than 50% female shares						
Haryana	4	4	0	36	49	13
West Bengal	20	20	0	33	48	15
Karnataka	19	16	–3	46	47	1
Bihar	5	6	1	29	47	18
Maharashtra	8	8	0	46	45	–1
Gujarat	9	6	–3	46	42	–4
Odisha	12	18	6	39	42	3
Assam	10	17	7	25	38	13
Madhya Pradesh	29	20	–9	43	37	–6
Jharkhand	20	15	–5	31	37	6
Uttar Pradesh	12	8	–4	17	35	18
J&K	12	21	9	19	28	9
India	16	15	–1	47	53	6

Note: Overall participation rate is the ratio of total persons who worked to total rural working-age population; female share of NREGA workers is the share of days worked by females to the total person-days worked in NREGA.
Source: Official NREGA records (www.nrega.nic.in).

rising female participation in NREGA, though there is uneven distribution of this participation at the State level and, as Desai *et al.* (2015) find, at the household level as well. The authors note that while lower-caste households do seem to participate at relatively high rates, poor households more generally seem to experience rationing, both at the level of the household, wherein they are unable to procure NREGA job cards, and at the level of individuals from the household who are able to procure work. As with much of the literature, Desai *et al.* (2015) attribute this phenomenon to failures of implementation and governance. They point out that variation in participation seems to be highest at the inter-village rather than inter-State level, and thus emphasise the role that quality of village governance plays in NREGA implementation. This variation in village-level participation could, of course, also be viewed in terms of the class–caste coalitional argument advanced by Marxian analyses.

Agrarian Crisis and Women's Work in the Rural Context

A key feature of Indian agriculture has been the steady decline in average landholdings among rural households with land, alongside a decline in the share of agricultural labour households (see also Ramachandran 2011; Rawal 2008). NSS data indicate that working-age members of households with more than 2 acres of land accounted for only 20 per cent of the rural working-age population in 2011–12, down from 32 per cent in 1993–94. At the same time, working-age members of marginal farmer households (with less than 2 acres of land) accounted for 18 per cent of the rural working-age population in 2011–12, as compared to 11 per cent in 1993–94. Combining working-age members of marginal farmer households with members of households whose income is primarily from casual labour gives us 60 per cent of the rural working-age population in 2011–12, as compared to 50 per cent in 1993–94.

The liberalisation policies implemented in the Indian economy – ostensibly designed to make production globally competitive, reduce barriers to trade, and shrink the role of the state through reductions in subsidies or licensing requirements – have hit the growing number of marginal farmers and the landless in India's rural economy particularly hard. While there are regional variations in the impacts of these policies, overall declines in agricultural extension services, credit, and price support systems have meant greater risk for famers even as underlying structural issues of rising costs, high levels of indebtedness, and vulnerability to rainfall shocks remain, leading to continuing reports of farmer suicides in different parts of the country. Agricultural productivity and employment declined over this entire period, alongside a decline in the number of agricultural wage workers and days of employment available to manual rural workers (Thomas 2012; Ramachandran 2011). For vulnerable marginal farmer and labouring households, migration, debt, and exploitative employment relations characterise the battle for survival in rural India (da Corta and Venkateshwarlu 1999; Mosse *et al.* 2002; Breman 2010; Guérin 2013).

Several studies have shown agrarian crisis and rural distress in some regions of India, with widening rural–urban and occupational inequalities across the country, and, most importantly, growing insecurity in livelihoods for large numbers of those who continue to be employed in the rural economy (Reddy and Mishra 2010; Shah and Harriss-White 2011). Contra Lewis (1954), the capitalist industrial sector in India has failed to absorb the surplus labour released from the agricultural sector, redirecting it instead into a large and growing informal economy characterised by casualisation and flexible employment (Harriss-White 2003; Shah and Harriss-White 2011), increasing temporary and circular migration out of rural areas, and creating livelihoods that are spatially fragmented.

NREGA was, of course, designed as a response to agrarian distress. The programme arose from significant grassroots struggles in response to the lack of employment, which in turn led to policy discussions, court rulings, and political negotiation. This was not a hand-out from the elites but rather a programme wrested from a reluctant state (Khera 2011; see also Drèze 2011 for a history). The provision of guaranteed employment through an Act made it an "enforceable obligation" of the state, one that could be demanded by right and not easily abandoned according to the whims of government or bureaucracy (Drèze 2011, p. 9). Given the decline in agricultural employment, NREGA was designed to provide a buffer against poverty and distress migration, as well as to enhance the bargaining power of agricultural workers, create assets in rural areas, and revitalise local institutions such as village panchayats and assemblies (Drèze 2011).

The distribution of agrarian distress is, however, shaped by gender and class. The ratio of rural working-age females to their male counterparts for all agricultural work has declined from 49 women per 100 men to 40 women per 100 men (see Table 13.3), with the biggest decline for women seen in absolute agricultural employment (Kannan and Raveendran 2012). This decline for women appears especially concentrated amongst marginal farmer and casual labour households, with women in these households leaving the labour force to a greater extent than women in households with land and/or sources of non-agricultural self-employment (Rao 2018). When compared to Table 13.3, Table 13.4 indicates that women's share in the agricultural work force among both marginal farmer households and casual labour households is lower than that of the rural working-age population as a whole.

Table 13.3 *Principal status occupation as a share of working-age persons, rural India, 1993–94 and 2011–12* in per cent

	Agriculture	Manufacturing	Construction	Trade/ hospitality	Transport
1993–94					
Men	62	6	3	5	2
Women	31	3	0	1	0
Share of women in work force	49	49	10	15	1
2011–12					
Men	47	7	11	7	3
Women	19	2	1	1	0
Share of women in work force	40	28	12	13	0

Source: Authors' calculations based on NSSO's EUS data for 1993–94 and 2011–12.

Table 13.4 *Employment by class and gender, rural India, 2011–12* in per cent

	Agriculture	Manufacturing	Construction	Trade/ hospitality	Transport
Casual labour households					
Men	41	8	21	3	4
Women	20	3	3	0	0
Share of women in work force	34	27	12	13	1
Marginal farmer households					
Men	73	1	2	2	1
Women	22	1	0	0	0
Share of women in work force	23	34	10	16	1

Note: Type of household is determined by primary source of income.
Source: Authors' calculations based on NSSO's EUS data for 2011–12.

Thus, we might expect more demand for NREGA work from women than from men, particularly women from marginal farmer and casual labour households, based on NSS data, which show that 73 per cent of women participating in NREGA came from marginal farmer, non-agricultural worker, and agricultural worker households.[4] Notably, as shown in Table 13.5,

[4] These class categories are constructed using principal source of income and landholdings, as described in Vakulabharanam and Motiram (2016).

Table 13.5 *Women NREGA participants by household class status, rural India, 2011–12* in per cent

Household class status	Women NREGA participants
Rich farmer	2
Middle farmer	6
Small farmer	9
Marginal farmer and manual labour	73
Others	10

Source: Authors' calculations based on NSSO's EUS data for 2011–12.

15 per cent of women participating in NREGA were from households with landholdings between 2 and 10 acres, which suggests some demand accruing from women who belong to somewhat "better-off" rural households as well. If this demand is indicative of the pervasiveness of agrarian distress across rural classes, the case for expansion of NREGA is further bolstered. To the extent, therefore, that in addition to the poor, the "nearly poor" have also benefited from the livelihood support and social insurance provided by NREGA in the face of economic insecurity, the programme has economic and political benefits in terms of "widening the constituency" of such entitlement programmes (Jenkins and Manor 2017, p. 9).

The economic and political benefits of NREGA depend, however, on the particular set of livelihood strategies available to and adopted by households. In contexts where men who have also lost agricultural employment are unable to find alternative sources of employment, it may be the case that they monopolise the family entitlement to NREGA work, thereby reducing the female share of person-days.

Another response to agrarian distress is migration, and here too, the nature of the migration matters. There are regions where family migration to urban or rural construction sites is relatively common; in this case, women are not necessarily more likely to participate in NREGA. However, because male migration streams are more common, we would expect female shares of NREGA participation to be much higher. Interestingly, the literature suggests that family migration is more common among unskilled and poorer households (Mosse, Gupta, and Shah 2005). If this is true, then it might indicate that rural women from better-off households, who are less likely to migrate themselves, are more likely to be in a position to demand and gain NREGA work.

Non-Farm Employment and Discouragement

The unsustainability of agriculture alone as a source of livelihood has meant that rural households must increasingly look towards the non-agricultural sector. At the same time, the lack of absorption by the urban formal manufacturing sector has meant that rural workers find themselves in the rural unorganised or informal sectors (Shah and Harriss-White 2011). However, women's share of work in these sectors has barely grown. Most of the growth in rural non-agricultural employment has come in sectors such as trade/hospitality and construction, which are still dominated by men. As indicated by Table 13.3, rural construction work, one of the fastest growing employment categories in rural India through the 2000s, has consisted almost entirely of wage work for men and has absorbed some of the male labour force released from agriculture (Thomas 2012; see also Venkatesh 2013). Women's share in construction work has increased only slightly, from 10 to 12 per cent. Meanwhile, the share of women in manufacturing has shrunk (the sector overall has been stagnant), and the share of women in other sectors like transport and trade/hospitality has remained extremely low, even as the overall share of employment in these sectors has increased by around 40 per cent.

In Table 13.4, we disaggregated rural non-agricultural employment figures for marginal farmer and casual labour households. Apart from casual wage work in construction for men in casual labour households, these two household groups did not demonstrate particularly high participation in non-agricultural employment. India's failure to create decent non-farm work has been widely noted, but Table 13.4 shows the disproportionate negative effect for marginalised classes. Among those who participated in non-agricultural work, however, women's share was consistently low. Thus, while women's share of agricultural work in these two household groups was lower than for the rural working-age population as a whole, women's share of the non-agricultural work force was not high enough to compensate. To the extent that women have lost work due to shrinking agricultural employment, these figures suggest they were unable to compensate for that lost work in the rural non-farm sector.

In other words, the pattern of non-agricultural employment growth in rural India remains uneven and gendered, indicating that NREGA is a relatively more reliable way for rural women to access employment, even if for only a few days every year. Paradoxically, this would then mean that it is in regions where non-agricultural employment has grown, providing opportunities for men, that women's *share* of participation in NREGA would be relatively high. Thus, for example, we note that women's participation in NREGA in 2011–12 was positively correlated with their spouses being engaged in non-agricultural employment (Ramnarain and Rao 2018).

Reproductive Work Burden and NREGA

In the literature on declining labour force participation rate (LFPR) for women in rural India, one of the explanations provided for the decline in women's participation is an income effect. That is, rising family incomes result in women's withdrawal from the market due to the status effects of such withdrawal (Himanshu 2011; Rangarajan, Seema, and Vibeesh 2014; Eswaran, Ramaswami, and Wadhwa 2013; Neff, Sen, and Kling 2012).

NREGA work is designed to be hard manual labour, and it is the physical arduousness of this work that acts as a screening mechanism for applicants. Due to this nature of NREGA work, it is assumed that only the poorest and neediest of households and persons will avail such physically challenging employment. That women are increasingly those availing this type of work, however, flies in the face of the income-effect narrative. Clearly, where such work *is* available, as in the case of NREGA, women seem to be demanding it in large numbers. This demand is in spite of the work being "outside" the home and physically arduous, all features of low-status work. States like Punjab or Bihar are striking in this regard, as the shares of women's participation in NREGA have risen by almost 20 percentage points (Table 13.2) *without* apparently much change in women's overall LFPR.

Women's participation in NREGA aligns with two other alternative explanations for the decline in women's LFPR. First, some studies refer to a strong discouraged-worker effect for women, where women's employment has been disproportionately affected by the decline in agricultural work (Kannan and Raveendran 2012; Chowdhury 2011); this is an explanation discussed for NREGA in previous sections. In addition, a second factor comes into play from feminist economics, which argues that any consideration of changes in women's paid work must be connected to changes in their unpaid labour of social reproduction. Indeed, another explanation for falling LFPR is given in studies which argue that it may be the case that women's work burden has merely shifted from the public to the private sphere, and is prone to measurement error due to the lack of social recognition of women's work as work (Hirway 2012; Azam 2012; Naidu and Rao 2018).

Though the absence of other feasible work opportunities for women may explain their relatively high demand for NREGA work, here we try to theorise how women's work in NREGA may intersect with what some have termed "women's domestic/care responsibilities," and what we, following terminology from feminist political economy, specifically term women's "labour of social reproduction." Following Bezanson and Luxton (2006), we define the labour of social reproduction as the labour involved in the various activities and processes that reproduce and maintain people on a daily basis as well as across generations. The labour of social reproduction thus includes work that goes into the maintenance and regeneration of workers outside the production process, which enables their participation in it; the work of caring and maintenance of non-workers outside production processes (viz. the elderly, children, the sick, and the disabled); and work that produces new workers themselves (Bhattacharya, ed. 2017).

This work of social reproduction tends to largely be performed by women in many societies of the global South due to existing norms around the gender division of labour. Since a large proportion of this work is performed in the private sphere, i.e. within the household, it also tends to remain invisible, or is inadequately captured in statistical measurement such as in labour force participation statistics. In addition, scholars have speculated that women's labour of social reproduction may have increased due to environmental destruction, and increased barriers faced by rural communities in terms of access to common lands from which fuel, fodder or food could be foraged (Chandrasekhar and Ghosh 2011; Levien 2017).

What, then, is the connection between the labour of social reproduction and women's participation in NREGA? Based on an analysis of 2011–12 NSS data, we find that 40 per cent of women who participated in NREGA were principal status domestic and allied workers, or those "not in the labour force" based on the NSS's definition of the term (Ramnarain and Rao 2018).[5] That is, 40 per cent of women participating in NREGA combined their reproductive responsibilities (i.e. their domestic and allied work) with NREGA work, making NREGA potentially their primary source of cash earnings. The demand for NREGA work illustrates, therefore, that women would engage in the labour force if such work was easily accessible and flexible enough to accommodate with their relatively inflexible – and arguably increasing – labour of social reproduction.

CONCLUSION

The existing social science literature largely agrees that NREGA has helped the rural economy along various dimensions, even if its impact has been miniscule and unevenly targeted for macro-level effects. This chapter intervenes in this

---

[5] This result is corroborated by Desai *et al.* (2015) using a different dataset, the IDHS2.

literature to point out the incomplete understanding of how NREGA has been increasingly availed by women workers. NREGA was designed as a response to the decline of agricultural employment without a corresponding increase in decent non-agricultural work. The design of the programme has always acknowledged the role of demand-side factors driving participation, yet this perspective is missing with respect to gendered patterns of participation. This chapter argues for a feminist political economy approach that looks at the macro-structural economic forces shaping NREGA participation in a gendered and classed manner.

We have outlined three central propositions that require further empirical investigation: NREGA participation for women is likely to be higher in regions with a decline in women's participation in agriculture; women's share of NREGA participation is higher in regions where men dominate in non-agricultural work; and the particular forms of women's reproductive labour shape their ability to participate in NREGA work. Taking these factors together, women's participation in NREGA may not unambiguously be a cause for celebration, but should provoke further attention to and analysis of the exclusionary nature of recent economic growth in India. While the programme's role as a social safety net is important, recognition of the connections between women's reproductive and productive work in particular has implications for the programme's continued effectiveness and expansion. Karat (2009) points out, for instance, the restrictive nature of works taken up under NREGA, which do not account for the hours women may spend "climbing up dangerous rocky hillsides, collecting fodder and carrying the huge bundles back to their village . . . work which is fulfilling a social responsibility." In this regard, the state must find ways to subsidise women's allied work burdens, or even expand NREGA to include payment for such work. Further, NREGA projects themselves could be directed at improving the local village infrastructure of social provisioning, ideally in consultation with the women who perform this labour. It is our hope that explicitly drawing attention to these connections will lead to more research on the links between women's labour of social reproduction and their participation in all forms of paid work, including NREGA.

REFERENCES

Ambasta, Pramathesh, Shankar, Vijay P. S., and Shah, Mihir (2008), 'Two Years of NREGA: The Road Ahead," *Economic and Political Weekly*, vol. 43, no. 8, February, pp. 41–50.

Armstrong, Elisabeth (2014), *Gender and Neoliberalism: The All India Democratic Women's Association and Globalisation Politics*, Routledge, New York.

Azam, Mehtabul (2012), "The Impact of Indian Job Guarantee Scheme on Labour Market Outcomes: Evidence from a Natural Experiment," Discussion Paper No. 6548, Institute for the Study of Labour (IZA), Bonn, Germany, available at ftp.iza.org/dp6548.pdf, viewed on 16 June 2019.

Banerjee, Kaustav, and Saha, Partha (2010), "The NREGA, the Maoists and the Developmental Woes of the Indian State," *Economic and Political Weekly*, vol. 45, no. 28, pp. 42–47.

Basole, A. (2019), "State of Working India," Centre for Sustainable Employment, Azim Premji University, Bangalore, available at: https://cse.azimpremjiuniversity.edu.in/wp-content/uploads/2019/04/State_of_Working_India_2019.pdf

Bezanson, Kate, and Luxton, Meg (2006), "Introduction: Social Reproduction and Feminist Political Economy," in Meg Luxton and Kate Bezanson (eds.), *Social Reproduction: Feminist Political Economy Challenges Neo-Liberalism*, McGill-Queen's University Press, Montreal, pp. 3–10.

Bhatia, Bela, and Drèze, Jean (2006), "Employment Guarantee in Jharkhand: Ground Realities," *Economic and Political Weekly*, vol. 41, no. 29, July, pp. 3198–202.

Bhattacharya, Tithi (ed.) (2017), *Social Reproduction Theory: Remapping Class, Recentering Oppression*, Pluto Press, London.

Breman, Jan (2010), *Outcast Labour in Asia: Circulation and Informalisation of the Workforce at the Bottom of the Economy*, Oxford University Press, New Delhi.

Carswell, G., and De Neve, G. (2014), "MGNREGA in Tamil Nadu: A story of success and transformation?" *Journal of Agrarian Change*, vol. 14, no. 4, pp. 564–85.

Chandrasekhar, C. P., and Ghosh, Jayati (2011), "Latest Employment Trends from the NSSO," *The Hindu Business Line*, 12 July available at https://www.thehindubusinessline.com/opinion/columns/c-p-chandrasekhar/Latest-employment-trends-from-the-NSSO/article20304971.ece, viewed on 8 June 2019.

Chibber, Vivek (2012), "Organised Interests, Development Strategies and Social Policies," in R. Nagaraj (ed.), *Growth, Inequality and Social Development in India*, Palgrave Macmillan, London, pp. 168–93.

Chowdhury, Subhanil (2011), "Employment in India: What Does the Latest Data Show?" *Economic and Political Weekly*, vol. 34, no. 32, August, pp. 23–26.

da Corta, Lucia, and Venkateshwarlu, Davuluri (1999), "Unfree Relations and the Feminisation of Agricultural Labour in Andhra Pradesh, 1970–95," *The Journal of Peasant Studies*, vol. 26, no. 2–3, pp. 71–139.

Datta, Soumyendra Kishore, and Singh, Krishna (2012), "Women's Job Participation in and Efficiency of NREGA Programme: Case Study of a Poor District in India," *International Journal of Public Administration*, vol. 35, no. 7, May, pp. 448–57.

Deere, Carmen Diana (1990), *Household and Class Relations: Peasants and Landlords in Northern Peru*, University of California Press, Berkeley.

Department of Rural Development (2013), "MGNREGA Operational Guidelines 2013, 4th Edition," Ministry of Rural Development, Government of India, New Delhi, available at https://nrega.nic.in/Circular_Archive/archive/Operational_guidelines_4thEdition_eng_2013.pdf, viewed on 15 June 2019.

Department of Rural Development (2020), "Employment generated during 2017–18," Ministry of Rural Development, Government of India, New Delhi, available at http://mnregaweb4.nic.in/netnrega/citizen_html/demregister.aspx?lflag=eng&fin_year=

2017-2018&source=national&labels=labels&Digest=cT/J7ChEq5LOfEr0AmsuAQ, viewed on 4 October 2019.

Desai, Sonalde, Vashishtha, Prem, and Joshi, Omkar (2015),"Mahatma Gandhi National Rural Employment Guarantee Act: A Catalyst for Rural Transformation," National Council for Applied Economic Research, New Delhi.

Dev, S. Mahendra (1995), "Alleviating Poverty: Maharashtra Employment Guarantee Scheme," *Economic and Political Weekly*, vol. 30, no. 41–42, October, pp. 2663–676.

Drèze, Jean (2007), "NREGA: Dismantling the Contractor Raj," *The Hindu*, 20 November, available at https://www.thehindu.com/todays-paper/tp-opinion/NREGA-Dismantling-the-contractor-raj/article14878947.ece, viewed on 15 June 2019.

Drèze, Jean (2011), "Employment Guarantee and the Right to Work," in Reetika Khera (ed.), *The Battle for Employment Guarantee*, Oxford University Press, New Delhi.

Eswaran, Mukesh, Ramaswami, Bharat, and Wadhwa, Wlima (2013), "Status, Caste, and the Time Allocation of Women in Rural India," *Economic Development and Cultural Change*, vol. 61, no. 2, January, pp. 311–33.

Gill, Sucha Singh, Singh, Sukhwinder, and Brar, Jaswinder Singh (2013), "Functioning of NREGS in a Prosperous State: A Study in Punjab," in K. P. Kannan and Jan Breman (eds.), *The Long Road to Social Security: Assessing the Implementation of National Social Security Initiatives for the Working Poor in India*, Oxford University Press, New Delhi.

Guérin, Isabelle (2013), "Bonded Labour, Agrarian Changes and Capitalism: Emerging Patterns in South India," *Journal of Agrarian Change*, vol. 13, no. 3, June, pp. 405–23.

Gupta, Smita (2009), "Women in India's National Rural Employment Guarantee Scheme," in Shahra Razavi (ed.), *The Gendered Impacts of Liberalization: Towards "Embedded Liberalism"?*, Routledge, New York, pp. 327–56.

Harriss-White, Barbara (2003), *India Working: Essays on Society and Economy*, Vol. 8, Cambridge University Press, Cambridge.

Himanshu (2011), "Employment Trends in India: A Re-examination," *Economic and Political Weekly*, vol. 46, no. 37, September, pp. 43–59.

Hirway, Indira (2012), "Missing Labour Force: An Explanation," *Economic and Political Weekly*, vol. 47, no. 37, September, pp. 67–72.

Jackson, Cecile, and Rao, Nitya (2009),"Gender Inequality and Agrarian Change in Liberalising India," in Shahra Razavi (ed.), *Gendered Impacts of Liberalization: Towards "Embedded Liberalism"?*, Routledge, New York, pp. 63–98.

Jakimow, Tanya (2014), "'Breaking the Backbone of Farmers': Contestations in a Rural Employment Guarantee Scheme," *Journal of Peasant Studies*, vol. 41, no. 2, March, pp. 263–81.

Jeffrey, Craig, and Lerche, Jens (2000), "Stating the Difference: State, Discourse and Class Reproduction in Uttar Pradesh, India," *Development and Change*, vol. 31, no. 4. pp. 857–78.

Jenkins, Rob, and Manor, James (2017), *Politics and the Right to Work: India's National Rural Employment Guarantee Act*, Oxford University Press, Oxford.

Kannan, K. P., and Jagajeevan, N. (2013), "Beneficiary as Agency: Role of Women's Agency and the Panchayat in Implementing NREGA: AStudy in Kerala," in K. P. Kannan and Jan Breman (eds.), *The Long Road to Social Security: Assessing the Implementation of National Social Security Initiatives for the Working Poor in India*, Oxford University Press, New Delhi.

Kannan, K. P., and Raveendran, G. (2012), "Counting and Profiling the Missing Labour Force," *Economic and Political Weekly*, vol. 47, no. 6, February, pp. 77–80.

Karat, Brinda (2009), "Rejigging NREGA, the Wrong Way," *Indian Express*, 3 September 3, available at https://indianexpress.com/article/opinion/columns/rejigging-nrega-the-wrong-way/, viewed on 23 December 2019.

Khera, Reetika (2011), "The Battle for Employment Guarantee," in Reetika Khera (ed.), *The Battle for Employment Guarantee*, Oxford University Press, New Delhi.

Khera, Reetika, and Nayak, Nandini (2009),"Women Workers and Perceptions of the National Rural Employment Guarantee Act," *Economic and Political Weekly*, vol. 44, no. 43, October, pp. 49–57.

Krook, Mona Lena (2006), "Gender Quotas, Norms, and Politics," *Politics and Gender*, vol. 2, no. 1, March, pp. 110–18.

Kumbhar, Rathi Kanta (2013), "Structural Legacy, Inefficacy and Weakening Social Securities: A Study of NREGS in a Panchayat in Odisha," in K. P. Kannan and Jan Breman (eds.), *The Long Road to Social Security: Assessing the Implementation of National Social Security Initiatives for the Working Poor in India*, Oxford University Press, New York.

Levien, Michael (2017), "Gender and Land Dispossession: A Comparative Analysis," *The Journal of Peasant Studies*, vol. 44, no. 6, October, pp. 1111–134.

Lewis, W. Arthur (1954), "Economic Development with Unlimited Supplies of Labour," *The Manchester School*, vol. 22, no. 2, May, pp. 139–91.

McCartney, Matthew, and Roy, Indrajit (2016), "A Consensus Unravels: NREGA and the Paradox of Rules-Based Welfare in India," *The European Journal of Development Research*, vol. 28, no.4, September, pp. 588–604.

Menon, Sudha Venu (2008), "Right to Information Act and NREGA: Reflections on Rajasthan," MPRA Paper No. 7351, Munich Personal RePEC Archive (MPRA), Munich, Germany, available at https://mpra.ub.uni-muenchen.de/7351/, viewed on 15 June 2019.

Mosse, David, Gupta, Sanjeev, and Shah, Vidya (2005), "On the Margins in the City: Adivasi Seasonal Labour Migration in Western India," *Economic and Political Weekly*, vol. 40, no. 28, pp. 3025–38.

Mosse, David, Gupta, Sanjeev, Mehta, Mona, Shah, Vidya, Rees, Julia fnms, and KRIBP Project Team (2002), "Brokered Livelihoods: Debt, Labour Migration, and Development in Tribal Western India," *Journal of Development Studies*, vol. 38, no. 5, pp. 59–88.

Naidu, Sirisha C., and Rao, Smriti (2018), "Reproductive Work and Female Labor Force Participation in Rural India," Working Paper Series, No. 458, Political Economy Research Institute (PERI), University of Massachusetts Amherst, available at https://www.peri.umass.edu/publication/item/1070-reproductive-work-and-female-labor-force-participation-in-rural-india, viewed on 10 June 2019.

Narayanan, Sudha, and Das, Upasak (2014),"Women Participation and Rationing in the Employment Guarantee Scheme," *Economic and Political Weekly*, vol. 49, no. 46, November, pp. 46–53.

National Sample Survey Organisation (NSSO) (1997), "Employment and Unemployment Situation in India, 1993–94," National Sample Survey 50th Round, Report No. 409,

Ministry of Statistics and Programme Implementation (MoSPI), Government of India, New Delhi.

National Sample Survey Organisation (NSSO) (2011), "Employment and Unemployment Situation in India, 2009–10," National Sample Survey 66th Round, Report No. 537, Ministry of Statistics and Programme Implementation (MoSPI), Government of India, New Delhi.

Neff, Daniel F., Sen, Kunal, and Kling, Veronika (2012),"The Puzzling Decline in Rural Women's Labor Force Participation in India: A Reexamination," GIGA Working Papers, No. 196, German Institute of Global and Area Studies (GIGA), Hamburg, Germany, available at http://dx.doi.org/10.2139/ssrn.2143122, viewed 6 September 2019.

Pankaj, Ashok, and Tankha, Rukmini (2010),"Empowerment Effects of the NREGS on Women Workers: A Study in Four States," *Economic and Political Weekly*, vol. 45, no. 30, July, pp. 45–55.

Patnaik, Utsa (2002), "Deflation and Deja Vu: Indian Agriculture in the World Economy," in V. K. Ramachandran and Madhura Swaminathan (eds.), *Agrarian Studies: Essays on Agrarian Relations in Less-Developed Countries*, Tulika Books, New Delhi, pp. 111–43.

Pattenden, Jonathan (2010), "A Neoliberalisation of Civil Society? Self-Help Groups and the Labouring Class Poor in Rural South India," *The Journal of Peasant Studies*, vol. 37, no. 3, July, pp. 485–512.

Pattenden, Jonathan, (2011a), "Gatekeeping as Accumulation and Domination: Decentralization and Class Relations in Rural South India," *Journal of Agrarian Change*, vol. 11, no. 2, March, pp. 164–94.

Pattenden, Jonathan, (2011b), "Social Protection and Class Relations: Evidence from Scheduled Caste Women's Associations in Rural South India," *Development and Change*, vol. 42, no. 2, April, pp. 469–98.

Pattenden, Jonathan, (2015), "Class and Social Policy: The National Rural Employment Guarantee Scheme in Karnataka, India," *Journal of Agrarian Change*, vol. 17, no. 1, August, pp. 43–66.

Pellissery, Sony, and Jalan, Sumit Kumar (2011),"Towards Transformative Social Protection: A Gendered Analysis of the Employment Guarantee Act of India (MGNREGA)," *Gender and Development*, vol. 19, no. 2, July, pp. 283–94.

Ramachandran, V. K. (2011), "The State of Agrarian Relations in India Today," *The Marxist*, vol. 27, nos. 1–2, January–June, pp. 51–89.

Rangarajan, C., Seema, A., and Vibeesh, E. M. (2014), "Developments in the Workforce between 2009–10 and 2011–12," *Economic and Political Weekly*, vol. 49, no. 23, June, pp. 117–21.

Ramnarain, Smita, and Rao, Smriti (2018), "NREG and Rural Economies: The Role of Gender and Class," paper presented at the Union of Radical Political Economics 50th Annual Conference, Amherst, Massachusetts, 27–30 September.

Rao, Smriti (2018), "Gender and Class Relations in Rural India," *Journal of Peasant Studies*, vol. 45, nos. 5–6, October, pp. 950–68.

Rawal, Vikas (2008), "Ownership Holdings of Land in Rural India: Putting the Record Straight," *Economic and Political Weekly*, vol. 43, no. 10, March, pp. 43–47.

Reddy, C. Sheela (2013), "Innovation, Transparency and Governance: A Study of NREGS in Andhra Pradesh," *Journal of Rural Development*, vol. 32, no. 2, pp. 107–20.

Reddy, D. Narasimha, Reddy, A. Amarender, and Bantilan, M. C. S. (2014), "The Impact of Mahatma Gandhi National Rural Employment Guarantee Act (MGNREGA) on Rural Labour Markets and Agriculture," *India Review*, vol. 13, no. 3, August, pp. 251–73.

Reddy, D. Narasimha, and Mishra, Srijit (2010), "Agriculture in the Reforms Regime," in D. Narasimha Reddy and Srijit Mishra (eds.), *Agrarian Crisis in India*, Oxford University Press, New Delhi, pp. 3–43.

Reddy, D. Narasimha, Tankha, Rukini, Upendranadh, C., and Sharma, Alakh N. (2010), "National Rural Employment Guarantee as Social Protection," *IDS Bulletin*, vol. 41, no. 4, July, pp. 63–76.

Roy, Indrajit (2015), "Class Politics and Social Protection: The Implementation of India's MGNREGA," ESID Working Paper No. 46, Effective States and Inclusive Development Research Centre (ESID), Manchester, UK, available at http://www.effective-states.org/wp-content/uploads/working_papers/final-pdfs/esid_wp_46_roy.pdf, viewed on 5 June 2019.

Shah, Alpa, and Harriss-White, Barbara (2011), "Resurrecting Scholarship on Agrarian Transformations," *Economic and Political Weekly*, vol. 46, no. 39, September, pp. 13–18.

Sudarshan, Ratna M., Bhattacharya, Rina, and Fernandez, Grace (2010), "Women's Participation in the NREGA: Some Observations from Fieldwork in Himachal Pradesh, Kerala and Rajasthan," *IDS Bulletin*, vol. 41, no. 4, July, pp. 77–83.

Swaminathan, Madhura (2019), "Public Support for Rural Households," in Madhura Swaminathan and Ranjini Basu (eds.), *Socio-Economic Surveys of Three Villages in Tripura*, Tulika Books, New Delhi, pp. 365–74.

Thomas, Jayan Jose (2012), "India's Labour Market during the 2000s: Surveying the Changes," *Economic and Political Weekly*, vol. 47, no. 51, December, pp. 39–51.

Vakulabharanam, Vamsi, and Motiram, Sripad (2016), "Mobility and Inequality in Neoliberal India," *Contemporary South Asia*, vol. 24, no. 3, August, pp. 257–70.

Vanaik, Achin, and Siddhartha (2008), "Bank Payments: End of Corruption in NREGA?" *Economic and Political Weekly*, vol. 43, no. 17, April–May, pp. 35–39.

Veeraraghavan, Rajesh (2017), "Strategies for Synergy in a High Modernist Project: Two Community Responses to India's NREGA Rural Work Programme," *World Development*, vol. 99, November, pp. 203–13.

Venkatesh, P. (2013), "Recent Trends in Rural Employment and Wages in India: Has the Growth Benefited the Agricultural Labourers?" *Agricultural Economics Research Review*, vol. 26, September, pp. 13–20.

V

Women's Wages and Earnings

14

Women's Work and Earnings in Nineteenth-Century Rural Bihar

Madhavi Jha

Women's work and labour have not received much attention in Indian historiography.[1] Scholars have pointed out the urban and industrial bias in labour historiography that has led to further marginalisation of rural women's work in history writing (Bhattacharya 2006, pp. 147–61; Joshi 2008, pp. 439–54; Upadhyay 2001, pp. 87–117). Both undercounting and the lack of identifying women's work as work make it difficult to give a comprehensive picture of what women did for their quotidian existence in a different historical period. This "gap" or "invisibility" fuels stereotypes like the "male breadwinner" that entrench unequal gender relations in work spaces and beyond.[2] To address this gap, this chapter reconstructs the world of work of rural women, and analyses the contribution of women from rural households in nineteenth-century Bihar.[3]

In India's rural areas, women worked at various sites and types of work, as seen in the surveys by Chowdhry (1994) for Haryana, Maskiell (1990, pp. 35–72) for Punjab, and Sen (1999, pp. 54–89) for Bengal. As Chowdhry (1994, pp. 24–57) shows, women were indispensable to the Haryanvi economy with its peasant base and high male migration. They worked in a number of agricultural operations and also took care of cattle, which was of immense importance to dryland farming. In Punjab, the interdependence of men and women's work was established by Maskiell (1990). In both Punjab and Bengal, women were involved in a number of tasks apart from

---

[1] There have been a few works that focus on women's labour in factories, including R. Kumar (1991), Sen (1999), and Joshi (2005).

[2] For a review of the male breadwinner debate in the Indian historical context, see Joshi (2002), pp. 261–74.

[3] Much of the history writing on nineteenth- and twentieth-century Bihar has focused on the impact of colonial policies on agrarian relations and existing political and social structures; see Henningham (1983), pp. 35–55; Pouchepadass (1990); Robb (1992), pp. 97–119; Yang (1979a), pp. 247–64; and Yang (1989). Different aspects of peasant response and choices have also been studied; see Das (1982); Henningham (1979), pp. 53–75; A. Kumar (2001); and Yang (1979b), pp. 37–58.

work in the fields, such as processing grain, spinning cotton, collecting fuel, and selling household artisanal products.

Historical writings on women's labour emphasise that the nature of work done by women depended on the social rank – the caste and class – of the households to which they belonged. Maskiell (1990) describes one of the main determining factors of women's work to be kinship ties. The family and extended family controlled the deployment of women's labour. This was true of all classes of women, though the exact nature of this control underwent change depending on class and caste. The caste and class location of the marital household decided the kind of work women did, though women also had access to some resources they brought from their natal homes. Where women were confined within the household, they carried on tasks such as grain processing and weaving.

The present chapter relies on statistical reports, official reports, and gazetteers from the nineteenth century that focus on different regions of the present-day state of Bihar.[4] The main source for the early part of the nineteenth century is the Buchanan-Hamilton report. Dr Francis Buchanan[5] was instructed by the Governor General in Council to collect statistical information from the province of Bengal.[6] The results of Buchanan's investigation between 1807 and 1813 were reported in five volumes spanning the then districts of Purnea, Bhagalpur, Patna, Behar, and Shahabad.[7] Cohn (1987, pp. 224–55) remarked that at this early stage of colonial rule, the British were preoccupied with the need to gather information for the purpose of revenue collection. A classification of tribes and castes was not yet the main focus; the shift from a descriptive narrative to a classificatory one occurred in the later part of the nineteenth century. Amin (1989, pp. xxx–xxxiii), speaking of the colonial knowledge produced in the early part of the nineteenth century, stated that while the reports were indeed based on "expert" information provided by local Indian agents, English authors were more familiar with the countryside and wrote much of the report themselves. He gave the example of the Buchanan-Hamilton report in this context. The descriptive nature of this report has

---

[4] In the nineteenth century, the present-day state of Bihar was part of the Bengal Presidency (1757–1912).

[5] Apart from being a trained physician, Dr Francis Buchanan-Hamilton was a botanist, geologist, mineralogist, zoologist, and geographer. He conducted a survey of Mysore prior to the statistical survey of the province of Bengal; see Oldham (1930) and Vicziany (1986), pp. 625–60.

[6] "Letter from the Governor General in Council to Dr Francis Buchanan with the subject of 'Instructions to Dr. Francis Buchanan for conducting a statistical survey of Bengal'," file no. 18, Home Department (Public), 11 September 1807, National Archives of India (NAI), New Delhi.

[7] Behar corresponds to areas around present-day Gaya, including the districts of Arwal, Nawada, Jahanabad, Aurangabad, and Rohtas.

allowed for the following investigation into the world of women's work in nineteenth-century Bihar.

In the following sections, we look at three aspects of women's work in rural Bihar: work in the fields, which included different agricultural operations; women's earnings; grain processing; and fuel collection and preparation. Women predominantly engaged in the latter two tasks, which generated part of the household income.[8] Women were also a crucial part of the production of different artisanal products in rural areas, notably those made by spinning.[9] This chapter seeks to determine the kind of contribution women made to the household income by examining both household budget estimates and the work done by women.

WOMEN'S WORK IN THE FIELD: VARIATIONS BY CLASS

Women's work in rural areas depended on the type of household to which they belonged, more specifically the relationship of the household to land and the types of production activities that it engaged in. The Buchanan-Hamilton report gives a rich description of the different types of classes (with several internal divisions) found in rural Bihar. These classes were defined on the basis of land ownership and occupation. The report broadly identifies four such classes, of which the first two – which he identified as *ashraf* and traders (*beniya bakali*s or *dokandar*s) – were characterised by their freedom from manual work.[10] The visibility of women's labour in the fields was crucial to maintenance of the *ashraf* rank. This becomes evident in the case of the *sheykh*s (one of the *ashraf* groups) in Purnea:

> These sheykhs are in general cultivators, and seem much fonder of the plough than any other profession. In some parts they have subdivided themselves variously, in others they are all without distinction called sheykhs. The chief cause of difference seems to have arisen from those who as much as possible imitate the nobler tribes in concealing their women, while others are not at this pain, which to a farmer is always attended with an excessive inconvenience.

---

[8] In addition, the Buchanan-Hamilton report also lists "dancing and singing girls" as a large category of remunerated work for women.

[9] In the case of cotton and silk weaving, women and men worked as a single unit, though weaving was constructed as a masculine skill by the end of the nineteenth century. We also find reference of women's contribution to production of lac bracelets, lime burning, processing milk products, and making torches and leaf platters.

[10] These were broad classes with a number of castes within them, and varied for the different regions that Buchanan surveyed. The present chapter translates the caste or occupational group names as given in the Buchanan-Hamilton report.

(Buchanan 1928, p. 197)

The remaining classes and the local variations and divisions between them constituted the majority of agricultural cultivators, and usually the same people could be found working in various capacities such as seasonally hired ploughmen and day labourers who worked for a daily wage. Much of the artisanal class, called *pangeh pauniya*s or *karigar*, worked as cultivators. For example, it is remarked that in Shahabad, "at least two thirds of the artificers, who cultivate, do so as day labourers, and not above one-third hold the plough" (Buchanan 1934b, p. 152), and that "among the cultivating tribes, taking hire is not considered disgraceful, and many even of the artificers gain a part of their subsistence by weeding and transplanting and reaping" (*ibid.*, p. 343). Similarly in Patna and Behar, the artisans not only leased land, but also ploughed it with their own labour or acted as day labourers. It is stated that "they cultivate the ground, when they do not find employment at their trade, or one brother cultivates the farm and the other follows the duties of his profession" (*ibid.*, p. 265).

A fourth class has been called *karindagan* (labourers) or *jotiya*s. They are often mentioned as those whose "proper duty" was to work on land. However, as we have seen, there was no social class from which some proportion of families did not work as cultivators. This class comprised domestic and field servants, and also those who hired out their labour as day labourers or as ploughmen. It bears repetition, though, that the dividing line between artisans and labourers was blurred, and many artisans hired themselves out as day labourers or ploughmen. It was the nature of tenure that determined the remuneration and conditions of work. As mentioned earlier, usually the labourers were either hired seasonally or as day labourers; however, there were many local variations.

A large number of women were involved in agricultural production, especially those from households that hired out their labour as ploughmen or as day labourers. The work was seasonal and determined by the paddy-dominated agricultural rhythm of the region. Though there is no evidence of women holding the plough, there is ample evidence of their presence in other agricultural activities, especially reaping and threshing during the harvest season, and weeding and transplanting in other seasons.

Women's Earnings

Was women's labour in the fields remunerative? In order to answer this question, we look at the different types of household budgets found in the Buchanan-Hamilton report for the early part of the nineteenth century. We also present some household estimates from the later part of the century.

In Shahabad, a ploughman was engaged for the entire season on payment of an advance that varied between one and two rupees, along with a daily allowance of three *sers*[11] of coarse grain. Instead of money, in many places, a plot of land was given, from which he could retain half of the produce. Sometimes a daily allowance of parched grain was given in addition to coarse grain. It is reported that there was no idle period (period of no work on land), though much of the earnings was concentrated in harvest time. The season for which the advance was paid lasted four months in a year, and during the remaining months, the ploughmen repaired huts and fences for 2.5 *sers* of grain daily and also cultivated cotton, of which they kept three-eighths of the produce for their labour (watering, weeding, hoeing, ploughing, and gathering). Their whole earnings (mostly in the form of coarse grain) was calculated to be no more than Rs 26.5 per year, considered to be below subsistence level for a family with an average of five members. Buchanan mentions that he could not get "an account of how the difference is procured" (1934b, pp. 341–44). This deficit was in all probability eliminated by the earnings of women and children, as was the case in other districts.

In Purnea, the daily wages for ploughing were low but much of the profit accrued during harvest time. Here, a ploughman was engaged for nine months, and there was another category of seasonal workers who tended cattle. Given four members in a ploughman's family and an estimated expense of Rs 24 per year, the district calculated the allowance for ploughing as Rs 6 (Rs 4.5 in cash and a quarter of grain or food per day, which amounted to about Rs 1.5), leaving a balance of Rs 18. The rate for beating rice was low in Purnea as compared to other districts, and a woman earned Rs 6 working for ten months in a year. An income of Rs 3.5 was earned from spinning. Hence, working in these two occupations, women reduced the household deficit to Rs 8.5, which was made up by profits during harvest or by borrowing. During harvest, income came from women's labour in reaping and threshing, and from "customary presents" called *lora* and *kuri*[12] amounting to Rs 4.75. In addition, women earned a considerable sum from weeding at this time. A good portion of the harvest profits was also made by "pilfering" (similar to gleaning) the remaining harvest, in which women played an important role. Buchanan remarked, "it would thus appear that, notwithstanding the low price of cleaning grain, the women actually earn more than men" (1928, p. 444).

In Bhagalpur, the daily allowance for ploughing was three *sers* of rice in the husk or another coarse grain, for which a ploughman had to work between

---

[11] One *ser* was equal to one kilogram approximately.

[12] *Lora* and *kuri* refer to "customary rights" of labourers during harvesting, which included gleaning.

six to nine hours, depending on the number of bullocks yoked to the plough. It is mentioned that the allowance for weeding and transplanting was slightly higher than that for ploughing. Servants, as opposed to day labourers, secured the profits of harvest, which was done twice annually in this district. To meet the annual household expense of Rs 24, the ploughman contributed Rs 15, and the rest was derived from advances and women who, like in Purnea, "pilfered" or gleaned the remaining harvest. It is mentioned that "most of the reapers having a strong fellow feeling leave her a large quantity of ears," however, "owing to the extravagant jealousy of men here, the women can on whole gain less than that in Purnea" (Martin 1838, p. 226).

In the districts of Patna and Behar, much of the land was cultivated by hired servants. The ploughmen here were called *kamiya*s, and a major difference between their terms of hire and those of their counterparts in other districts was that the repayment of advance was carried over to the next generation.[13] Given this situation, it is interesting to note that in these districts, "within the memory of man the price necessary to be advanced to servants has doubled. Formerly, no one gave more than Rs 20 and now they are content to give Rs 40" (Buchanan 1934a, p. 555). Buchanan attributes this to the general rise in the price of money or inflation; however, we do not see this effect of inflation in the other districts. As mentioned earlier, in Shahabad, where ploughmen were also seasonally engaged, the amount of advance varied between one and two rupees (*ibid.*, p. 341). In places in the vicinity of Behar, in Bhagalpur district, it was noted that ploughmen "sold" themselves for the duration of the ploughing season. Here, the range of advance given was between Rs 5 and Rs 20.

In Behar and Patna, like in other places, ploughmen were occasionally given land (in this case, between 6 and 20 *katha*s),[14] for which they procured seeds independently and used the master's plough. They paid half of their produce as rent. The daily allowance for ploughing was three *ser*s of grain or, in some places, 1.5 to 2 paisas with half a *ser* of parched grain. They were required to work for nine hours and received additional allowance for extra work. The districts' accounts show a detailed break-up of their annual income from two different *pargana*s – Azimabad and Nawada. The difference between the two was that Nawada was "one of the poorer and least cultivated parts of

---

[13] Prakash (1990) has studied the *kamauti* (debt repayment through physical labour) system in south Bihar, emphasising the role of colonial discourse that reconceptualised the dependence of the *kamiya*s on the *malik*s (masters) as unfreedom of the former. The universe of caste where dominance existed along with contestations (as powerfully narrated in oral traditions) was replaced in the British reconstitution of the *kamiya–malik* relationship through the power of debt bondage.

[14] *Katha* as a unit of area differs from region to region. In Patna one *katha* is equivalent to 1,350 square feet, and one acre is about 32 *katha*s.

Table 14.1 *Yearly income of ploughmen, Azimabad* money in paisa, grain in *ser*

Activity	Remuneration		
	Money	Parched grain	Grain
182 days ploughing	364	91	0
60 days watering	180	30	0
45 days reaping	0	0	310
45 days threshing and cleaning	0	22	40
45 days repairing master's house	45	0	0
15 days idle	0	0	0

Source: Buchanan (1934a), p. 556.

the district, where the assessment is low, and where a large proportion of the expense of labour is thrown on the harvest, most of the rent being obtained by a division of the crop" (Buchanan 1934a, p. 557).

If each of the forms of remuneration is converted to money, then the total annual income was Rs 16.6, from which Rs 2 was subtracted for losses during sickness. The income was supplemented by the earnings of other family members. Women earned almost as high a wage as ploughmen, through agricultural activities like reaping, weeding, and transplanting. They could also get the same amount from beating rice, but this was considered as an occupation given to more "interruptions." A woman's income was estimated at Rs 8, which, added to the Rs 4.5 earned from tending cattle (by a younger or elderly person), brought the household income for a family of five to Rs 26.5.

In Nawada, the idle period was calculated as one month, during which income came from cultivating one's own plot of about one *bigha*,[15] from which half of the produce was kept, yielding an income of 1 rupee and 6.5 annas.[16] Converting kind to cash, Buchanan calculated the total amount of yearly income earned by the ploughmen as Rs 22 and 1.5 annas. Buchanan took into consideration that ploughmen in these parts were hardly given any advances and were hence reliant only on what they earned. *Lara*, or the produce gleaned during harvest, was mostly collected by women, and it can be therefore noted that the grain collected was almost double the income obtained from either ploughing or reaping. This probably formed the most important source of income for women, as opposed to cleaning grains or spinning in other districts, as it is mentioned that "the woman while collecting the lara cannot do any other work" (Buchanan 1934a, p. 557). Also, like in

[15] One *bigha* is equal to 20 *katha*s and 1 acre is 1.6 *bigha*s.
[16] One anna was one-sixteenth of a rupee, and one paisa was one-fourth of an anna.

Table 14.2 *Yearly income of ploughmen, Nawada* in *sers*

Activity	Remuneration	
	Grain	Parched grain
6 months ploughing	546	91
1 month watering	90	15
1 month repairing master's house	90	15
2 months reaping (up to 21 bundles)	600	
2 months reaping (*ati*)	360	
2 months reaping (*lara*)	1050	
1 month threshing	0	

Source: Buchanan (1934a), p. 557.

Azimabad, women most probably worked in other agricultural activities like reaping, weeding, and transplanting.

In the case of day labourers too, family income estimates show that women's labour formed a crucial part of the household income. In Shahabad, the lowest rate received for reaping was 3.75 per cent of the gross produce and the highest was 8.75 per cent (Buchanan 1934b, p. 302). The rate of hire for day labourers and ploughmen was the same: three *sers* of coarse grain along with a daily allowance of parched grain. It was noted that "their wives in transplanting make as much as themselves" (*ibid.*, p. 343). In Purnea, people hired by the day for weeding and transplanting or for ploughing managed to earn Rs 12 per year, working for 270 days. Again, it was noted that the "wives often labour at the same employment, and will make fully as much" (*ibid.*, p. 446). Even though the wages of both types of labour were similar, day labourers could not procure advances easily or earn as much as the monthly or seasonal cultivators did during harvest. In Patna and Behar, day labourers were employed in large numbers for transplanting rice and watering winter crops, for which they earned one-third more grain than for other agricultural activities like weeding. Buchanan remarked that "notwithstanding the extreme jealousy of the men, the women day labourers make almost as much as the men, as they are employed to weed and transplant rice, receiving the same allowance as men and they also assist in harvest" (Buchanan 1934a, p. 558).

The gazetteers of different districts give information on the prevailing wages for agricultural labourers in the later part of the century. In all districts of the province, agricultural labourers were mostly paid a bare minimum, less than other kinds of labourers. In most places, during harvest, the labourers were given one sheaf out of every 21 sheaves they cut. In Gaya district, migrant labourers worked only during harvest and were given one out of every 16 sheaves they cut; the same was given to ploughmen (Grierson 1893, p. 152). The remuneration amounted to about two annas when converted in terms of money. In 1871, in Patna, the rate was three *sers* of paddy or one anna (O'Malley 1924, p. 117), whereas in Munger, by the end of the century, the value of grain given to the agricultural labourer was placed at five to six annas (O'Malley 1926a, p. 131). In Darbhanga, an adult male labourer received four *sers* of an inferior variety of rice or two annas, whereas women and boys received three *sers*, which amounted to one-and-a-half annas (O'Malley 1907, p. 84). A statistical account from Shahabad estimates that a labourer's family consisting of four members would require four *sers* of rice and pulses or three annas daily, to which the expense incurred on fuel and clothes was added (Ahamed 1874). The daily income of four annas was considered "even in ordinary times, hand to mouth existence" (*ibid.*, p. 21). Regarding women's work, it was stated that apart from reproductive activities, women performed "all domestic labour and are generally required at the sowing and reaping seasons for outdoor labour" (*ibid.*, p. 17).

In a detailed report on Gaya district, Grierson (1893) provided expenditure and income estimates according to type of household. The main three divisions of "poorer classes" made by him were cultivators, labourers, and artisans. He cautioned that the distinction between cultivators and labourers was not very well defined; those who subsisted on wage labour were classified as labourers and those who were assisted by wage labour fell in the category of cultivators. The artisanal classes that were surveyed included weavers, dyers, washermen, basket weavers, shepherds, braziers, goldsmiths, carpenters, blacksmiths, potters, barbers, and leather workers. Grierson found that around 70 per cent of the landholdings could not support their cultivators, who therefore had to depend on supplementary sources of income. To reach this conclusion, he analysed average figures of over 3,500 holdings and actual figures of four villages (Utrend, Pali, Pathra, and Gothi).

Women were employed in the fields during paddy transplantation. The wages at this time were four *sers* for men and three *sers* for women, along with an allowance of three-fourths *ser* of *sattu*[17] per head. Women also worked during harvest, and a husband–wife pair could earn up to 18 *sers* a day for a month (*ibid.*, p. 111). It was concluded that in two of the villages under study, Utrend and Pali, the supplemental income formed 38 per cent of the total income in the case of a cultivator household, of which around 30 per cent could be categorised as "miscellaneous." This miscellaneous category consisted of, amongst other things, "the profits of the manufacture of cow dung fuel,

---

[17] Flour of pulses, mostly gram.

Table 14.3 *Income estimates for a labourer household, Gaya district in rupees*

Activity	Remuneration
Harvesting, man and woman, for 1 month	11.25
Ploughing, man, for 8 months	18
Transplanting, man and woman, for 1 month	6.375
Opium tapping, woman, for 15 days	1.125
Cow dung, fuel, straw collection	5
Total	41.75

Source: Grierson (1893), p. 112.

home labour, such as spinning and the like, fish and jangal produce" (*ibid.*, p. 108). Much of this labour fell on women. Apart from working in the fields during the transplanting and reaping seasons, women in labourer households worked at "tapping poppy-heads and collecting opium . . . looking after household work, such as husking paddy, flour grinding, cooking, collecting fuel, and the like" (*ibid.*, p. 111). Estimates of the income earned by men and women from labourer households is given in Table 14.3.

GRAIN PROCESSING

It is clear from the above estimates that women's contribution to the household income also came from activities outside agricultural fields. In this section, we provide details of women's work in grain processing. Buchanan observed that in Patna and Behar, "except a very few great families, almost all the zamindars and farmers beat in their own houses whatever rice is required for family use; for they all rear this grain," and that this labour mainly fell on women (Buchanan 1934a, p. 494). A large number of women earned either a part or all their livelihood by processing grain. They were mainly employed by traders (called *beparis*, *baldiya* or *paikars*), who either supplied grain to the local market or exported it. Most of them bought grain in the husk and hired women to clean them. The general arrangement was that the women would receive a certain quantity of uncleaned grain (by weight) and would return a certain quantity of it cleaned, keeping the remaining grain as their profit. Buchanan calculated the profit that would accrue in different districts based on his experiments on how much cleaned grain could be obtained from a specific amount of uncleaned grain. In the case of rice, usually the grain was either cleaned by boiling, which yielded what was considered to be an inferior product to be used by the poor, or without boiling, which was said to produce a superior quality of grain.

For grain cleaned without boiling, 40 *sers* of cleaned rice was to be returned for 70 *sers* received in the husk in Purnea. According to Buchanan, 45 *sers* of cleaned rice could be obtained from 70 *sers* of uncleaned rice, and hence the profit would be 5 *sers*. A woman worker would also obtain 3.36 *sers* of broken grain that could not be sold but was equally nourishing and hence could be consumed. In the case of cleaning by boiling, a woman returned 8 *sers* of rice of the 13 *sers* she received and made a profit of 1.76 *sers*. This came to around 18 per cent, whereas in the earlier case of cleaning without boiling, the profit was around 11 per cent. Women usually worked in pairs and would clean 65 *sers* of rice in two days' time (Buchanan 1928, pp. 349–50), using both the *dhenki* and the common wooden mortar and pestle. The latter was mostly used for cleaning grains for household consumption and resulted in fewer broken grains. Though the use of the *dhenki* resulted in more broken grains, which were not saleable, the grains were considered equally nourishing (Buchanan 1934b, p. 350).

In Patna and Behar, wage rates were dependent on the quality of the grain. If a woman received good-quality rice that was to be cleaned by boiling, then, for 60 *sers* of rice received, she would return 40 *sers* of cleaned rice. In the case of inferior-quality grain, 40 *sers* of cleaned rice were returned for 65 *sers* of rice in the husk (Buchanan 1934a, p. 494). In these districts, women worked in groups of three, and according to Buchanan's calculation, each could earn up to five paisas per day. He compared this income to a day's hire for a labourer, which was six paisas (*ibid.*, p. 495). When the rice was cleaned without boiling, the resulting broken grains retained some sale value in these districts. Women workers gained small profits from bran and husk (*ibid.*, p. 496).

In Patna, Behar, and Purnea districts, irrespective of the rate of return to their labour, women earned the same profit, as they tended to adjust their quantity of work according to the prevailing wage rates. With respect to Purnea, "where the reward for cleaning rice is high, women clean little and where the reward is low, they work hard, so as to make almost as high wages" (Buchanan 1928, p. 351). Husking rice and spinning were the most widely diffused activities, and not always done for the market. Women also processed rice into different kinds of products like *lava* and *mudhi*. Notably, rice was not the common grain of the labouring classes, most of whom consumed coarse grains and their substitutes or supplements, such as *mahua* flowers, mango kernel, and *kend* fruit.

Parched grain or *sattu* formed an important part of the remuneration for working in the fields. Grain parchers belonged to a specific caste, *Kandu*, and in most of the districts, it was *Kandu* women who parched grains. In Shahabad, where the number of *Kandu* families was estimated at 2,300, it is mentioned that they, "although reckoned among artificers, in strict propriety should be considered as labourers of the soil; for it is the women alone that parch grain, and men cultivate the land, but chiefly as day labourers" (Buchanan 1934b, p. 198). Similarly, in Patna and Behar, "the *Kandu* men build houses and act as day labourers in agriculture, while their women parch grains" (Buchanan 1934a, p. 333). In Purnea, one-fourth of the *Kandu* men held the plough (Buchanan 1928, p. 220). Women who parched grains, also called *barbhunas*, often worked in pairs and sat in either a shop (usually not owned by them) or a house; they could parch up to 192 to 240 *sers* of grain in a day. The grains to be parched were provided by the customer, whereas the women collected the fuel that they needed to carry out this task. Women workers received one-twenty-fourth of the grain and could earn up to four to five *sers* daily (Buchanan 1934b, p. 402).

Since the second half of the century, the evidence of women's involvement in grain processing, especially cleaning rice, is sparse.[18] The statistical report from Shahabad mentioned earlier indicates that women were engaged in cleaning grain and that *dhenki* was in use (Ahamed 1874, p. 12). As mentioned in the last section, Grierson (1893) listed husking paddy and grinding flour as part of women's work. Amongst all the gazetteers, we find details of food processing by women only in the Purnea Gazetteer. It includes a description of two types of rice according to the distinct ways of husking it. Rice cleaned after boiling was called *ushna*, and rice cleaned without boiling was called *arwa*. Both the mortar and *dhenki* were in use; the former was used when there was a minimal quantity to be cleaned (O'Malley 1926b, p. 87). From Purnea we also get an account of the remuneration of women who were engaged in this occupation. For *arwa*, women gave back 40 *sers* of cleaned grain out of the 70 *sers* of grain in the husk received, and for *ushna*, the same amount was returned for 65 *sers* of the uncleaned grain received. Women worked in pairs and could produce 40 *sers* of cleaned rice using either method in two days. For *ushna*, they received 4.5 *sers* of cleaned rice and 0.5 *ser* of broken rice as remuneration, and for *arwa*, they were paid 5 *sers* of cleaned rice and 1.25 *sers* of broken rice. Hence, the daily earning of each woman ranged between 1 and 1.25 *sers* of cleaned rice (*ibid.*, p. 110).

---

[18] Mukherjee (1983) looks at the impact of the introduction of rice mills in early twentieth-century Bengal on the manual husking industry, which was dominated by women. It is argued that with the decline of the manual husking industry, women lost an employment opportunity, source of income, and control over vital resources, that is, their access to grains.

FUEL COLLECTION AND PREPARATION

An important part of women's work consisted of fuel collection and preparation. Apart from being used for cooking, traditional fire or firewood was the main source of heat during winter months. While reporting on the use of fuel in Purnea district, Buchanan remarked that "almost everyone in the four months of cold weather could in the morning kindle a fire, important considering the scantiness of clothes and shelter" (Buchanan 1928, p. 155). Fuel was also often an indispensable requirement of whatever the household manufactured for its own use or sale. Cow dung made into cakes and sometimes mixed with husks of rice was the most commonly used fuel. This was true even for a town like Patna, where "these cakes formed by far the greater part of the fuel and for eight or nine miles round, poor women attended carefully every herd of cattle, or even every plough, in order to procure a quantity sufficient" (Buchanan 1934a, p. 285). Cow dung cakes were "prepared in the dry season and are preserved in a quantity sufficient to last during the periodical rains" (Buchanan 1928, p. 154). Other sources of fuel like firewood were scarce as not everyone had access to wood from trees, which were said to be preserved "partly from religious motives and partly as they sheltered game" (Buchanan 1934b, p. 164). In Purnea, it was reported that the "owners of land have an utter abomination at allowing any planted trees to being cut, and the chief supply of wood, used for the fire, comes from mango trees that have decayed or from natural woods, which harbour so many destructive animals" (Buchanan 1928, p. 155). Another detriment to the use of firewood was that it was not readily available. However, the exception to this was in Bhagalpur district where firewood was abundant (Martin 1838, p. 99). Even here, cow dung formed a portion of the fuel used in addition to brushes and woody stems of various crops like *arhar* (a pulse) or cotton. In Behar and Patna, "stubble and the woody stems of all kinds of crops that have such and reeds" were carefully collected (Buchanan 1934a, p. 285).

In most places, it was the women from the *Goyala* caste who sold fuel. It is reported that in Shahabad, where the *Goyalas* tended the cattle of the rich, *Goyala* women were "much employed in forming cakes of cow dung for fuel; and make about as much by this employment as those of Behar" (Buchanan 1934b, p. 331). In Behar, *Goyala* women were "chiefly employed in collection and drying of the dung for fuel." Their remuneration depended on the location: "near the towns, a woman with this employment can make a rupee a month. In the country places she may make ten annas" (Buchanan 1934a, p. 542). This income has been compared by Buchanan with that gained from tending cattle, which was mostly done by older men and children. In Behar and Patna, the remuneration near the towns was 12 annas a month, and in the countryside, it was half of this (*ibid.*).

Information on the use of cow dung as fuel in the later part of the century is found in the "Report on Supply of Firewood and Timber," which covered the then districts of Patna, Gaya, Shahabad, Tirhoot, Saran, and Champaran (Bayley 1873, p. 4). In addition to the source of timber, rivers used to transport it through these districts, and regarding the existing nature of trade, the report also discussed the "nature of supply" of firewood wherein cow dung remained the major source of fuel, especially in the interior parts of these districts. It is reported that firewood was seldom sold in the interiors of Patna district. Instead, cultivators and other poorer classes dried and preserved cow dung in cakes, used leaves of trees collected from gardens and other places, and the stems and stumps of plants gathered from fields after harvest. In the north and north-western parts of Gaya as well as the interior and rural areas of Shahabad, wood was not easily available, and cow dung was used more commonly. The remaining districts (many of which fell in the erstwhile Bhagalpur district of the Buchanan-Hamilton report) had sufficient firewood and petty timber resources.

Furthermore, in Shahabad, cow dung, in addition to leaves, was the common source of fuel, not wood (Ahamed 1874, p. 16). For Gaya district, Grierson's (1893) report throws some light on the use of fuel and the involvement of women in the provisioning of fuel in the last decade of the century. As mentioned above, around 70 per cent of landholdings did not support their cultivators, who had to depend on supplemental sources of income for their subsistence. In the case of cultivator households, around 30 per cent of the supplemental income could be categorised as "miscellaneous." "Profit of the manufacture of cow dung fuel" formed a part of this income (*ibid.*, p. 108). Regarding fuel collection work done by women from labourer households, it was noted that "they sell cakes of cow dung fuel in the hot weather, a basketful every two or three days, for two Gorakhpuri pice" (*ibid.*, p. 111).[19] In this manner they could annually earn up to five rupees selling cow dung, fuel, and straw (*ibid.*, p. 112).

CONCLUSION

The above account of women's work in nineteenth-century rural Bihar illuminates the different types of remunerated activities that women performed. In the case of agriculture, it is clear that women were usually employed in the tasks that were paid less than other tasks, most importantly ploughing.

---

[19] One Gorakhpuri pice was equal to one-third of an anna.

However, the period of harvesting is identified as particularly profitable for women because of gleaning. In this context, the reduced importance of gleaning in the sources from the second half of the century is noteworthy. One finds that the form of remuneration for women's tasks both on the fields and outside was usually in kind.

Women were also a crucial part of the production of different artisanal products in rural areas, notably for those made by spinning. The Buchanan-Hamilton report also significantly mentions that in certain castes it was women who retailed the household produce, for example, the *Dahiyar*s, who made curd and butter, and the *Rangdhaluya*s, who worked in tin and pewter, and made ornaments. Buchanan also found women selling fish and vegetables in the markets. Markets hence become another site for women's work apart from fields, shops, and their own homes.

We have seen in the previous sections that the socio-economic location of the household was the most crucial factor in determining the types and sites of women's work. In analysing the income estimates of labouring peasant households, we found that men provided about half or slightly more than half of the total income, and other members of the family provided the rest. Many women worked in the fields, mostly in activities like weeding, transplanting and reaping, and gleaning. The budget deficit of the household was in many cases met by women's income gained from grain processing and the sale of fuel. It is clear that women's paid labour was an important part of the household budget in rural areas. Although the paid component of women's labour declined, and women's work became increasingly devalued and unrecognised by the end of the century (Sen 1999), rural women's work continued to be crucial for the social reproduction of the labouring poor, both in rural and urban areas.

REFERENCES

Ahamed, M. S. D. H. (1874), "Report on the Agricultural Statistics of Shahabad," Calcutta.

Amin, Shahid (1989), *A Glossary of North Indian Peasant Life*, Oxford University Press, New Delhi.

Bayley, Stuart Colvin (1873), "Report on the Supply of Firewood and Timber, 21st April 1873, File 5-2, Revenue Department," West Bengal State Archives (WBSA).

Bhattacharya, Sabyasachi (2006), "Paradigms in Historical Approach to Labour Studies on South Asia," in Jan Lucassen (ed.), *Global Labour History: A State of the Art*, Peter Lang, Bern, pp. 147–60.

Buchanan, Frances (1928), *An Account of the District of Purnea in 1809–1810*, Patna.

Buchanan, Frances (1934a), *An Account of the Districts of Behar and Patna in 1811–1812* (2 vols.), Patna.

Buchanan, Frances (1934b), *An Account of the District of Shahabad in 1812–13*, Patna.

Cohn, Bernard (1987), *An Anthropologist among Historians and Other Essays*, Oxford University Press, New Delhi.

Chowdhry, Prem (1994), *The Veiled Women: Shifting Gender Equations in Rural Haryana*, Oxford University Press, New Delhi.

Das, Arvind N. (ed.) (1982) *Agrarian Movement in India: Studies on Twentieth Century Bihar*, Frank Cass, London.

Grierson, George Abraham (1893), *Notes on the District of Gaya*, Calcutta, Bengal Secretariat Press.

Henningham, Stephen (1979), "Agrarian Relations in North Bihar: Peasant Protest and the Darbhanga Raj, 1919–20," *Indian Economic and Social History Review*, vol. 16, no. 53, January, pp. 53–75.

Henningham, Stephen (1983), "Bureaucracy and Control in India's Great Landed Estates: The Raj Darbhanga of Bihar, 1879 to 1950," *Modern Asian Studies*, vol. 17 no. 1, February, pp. 35–57.

Joshi, Chitra (2002), "Notes on the Breadwinner Debate: Gender and Household Strategies in Working-Class Families," *Studies in History*, vol. 18, no. 2, August, pp. 261–74.

Joshi, Chitra (2005), *Lost Worlds : Indian Labour and its Forgotten Histories*, Anthem, London.

Joshi, Chitra (2008), "Histories of Indian Labour: Predicaments and Possibilities," *History Compass*, vol. 6, no. 2, February, pp. 439–54.

Kumar, Arun (2001), *Rewriting the Language of Politics: Kisans in Colonial Bihar*, Manohar, New Delhi.

Kumar, Radha (1991) *City Lives: Women Workers in Bombay Cotton Textile Industry, 1911 to 1947*, unpublished PhD thesis, Jawaharlal Nehru University, New Delhi.

Martin, Montgomery (1838), *The History, Antiquities, Topography, and Statistics of Eastern India*, volume 2, William H. Allen and Co., London.

Maskiell, Mitchell (1990), "Gender, Kinship and Rural Work in Colonial Punjab," *Journal of Women's History*, vol. 2, no. 1, Spring, pp. 35–72.

Mukherjee, Mukul (1983), "Impact of Modernisation on Women's Work: A Case Study of the Rice-Husking Industry of Bengal," *Indian Economic and Social History Review*, vol. 20, no. 1, January, pp. 27–45.

O'Malley, L. S. S. (1907), *Bengal District Gazetteers, Darbhanga*, Calcutta.

O'Malley, L. S. S. (1924), *Bihar and Orissa District Gazetteer, Patna*, Patna.

O'Malley, L. S. S. (1926a), *Bihar and Orissa District Gazetteer, Monghyr*, Patna.

O'Malley, L. S. S. (1926b), *Bengal District Gazetteers, Purnea*, Calcutta.

Oldham, Charles Evelyn Arbuthnot William (1930), *Journal of Francis Buchanan Kept During the Survey of the District of Bhagalpur in 1810–1811*, Patna.

Pouchepadass, Jacques (1990), "The Market for Agricultural Labour in Colonial North Bihar 1860–1920," in Mark Holmstrom (ed.), *Work for Wages in South Asia*, Manohar, New Delhi, pp. 11–27.

Prakash, Gyan (1990), *Bonded Histories: Genealogies of Labour Servitude in Colonial India*, Cambridge University Press, New York.

Robb, Peter (1992) "Peasants' Choices? Indian Agriculture and the Limits of Commercialization in Nineteenth-Century Bihar," *The Economic History Review*, vol. 45, no. 1, February, pp. 97–119.

Sen, Samita (1999), *Women and Labour in Late Colonial India: The Bengal Jute Industry*, Cambridge University Press, New York.

Upadhyay, Shashi Bhushan (2001), "Indian Labour History: A Historiographic Survey," in Sabyasachi Bhattacharya (ed.), *Approaches to History: Essays in Indian Historiography*, Primus Books, Delhi, pp. 87–117.

Vicziany, Marika (1986), "Imperialism, Botany and Statistics in Early Nineteenth-Century India: The Surveys of Francis Buchanan (1762–1829)," *Modern Asian Studies*, vol. 20, no. 4, October, pp. 625–60.

Yang, Anand A. (1979a), "An Institutional Shelter: The Court of Wards in Late Nineteenth-Century Bihar," *Modern Asian Studies*, vol. 13, no. 2, April, pp. 247–64.

Yang, Anand A. (1979b), "Peasants on the Move: A Study of Internal Migration in India," *Journal of Interdisciplinary History*, vol. 10, no. 1, Summer, pp. 37–58.

Yang, Anand A. (1989), *The Limited Raj: Agrarian Relations in Colonial India, Saran District, 1793–1920*, Oxford University Press, Delhi.

15

Trends in Male and Female Wage Rates

Arindam Das

This chapter examines levels and trends in wage rates for male and female workers in rural India. According to the Periodic Labour Force Survey (PLFS) of 2017–18, about 25 per cent of rural households in India were casual labour households. A total of 28 per cent of all male and 32 per cent of all female workers in India were casual wage workers, with over 73 per cent of women workers participating in agriculture. Agriculture is the single largest employer of women in India. It is widely recognised that the wage labour force in rural India comes from the poorest and marginalised sections of rural society. Income poverty is much higher among manual worker households as compared to households dependent on other sources of income, on account of both underemployment or unemployment and low wages. The wage rate for agricultural labour is thus a key determinant of the earnings and well-being of manual worker households.

There are, however, substantial differences between the wages paid to male and female workers in different agricultural operations. The main objective of this chapter is to analyse wage rates as reported in *Wage Rates in Rural India* (WRRI) over a two-decade period, 1998–99 to 2018–19. This chapter also examines some factors that contribute to the gender gap in wage rates for agricultural and non-agricultural occupations.

DATA AND METHODOLOGY

There are two major data sources for agricultural and non-agricultural wage rates. One is *Agricultural Wages in India* (AWI), collected and reported by the Directorate of Economics and Statistics, Ministry of Agriculture, since 1951–52. However, the AWI data suffer from several limitations (Chavan and Bedamatta 2006; Kurosaki and Usami 2016). The other is *Wage Rates in Rural India* (WRRI) of the Labour Bureau, which is the most reliable official data source and is used in the present study (Usami 2011; Das and Usami 2017). WRRI is published monthly, and covers various agricultural and non-agricultural occupations of male and female workers in rural India.

A major constraint in using WRRI data is the change in classification of occupations that occurred in November 2013 (Das and Usami 2017). Until October 2013, wage data were collected for 11 agricultural and 7 non-agricultural occupations. Since November 2013, wage data for 25 occupations, including 12 agricultural and 13 non-agricultural occupations, have been collected. For agricultural occupations, operations are merged; that is, ploughing and tilling, sowing (or planting) with transplanting and weeding, and harvesting with winnowing and threshing, have been merged in the data series. This reclassification of occupations was done in order to capture changes in the occupational structure recommended by T. S. Papola committee (CSO 2013). It is known that female participation in agricultural occupations such as ploughing and plant protection work, as well as in non-agricultural occupations such as masonry, blacksmithery, and carpentry, is very low. Data on wage rates for these specific agricultural and non-agricultural occupations are not available for female workers. In this chapter, we confine our analysis to sowing/transplanting/weeding, harvesting/winnowing/threshing, and un-skilled non-agricultural labour, as data on wage rates for these occupations are available for both male and female workers.

To link the old and new series of WRRI, I have taken the simple average of sowing, transplanting, and weeding (hereafter STW) of the old series, and linked this figure with that of the new series of sowing which also includes planting, transplanting, and weeding. Similarly, I have taken a simple average of harvesting, winnowing, and threshing (hereafter HTW), and linked it with the corresponding figure in the new series. For unskilled non-agricultural labourers, I have taken unskilled labourer occupations from the old series and linked this with non-agricultural labourers from the new series. The nominal wage rates were then deflated by the Consumer Price Index for Agricultural Labourers (CPI-AL) and by the Consumer Price Index for Rural Labourers (CPI-RL) for agricultural and rural non-agricultural labourers, respectively, at 2009–10 prices. The WRRI provides average daily wage rates of various agricultural and non-agricultural occupations on a monthly basis. This chapter is based on average daily wage rates for male and female workers.

Level and Growth of Real Wage Rates

To examine levels and trends in daily wage rates, real wage rates for males and females have been estimated between 1998–99 and 2018–19 for sowing/transplanting/weeding (STW), harvesting/threshing/winnowing (HWT), and unskilled non-agricultural labourers, at 2009–10 prices. Figure 15.1 shows the trends in real agricultural and rural labour wage rates at the all-India level over

Figure 15.1 *Real wage rates for various agricultural and non-agricultural labourers (unskilled), 1998–99 to 2018–19* in Rs

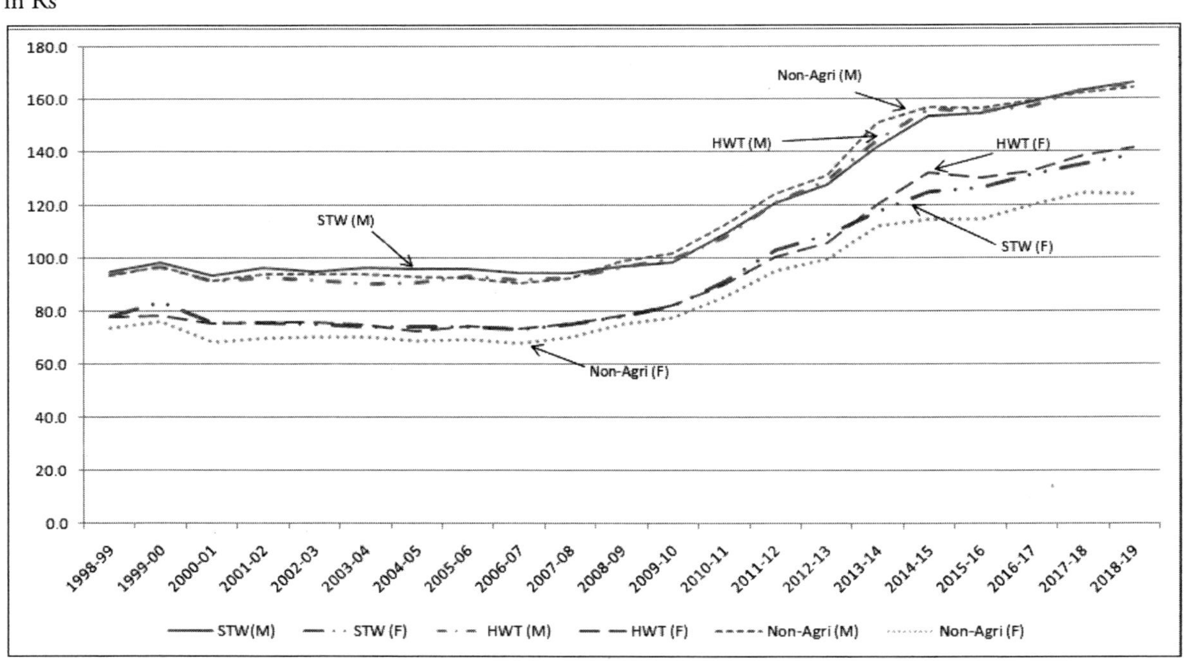

Note: "STW" stands for sowing/transplanting/weeding, "HTW" stands for harvesting/threshing/winnowing, "non-agri" stands for non-agricultural labourer (unskilled), "M" stands for male, and "F" stands for female.
Source: Computed from *Wage Rates in Rural India*, various years.

the last two decades. There is no significant difference in male wage rates for the three occupations at the all-India level. For a male labourer, wage rates for unskilled labour followed the same trend as wages for agricultural occupations. However, for a female labourer, the wage rates for unskilled labour were the lowest among the three occupations. This signifies that even with high growth in the non-agricultural sector (namely, the construction sector) in the last two decades, this sector did not play a significant enough role to raise wage rates for female unskilled non-agricultural labourers.

Based on trends in real wage rates (Figure 15.1), we have divided the period into three sub-periods: a period of stagnation (1998–99 to 2006–07), a period of rapid growth (2006–07 to 2014–15), and a period of stagnation (2014–15 to 2018–19). Average daily real wage rates of agricultural labourers show that between 1998–99 and 2006–07, real wage rates remained stagnant or declined at the all-India level. The real wage rates for male labourers ranged between Rs 94 and Rs 98 for sowing/transplanting/weeding, and Rs 90 and Rs 96 for harvesting/threshing/winnowing operations. For female labourers, the corresponding rates ranged between Rs 74 and Rs 83 for STW, and Rs 74 and Rs 78 for HWT at the all-India level. The growth rates in the first sub-period (1998–99 to 2006–07) for STW occupations were –0.1 per cent and –1.1 per cent for males and females, respectively, and for HWT occupations, they were –0.4 per cent and –0.8 per cent for males and females, respectively (Tables 15.1 and 15.2). In other words, the deceleration in real wage rates was more severe for female agricultural workers than for male workers. The prolonged stagnation in real wage rates between 1998–99 and 2007 was due to multiple droughts and a resulting decline in agricultural production. A study by Mahajan (2016) showed that while rainfall shocks caused a general decline in wages, it had more of an adverse impact on female wages than that of males. The real wage rates for unskilled non-agricultural occupations followed similar trends. The growth of wage rates for unskilled non-agricultural operations were –0.4 per cent and –0.1 per cent for males and females, respectively. In other words, despite significant growth of the Indian economy during this period, there was little impact on the wage rates of agricultural workers.

However, from 2006–07 up to 2014–15 (the second sub-period), rural wage rates for men and women across agricultural and non-agricultural occupations grew by more than 6 per cent per annum at the all-India level. The rate of growth in wage rates for female workers was higher than for male workers in all three occupations. Real wage rates for male labourers ranged from Rs 94 to Rs 153 for sowing/transplanting/weeding, and Rs 93 to Rs 156 for harvesting/threshing/winnowing occupations. For major agricultural occupations, data show that there was a higher growth in wage rates for female labourers than

Table 15.1 *Average annual rate of growth of wage rates for sowing/transplanting/weeding occupations, rural India, 1998–99 to 2018–19,* in per cent

States	Male			Female		
	1998–99 to 2006–07	2006–07 to 2014–15	2014–15 to 2018–19	1998–99 to 2006–07	2006–07 to 2014–15	2014–15 to 2018–19
Andhra Pradesh	2.4	6.2	3.7	1	7.3	4.3
Assam	3	4.1	4.3	–0.3	4.9	4
Bihar	1.6	10	4.3	1.8	9.4	4.8
Gujarat	0.7	4	3.4	0.5	4.9	3.9
Haryana	0.7	5.1	–1.8	2.2	5.4	–1.2
Karnataka	4.1	7.4	4.6	0.2	7.3	3.8
Kerala	0.7	5	0.4	0.3	8.6	0.4
Madhya Pradesh	–0.5	7.7	4	–1.4	9.1	3.4
Maharashtra	–0.5	6.1	2.5	–0.9	7	3.2
Manipur	1.3	9.2	–1.1	1.5	9.3	–2.1
Meghalaya	3.7	2.8	1.3	3.2	3.3	1.1
Odisha	3.3	6.4	3.2	2.9	7.8	3.5
Rajasthan	–2.1	6.9	–1.6	–2.8	6.6	2.9
Tamil Nadu	0.6	8.8	–0.9	–0.2	9.6	–0.9
Uttar Pradesh	0	6.9	5.1	0.4	6.9	5.8
West Bengal	2.6	5.8	3.3	2.7	6.8	2.1
All-India*	–0.1	6.5	2.1	–1.1	7.6	2.7

Note: * All-India refers to the average value for India, not just the States mentioned in the table.
Source: Computed from *Wage Rates in Rural India*, various issues; further, see Das and Usami (2017).

for male labourers at the all-India level. The growth rates for STW operations were 6.5 per cent and 7.6 per cent for males and females, respectively, and for HTW operations, they were 7.3 per cent and 7.9 per cent for males and females, respectively. The all-India female wage rate for STW increased from Rs 75.1 in 2007–08 to Rs 124.9 in 2014–15, and for HWT, it rose from Rs 75.3 in 2007–08 to Rs 132.1 in 2014–15.

Table 15.1 shows the above trend for STW operations in nine States. Some possible factors mentioned in the literature for high wage growth during this period are rise in agricultural productivity, stable agricultural prices (MSP), implementation of MGNREGS, growth in the construction sector, and stable rise of NSDP (Berg *et al.* 2012; Gulati, Jain, and Satija 2013; Jose 2013;

Table 15.2 *Average annual rate of growth of wage rates for harvesting/threshing/winnowing occupations, rural India, 1998–99 to 2018–19,* in per cent

States	Male			Female		
	1998–99 to 2006–07	2006–07 to 2014–15	2014–15 to 2018–19	1998–99 to 2006–07	2006–07 to 2014–15	2014–15 to 2018–19
Andhra Pradesh	1.1	5.6	5.4	–0.2	5.4	6.7
Assam	2.5	5.7	3.1	0.6	5.1	2.9
Bihar	3.1	9.1	3.5	3.8	8.9	2.3
Gujarat	–0.5	4	3	–0.1	4.3	2.9
Haryana	1.2	4.7	–1.5	1.9	4.9	–3.1
Karnataka	0.7	8	3.4	0.4	6.1	4.2
Kerala		8.9	–0.2	1.6	7.8	2.4
Madhya Pradesh	–0.6	8.9	2.3	–1.5	10	1.2
Maharashtra	1.2	6.8	4.3	–0.4	8.1	4.2
Manipur	0.1	10.7	–2.7	1	10.4	–2.5
Meghalaya	4.9	3.5	6.7	2.1	2.9	6.9
Odisha	2.5	8.8	2.1	1.2	10.3	1.8
Rajasthan	–4.3	8.5	–3.1	–4.8	8.1	0.6
Tamil Nadu	–1	10.5	–2.1	0.3	9.8	–4.3
Uttar Pradesh	0.1	7.4	4	–0.1	7	6
West Bengal	3.2	6.4	2.9	3.2	6.7	2
All-India*	–0.4	7.3	1.6	–0.8	7.9	1.9

Note: *All-India refers to the average value for India, not just the States mentioned in the table.
Source: Computed from *Wage Rates in Rural India*, various issues; further, see Das and Usami (2017).

Himanshu and Kundu 2016; Himanshu 2017). However, all these factors may not explain the growth in female wage rates specifically. MGNREGS may have had a greater influence on female agricultural wage rates in rural India (Chandrasekhar and Ghosh 2011). On the other hand, growth in the non-farm sector could have had a greater effect on male wage rates as compared to female wage rates. Since the overall participation of females in the non-agricultural sector (excluding MGNREGS) was quite low even after the 2000s, female participation in the non-farm sector increased only marginally over two decades. Thus, the impact of the growth in the non-farm sector on female wage rates requires further investigation.

The steady growth of wage rates for agricultural and non-agricultural occupations ceased after 2014–15. From 2015–16 onwards, growth of real wage rates for major agricultural operations started to decline and this continued till

Table 15.3 *Average annual rate of growth of wage rates for general non-agricultural occupations, rural India, 1998–99 to 2018–19,* in per cent

State	Male			Female		
	1998–99 to 2006–07	2006–07 to 2014–15	2014–15 to 2018–19	1998–99 to 2006–07	2006–07 to 2014–15	2014–15 to 2018–19
Andhra Pradesh	0.2	7.8	2.1	0.3	7.9	3.8
Assam	3.6	4.7	3	–0.1	7.4	3.2
Bihar	3	8.7	3.5	3.3	8.7	2.8
Gujarat	–0.7	4	2.2	–0.1	4.3	2.1
Haryana	0.4	5.3	–1.3	1.5	4.9	
Himachal Pradesh	2	3.6	4.4		4.9	
Jammu and Kashmir	1.1	8	–1.1			
Karnataka	1.4	6.6	0.8	0.9	6.6	3.1
Kerala	1.2	7.7	–2.6	3.2	4.5	
Madhya Pradesh	–0.8	7	4.8	–1.5	7.1	6.1
Maharashtra	–0.2	6.5	0	–1.3	6.4	1.6
Manipur	1.3	6.2		1.4	7.2	
Meghalaya	4.7	2.3	–0.8	–0.2	2.2	
Odisha	3	7.8	5.7	2	9.6	4
Punjab	–0.7	6	0.5	2.1	2.4	–0.4
Rajasthan	–1.1	7.4	–0.3	–0.3	7.8	–1.6
Tamil Nadu	1.7	8.7	–3	2.5	8.5	
Tripura	5.9	1.7	3.8	–	–	
Uttar Pradesh	0.1	7.6	4.6	0.6	8.1	4.2
West Bengal	2	6.9	3.9	2.4	6.7	0.6
All-India*	–0.4	7	1.3	–0.1	7.2	2.3

Note: *All-India refers to the average value for India, not just the States mentioned in the table.
Source: Computed from *Wage Rates in Rural India,* various issues; further, see Das and Usami (2017).

2017–18. The real wage rates for STW and HTW occupations, in absolute terms, increased by a mere Rs 8 to Rs 10 for both male and female labourers. The rate of growth of wage rates for major agricultural occupations declined to 2 per cent per annum during this four-year period. However, a marginal revival of real wage rates was observed in 2018–19 at the all-India level.

Wage rates for non-agricultural occupations followed a similar trend. At the all-India level, for males, absolute wage rates were higher for non-agricultural occupations than for agricultural ones. But in the case of female workers, non-agricultural wages were the lowest among all three occupations. Real wage rates for non-agricultural occupations for male and female labourers were stagnant from 1998–99 to 2006–07, following which they rose sharply and continued to rise till 2014–15. This sharp rising trend ended in 2015–16, recovering marginally in 2018–19. The long-term stagnation of wage rates could be explained by factors such as agrarian distress, stagnation in the construction industry, and increase in unemployment.

Gender Gap in Wage Rates

Women labourers are paid lower wages than male labourers across and within the different occupations discussed in recent literature. Das and Usami (2017) argue that despite a period of high growth in agricultural and non-agricultural wage rates, the gender gap in wage rates has not shown a tendency to fall. Similarly, a recent study by Jose (2017) shows that the gender gap in wage rates has not increased between 2005–06 and 2015–16. Himanshu (2017), using WRRI data, shows that the gender wage gap in rural areas had increased during the period of wage stagnation (2001–02 to 2007–08), but declined considerably after 2007 for both agricultural and non-agricultural occupations.

In this section, we examine the gender gap in wage rates for three major agricultural and non-agricultural occupations. Figure 15.2 shows the ratio of male to female wage rates for sowing/transplanting/weeding, harvesting/threshing/winnowing, and unskilled non-agricultural occupations, from 1998–99 to 2018–19.[1] It shows that male–female wage disparities have persisted over the last two decades at the all-India level. For all major agricultural occupations, the wage rates for female workers were four-fifths of male wage rates. The wage disparity for unskilled non-agricultural occupations was relatively higher than for agricultural occupations (STW and HWT). All-India male wages for STW were between 117 per cent and 125 per cent higher than that for females between 2001–02 and 2017–18, respectively. For unskilled non-agricultural occupations, all-India male wage rates ranged between 127 per cent to 133 per cent higher than that of females between 1998–99 and 2017–18.

The data show that between 1998–99 and 2006–07, the gender wage gap increased at the all-India level for STW and unskilled non-agricultural occupations. During this period, female labourers received 80 per cent of the wages received by male labourers for agricultural occupations. At the same time, male wage rates stagnated whereas female wage rates declined (–1.1 per cent) for STW occupations. For non-agricultural occupations, female wages were 75 per cent that of male labourers at the all-India level.

---

[1] This is an extension of the work of Das and Usami (2017).

Figure 15.2 *Ratio of male to female wage rates for STW, HWT, and unskilled non-agricultural occupations, 1998–99 to 2018–19*

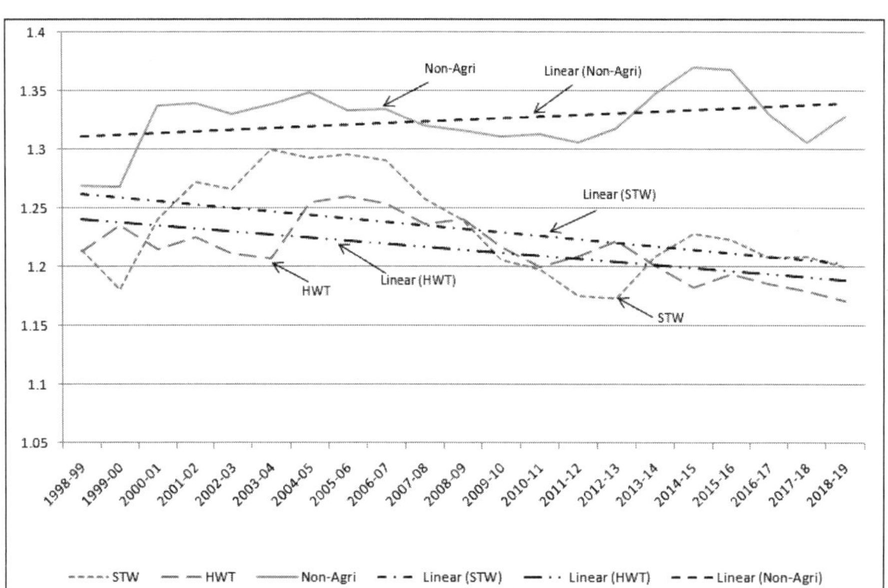

Source: Computed from *Wage Rates in Rural India*, various issues.

In the second sub-period, between 2007–08 and 2011–12, the gender gap in wage rates declined sharply at the all-India level for STW, but improved marginally for HTW due to higher growth in real wage rates for female labourers over male labourers. Even with persistent growth in unskilled non-agricultural occupations for male and female workers, the gender gap in wage rates either remained stagnant or only marginally improved at the all-India level in the second sub-period. However, a recent trend shows that the male–female wage disparity has persisted, showing no further decline between 2014–15 and 2018–19 for STW, HWT, and non-agricultural occupations. For STW and unskilled non-agricultural labour, the gender gap in wage rates increased between 2014–15 and 2017–18.

There was substantial variation in the gender disparity in wage rates across States: for example, the ratio of male to female wages varied from 104 per cent in Haryana to 158 per cent in Tamil Nadu for STW between 2016–17 and 2018–19. More precisely, the male–female wage gap was higher in the southern Indian States and lower in the northern and eastern Indian States[2]

---

[2] Studies by Boserup (1970), Srivastava and Singh (2006), Chavan and Bedamatta (2006), Usami (2011), Jose (2017), Das and Usami (2017) made similar observations. Jose (2017) shows that there was no reduction in gender wage disparity among the States.

(Appendix Figure 15.1). Let us look at carefully at the State-level analysis for STW, HWT, and unskilled non-agricultural wages.

First, for STW and HWT operations, the ratio shows that the male–female wage gap is relatively low in northern and eastern Indian States (Appendix Tables 15.1 and 15.2). The States of Bihar, Uttar Pradesh, West Bengal, Odisha, Haryana, and Assam saw male wages close to or below 117 per cent of female wages. The pattern was slightly different in the southern Indian States of Kerala, Karnataka, Andhra Pradesh, and Tamil Nadu, where the wage disparity was relatively large. The gender gap in wage rates was the highest in Tamil Nadu. In Kerala, which had the highest wage rates among all States for both males and females, the gender gap in wage rates continued to be high. The western Indian State of Maharashtra and the North Eastern State of Meghalaya also showed a high gender gap in wage rates. In terms of change, the male–female wage gap has narrowed in Kerala, Rajasthan, Gujarat, Madhya Pradesh, and Uttar Pradesh, whereas it has increased in Karnataka, Tamil Nadu, Maharashtra, and Assam over the two decades (Appendix Tables 15.1 and 15.2). The gender disparity in wage rates has stagnated in West Bengal, Bihar, Haryana, and Odisha.

The regional variation of male–female wage gap for unskilled non-agricultural occupations followed a pattern similar to that of agricultural occupations (Appendix Table 15.3). The gender wage disparity was relatively large in Karnataka, Andhra Pradesh, Tamil Nadu, and Maharashtra, as compared to Bihar, Gujarat, Haryana, and West Bengal.

Factors Affecting Gender Wage Differential

Neoclassical economics explains the wage differential in terms of marginal productivity theory, which argues that differences in the marginal productivity of male and female workers determine differences in wages (Skoufias 1994). Another argument, by Dobb (1955), is that for agricultural tasks, male and female workers are not strictly non-competing groups; that is, most operations can be carried out by both male and female workers. Mahajan (2016) argued that sudden change in rainfall patterns has a significant effect on female wage rates as compared to male wage rates. The implementation of MGNREGS has had the positive impact of reducing the gender wage gap, which is also discussed by Chandrasekhar and Ghosh (2011) and Berg *et al.* (2012). Other factors such as agro-ecology, cropping pattern, productivity, agricultural mechanisation, migration, and non-farm employment have differentiated impact on male and female wage rates. In this section, I explore four possible factors affecting the gender gap: level of wage rates, female labour supply (work participation rates), MGNREGS, and non-agricultural wages.

Level of wage rates by State
Figure 15.3 shows the gender wage gap with levels of wage rates for STW occupations for major States of India in 2017–18. The high-wage region shows a wide gender gap in wage rates, i.e. in States such as Kerala, Karnataka, and Tamil Nadu. These States did not historically belong to the high-wage regions, yet they had a wide gender gap. In States with low wage rates such as West Bengal, Bihar, Uttar Pradesh, Gujarat, and Madhya Pradesh, the gender gap in wage rates has narrowed. This does not hold for all States; the exceptions are Maharashtra, which has low wage rates but a high gender gap in wages, and Haryana, which has high wage rates and a low gender gap in wage rates. Thus, gender gaps in wage rates are clearly not associated with absolute wage rates.

Female work participation rates (FWPRs)
The relationship between gender differential in wage rates and female labour supply is widely discussed in the literature. Boserup (1970) first established the negative relationship between female labour supply and gender wage differential in developing countries. She argued that variation in the gender gap in wage rates was due to variation in female participation in the work force across rural India. The male–female wage gap was higher in the southern Indian States where female work participation rates (FWPRs) were higher than in lower wage gap States in northern India, where FWPR was low. Mahajan and Ramaswami (2017) tested the hypothesis and confirmed that female labour supply has a sizeable effect on the gender differential in wage rates. Usami (2011) also showed a significant correlation between FWPR and the female–male wage gap for various agricultural operations (e.g., 0.61 in 1999–2000 and 0.73 in 2004–05 for transplantation operations).

Figure 15.4 examines the correlation between female labour supply, i.e. female workers estimated by the EUS, and the gender wage gap for STW and unskilled non-agricultural labourers, with 2011–12 as the reference year. States where both the WPRs and the gender gap in wage rates were low are the northern States of Bihar, West Bengal, and Uttar Pradesh. Conversely, southern States like Tamil Nadu and Andhra Pradesh had high gender gap and high WPRs. However, the negative relations between WPR and gender gap does not hold true for all States (Table 15.4). For example, in Kerala and Karnataka, the WPR is relatively low (medium category) but the gender wage gap is high, and in Rajasthan, the WPR is high but the gender wage gap is relatively low.

National Rural Employment Guarantee Scheme (NREGS)
Chandrasekhar and Ghosh (2011), Berg *et al.* (2012), and Azam (2012) claim that the rise in wage rates for unskilled labourers was due to the

Figure 15.3 *Gender gap and level of wages for agricultural occupations,* in Rs per day

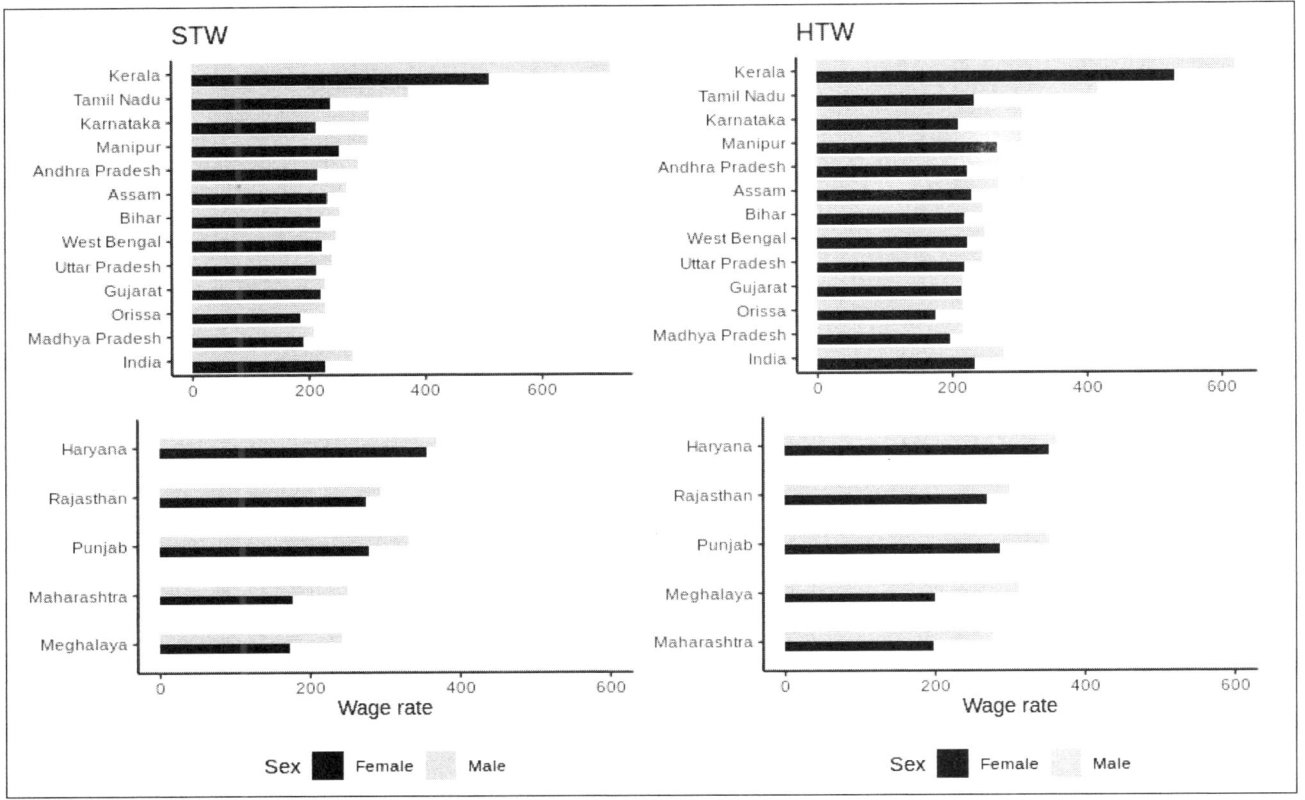

Source: Computed from *Wage Rates in Rural India,* 2017–18.

Figure 15.4 *Gender gap in wage rates and female work participation rates, 2011–12*

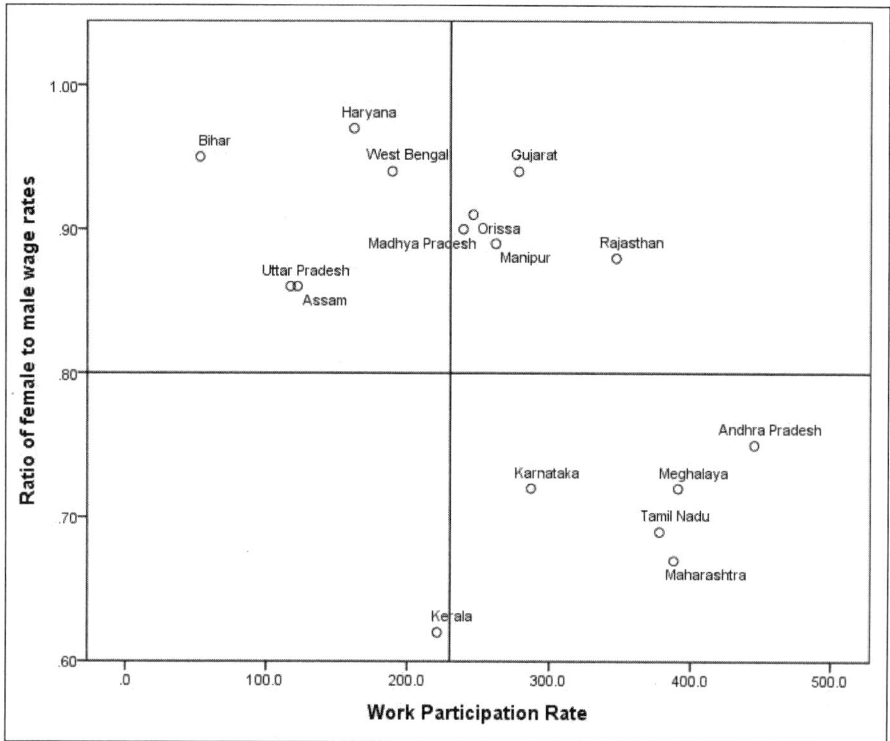

Source: Computed from the Labour Bureau's *Wage Rates in Rural India* and NSSO's Employment and Unemployment Survey, 2011–12.

implementation of NREGS after 2005. However, Dutta *et al.* (2012) argue that this increase cannot be entirely attributed to the scheme. The growth in agriculture and construction together with the implementation of NREGS might have triggered growth in farm wages (Gulati, Jain, and Satija 2013; Himanshu and Kundu 2016).

Wages were paid for NREGS work according to the State-wise statutory minimum wage rate until 2008–09. Since 2009–10, the wage rate for NREGA work has been fixed and notified by the Ministry of Rural Development[3] (MGNREGA Section 6 [1]). It was announced in March 2011 that the wage revision indexed to CPI-AL would be done annually and become effective on 1 April of each year. In 2018, the government considered a proposal to change the wage calculation methodology from CPI-AL to CPI-Rural. Since 2012–13, the average wages paid under NREGS are less than the corresponding

---

[3] Notification of revised wage rates under section 6 (1) of the MGNREG Act, 2005.

Table 15.4 *Gender gap in wage rates and work participation rates*

State	WPR*	Gender gap for STW operations**	Level of parti-cipation#	Level of gender gap in wage rates	Category
Andhra Pradesh	445	0.75	High	High	I
Maharashtra	388	0.67	High	High	I
Meghalaya	391	0.72	High	High	I
Tamil Nadu	378	0.69	High	High	I
West Bengal	189	0.94	Low	Low	II
Haryana	162	0.97	Low	Low	II
Assam	122	0.86	Low	Low	II
Uttar Pradesh	117	0.86	Low	Low	II
Bihar	53	0.95	Low	Low	II
Karnataka	287	0.72	Medium	High	III
Kerala	221	0.62	Medium	High	III
Odisha	246	0.91	Medium	Low	IV
Madhya Pradesh	239	0.9	Medium	Low	IV
Manipur	262	0.89	Medium	Low	IV
Gujarat	278	0.94	Medium	Low	IV
Rajasthan	347	0.88	High	Low	V

Note: * NSS-EUS, 2011–12. ** Ratio of female to male wage rates. # Based on WPR.
Source: Computed from *Wage Rates in Rural India*, various issues, and NSSO's Employment and Unemployment Survey, 2011–12.

State minimum wages, as well as the prevailing wage rates for agricultural and non-agricultural occupations. Secondly, the NREGS wage rates are piece-rated, and so the actual payments made to male and female workers based on the completion of tasks are different.

Table 15.5 compares the average wage rates under NREGS for female STW workers in 2007–08, 2010–11, and 2013–14. It is assumed that employment generation under NREGS will result in increased market wage rates, in particular for female labourers.

There is no clear picture of the effect of NREGS on market wage rates. In 2007–08, average wages paid under NREGS were lower than the market wages (STW) for female labourers across States. In other words, the market wage rates for female workers were lower than the minimum wages and average wages paid under NREGS. In 2010–11, the average wages paid under NREGS were lower than the wage rates for female STW workers in six States – Andhra Pradesh, Haryana, Kerala, Rajasthan, Tamil Nadu, and Odisha, all of which have relatively high wage rates. In States such as Rajasthan and Tamil

Table 15.5 *Difference between average wages paid under NREGS and nominal wage rates for female STW workers, 2007–08, 2010–11, and 2013–14* in Rs

State	2007–08			2010–11			2013–14		
	Average NREGS wage	Female STW wage	Difference	Average NREGS wage	Female STW wage	Difference	Average NREGS wage	Female STW wage	Difference
Assam	75	68	–7	116	98	–18	153	162	9
Bihar	83	54	–29	115	92	–23	143	157	14
Gujarat	57	61	4	104	79	–25	126	146	20
Uttar Pradesh	62	62	0	113	96	–17	140	150	10
West Bengal	85	65	–20	115	99	–16	147	176	29
Karnataka	88	47	–41	143	77	–66	201	146	–55
Madhya Pradesh	61	45	–16	120	75	–45	135	126	–9
Maharashtra	78	47	–31	137	80	–57	157	134	–23
Andhra Pradesh	NA	54		111	117	6	112	156	44
Haryana	125	104	–21	169	188	19	211	288	77
Kerala	118	118	0	129	176	47	139	405	266
Rajasthan	84	67	–17	87	112	25	99	174	75
Tamil Nadu	NA	53		84	110	26	99	175	76
Odisha	83	43	–40	96	109	13	131	133	2

Source: http://nrega.nic.in/netnrega/home.aspx, Ministry of Rural Development, and *Wage Rates in Rural India*, various issues.

Nadu, where performance of NREGS is relatively better, wage rates for female workers are higher than the NREGS wage rate. It is important to note that the gap between market wage rates and wages paid under NRGES increased from 2007–08 to 2010–11 for Assam, Gujarat, Uttar Pradesh, West Bengal, Karnataka, Madhya Pradesh, and Maharashtra. This implies that NREGS had minimum impact on female STW wages. However, the trend reversed since 2013–14, when market wage rates for female workers overtook NREGS wages in all States except Karnataka, Madhya Pradesh, and Maharashtra. In these States, female STW wage rates were lower than wages paid under NREGS between 2007–08 and 2013–14. The ratio of wage paid under MGNREGS to female STW wage rates were calculated and correlated with growth rates for STW operations in 2013–14. The correlation coefficient between the two indicators was 0.31, which indicates no significant impact of MGNREGS on wage rates. Hence, NREGS was not the sole reason for the high growth in wage rates for female workers between 2007–08 and 2013–14.

Female labourers in agricultural and non-agricultural occupations
The rapid rise in real wage rates after 2007 and the decline in gender gap in wage rates were accompanied by growth in non-farm employment, as discussed extensively in the literature (Himanshu 2017; Gulati *et al.* 2013). Within the non-agricultural sector, growth in the construction sector and implementation of MGNREGS contributed to a sharp rise in wage rates. In other words, we can argue that rise in demand for non-agricultural employment led to a decrease in the supply of labour and an increase in wage rates in agriculture. Table 15.6 examines the pattern of wage differential between agricultural and non-agricultural occupations over the last two decades for female labourers. The ratio of wages between unskilled non-agricultural labour and STW was computed. Three-year averages were taken for comparison at the beginning and end of the period under study.

Table 15.6 and 15.7 show the ratio between unskilled non-agricultural and agricultural wage rates for females and males. Except in Tamil Nadu, Haryana, and Andhra Pradesh, unskilled non-agricultural wages were lower than those for STW between 1998–99 and 2000–01. During the high-growth period (2007–08 to 2014–15), unskilled non-agricultural wage rates overtook agricultural wage rates (STW) for most States.

There was substantial regional variation. When compared to STW, the wage rates for unskilled non-agricultural labour were consistently lower by more than 10 per cent in Madhya Pradesh, Maharashtra, Andhra Pradesh, and Karnataka from 1998–99 to 2018–19. Except for Madhya Pradesh, these States have high gender gaps in wage rates, and non-agricultural wage rates

Table 15.6 *Wage ratios between unskilled non-agricultural and sowing/transplanting/ winnowing occupations for female labourers, 1998–99 to 2016–17*

States	1998–99 to 2000–01	2006–07 to 2008–09	2015–16 to 2017–18
Uttar Pradesh	0.99	0.99	1.07
West Bengal	0.91	0.88	1.05
Gujarat	0.96	0.97	1.13
Assam	0.77	0.83	1.15
Haryana	1.06	1.02	NA
Bihar	0.91	1.02	1.01
Kerala	0.94	1.15	NA
Odisha	0.98	1.04	1.17
Rajasthan	0.97	1.12	NA
Tamil Nadu	1.03	1.24	1.24
Andhra Pradesh	0.99	0.92	0.87
Madhya Pradesh	0.87	0.87	0.89
Maharashtra	0.84	0.84	0.87
Karnataka	0.85	0.91	0.88
All-India	0.93	0.94	0.95

Source: Computed from *Wage Rates in Rural India*, various issues.

did not have a significant impact on female wage rates and gender gap in wage rates. In Tamil Nadu, where the unskilled non-agricultural wage rates for females were higher as compared to other States, the gender wage gap continued to widen between 2007–08 and 2014–15.

In Bihar, Kerala, Odisha, and Rajasthan, unskilled non-agricultural wage rates were overtaken by wage rates for female STW occupations in the high-growth period (2007–08 to 2014–14). In addition, the wage gap declined in Kerala, Odisha, and Rajasthan. Thus, non-agricultural wages have had a significant impact on agricultural wage rates and also helped in improving the gender gap in wage rates. In Rajasthan, the implementation and performance of MGNREGS might have raised unskilled non-agricultural wages and agricultural wages. In Kerala, the performance of the construction sector had a significant impact on female wage rates. In Bihar and Odisha, the rise in non-farm employment and male out-migration might have had an impact on wage rates in the rural areas.

Between 1998–99 and 2011–12, unskilled non-agricultural wages were lower than agricultural wages in Uttar Pradesh, West Bengal, Gujarat, and Assam. Overall work participation rates and participation in non-farm employment in these States were very low. Thus, unskilled non-agricultural

Table 15.7 *Wage ratios between unskilled non-agricultural and sowing/transplanting/ winnowing occupations for male labourers, 1998–99 to 2016–17*

States	1998–99 to 2000–01	2006–07 to 2008–09	2015–16 to 2017–18
Andhra Pradesh	1.08	0.94	0.91
Assam	0.93	0.98	0.95
Bihar	0.94	1.04	0.92
Gujarat	0.94	0.90	0.97
Haryana	1.02	1.01	0.94
Karnataka	0.83	0.89	0.84
Kerala	0.94	0.83	0.90
Madhya Pradesh	0.86	0.85	0.96
Maharashtra	0.86	0.85	0.90
Odisha	0.94	0.97	1.00
Rajasthan	0.89	0.99	1.04
Tamil Nadu	0.98	1.07	1.12
Uttar Pradesh	1.02	1.03	1.03
West Bengal	0.93	0.89	1.13
All-India	0.99	0.99	1.00

Source: Computed from *Wage Rates in Rural India,* various issues.

wage rates did not have a significant impact on the gender gap in wage rates. However, the trends reversed from 2014 onwards.

CONCLUSION

This chapter examined trends in wage rates of male and female workers and the gender gap in wage rates in rural India for the period 1998–99 to 2018–19 using the Wage Rates in Rural India database as reported in the *Indian Labour Journal.*

A period of wage stagnation (1998–99 to 2006–07) was followed by significant growth in rural wage rates for men and women across all occupations and States until 2014–15. For major agricultural occupations, the data show that there was higher growth in wage rates for female workers than for males at the all-India level. For sowing/transplanting/weeding operations, the growth rate of female wages was higher than that of male wages in nine States. In the period of stagnation (1998–99 to 2006–07), deceleration of female wage rates was more severe than of male wage rates.

An indicator of labour market discrimination against women is the gender wage gap. For three major rural occupations (sowing/transplanting/weeding, harvesting/winnowing/threshing, and unskilled non-agricultural), wage rates for female workers were lower than for male workers at the all-India level. Among the three occupations, female wage rates were lowest for unskilled non-agricultural occupations. For agricultural operations such as sowing/transplanting/weeding and harvesting/winnowing/threshing, female wage rates were four-fifths of male wage rates at the all-India level. Between 1998–99 and 2005–06 (a period of stagnation), the gender gap in wage rates was either stagnant or increasing across States and at the all-India level, but during the period of wage growth (2006–07 to 2014–15), the gap declined marginally. In the last five years (2014–15 to 2018–19), the gap has either stagnated or increased marginally.

Finally, there was substantial variation in the gender gap in wage rates across States; it was relatively high in Kerala, Tamil Nadu, Andhra Pradesh, Karnataka, and Maharashtra, as compared to Bihar, Gujarat, Haryana, Manipur, and West Bengal. In other words, the south and west versus north and east dichotomy persists in the recent period.

Changes in the gender wage gap were examined by looking at the following factors: regional variation in wage rates, variation in female labour supply, NREGS, and growth in non-agricultural sector. It was found that:

(i) The gender gap in wage rates is influenced by the level of wage rates. The gap is larger in high wage rate regions such as Kerala, Tamil Nadu, and Karnataka; it is smaller in low wage rate regions like West Bengal, Bihar, and Uttar Pradesh.

(ii) The gender wage gap is not negatively correlated to female labour supply; the relation between the two is more complex.

(iii) The implementation of NREGS has had a favourable impact on female wage rates in the low wage rate regions, leading to a reduction in the gender gap in wage rates till 2013–14. In the following year, NREGS wages were revised but remained below market wage rates.

(iv) In the last two decades, the shift of male labourers from agriculture to non-agriculture has had a greater impact on male wage rates, associated with a stagnation or increase in the gender wage gap between 1998–99 and 2008–09. After 2008–09, unskilled non-agriculture wages were higher than agricultural wages for females, except in Maharashtra, Karnataka, Madhya Pradesh, and Andhra Pradesh. This may have pushed up female wage rates in agriculture, thus lowering the gender gap in agricultural wage rates in the period of rapid wage growth (2007–08 to 2014–15).

I am grateful to Yoshifumi Usami for detailed comments and suggestions, and Rakesh Kumar Mahato for research assistance. Research for this paper was supported by a grant from Azim Premji University (project titled "Wage Rates in Rural India: Trends and Determinants").

References

Azam, Mehtabul (2012), "The Impact of Indian Job Guarantee Scheme on Labor Market Outcomes: Evidence from a Natural Experiment," IZA Working Paper 6548.

Berg, Erlend, Bhattacharyya, Sambit, Durgam, Rajasekhar, and Ramachandra, Manjula (2012), "Can Rural Public Works Affect Agricultural Wages? Evidence from India," CSAE Working Paper WPS/2012–05, Centre for the Study of African Economies, Department of Economics, University of Oxford.

Boserup, E. (1970), *Woman's Role in Economic Development*, Earthscan Publications, London.

Central Statistical Office (CSO) (2013), "Key Indicators of Employment and Unemployment in India: 2011–12," National Sample Survey Office, Ministry of Statistics and Programme Implementation, Government of India.

Chandrasekhar, C. P., and Ghosh, Jayati (2011), "Public Work and Wages in Rural India," http://www.macroscan.org/fet/jan11/fet110111 public works.htm, viewed on 30 March 2020.

Chavan, Pallavi, and Rajshree Bedamatta (2006), "Trends in Agricultural Wages in India, 1964–65 to 1999–2000," *Economic and Political Weekly*, vol. XLI, no. 38, pp. 4041–51.

Das, Arindam, and Usami, Yoshifumi (2017), "Wage Rates in Rural India, 1998–99 to 2016–17," *Review of Agrarian Studies*, 7, 2, http://www.ras.org.in/wage_rates_in_rural_india_1998.

Dobb, Maurice (1955), *Wages*, Cambridge Economic Handbook, Volume VI.

Emmanuel Skoufias (1994), "Using Shadow Wages to Estimate Labor Supply of Agricultural Households," *American Journal of Agricultural Economics*, vol. 76, issue 2, May, pp. 215–27.

Government of India (GOI), Ministry of Labour and Employment, Labour Bureau, *Wage Rates in Rural India*, various issues.

Gulati, Ashok, Jain, Surbhi, and Satija, Nidhi (2013), "Rising Farm Wages in India: The 'Pull' and 'Push' Factors," Discussion Paper No. 5, Commission for Agricultural Costs and Prices, Ministry of Agriculture, Government of India, New Delhi.

Himanshu (2017), "Growth, Structural Change and Wages in India: Recent Trends," *Indian Journal of Labour Economics*, vol. 60, issue 3, pp. 309–31.

Himanshu, and Kundu, Sujata (2016), "Rural Wages in India: Recent Trends and Determinants," *Indian Journal of Labour Economics*, vol. 59, issue 2, pp. 217–44.

Jose, A. V. (2013), "Changes in Wages and Earnings of Rural Labourers," *Economic and Political Weekly*, vol. XLVIII, no. 26/27, pp. 107–14.

Jose, A. V. (2017), "Agriculture wages in India," *Indian Journal of Labour Economics*, vol. 60, issue 3, pp. 333–45.

Kurosaki, Takashi and Usami, Yoshifumi (2016), "A Note on the Reliability of Agricultural Wage Data in India: Reconciliation of Monthly AWI Data for District-Level Analysis," *Review of Agrarian Studies*, vol. 6, no. 1.

Mahajan, Kanika (2016), "Rainfall Shocks and the Gender Wage Gap: Evidence from Indian Agriculture," *World Development*.

Mahajan, Kanika, and Ramaswami, Bharat (2017), "Caste, Female Labour Supply, and the Gender Wage Gap in India: Boserup Revisited," *Economic Development and Cultural Change*, vol. 65 (2), University of Chicago Press.

Ramachandran, V. K. (1990), *Wage Labour and Unfreedom in Agriculture: An Indian Case Study*, Clarendon Press, Oxford.

Srivastava, Ravi, and Singh, Richa (2006), "Rural Wages during the 1990s: A Re-estimation," *Economic and Political Weekly*, issue no. 38, pp. 4053–62.

Usami, Yoshifumi (2011), "A Note on Recent Trends in Wage Rates in Rural India," *Review of Agrarian Studies*, http://ras.org.in/a_note_on_recent_trends_in_wage_rates_in_rural_india, viewed on 30 March 2020.

Usami, Yoshifumi (2012), "Recent Trends in Wage Rates In Rural India: An Update," *Review of Agrarian Studies*, http://ras.org.in/recent_trends_in_wage_rates_in_rural_india, viewed on 30 March 2020.

APPENDIX

Appendix Figure 15.1 *Male to female wage ratio across states*

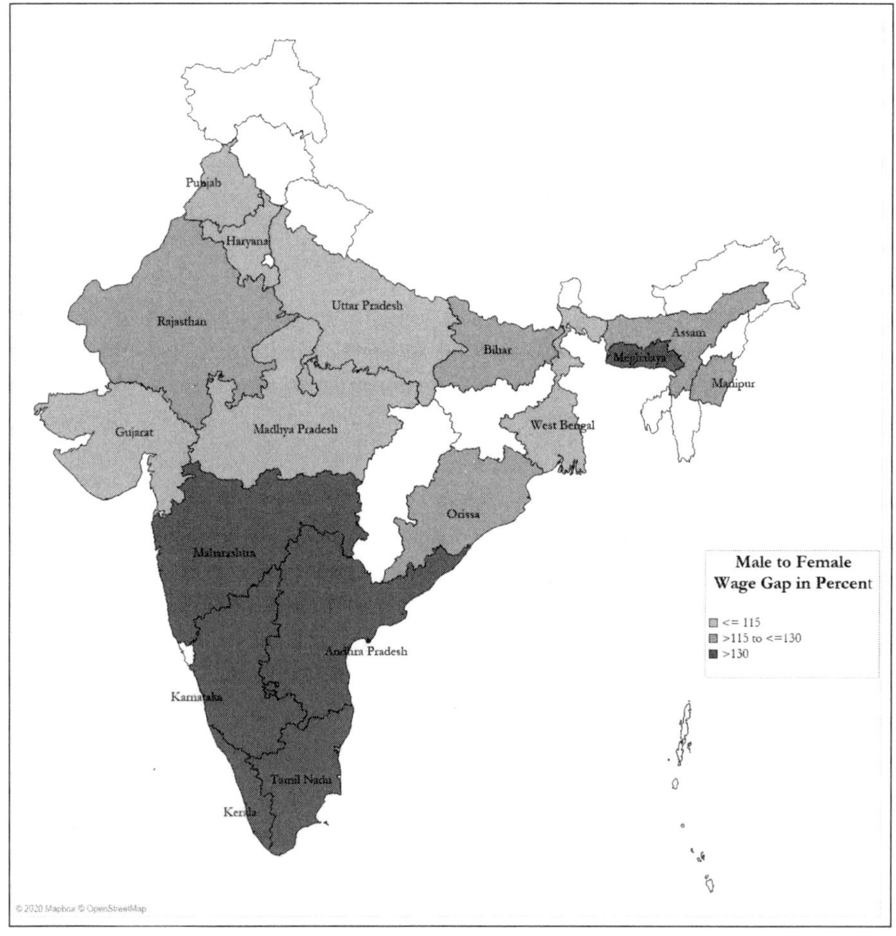

Source: *Wage Rates in Rural India*, 2018–19.

Appendix Table 15.1 *Changes in male–female ratio of wage rates for sowing/transplanting/ weeding (STW)*

States	1998–99 to 2000–01	2005–06 to 2007–08	2011–12 to 2013–14	2016–17 to 2018–19
Kerala	1.46	1.81	1.64	1.38
Tamil Nadu	1.57	1.64	1.50	1.58
Maharashtra	1.43	1.52	1.48	1.45
Karnataka	1.37	1.40	1.44	1.43
Meghalaya	1.37	1.40	1.38	1.37
Andhra Pradesh	1.32	1.39	1.28	1.31
Rajasthan	1.27	1.34	1.20	1.13
Uttar Pradesh	1.20	1.18	1.19	1.13
Odisha	1.17	1.25	1.14	1.22
Madhya Pradesh	1.15	1.19	1.14	1.09
Bihar	1.11	1.10	1.12	1.17
Punjab	NA	NA	NA	1.18
Manipur	1.06	1.10	1.13	1.19
Haryana	1.16	1.05	1.03	1.04
Gujarat	1.10	1.12	1.07	1.04
West Bengal	1.10	1.11	1.06	1.12
Assam	0.94	1.16	1.09	1.16
All-India	1.21	1.28	1.19	1.21

Note: Three-year average to compare the beginning and end of the sub-periods.
Source: Computed from *Wage Rates in Rural India*, various issues.

Appendix Table 15.2 *Changes in male–female ratio of wage rates for harvesting/threshing/winnowing (HTW)*

States	1998–99 to 2000–01	2005–06 to 2007–08	2011–12 to 2013–14	2016–17 to 2018–19
Tamil Nadu	1.51	1.40	1.44	1.74
Maharashtra	1.42	1.57	1.50	1.43
Kerala	1.34	1.21	1.26	1.22
Karnataka	1.32	1.32	1.44	1.44
Andhra Pradesh	1.26	1.36	1.38	1.26
Meghalaya	1.23	1.45	1.50	1.59
Punjab	1.24	NA	NA	1.17
Odisha	1.17	1.29	1.30	1.20
Bihar	1.18	1.11	1.12	1.12
Uttar Pradesh	1.16	1.15	1.13	1.12
Madhya Pradesh	1.13	1.19	1.13	1.11
Manipur	1.14	1.10	1.12	1.11
Rajasthan	1.11	1.14	1.07	1.11
West Bengal	1.10	1.10	1.10	1.13
Gujarat	1.07	1.04	1.00	1.02
Haryana	1.04	1.02	1.01	1.03
Assam	0.97	1.08	1.15	1.18
All-India	1.22	1.25	1.21	1.18

Note: Three-year average to compare the beginning and end of the sub-periods.
Source: Computed from *Wage Rates in Rural India*, various issues.

Appendix Table 15.3 *Changes in male–female ratio of wage rates for unskilled non-agricultural labourers*

States	1998–99 to 2000–01	2005–06 to 2007–08	2011–12 to 2013–14	2016–17 to 2018–19
Meghalaya	1.73	1.55	1.55	NA
Kerala	1.46	1.29	1.55	NA
Tamil Nadu	1.50	1.40	1.40	1.40
Maharashtra	1.47	1.56	1.56	1.53
Andhra Pradesh	1.40	1.38	1.37	1.41
Karnataka	1.34	1.38	1.39	1.28
Uttar Pradesh	1.23	1.21	1.20	1.16
Rajasthan	1.16	1.11	1.09	1.14
Assam	1.14	1.40	1.22	1.01
Bihar	1.15	1.12	1.14	1.19
Madhya Pradesh	1.13	1.16	1.16	1.12
Odisha	1.12	1.20	1.10	1.13
West Bengal	1.13	1.12	1.15	1.26
Haryana	1.11	1.06	1.07	NA
Gujarat	1.08	1.04	1.03	0.97
Manipur	1.10	1.11	1.07	NA
Himachal Pradesh	NA	NA	0.92	NA
All-India	1.29	1.33	1.33	1.32

Note: Three-year average to compare the beginning and end of the sub-periods.
Source: Computed from *Wage Rates in Rural India*, various issues.

16

The Gender Gap in Wage Rates
Exploring the Role of Female Labour Supply with Evidence from PARI Villages

Arindam Das

This chapter describes and examines the possible factors determining female wage rates and the gender wage differential for agricultural field operations, drawing from village surveys conducted under the Project on Agrarian Relations in India (PARI) by the Foundation for Agrarian Studies (FAS). The gender gap in wage rates can be attributed to multiple factors, and varies according to cropping pattern, crop operation, agro-ecology, forms of wages, level of mechanisation, male out-migration, urbanisation, and participation in non-farm employment. The primary survey data allow for an examination of some of these factors.

In this chapter, we first discuss the extent and magnitude of the gender gap in wage rates, followed by an explanation of the composition of female labour supply, to understand who participates in the wage labour market and what determines their participation. Later, we explore how the variation in female labour supply influences women's wages and leads to variation in the gender differential in wage rates.

DATABASE AND METHODOLOGY

Data on wage rates for wage-worker households from 16 villages across 9 States of India have been used for the analysis. These villages belong to different agro-ecological zones, and have varying cropping patterns and different socio-economic indicators. The villages were surveyed by FAS between 2005 and 2012. A brief description of the survey villages is given in Appendix Table 16.1.

An important feature of the PARI village data is that wage data are collected at a disaggregated level: for wage workers, data are collected by gender, crop operation, season, type of wage contract, work hours, and mode of payment (cash and kind). The PARI village surveys also collect data on different socio-economic indicators, such as landholding, cropping pattern, crop production by operational holding, education, occupation, and employment. The PARI data cover two types of wage contracts prevalent in the villages: piece-rated and daily-rated. In piece-rated contracts, wages were paid based on either acreage or volume of production. As discussed in the literature, there has been a shift from daily-rated to piece-rated wage contracts in many of the villages (Ramachandran 1990; Dhar 2017). However, given that most official databases do not collect and include data on piece-rated wage contracts, these have been excluded from the analysis so as to allow for comparability with secondary data.

For the analysis, we took the simple average of daily wage rates for sowing, transplanting, weeding, and harvesting operations, normalised to eight hours of employment in wage work. Further, if any person was employed for at least one day, wage work was included in the calculation. The nominal wages were adjusted by the consumer price index for agricultural labourers (CPI-AL) with 2009–10 as the base year.

VARIATION IN WAGE RATES

Ramachandran (1990) and Dhar (2011) show that wage rates in agriculture vary by crop, crop operation, gender, and type of wage contract. Appendix Table 16.2 in this chapter gives the average daily wage rates for sowing, transplanting, weeding, and harvesting operations deflated by 2009–10 prices for 14 out of the 16 study villages. Overall, it can be seen that female wage rates were lower than male wage rates for female-specific operations such as sowing, transplanting, and weeding. Among the 16 villages, women were paid slightly higher wages in Rewasi (Sikar district, Rajasthan) – Rs 158, Bukkacherla (Anantapur district, Andhra Pradesh) – Rs 118, and Panahar (Bankura district, West Bengal) – Rs 91. At the lower end were Katkuian (West Champaran district, Bihar), Mahatwar (Balia district, Uttar Pradesh), Zhapur (Kalaburagi district, Karnataka), and 25F Gulabewala (Sri Ganganagar district, Rajasthan), where wages ranged from Rs 40 to Rs 55 per day. For each crop operation, the average male daily wage rates were higher than female wage rates in all the study villages, with two exceptions of Panahar and Rewasi where male and female wage rates were equal. In Rewasi all workers received a daily wage of Rs 158, the highest across all study villages.

The wage rates for harvesting were higher than those for sowing, transplanting, and weeding operations in the case of female workers across all the villages. In Warwat Khanderao and Nimshirgaon (both in Maharashtra), female wage rates for harvesting were higher than for sowing, transplanting, and weeding by Rs 20 to Rs 30 in absolute terms. This may be due to cotton cultivation in Warwat Khanderao and horticulture in Nimshirgaon, as both types of cultivation used female labour for the harvesting/plucking operation.

GENDER GAP IN WAGE RATES

With two exceptions, the gender wage differential persisted in all the study villages for every crop operation. The regional pattern of the gender wage gap for these operations does not always align with that given by official sources such as *Wage Rates in Rural India* (WRRI). I have previously argued that there is a north–east and west–south dichotomy in the gender gap in wage rates, wherein the wage gap is higher in southern and western States as compared to northern and eastern States (see chapter 15 in this volume). Village data show that along with spatial variation, agro-ecology and cropping pattern play a significant role in the gender gap in agricultural wage rates. The gender wage gap was relatively large in southern (Ananthavaram, Bukkacherla, and Kothapalli in Andhra Pradesh; Siresandra, Zhapur, and Alabujanahalli in Karnataka), western (Nimshirgaon and Warwat Khanderao in Maharashtra), and some eastern (Katkuian and Nayanagar in Bihar; Kalmandasguri in West Bengal) villages. In other eastern villages (Amarsinghi and Panahar in West Bengal), the gender gap in wage rates was small. Further, the gender wage gap between men and women was not uniform across villages within States. For example, the female to male wage ratio was relatively low in Amarsinghi (Malda district, West Bengal) and Panahar (Bankura district, West Bengal), between 0.85 and 0.98, whereas it was higher in Kalmandasguri, North Bengal, ranging from 0.69 to 0.82 for various agricultural operations.

The data suggest a relatively large wage disparity in rainfed single-crop villages such as Warwat Khanderao, Kalmandasguri, and Zhapur (ranging between 0.4 to 0.7), whereas the disparity was minimal in the irrigated multi-crop village of Panahar (0.98). The gender gap in wage rates was high in villages with sugarcane and paddy cultivation, such as Katkuian, Nimshirgaon, and Alabujanahalli.

The village data show that the gender gap in wage rates was higher for harvesting/threshing/winnowing (HTW) operations than for sowing/transplanting/weeding (STW) operations in Zhapur, Katkuian, Kalmandasguri, and Bukkacherla (Table 16.1). These villages either lie in rainfed regions and cultivate only a single crop or lie in areas growing commercial crops (sugarcane). In Alabujanahalli, Ananthavaram, Siresandra, Nayanagar, Nimshirgaon, 25F Gulabewala, Harevli, Warwat Khanderao, and Gharsondi, the gender differential in wage rates was lower for HTW operations than for

 325

Table 16.1 *Female to male wage ratios by agricultural operation, study villages*

Village	State	Sowing	Transplanting	Weeding	Harvesting
Ananthavaram	Andhra Pradesh	0.59	0.54	0.82	0.71
Bukkacherla	Andhra Pradesh	0.91	0.83	0.7	0.76
Harevli	Uttar Pradesh	0.8	0.81	0.84	0.88
25F Gulabewala	Rajasthan	–	–	0.67	0.73
Warwat Khanderao	Maharashtra	0.88	–	0.77	0.97
Nimshirgaon	Maharashtra	0.81	–	0.84	0.83
Gharsondi	Madhya Pradesh	–	–	0.92	0.94
Zhapur	Karnataka	0.44		0.44	0.48
Alabujanahalli	Karnataka	0.56	0.47	0.53	0.51
Siresandra	Karnataka	0.56		0.8	0.66
Panahar	West Bengal	1	0.99	1	0.98
Kalmandasguri	West Bengal	0.69	0.82	0.81	0.72
Amarsinghi	West Bengal	–	0.99	0.86	0.9
Rewasi	Rajasthan	–	–	1	1
Nayanagar	Bihar	0.65	–	0.76	0.69
Katkuian	Bihar	0.4	0.69	0.6	0.48

Source: PARI survey data.

STW operations. In these villages, the major crops were paddy, cotton, and vegetables.

Paddy absorbs a large proportion of female labour (Ramachandran 1990; Niyati, chapter 6 in this volume), with participation of female labour being much higher for irrigated paddy than for rainfed paddy. In paddy cultivation, transplanting, which is still a non-mechanised operation, required more female labour than any other operation. Women were also hired for weeding, harvesting, and post-harvesting operations. On the other hand, female participation in cultivation of coarse grain and wheat was seen to be consistently low. In sugarcane and cotton, overall female labour absorption was low except in some operations. Based on the above discussion, we have divided the 16 study villages into three regions based on the main crops grown: rice-growing villages; sugarcane-growing villages; and villages with mixed cropping including wheat, coarse grains, cotton, and vegetables.

In the rice-growing villages (Appendix Table 16.3) of Panahar and Amarsinghi in West Bengal, the wage gap was narrow (0.9 to 0.98). In Kalmandasguri, in addition to rice, potato and jute were important crops (Sarkar 2017b). The gender wage gap was large in Kalmandasguri (0.82 for transplanting and 0.72 for harvesting). In Ananthavaram village of Andhra Pradesh, the gender gap in wage rates was even larger (0.54 for transplanting and 0.71 for harvesting).

In the mixed-crop villages, there were some interesting variations (Appendix Table 16.4). While there was a gender wage gap in all the villages except Rewasi, it was lower in cotton-growing villages like Warwat Khanderao. This probably reflects the higher demand for female labour in cotton-picking operations. A mixed cropping pattern was only one of the factors affecting wage rates. In rainfed villages such as Bukkacherla, Siresandra, and Zhapur, women received much lower wages than men across all agricultural operations. This may reflect an overall lower demand for labour in unirrigated agriculture.

In villages with sugarcane cultivation, we see a mixed pattern. The wage gap was 0.8 in Nimshirgaon and Harevli, and 0.5 in Katkuian and Alabujanahalli. As previously stated, this analysis suggests that a combination of factors influenced wage rates.

Factors Affecting Female Labour Supply in Agriculture

Female labour supply (and female work participation) is likely to be an important factor in the setting of female wage rates. To understand female work participation in agriculture, this sub-section draws from Dhar (2013 and 2017), Usami (chapter 3 in this volume), and Ramachandran (chapter 4 in this volume). In the PARI village surveys, all persons who are reported as being engaged in an economically productive activity as their primary, secondary or tertiary activity are categorised as workers. A worker is defined as an individual above the age of 15 years who has undertaken any economic activity, either directly as part of a production process or under supervision, for at least one day in the reference year. Animal husbandry performed by an individual is considered as work in the definition, whereas housework is excluded from the definition.

In the study villages, women were largely engaged in animal husbandry, family labour or supervision in their own field, and agricultural labour. Female participation in non-agricultural activities was very limited due to the unavailability of non-farm employment in the vicinity of the village. Female agricultural labour from manual worker and small peasant households were the primary source of supply in the wage market. Apart from this, female family labour from small peasant households was a major source of supply for non-mechanised operations. Female work participation rates were low among landlord, rich peasant, and upper-caste Hindu households. Women were also employed in the construction and mining sector in Zhapur, and

MGNREGS in Panahar, Nayanagar, and Alabujanahalli. The share of female workers among all females ranged from 36 to 76 per cent in the study villages.

To understand female labour supply, we examined the share of female agriculture workers among all female workers.[1] Except in Rewasi, more than one-third of women workers were agricultural labourers. However, there was substantial variation across villages. The share of female agricultural labourers among total female workers was more than 50 per cent in 25F Gulabewala, Ananthavaram, Harevli, Warwat Khanderao, Kalmandasguri, Bukkacherla, and Zhapur. In Alabujanahalli, Panahar, Amarsinghi, Katkuian, and Nayanagar, the proportion was less than 50 per cent.

We explore three factors that determine female labour supply at the village level: incidence of landlessness, size of manual labour work force, and social composition of the population.

First, the correlation coefficient between the incidence of landlessness and the female agricultural labour force was 0.6 (Figure 16.1).[2] The proportion of female agriculture labourers among all female workers was relatively high in villages where the proportion of landless households was high. For example, the proportion of female agricultural labourers was more than 50 per cent in 25F Gulabewala, Ananthavaram, and Nayanagar, where the proportion of landless households was also more than 50 per cent. The proportion of female agricultural labourers was low in Alabujanahalli and Nimshirgaon, where the proportion of landlessness was also low. Alabujanahalli[3] and Nimshirgaon[4] belonged to prosperous regions, and an income effect could be a reason for non-participation of women workers in the wage labour market. Female workers were also employed in sericulture activities as family labour or on daily-rated contracts in Alabujanahalli and Siresandra. In the eastern Indian villages surveyed, the proportion of female agriculture labourers was relatively low (less than 50 per cent of all workers), irrespective of the magnitude of landlessness.

Secondly, workers from manual worker households were major sources of labour supply to the wage labour market. We define manual worker households as those households whose main source of income comes from wage work. The participation in wage work of women from manual worker households was very high, at 35 to 65 per cent, in the study villages (Nagbhushan, chapter

---

[1] A worker is defined as one who has participated in at least one day of agricultural activity outside the house as wage work.

[2] Statistically significant at 5 per cent level of confidence, where p value is 0.02.

[3] Alabujanahalli is located close to Maddur and Mandya towns.

[4] Nimshirgaon is part of an industrial belt in western Maharashtra, and is surrounded by towns such as Jaysingpur, Kolhapur, Shirol, and Sangli. Owing to this, non-agricultural employment, mainly in the construction sector and small factories, was an important source of employment for male workers.

Figure 16.1 *Regression plot between shares of female agricultural labourers among total female workers and share of landless households among all households*

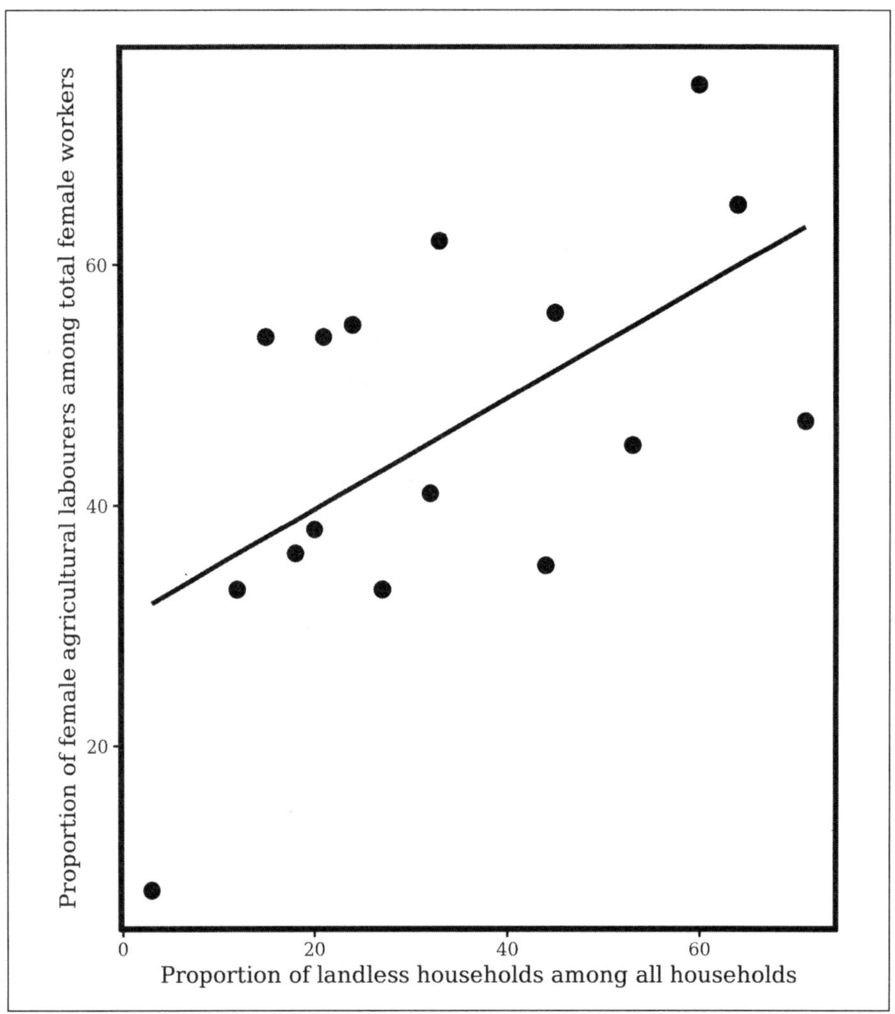

Source: PARI survey data.

11 in this volume). Thus, the variation in the proportion of female agricultural labourers depends on the share of manual worker households in total village households (Table 16.2). However, women wage workers from manual worker households alone do not form the class of workers who are employed in wage work. Women from small peasant[5] households participate in cultivation as

---

[5] The definition of a small peasant is a peasant with an operational holding of less than 2 hectares, or 6 hectares of unirrigated land, or any combination thereof. The manual worker households that

Table 16.2 *Proportion of manual worker and small peasant households in total households, and the share of female agricultural labourers among total female workers, study villages* in per cent

Village	State	Share of manual worker households among total households	Share of small peasant households in total households	Share of female agricultural labourers among total female workers
25F Gulabewala	Rajasthan	56	1	65
Zhapur	Karnataka	47	24	56
Ananthavaram	Andhra Pradesh	25	34	75
Kalmandasguri	West Bengal	44	46	54
Siresandra	Karnataka	16	71	33
Harevli	Uttar Pradesh	25	41	62
Nayanagar	Bihar	61	25	47
Nimshirgaon	Maharashtra	39	31	33
Gharsondi	Madhya Pradesh	27	27	38
Bukkacherla	Andhra Pradesh	20	37	54
Rewasi	Rajasthan	18	49	8
Alabujanahalli	Karnataka	30	47	36
Katkuian	Bihar	63	24	45
Warwat Khanderao	Maharashtra	40	42	55
Panahar	West Bengal	30	58	35
Amarsinghi	West Bengal	28	43	41

Source: PARI survey data.

family labour and also work outside the household as wage labour during times of seasonal demand in agriculture (Ramachandran, chapter 4 in this volume). The village evidence shows increasing participation of female wage workers from peasant households in the villages surveyed in southern India, as compared to those surveyed in the northern and eastern parts of the country. The increase in supply of female workers can influence wage rates.

Thirdly, Scheduled Caste (SC) and Scheduled Tribe (ST) households represented a significant proportion of all manual worker households. The proportion of SC households as a proportion of total manual worker households varied from 18 per cent in Nayanagar to 81 per cent in Panahar (Nagbhushan,

depend on incomes from business, salaries or remittances and are without operational holdings, are excluded from small peasant households (Sivamurugan and Swaminathan 2017).

Figure 16.2 *Regression plot between shares of female agricultural labourers among total female workers and SC/ST households among total households, study villages*

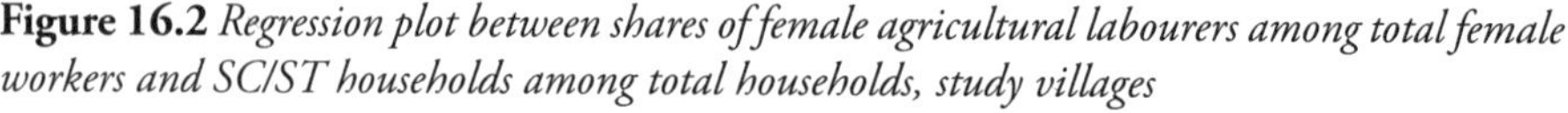

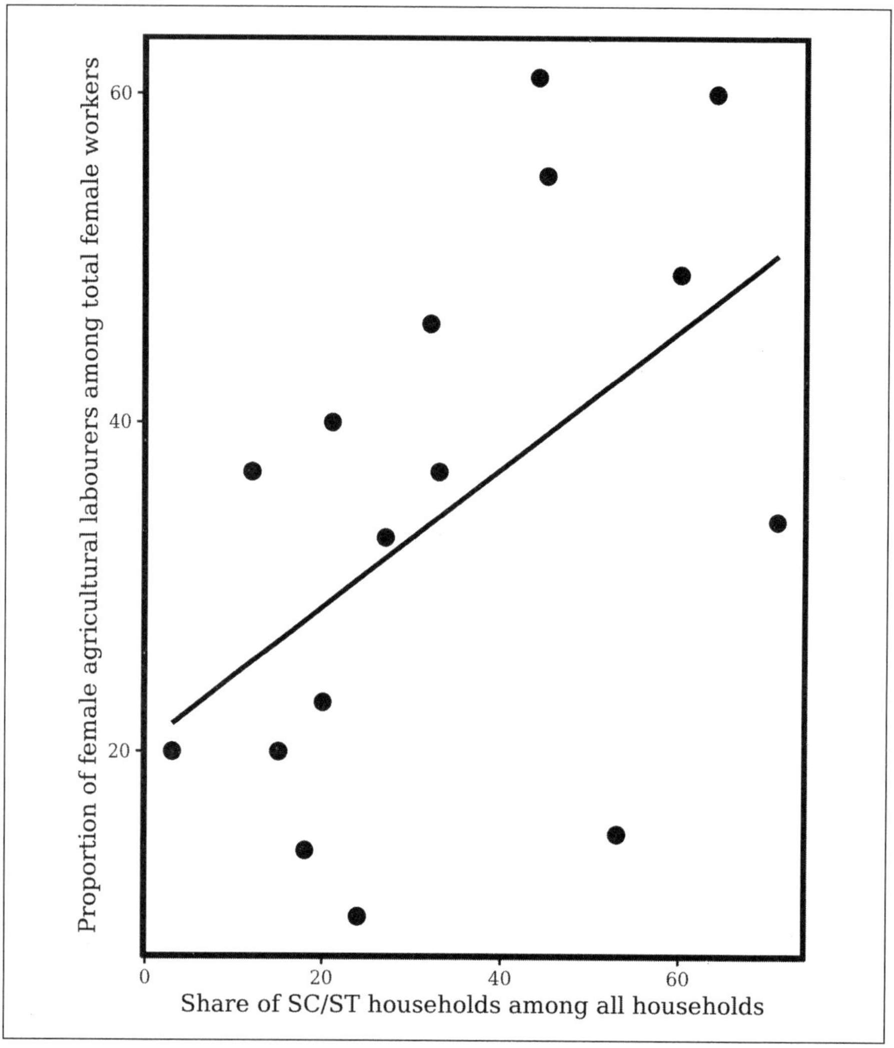

Source: PARI survey data.

chapter 11 in this volume). Thus, female labour supply also depended on the composition of social groups in the village. Village data confirmed a positive correlation between female work participation in wage work and female workers belonging to SC and ST communities. The data showed that female labour supply was higher in villages with a higher proportion of SC and ST households. In Nayanagar, Panahar, Nimshirgaon, and Zhapur, 60 per cent or more of total female wage labourers belonged to SC and ST households.

The share of female agricultural labour supply was lower wherever the share of SC and ST households was low. In Kalmandasguri, Katkuian, and Warwat Khanderao, females from Muslim and OBC (Other Backward Classes) households constituted the female labour supply. Excluding the exceptional cases of Kalmandasguri, Katkuian, and Warwat Khanderao, the coefficient of correlation between the share of female agricultural labourers among total female workers and the share of SC and ST households among total households was 0.51.[6]

FEMALE LABOUR SUPPLY AND GENDER WAGE GAP

Here, we examine the relationship between female agricultural labour supply and the gender gap in wage rates in the study villages (Figure 16.3). The variation in female agricultural labour supply could be one of the major causes for the gender gap in wage rates. For harvesting operations, female labourers received 75 per cent of male wages in villages where the proportion of female agricultural labourers was more than 50 per cent of all female workers. For instance, in Ananthavaram, Katkuian, Nayanagar, Zhapur, and 25F Gulabewala, female agricultural labourers accounted for more than 50 per cent of female workers and received less than 75 per cent of male wage rates. On the other hand, the relative gender gap in wage rates was low in villages such as Rewasi, where only 5 per cent of households were landless and female labour supply was low.

Excluding exceptional villages, the correlation coefficient between the proportion of female agricultural labourers and gender gap in wage rates was negative (–0.4) for all study villages taken together; that is, higher labour supply was associated with a higher gender wage gap (lower female to male wage ratio). The variations across villages can be better understood by looking at Figure 16.3. The four quadrants are defined based on mean gender wage gap (on y-axis) and mean share of female agricultural labourers in total female workers (on x-axis). The intersection point gives mean gender gap and mean share of female agricultural labourers in total workers. The shaded area is the confidence interval along the negatively sloped linear line. We identify four categories of villages and provide some very preliminary explanations.

Category I (right-hand side lower quadrant) includes Ananthavaram, 25F Gulabewala, Kalmandasguri, Zhapur, and Bukkacherla. There are two types of villages here: irrigated villages and rainfed villages with high gender gap in wage rates. The share of female agricultural labourers in total female workers

---

[6] Statistically significant at 10 per cent level of confidence, where p value is 0.10.

was high in the irrigated, paddy-growing, and coastal village of Ananthavaram, and the cotton- and wheat-growing village of 25F Gulabewala. In these villages, Gini coefficients of the distribution of household ownership holdings of land were very high (0.8 to 0.9). The gender gap in wages was also high: female workers received at most 72 per cent of male wages.

Bukkacherla and Kalmandasguri are rainfed, single-crop villages wherein both the proportion of female agricultural labourers and the gender gap in wage rates were high. In these villages, low productivity and profitability from crop production were associated with lack of employment opportunities and poverty among households. Female labourers from small peasant households also worked as wage labour during times of seasonal demand. The male

Figure 16.3 *Plot between gender (female to male) wage gap and share of female agricultural labourers in total female workers*

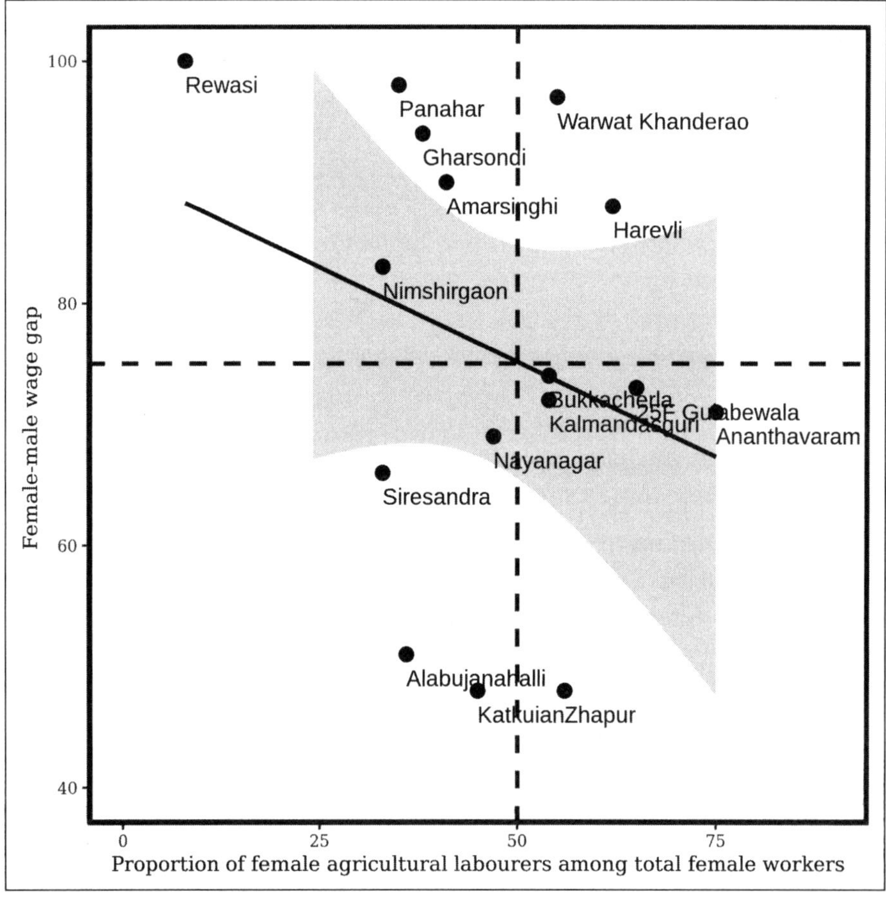

Source: PARI survey data.

workers of these households often migrated to cities for higher-paying, non-agricultural activities, which led to higher male wages.

Zhapur is an exception. Here, female wages were 48 per cent of male wages despite female agricultural labourers comprising 50 per cent of all female workers. This could be because of higher demand for male labour and availability of wage employment for men (in stone-quarrying and stone-crushing units) in Zhapur.

Category II villages are Alabujanahalli, Siresandra, Nayanagar, and Katkuian. These are villages in the lower left quadrant, that is, with a high gender gap in wage rates (48 to 65 per cent) but relatively low share of female agricultural labourer among total female workers (less than 50 per cent). The gap could be explained by the gender division of labour with respect to crops and their operations. For example, in Alabujanajhalli, about 64 per cent of land under cultivation was under sugarcane and other perennial crops. These crops generated employment primarily for male labourers, for example, weeding by use of bullocks in the sugarcane fields. Sugarcane was an important crop in Katkuian too. In sugarcane operations, female workers received one-third of male wages, while the wage gap was smaller for paddy transplanting and weeding operations.

In Nayanagar, multiple crops were grown. The reasons for the gender gap here needs to be studied further, but it may have been on account of a high degree of inequality in the ownership of landholdings, and the control of landlord and rich peasant Bhumihar households over the level of wage rates.

Category III villages are Panahar, Amarsinghi, Nimshirgaon, Gharsondi, and Rewasi. In this category, both the gender gap in wage rates and the proportion of female agricultural labourers in total female workers were low (upper left quadrant). Except for Rewasi, the general level of wages was low in these villages.

Panahar and Amarsinghi are irrigated, paddy-growing villages in West Bengal. Agriculture was the major source of employment for both male and female workers in these villages, and equal minimum wages in agriculture may be a factor contributing to the low wage gap. In Rewasi too, male and female wages were equal, but female labour use in agriculture was exceptionally low. Nimshirgaon has a diverse cropping pattern with sugarcane as the major crop, and flowers, fruits, and vegetables on irrigated land. The gender gap in wage rates may be smaller here due to the high demand for female labour in horticulture.

Category IV villages are Warwat Khanderao and Harevli (top right quadrant), villages with a relatively low gender gap in wage rates and a high proportion of female agricultural labourers in total female workers. In Warwat

Khanderao, the major crop cultivated was cotton, which provided about 76 per cent of total employment for male and female workers. In cotton cultivation, female labour was mainly absorbed in weeding and cotton-picking operations.

SOME FINAL OBSERVATIONS

This chapter is a preliminary exploration of the level of female wage rates and the gender gap in wage rates, using village-level data from 16 villages in 9 States, located in different agro-ecological zones. The village surveys provided disaggregated data on wages by crop and crop operation, type of wage contract, and gender; this level of information is not available in official statistics such as WRRI.

The village survey data showed that the level of wages for women was generally low. Average daily wage rates varied significantly within and across crop operations, and across the villages. The level of wages was lowest in rainfed, single crop-growing villages. Male workers received relatively higher wages in the villages surveyed in southern India, whereas female workers received better wages in Rewasi (Rajasthan) and Panahar (West Bengal).

Except for these two villages, wage discrimination against women in the form of a gender wage gap was experienced by all female labourers. Male and female labourers were differentially paid for the same operation. Further, female workers received lower wages than their male counterparts in operations such as transplanting and weeding, in which female participation rates were very high. This chapter tries to argue that the gender gap in wage rates is not a State-specific phenomenon, but can be attributed to agro-ecology, cropping pattern, crop intensity, and the supply of female agricultural labour.

The chapter explored the relationship between supply of female agricultural labour (or size of the female agricultural work force) and the gender wage gap. We found that the proportion of female agricultural labourers was associated positively with the degree of landlessness, the proportion of the manual labour work force, and the proportion of households from Scheduled Castes and Scheduled Tribes. We, however, observed a more complex relationship between the proportion of female agricultural labourers and the gender gap in wage rates. The gender gap in wage rates was high in Ananthavaram and 25F Gulabewala villages, where the share of female agriculture labourers among all female labourers was high. In Panahar and Gharsondi villages with a low labour supply, the gender wage gap was small. However, some villages did not fit into this pattern, and this relationship between labour supply and gender wage gap needs to be tested more rigorously in future research.

I am grateful to Madhura Swaminathan and Shruti Nagbhushan for their detailed comments and suggestions. I would also like to thank Rakesh Kumar Mahato, Subhajit Patra, and Ritam Dutta for their assistance with data-processing. Research for this paper was supported by a grant from Azim Premji University (project titled "Wage Rates in Rural India: Trends and Determinants").

BIBLIOGRAPHY

Dhar, Niladri Sekhar (2011), "Employment and Earnings of Labour Households in Rural India: A Study on Andhra Pradesh," PhD thesis submitted to the University of Calcutta.

Dhar, Niladri Sekhar, with Kaur, Navpreet (2013), "Features of Rural Underemployment in India: Evidence from Nine Villages," *Review of Agrarian Studies*, vol. 3, no. 1, January–June, pp. 14–54, available at http://ras.org.in/features_of_rural_underemployment_in_india, viewed on 30 March 2020.

Dhar, Niladri Sekhar, with Patra, Subhajit (2017), "Labour in Small Farms: Evidence from Village Studies," in Madhura Swaminathan and Sandipan Baksi (eds.), *How Do Small Farmers Fare? Evidence from Village Studies in India*, Tulika Books, New Delhi, pp. 62–94.

Jose, A. V. (2017), "Agriculture Wages in Indian States," *Indian Journal of Labour Economics*, vol. 60, September, pp. 333–45.

Mahajan, Kanika, and Ramaswami, Bharat (2017), "Caste, Female Labour Supply, and the Gender Wage Gap in India: Boserup Revisited," *Economic Development and Cultural Change*, vol. 65, no. 2, January, pp. 339–78.

Ramachandran, V. K. (1990), *Wage Labour and Unfreedom in Agriculture: An Indian Case Study*, Clarendon Press, Oxford.

Sarkar, Biplab (2017a), "The Economics of Household Farming: A Study with Special Reference to West Bengal," PhD thesis submitted to the University of North Bengal.

Sarkar, Biplab (2017b), "Cropping Pattern, Yield, and Crop Income: Findings from Three Village Surveyed in Karnataka," in Madhura Swaminathan and Arindam Das (eds.), *Socio-economic Surveys of Three Villages in Karnataka: A Study of Agrarian Relations*, Tulika Books, New Delhi.

Sivamurugan, T., and Swaminathan, Madhura (2017), "PARI Villages: An Introduction," in Madhura Swaminathan and Sandipan Baksi (eds.), *How Do Small Farmers Fare? Evidence from Village Studies in India*, Tulika Books, New Delhi, pp. 25–61.

Appendix Table 16.1 *Agro-ecological features of 16 villages studied under the Project on Agrarian Relations in India (PARI), 2005–12*

Village	District	State	Agro-ecological zone*	Agro-ecological features
Ananthavaram	Guntur	Andhra Pradesh	Krishna-Godavari Zone	Paddy-dominated area
Bukkacherla	Anantapur	Andhra Pradesh	Scarce Rainfall Zone of Rayalaseema	Dry and drought-prone
Harevli	Bijnor	Uttar Pradesh	Bhabar and Tarai Zone	Canal and groundwater irrigation; wheat/sugarcane
25F Gulabewala	Sri Ganganagar	Rajasthan	Irrigated North-Western Plain Zone	Canal and groundwater irrigation; cotton, wheat and mustard
Rewasi	Sikar	Rajasthan	Transitional Plain Zone of Inland Drainage	Unirrigated; pearl millet/wheat and mustard
Nimshirgaon	Kolhapur	Maharashtra	South Konkan Coastal Zone	Groundwater irrigation; sugarcane and multi-crop system
Warwat Khanderao	Buldhana	Maharashtra	Western Maharashtra Plain Zone	Unirrigated; cotton
Gharsondi	Gwalior	Madhya Pradesh	Gird Zone	Limited canal and groundwater irrigation; soyabean, wheat, and mustard
Alabujanahalli	Mandya	Karnataka	Southern Dry Zone	Canal irrigation; sugarcane, paddy, ragi, and sericulture
Siresandra	Kolar	Karnataka	Eastern Dry Zone	Groundwater irrigation; ragi, vegetable, and sericulture
Zhapur	Kalaburagi	Karnataka	North East Dry Zone	Unirrigated; millets, oilseeds, non-agricultural employment in stone quarries
Kalmandasguri	Cooch Behar	West Bengal	Terai Zone	Unirrigated; paddy, jute, and potato
Amarsinghi	Malda	West Bengal	New Alluvial Zone	Groundwater irrigation; aman/boro paddy and jute
Panahar	Bankura	West Bengal	Old Alluvial Zone	Groundwater irrigation; aman/boro paddy, potato, and sesame
Katkuian	West Champaran	Bihar	North-West Alluvial Gangetic Region	Canal and groundwater irrigation; sugarcane, paddy, and wheat
Nayanagar	Samastipur	Bihar	North-West Alluvial Gangetic Region	Groundwater irrigation; paddy, wheat, and maize

Note: * Agro-ecological zones are given as per the National Agricultural Research Project (NARP) classification.
Source: PARI village data.

Appendix Table 16.2 *Average daily wage rates for female and male workers, study villages, at 2009–10 prices in Rs*

Village	State	Sowing		Transplanting		Weeding		Harvesting	
		Female	Male	Female	Male	Female	Male	Female	Male
Ananthavaram	Andhra Pradesh	82	139	68	126	66	81	82	116
Harevli	Uttar Pradesh	53	66	49	61	53	63	63	73
25F Gulabewala	Rajasthan	–	58	–	–	34	50	41	56
Nimshirgaon	Maharashtra	71	88	–	–	66	78	88	106
Gharsondi	Madhya Pradesh		84	61	66	61	66	68	71
Zhapur	Karnataka	52	119	–	–	52	120	56	116
Alabujanahalli	Karnataka	86	155	72	155	82	156	79	155
Siresandra	Karnataka	79	141	–	–	80	100	80	121
Panahar	West Bengal	91	91	91	92	90	90	90	92
Kalmandasguri	West Bengal	70	101	77	94	81	100	76	105
Amarsinghi	West Bengal	–	–	93	94	74	86	91	101
Rewasi	Rajasthan	–	–	–	–	156	156	158	158
Nayanagar	Bihar	54	83	–	–	52	69	51	74
Katkuian	Bihar	42	105	45	64	40	66	40	83
Range	All villages	42–91	58–155	45–93	61–126	34–156	50–156	40–158	56–158

Source: PARI survey data.

Appendix Table 16.3 *Paddy as the major crop grown and female-to-male wage ratio for transplanting and harvesting operations, study villages*

Village	State	Cropping pattern (GCA)		Female-to-male wages	
		1st	2nd	Trans-planting	Harves-ting
Panahar	West Bengal	Aman paddy (41)	Boro paddy (19), potato (23)	0.99	0.98
Amarsinghi	West Bengal	Aman paddy (35)	Boro paddy (30)	0.99	0.90
Kalmandasguri	West Bengal	Aman paddy (49)	Jute (27), potato (16)	0.82	0.72
Ananthavaram	Andhra Pradesh	Paddy (47.5)	Maize (27.6), black gram (12.5)	0.54	0.71

Note: Figures in parentheses show area under different crops as a proportion of the total gross cropped area (GCA).
Source: PARI survey data.

Appendix Table 16.4 *Vegetable, cotton, pulses, wheat, and soyabean as major crops grown, and female-to-male wage ratio for sowing and harvesting operations, study villages*

Village	State	Cropping pattern (GCA)		Female-to-male wages	
		1st	2nd	Sowing	Harvesting
Rewasi	Rajasthan	Pearl millet intercrop	Wheat, mustard	1	1
Gharsondi	Madhya Pradesh	Soyabean (32.8)	Wheat (27.9)	–	0.94
Bukkacherla	Andhra Pradesh	Groundnut (74.2)	NA	0.91	0.74
Nayanagar	Bihar	Wheat (28)	Maize (22), sugarcane (16)	0.65	0.69
25F Gulabewala	Rajasthan	Cotton (21)	Rapeseed (34), wheat (26)	–	0.73
Siresandra	Karnataka	Finger millet intercrop (33)	Mulberry (22), vegetables (18)	0.56	0.66
Zhapur	Karnataka	Pigeon pea intercrop (40)	Pigeon pea (31)	0.44	0.48

Note: Figures in parentheses show area under different crops as a proportion of the total gross cropped area (GCA).
Source: PARI village data.

Appendix Table 16.5 *Sugarcane as the major crop grown and female-to-male wage ratio for harvesting operations, study villages*

Village	State	Cropping pattern (GCA)		Female-to-male wages	
		1st	2nd	Sowing	Harvesting
Harevli	Uttar Pradesh	Sugarcane (61)	Wheat and intercrop (25.6)	0.8	0.88
Nimshirgaon	Maharashtra	Sugarcane (34)	Soyabean (23.5), Sorghum (17.9)	0.81	0.83
Alabujanahalli	Karnataka	Sugarcane (36)	Paddy (40)	0.56	0.51
Katkuian	Bihar	Sugarcane (41)	Paddy (37), wheat (11)	0.4	0.48

Note: Figures in parentheses show area under different crops as a proportion of the total gross cropped area (GCA).
Source: PARI village data.

Appendix Table 16.6 *Share of landless households and SC/ST households among total households, and share of female agricultural labourers among all female workers, study villages in per cent*

Village	State	Share of landless households among all households	Share of SC/ST households among all households	Share of female agricultural labourers among total female workers
25F Gulabewala	Rajasthan	64	60	65
Zhapur	Karnataka	45	55	56
Ananthavaram	Andhra Pradesh	60	49	75
Kalmandasguri	West Bengal	21	40	54
Siresandra	Karnataka	12	37	33
Harevli	Uttar Pradesh	33	37	62
Nayanagar	Bihar	71	34	47
Nimshirgaon	Maharashtra	27	33	33
Gharsondi	Madhya Pradesh	20	23	38
Bukkacherla	Andhra Pradesh	15	20	54
Rewasi	Rajasthan	3	20	8
Alabujanahalli	Karnataka	18	14	36
Katkuian	Bihar	53	15	45
Warwat Khanderao	Maharashtra	24	10	55
Panahar	West Bengal	44	61	35
Amarsinghi	West Bengal	32	46	41

Source: PARI survey data.

VI

Access to Finance

17

Women's Access to Banking in India
Policy Context, Trends, and Predictors

Pallavi Chavan[1]

Historically, formal finance has sidestepped women and their credit needs. This is because formal finance typically relies on security, which women often lack owing to their limited access to wealth, education, secure job opportunities, and property rights. The absence of formal finance can itself hinder women's access to education, employment, and the means of production, thus limiting their participation in economic activity over time.

Microfinance has become almost synonymous with women's finance in many developing countries. Since its origin in the late 1980s, microfinance has been regarded as an innovative means of lending to women from economically backward sections by organising them into groups. The "social collateral" of the group is expected to address the absence of physical collateral (Haldar and Stiglitz 2016, p. 471). The growth of microfinance also needs to be seen in light of the wave of financial liberalisation since the 1990s. The self-regulated, for-profit form of microfinance is consistent with the economics of financial liberalisation.[2]

Equating women's finance with microfinance limits the scope of women's finance because it assumes that the credit needs of women may not just start

[1] This article was first published in *Review of Agrarian Studies*, vol. 10, no. 1.

[2] Formal financial institutions in this chapter typically refer to commercial banks and non-banking financial institutions that are regulated/supervised by public regulatory authorities (Beck 2015). By contrast, informal sources include moneylenders, and friends and family, who are completely unregulated (*ibid.*). Between these two ends lie an array of semi-formal institutions that are self-regulated or relatively less regulated. Microfinance evolved in Bangladesh with Grameen, a non-governmental non-profit lending institution. At present, microfinance institutions include a wide array of institutions, including non-banking financial companies, credit unions/cooperatives, trusts, as also commercial banks, with differences in the degree and type of regulation. These microfinance institutions operate either on the principle of "double-bottom line" (profits and social impact) or "triple-bottom line" (including environmental impact) underlining the role of profits in their operations (*ibid.*, p. 3).

small, but may also remain small over time.[3] Further, the for-profit nature of microfinance can be detrimental to the cause of women's finance. Evidence from India as well as other developing countries shows that microfinance institutions, aspiring for higher profits through high interest rates and lower default rates, take to coercion in lending and recovery, and have caused debt-related distress among women (Karim 2011; Ramakumar 2010). In fact, for-profit microfinance quite consciously factors in the restricted physical mobility of women in traditional environments as contributing to low credit risk (Beck 2015).

The tendency to equate women's finance with microfinance is reflected in the literature, with studies on women's finance from most countries focusing on the social and economic outcomes of microfinance.[4] By contrast, there is limited discussion on women's access to formal or bank finance, an issue that this chapter aims to address in the Indian context. India offers an interesting case for women's banking for various reasons. First, India has a rich history of social banking aimed at extending basic banking services to underserved sections of society. Secondly, banks have been the most important source of formal finance in India.[5] They have also been instrumental in providing microfinance by way of lending to women's groups directly and to microfinance institutions for on-lending, as will be discussed later. Hence, an analysis of women's banking can cover the entire gamut of formal financial services available to women in the Indian context.

The chapter analyses Indian banking policy from a gender perspective and quantifies the gender gap in banking services. The term gender gap is defined flexibly in the context of each banking service discussed here. It broadly refers to the gap between the coverage of or access to a given banking service for women vis-à-vis men. While the chapter discusses all major banking services, including deposit, credit and payments services, it focuses on credit as credit supports both production-related activities and consumption smoothing, particularly when the social security system is weak.

The next section of this chapter discusses major phases of Indian banking policy since bank nationalisation. It illustrates the changing perception of banks as purveyors of basic banking services to the Indian population, women

---

[3] Microfinance is defined by small-sized unsecured loans. To illustrate, the cap on individual micro-loans in India is set at Rs 0.125 million (RBI 2019b). Systemically, microfinance accounts for a small portion of total formal finance. For instance, microfinance was only 2 per cent of total bank credit in India in 2017–18 (MFIN 2018; Basic Statistical Returns of Scheduled Commercial Banks in India, RBI).

[4] See Singh (2018) for a review of the literature on microfinance, and its effects on various financial and social indicators concerning the poor, particularly poor women.

[5] Banks accounted for 61 per cent of the total formal debt of households in 2013 (NSSO 2014).

included. The third section discusses the literature on women's access to banking in India. The literature is small, owing partly to data limitations. Issues of data are discussed in the fourth section. The fifth and sixth sections analyse women's access to each of the banking services as compared to men's access. The seventh section estimates predictors of access to banking for women, and is followed by a concluding eighth section.

Banks as Purveyors of Basic (Banking) Services: Policy Insights

Based on the role that banks have played as purveyors of basic banking services, it is possible to divide Indian banking policy into two broad phases: the phase of bank nationalisation starting in 1969, and the phase of financial liberalisation from 1991. In this chapter, the policy of financial inclusion, begun in 2005, is treated as a continuation of the policy of financial liberalisation.

Phase of Bank Nationalisation

This phase began with the nationalisation of 14 major banks in 1969; six more banks were nationalised in 1980. Prior to nationalisation, a large part of the Indian banking sector (except the State Bank of India, which was nationalised in 1955) was controlled by and primarily served the credit needs of a few industrial houses (Goyal 1967).

Three policy instruments brought banks closer to the masses: namely, (i) branch licensing, (ii) directed lending programme known as priority sector lending, and (iii) interest rate regulations (Chavan 2017). The branch licensing policy, mainly through the 1:4 rule (of opening at least four branches in unbanked rural areas for every one branch in metropolitan/port areas), ensured the spread of bank branches to unbanked/underbanked areas. Priority sector lending was aimed at redistribution of bank credit in favour of underserved sectors or segments, including agriculture, small-scale industries, and socio-economically "weaker" sections. In addition, there were numerous policy interventions for redistribution, including the creation of Regional Rural Banks (RRBs) for targeted lending to socio-economically weaker sections in rural areas.

This phase is often described as the social banking phase, aimed at "elevation of the entitlements of previously disadvantaged groups [and sectors/activities] to formal credit, even though it might have entailed a weakening of the [more prudent] conventional banking practice[s]" (Wiggins and Rajendran 1987). The "conventional banking practices" included "commercial stability through deposit mobilisation, high recovery rates and caution in lending decisions" (*ibid.*). Evidently, the objective of redistribution was given priority over the profitability and commercial viability of banks.

Although critics associate this phase with "financial repression," they agree that India witnessed a significant increase in the overall (and household) savings and investment rates during this phase, which is not typically indicative of a repressive policy regime (Joshi and Little 1994). Studies also highlight the expansion of bank branches, particularly in rural areas and underbanked geographical regions, and increased growth of agricultural credit and credit to economically weaker sections during this phase (Shetty 2005).

Phase of Financial Liberalisation

The phase of financial liberalisation is generally associated with structural reforms triggered by the balance of payments crisis in 1991. This phase witnessed either withdrawal or dilution of most measures adopted earlier in order to give more importance to the profitability and efficiency of banks. Needless to say, this phase changed the perception of banks as purveyors of basic banking. Two quotations from official sources summarise this change. First, the Committee on the Financial Systems (CFS), while offering a blueprint for financial liberalisation, argued that "the pursuit of the redistributive objective should use the instrumentality of the fiscal rather than the credit system" (RBI 1991). Secondly, although it was acknowledged that the previous phase had achieved considerable expansion of banking, its redistributive policies were viewed as responsible for the weak profitability of banks, and hence it was declared that social banking had "outlived its purpose" and banks had to move towards "more commercial modes of operation" (RBI 2001).

Consequently, branch licensing policy was liberalised by withdrawing the 1:4 norm. Priority sector targets were neither withdrawn nor reduced but there were definitional changes, particularly in the case of agriculture – a key priority sector.[6] These changes altered the nature of agricultural credit, tilting it in favour of large-scale, commercial, capital-intensive agricultural production, and away from marginal and small farmers (Ramakumar and Chavan 2014). Finally, there was almost complete deregulation of interest rates, putting an end to cross-subsidisation of borrowers by banks (Mohanty 2010).[7]

The effects of these changes could be seen during the 1990s and early 2000s in the form of a fall in the number of rural bank branches; a widening

---

[6] There was a widening of the definitions under both constituents of agricultural credit: direct and indirect agricultural credit (Ramakumar and Chavan 2014).

[7] There were also policy changes that led to diversification to infrastructural and core industrial financing on a large scale (Chavan 2017).

differential in banking spread between rural and urban areas, and economically backward and vanguard regions; a steep fall in agricultural credit growth; and a decline in the share of small-sized agricultural loans (Shetty 2005; Subbarao 2012).

Policy of financial inclusion

The policy on financial inclusion was adopted in 2005. Officially, financial inclusion was defined as:

> the process of ensuring access to appropriate financial products and services (read deposit, payments, credit and insurance) needed by all sections of the society in general and vulnerable groups such as low income groups in particular at an affordable cost in a fair and transparent manner by regulated mainstream institutional players. (Chakrabarty 2011)

Notwithstanding the emphasis on universal provision of basic services, financial inclusion can be viewed as a continuation of the policy of financial liberalisation. This is because inclusion has to be pursued while taking into account "business considerations" to ensure the "long-term sustainability of the process" (RBI 2008a). The emphasis on making inclusion profitable for banks underlines a disregard for cross-subsidisation. This emphasis is reflected in the way inclusion has been pursued since 2005:

(i) There is a greater thrust on mobilising small-sized deposits as compared to giving small-sized credit as part of financial inclusion. This is because deposits are a cheap and stable source of funding for banks (Khan 2011). In comparison, the transaction costs associated with the financing of a large number of small borrowers are high.

(ii) There is a greater thrust on non-branch means of banking, such as through agents or business correspondents (BCs), as compared to brick-and-mortar branches. Again, this is because of the high operating costs for opening and maintaining branches as compared to agents.

(iii) The idea of involving private institutions, including for-profit microfinance institutions, small finance banks (specialising in small-sized loans), and payments banks (specialising in small-sized payments services), reflects the thrust on commercially oriented financial inclusion. The new-generation private institutions for financial inclusion are different from the old-generation public institutions, such as RRBs.

Furthermore, there has been little or no reversal in the process of (i) liberalising interest rates, and (ii) changing the definition of priority sectors in favour of large-sized loans during the period of financial inclusion. High interest rates (such as on microfinance) are, in fact, justified given the high transaction costs associated with extending small-sized loans.[8] A few large-sized loans, unlike a large number of small-sized loans, help in achieving the priority sector targets at lower transaction costs.

Although financial inclusion has essentially been a continuation of the policy of financial liberalisation, there has been a return of some policy mandates from the bank nationalisation phase, although in a diluted form. First, banks were instructed in 2011 to open at least 25 per cent of their total branches in a year in unbanked rural centres – a 4:1 norm as against the previous 1:4 norm. However, the mandate of opening bank branches in rural areas was modified in 2015 in conformity with the commercial approach to financial inclusion. Branches were replaced by banking outlets (defined as fixed point outlets manned by a banking correspondent/bank staff, which operated five days a week for four hours a day), and banks were instructed to open at least 25 per cent of such banking outlets in a year in unbanked rural centres.

Secondly, banks were asked to adopt board-approved financial inclusion plans (since 2010) and achieve targets under these plans for opening branches, small-sized (savings) deposit accounts and debit cards, and providing small-sized overdrafts. In 2014, the Prime Minister's Jan Dhan Yojana (PMJDY) (translated as the Prime Minister's People's Money Scheme) was introduced for accelerating the pace of financial inclusion. As part of financial inclusion plans and PMJDY, there has been a striking increase in the number of banking agents/business correspondents employed by banks, small-sized deposit accounts, and debit cards (issued against these deposit accounts). However, the emphasis on mobilising deposits has been greater than that on extending credit, in line with the commercially oriented approach towards financial inclusion.[9]

Banking Policy and Women

All the policies discussed above apply to women. Additionally, there are some policies that are specifically directed towards women.

---

[8] It has been argued that "freedom from poverty is not for free. The poor are willing and capable to pay the cost" (RBI 1999, cited in Ramakumar 2010). Although, following the crisis in the microfinance sector in 2010, interest rates on microfinance were capped, they have been liberalised since then (Chavan and Dutta 2019).

[9] In 2018, deposit accounts and debit cards were 355 million and 276 million, respectively. However, overdrafts worked out to only 0.4 per cent of the total amount of deposits mobilised; see https://pmjdy.gov.in.

1. *Adoption of microfinance.* Banks in India took a lead in providing microfinance to women from economically backward sections. While the bank-led microfinance model was more popular initially, the self-regulated and profit-oriented microfinance institution-led model emerged as a faster growing alternative in the 2000s (RBI 2008b). Over time, the onerous lending and recovery practices of microfinance institutions came to light, prompting the Reserve Bank of India to place them under a stricter regulatory purview in 2010, and prescribing ceilings on their interest rates and margins to be eligible for priority sector credit from banks, as banks had been a major source of funds for these institutions.[10] Unlike in other countries, banks in India have been direct lenders to self-help groups under the bank-led model, and to microfinance institutions under the microfinance institution-led model, for on-lending to self-help groups.

2. *Inclusion of women under priority sector.* Although socio-economically "weaker sections" was a priority sector category from the early 1970s, it did not explicitly include women till 2013. Originally, weaker sections were defined as small and marginal farmers, agricultural labourers, and Scheduled Castes and Scheduled Tribes. Later, self-help groups were included as a part of weaker sections (Chavan 2012). In 2013, for the first time, women were explicitly mentioned as a weaker section, by including loans to individual women beneficiaries of up to Rs 50,000 (increased to Rs 0.1 million in 2015) in the priority sector.

3. *Creation of a women-oriented bank.* Bharatiya Mahila Bank, a public sector bank with the mandate to cater to the banking needs of women, was created in 2013. While all board members of the Bank were women, its branches were manned by both men and women. It lent primarily to women but solicited deposits from both women and men (Gaikwad 2014).[11] Loans to women were charged a slightly lower interest rate than loans to men.

Although the Bank was described as a women-oriented bank, it was governed by the same set of regulations, including priority sector lending and branch authorisation policies, as any other commercial bank. Hence, strictly speaking, it was not a differentiated public institution, like a Regional Rural Bank.[12] Moreover, rapid branch expansion and brand building, which are needed for any new commercial bank to compete effectively with existing

---

[10] See RBI circular, "Bank Loans to MFIs Priority Sector Status," 3 May 2011, available at https://www.rbi.org.in/scripts/NotificationUser.aspx?Id=6381&Mode=0.

[11] Apart from offering retail loans to women, industrial loans were offered for beauty parlours, child care centres and catering services, as sectors with self-employment opportunities for women (*ibid.*).

[12] Regional Rural Banks were created to meet the credit needs exclusively of its targeted sections, such as small and marginal farmers.

banks, was seen to be missing in the case of the Bharatiya Mahila Bank (Bandyopadhyay 2014). The Bank thrived on treasury profits for a few years before it was merged with the State Bank of India in 2017.

4. *Interest subvention.* Although interest rates were largely deregulated as part of financial liberalisation, since 2007, a subvention has been offered to women's self-help groups for loans up to Rs 0.3 million. The effective rate thus works out to 7 per cent for women's groups (going down further to 4 per cent if the group repays on time).

5. *Targeted allocation of credit.* In 2000, the central government created a 14-point programme to give dedicated attention to women's credit needs. It included introducing women's cells in banks and stipulating a 5 per cent target of total credit for women. Although women were explicitly included under "weaker sections" as a priority sector only in 2013, the overall target for women's credit has been binding on banks since 2000. Although the target brought in a focus on women in credit allocation, it has limited relevance as: (i) it was fixed at a low level that did not adequately represent women's contribution to economic activity, and was kept unchanged over time; and (ii) being an overall target, it is hard to infer how the allocated credit reached women from economically backward sections.

A Review of Studies on Women and Banking

The empirical literature on gender gap in formal finance is limited. Research has, however, increased with the availability of gender-wise data on banking from the World Bank through its periodic Global Financial Index (Findex) surveys, begun in 2011. The following are the major observations from research based on cross-country data from Findex.

1. *Negative effect of gender on financial inclusion.* The studies are unanimous in their conclusion that gender has a negative effect on financial inclusion across countries, with women having lower access (in terms of both ownership and usage) to banking services than men (Kunt *et al.* 2013; Deléchat *et al.* 2018). Women are even more under-represented in business banking; their share in business loan portfolio declines as the size of business increases (Deléchat *et al.* 2018).

2. *Wider gender gap in developing countries.* While access to banking for women is generally low across countries, women from developing countries are worse off than those in developed countries (Kunt *et al.* 2013). Gender affects women's access to banking both directly and indirectly, through its effect on women's access to employment, income, and education (*ibid.*).

3. *Direct discrimination and indirect barriers to access for women.* Some studies

report direct gender discrimination by banks (Safavian 2012, cited in Kunt *et al.* 2013). To illustrate, women were charged higher interest rates than men in India (Vani, Bhattacharjee, and Rajeev 2011; RBI 2015b). The inability to provide collateral, low financial literacy, poor credit histories, and restrictions on physical mobility are factors that indirectly affect women's access to credit (Narain 2009; Coleman 2002).

In India, there are a few studies that show restricted access to formal credit for female-headed households as compared to male-headed households, particularly in rural areas (Vani, Bhattacharjee, and Rajeev 2011). There are also studies which argue that the decline in rural branches after financial liberalisation disproportionately affected the availability of credit for rural women, notwithstanding the rapid growth of microfinance (Chavan 2012). With the onset of the Prime Minister's Jan Dhan Yojana, there has been an expansion in the ownership of bank accounts among women, but the usage of these accounts has remained low (Kohli 2018).

Gender-Disaggregated Banking Data

Global Findex is the only source of gender-wise and country-wise data on ownership and use of banking services. There have been three rounds of Findex: in 2011, 2014, and 2017. In 2017, it covered a random sample of 150,000 adults (15 years and above) from 144 countries including India (representing 97 per cent of the world's population) (Kunt *et al.* 2017). In this chapter, Findex is used to compare India with other countries with regard to financial inclusion of women.

I use data from the Reserve Bank of India's *Basic Statistical Returns of Scheduled Commercial Banks in India* (BSR) from 1996 onwards to analyse trends in women's access to banking. Gender-wise data for earlier years are not publicly accessible. I also use data from the Consumer Pyramids survey of the Centre for Monitoring Indian Economy (CMIE) to identify the predictors of women's access to banking. Consumer Pyramids provides longitudinal panel data on a sample of households from 514 districts across 27 States.[13] Every sample household is interviewed thrice every year. I have used data from January 2014 to December 2018. Consumer Pyramids provides data on bank deposits at the individual level, but the data on bank credit are available only at the household level. Thus, the predictors for ownership of bank deposits are analysed for individual women, while those for access to bank credit are

---

[13] See https://consumerpyramidsdx.cmie.com.

attempted for female-headed households. I use a balanced panel of 6,276,118 individuals and 1,924,097 households.[14]

The head of a household is generally identified based on recognition and management of the functions of the household (Ramachandran, Swaminathan, and Rawal 2001).[15] As no large-scale survey, including Consumer Pyramids and All-India Debt and Investment Survey, provides a definition of a female-headed household, the tendency of the enumerator to identify a female-headed household based on recognition alone cannot be ruled out. Hence, a household whose chief earner/decision-maker is a woman may still be recognised by its adult male member and classified as a male-headed household. Such a bias can result in undercounting of female-headed households (*ibid.*; Agarwal 1986).

Only about 12 per cent of households in Consumer Pyramids are female-headed households; the corresponding proportion is 10 per cent in the All-India Debt and Investment Survey (2012–13). Households reported as female-headed households are generally headed by widows/separated women (explicitly marked by the absence of an adult man), corroborating the recognition bias discussed earlier. I use the data on female-headed households from Consumer Pyramids, acknowledging that the count may be a conservative one.

WOMEN'S ACCESS TO BANKING: INDIA COMPARED WITH OTHER COUNTRIES

Bank Deposits

In comparison with the world average and the average for BRIICS (Brazil, Russia, India, Indonesia, China, and South Africa) countries, India showed the most rapid increase in the percentage of adults owning deposit accounts in financial institutions (read banks in the Indian context) between 2011 and 2017, the period coinciding with the policy of financial inclusion and Prime Minister's Jan Dhan Yojana (Figure 17.1).[16] The reduction in gender

---

[14] About 60 per cent of the sample of Consumer Pyramids is from urban areas (CMIE 2019). The issue of oversampling of urban households is addressed by weighting every estimation by the sample weights provided in the database. The weights reflect the inverse of the sampling probability for each household.

[15] The Census of India notes that, "The head of household for census purposes is a person who is *recognised* as such by the household. She or he is generally the person who bears the chief responsibility for *managing* the affairs of the household and takes decisions on behalf of the household" (Census of India 2000, p. 48; emphasis added).

[16] The definition of (formal) financial institution in Findex includes "all types of financial institutions that offer deposit, checking, and savings accounts – including banks, credit unions, microfinance institutions, and post offices – and that fall under prudential regulation by a government body" (Kunt *et al.* 2017). In India, banks can be taken as a proxy for financial institutions given their key role in both deposit mobilisation and credit.

Figure 17.1 *Adult population with deposit accounts in financial institutions, India and BRIICS countries, 2011, 2014, and 2017,* in per cent

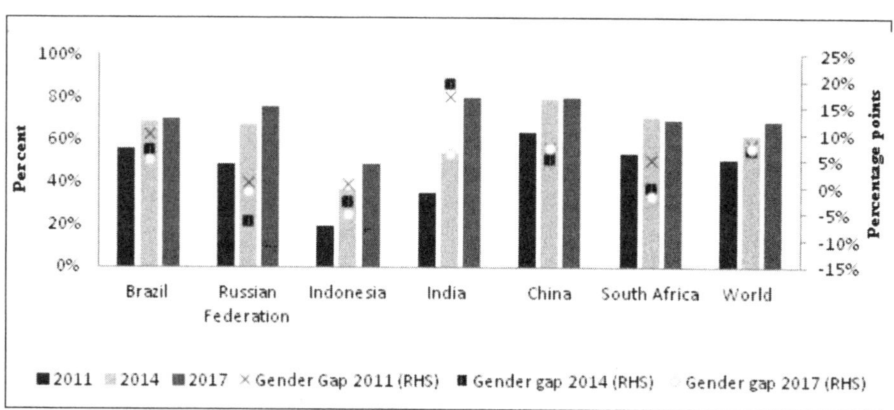

Source: Findex, World Bank.

Figure 17.2 *Extent of usage of bank deposit accounts, by gender, India and BRIICS countries, 2014 and 2017,* in per cent

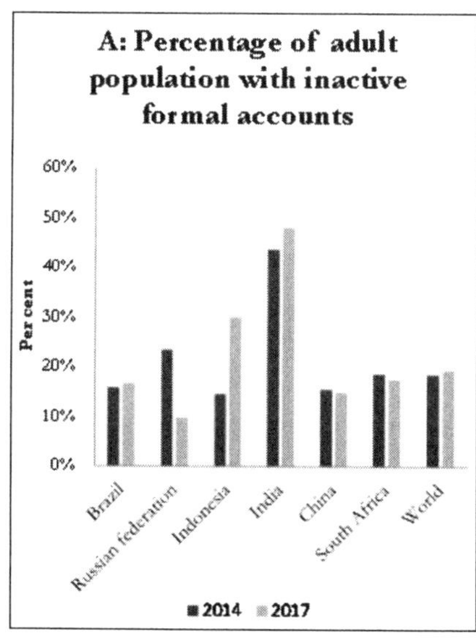

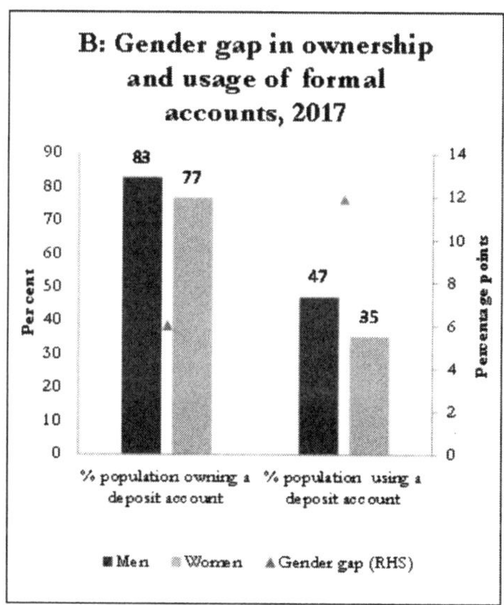

Source: Findex, World Bank.

gap (difference between the percentages of men and women) in owning an account too was the largest for India between 2011 and 2017, but the gap, at 6 percentage points, still remained the second highest after China among the BRIICS countries.

Owning a deposit is perhaps the first step in initiating customers into banking.

With regard to the second step of usage of accounts for savings or payments, India's performance was rather poor. Between 2014 and 2017, as the percentage of adults owning deposit accounts increased, the percentage of adults with inactive accounts (zero deposit or withdrawal during the preceding 12 months) too increased (Figure 17.2A). In 2017, the only year for which gender-wise data on usage are available, only 35 per cent of India's women actually *used* a bank account (Figure 17.2B). This was an average for all women; the percentage would be lower for women from the economically weaker sections.[17]

According to Findex, the main reason for not using bank accounts was insufficiency of funds (about 54 per cent of adults reported this as the reason in 2017). Insufficiency of funds is likely to be a stronger reason for women than for men, given their poorer access to economic opportunities.

Retail Payments

Generally, there are four phases in the evolution of the payments system of any country: cash or paper-based, card-based, web-based, and mobile phone-based (Credit Suisse 2016). In India, there has been a proliferation of the means of retail payment as part of financial inclusion, which include card-based (credit and debit cards), web-based (National Electronic Fund Transfer and

Figure 17.3 *Adult population owning a debit card, India, 2011, 2014, and 2017*, in per cent

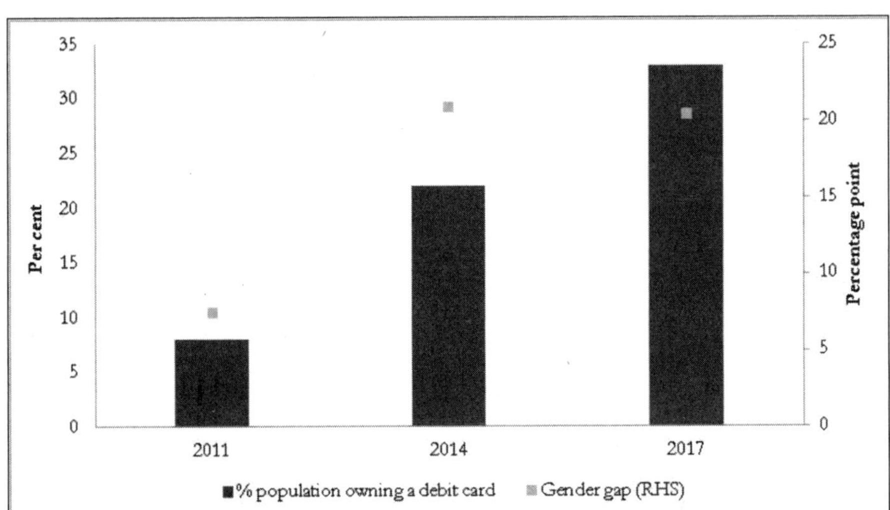

Source: Findex, World Bank.

[17] Unfortunately, Findex does not publish disaggregated data on usage.

Immediate Payments Switch), and mobile phone-based (Unified Payments Interface) payments (RBI 2019a). Given the paucity of gender-wise data, in this chapter I study one of the most basic means of payment, namely debit cards.[18]

Although the percentage of adults owning debit cards rose between 2011 and 2017, the gender gap widened (Figure 17.3). In 2017, only 22 per cent of women had a debit card as against 43 per cent of men. Although Findex does not give data on usage of debit cards, the gender gap in usage of cards is likely to be wider than in deposits. This is because, apart from insufficiency of funds, the availability of payments infrastructure can further constrain the usage of debit cards.

Bank Credit

India continued to lag far behind the world and other BRIICS countries in terms of access to formal (bank) credit.[19] There was a wide divergence between the share of adults possessing bank deposits and adults accessing bank

Figure 17.4 *Adult population accessing formal credit, India and BRIICS countries, 2011, 2014, and 2017,* in per cent

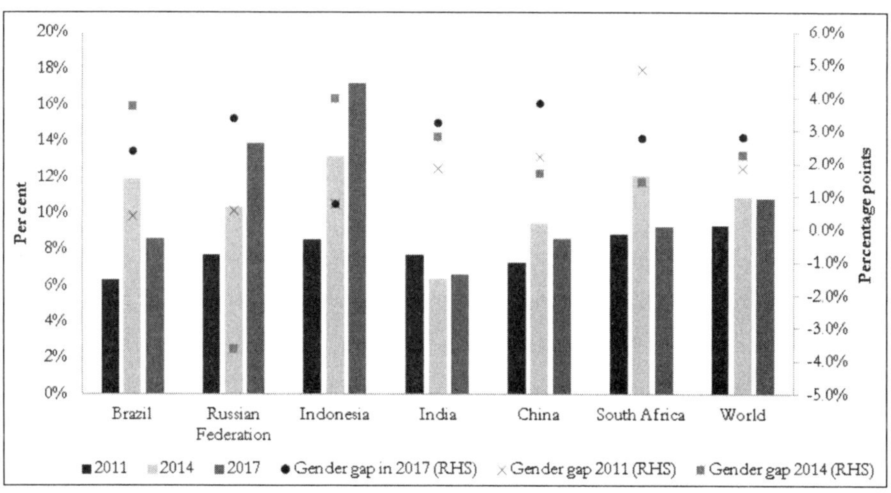

Source: Findex, World Bank.

[18] Although Findex provides data on gender-wise ownership of both debit and credit cards, I use only the former as the penetration of credit cards is extremely limited in India with a credit-to-debit card ratio of only 4 per cent (RBI 2018).

[19] The three major formal institutions providing retail credit in India are commercial banks (including Regional Rural Banks), cooperative banks, and non-banking financial companies. Of these, banks' share in total retail credit provided by all three agencies was 87 per cent; calculation based on RBI (2018).

credit in India. The divergence corroborated the deposit-centric approach of financial inclusion. The gender gap in credit access in India was second to China (Figure 17.4). In 2017, only 5 per cent of India's women accessed bank credit. The corresponding proportion was 7 per cent in both China and Brazil.

Trends in Women's Access to Banking in India

Women's share in total bank credit has shown a steady rise over the last two decades, but the rise has been far slower than for men (Figure 17.5A). Total bank credit includes credit going to institutions (including public and private corporate, cooperative, microfinance, and non-profit sectors) and households (including individuals – men and women, and "other household" entities – proprietorial/partnership firms, joint families, joint liability groups/non-governmental organisations/trusts).[20] In order to analyse the gender gap, it is necessary to separate credit to individuals from total credit. The growing divergence between the shares of individuals and women in Figure 17.5A reflects the share of men. In 2017, women accounted for about 7 per cent of total bank credit, and men's share was about 30 per cent (Figure 17.5A).

Women get access to bank credit not just as individuals, but also as the primary beneficiaries of credit given to microfinance institutions, self-help groups, and joint liability groups. Hence, I have added credit to microfinance institutions (MFIs), and joint liability groups (JLGs)/trusts/non-governmental organisations (NGOs) to the credit going to (individual) women, to arrive at a revised estimate of women's credit.[21] As per the revised estimate, women accounted for about 28 per cent of the total credit going to all individuals + microfinance institutions + joint liability groups/trusts/non-governmental organisations (or 8 per cent of total bank credit) in 2017 (Figure 17.5B).

To make the gender gap more meaningful, I looked beyond bank credit received by women, to the credit that they are entitled to get. To ascertain entitlements, I have first used the share of women in total population. An average woman receives only a fraction of the credit received by a man; in 2017, the ratio of credit amount per woman (including credit given to MFIs + JLGs/trusts/NGOs) to credit amount per man was 29 per cent (Figure 17.6).

---

[20] See the organisation-wise division of bank credit in Reserve Bank of India, Basic Statistical Returns of Scheduled Commercial Banks in India. Joint liability groups are a new variant of group lending; details are available at https://www.rbi.org.in/Scripts/NotificationUser. aspx?Id=9336&Mode=0#APP.

[21] This may be an overestimate as the data are not provided separately for joint liability groups. Joint liability groups are clubbed with trusts and non-governmental organisations, although in the case of the latter, credit may not necessarily be going to women.

Figure 17.5 *Share of women in total bank credit/credit to individuals in India,* in per cent

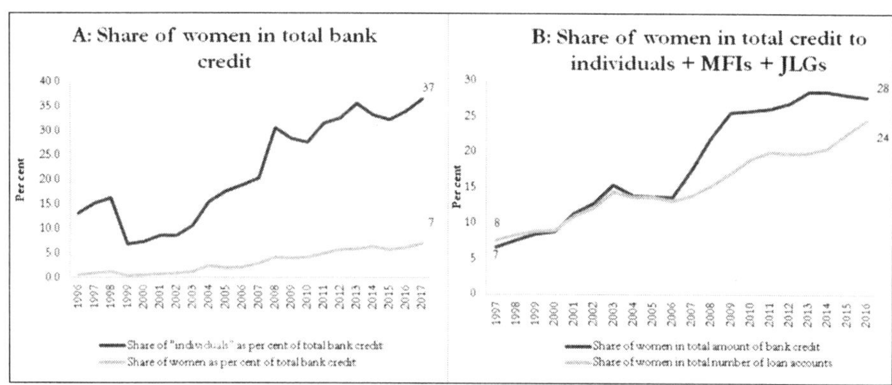

Note: Shares in Figure 17.5B are based on three-year moving averages.
Source: Reserve Bank of India (RBI), *Basic Statistical Returns of Scheduled Commercial Banks in India,* various issues.

Figure 17.6 *Relative amount of credit to and deposit from women vis-à-vis men, India, 1997–2016,* in per cent

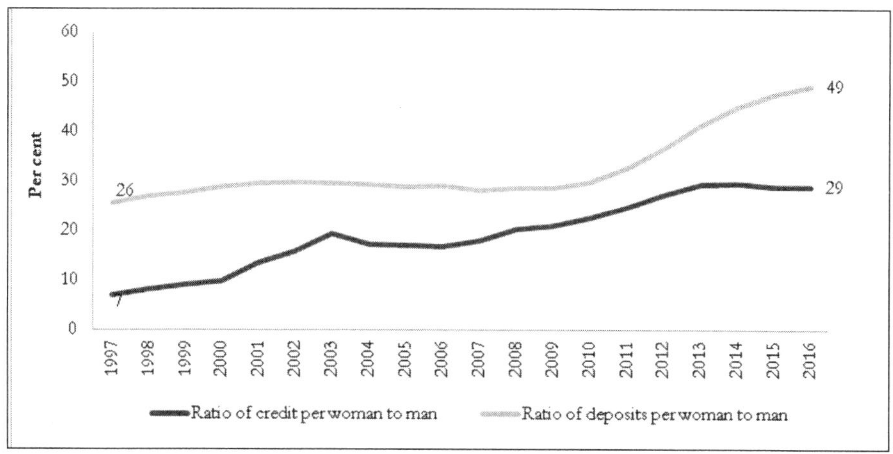

Notes: Shares are three-year moving averages to smooth out variations.
Credit to women includes credit given individually to women + MFIs + JLGs/trusts/NGOs. Credit figures are normalised by population of men and women.
Source: Reserve Bank of India (RBI), *Basic Statistical Returns of Scheduled Commercial Banks in India,* various issues; www.censusindia.gov.in.

The ratio was 23 per cent when only the credit going to individual women (excluding MFIs + JLGs/trusts/NGOs) was considered.

A second yardstick to measure women's entitlement to bank credit is their contribution to banks by way of deposits. In 2017, credit received by women

Figure 17.7 *Credit to deposit ratio by gender, India, 1996–2017*, in per cent

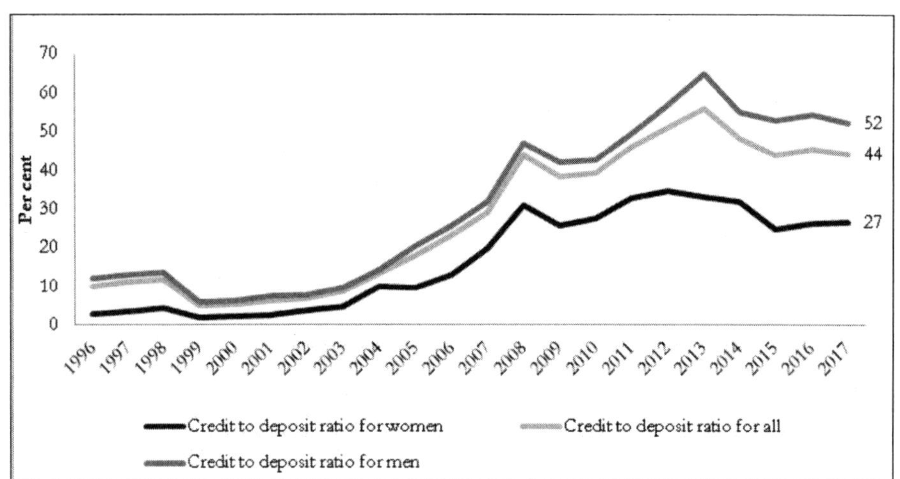

Source: Reserve Bank of India (RBI), *Basic Statistical Returns of Scheduled Commercial Banks in India*, various issues; www.censusindia.gov.in.

was only 27 per cent of the deposits they contributed, against 52 per cent for men (Figure 17.7). The credit-to-deposit ratio of women was only half that of men. A lower credit-to-deposit ratio for women is an advantage for banks from the point of view of liquidity. However, for women, it is a sign of credit deprivation.

Gender Gap by Geographical Regions

While there has been an increase in the amount of bank credit going to women (relative to men) in every geographical region, the ratio in each region still remains close to 25 per cent (Figure 17.8). Leading all the regions is the southern region (comprising Andhra Pradesh, Telangana, Karnataka, Kerala, and Tamil Nadu), which is the most well-banked and economically vanguard region (with a higher average State domestic product per capita in India) (Chavan 2017).

Interestingly, it is hard to establish any direct correlation between women's relative share in credit in a region and the state of banking and economic development of that region, as the second lowest gender gap was in the north-eastern region (comprising Assam, Arunachal Pradesh, Mizoram, Manipur, Meghalaya, Nagaland, Tripura, and Sikkim), the most underbanked region of India (*ibid.*).

Women from the southern and north-eastern regions have been ahead not

Figure 17.8 *Relative amount of credit to women vis-à-vis men by regions, India, 2001–16,* in per cent

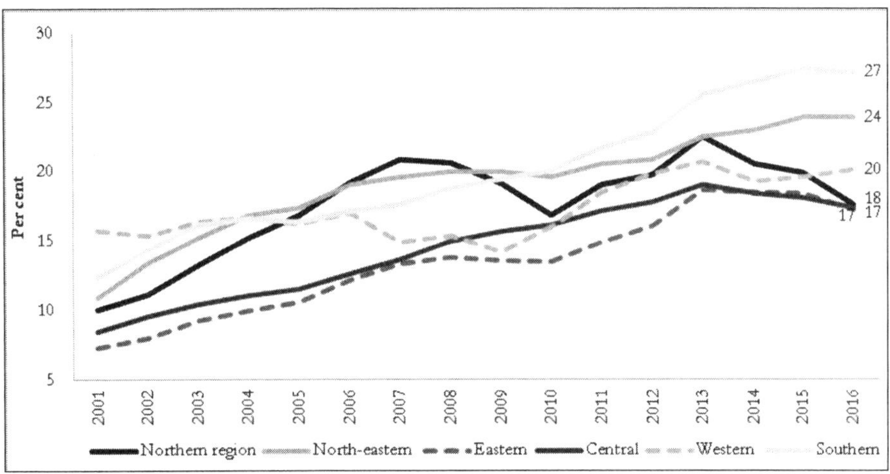

Notes: The figures are three-year moving averages. The figures are worked out dividing the per capita amount of bank credit to women vis-à-vis men in a given region.

Southern region: Andhra Pradesh, Telangana, Karnataka, Kerala, Tamil Nadu; north-eastern region: Assam, Arunachal Pradesh, Mizoram, Manipur, Meghalaya, Nagaland, Tripura, Sikkim; central region: Madhya Pradesh, Chattisgarh, Uttar Pradesh, Uttarakhand; eastern region: Bihar, Jharkhand, Odisha, West Bengal; western region: Goa, Gujarat, Maharashtra; and northern region: Delhi, Haryana, Himachal Pradesh, Jammu and Kashmir, Punjab, Rajasthan.

Source: Reserve Bank of India (RBI), *Basic Statistical Returns of Scheduled Commercial Banks in India*, various issues; www.censusindia.gov.in.

just in terms of the relative amount of bank credit, but they also obtain a larger share of what they contribute as deposits than women in other regions. The differential between the ratio of deposits by women to men and the ratio of credit obtained by women to men has been fairly narrow in these two regions (Figure 17.9). However, the gap between the ratio of deposits by women to men and the ratio of credit obtained by women to men has unmistakably widened in recent years. In other words, across regions, women's contribution to total deposits has outpaced their share in total credit relative to men.

Gender Gap in Rural and Urban Areas

Women from rural India are most deprived in terms of access to bank credit; they fare poorly compared to rural men, urban women, and urban men (Chavan 2008; Chavan 2016). However, there have been significant gains for

Figure 17.9 *Differential between the ratio of deposits contributed by women to men and the ratio of credit accessed by women to men, India, 2002–2016, by region*

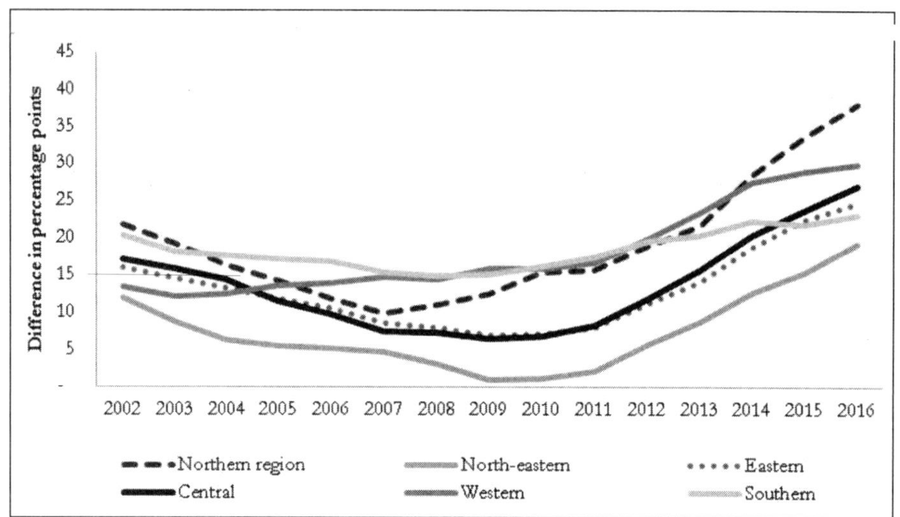

Note: The difference is worked out between three-year moving averages of the amount of deposits per woman to man and the amount of credit per woman to man.
Source: Reserve Bank of India (RBI), *Basic Statistical Returns of Scheduled Commercial Banks in India*, various issues; www.censusindia.gov.in.

Figure 17.10 *Relative amount of credit to rural/urban women vis-à-vis rural/urban men, India, 2001–16*, in per cent

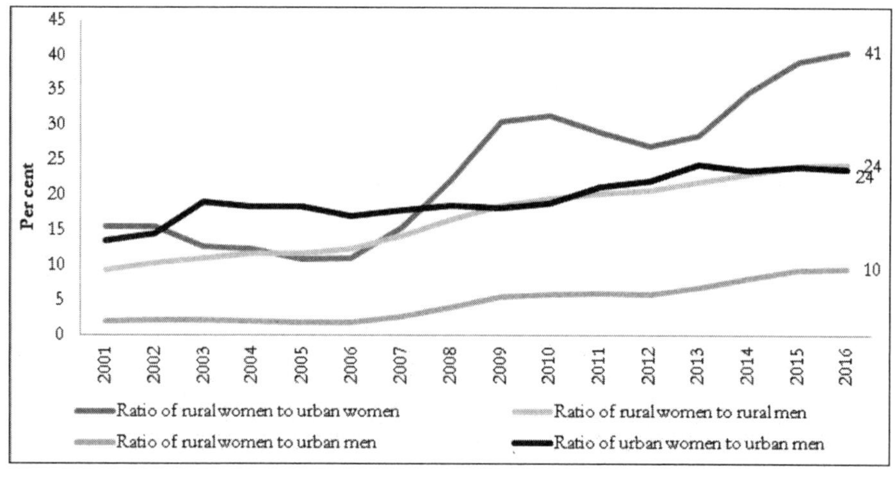

Source: Reserve Bank of India (RBI), *Basic Statistical Returns of Scheduled Commercial Banks in India*, various issues; www.censusindia.gov.in.

rural women in recent years, which have not only narrowed the gap between them and rural men, but have also brought them closer to urban women in terms of access of credit. The gains for rural women in terms of bank credit have come about after 2006, coinciding with the period of financial inclusion (Figure 17.10).

On average, rural women obtained 41 per cent of the credit obtained by urban women in 2016, but the ratio has shown a rising trend during the last decade.[22] In comparison, rural women obtained only 24 per cent of the credit given to rural men in 2016, underlining the stark gender gap in rural areas. The gender gap in urban areas has been as wide as in rural areas, with urban women getting 24 per cent of the credit given to urban men in 2016. Evidently, gender matters more than location when it comes to access to credit.

Gender Gap among Cultivators

The gender gap among cultivators in access to agricultural credit has been fairly large. Looking at data on the number of cultivators from the Census of India 2011, only 26 per cent of female cultivators had access to "direct"

Figure 17.11 *Coverage of cultivators by direct agricultural credit, by gender and region, India, 2011,* in per cent

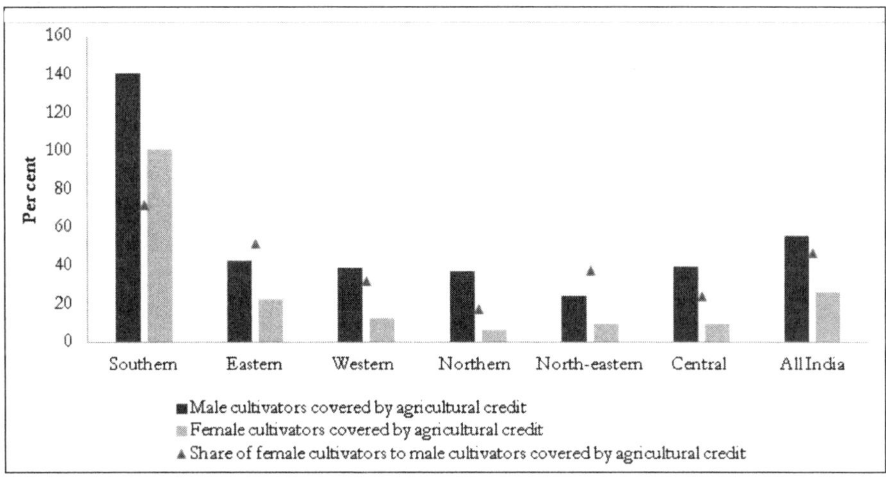

Source: Reserve Bank of India (RBI), *Basic Statistical Returns of Scheduled Commercial Banks in India,* various issues; www.censusindia.gov.in.

[22] This is a three-year moving average taking data from 2015 to 2017, and is reported against 2016.

agricultural credit while the corresponding percentage was 55 per cent for male cultivators.[23]

There are also regional disparities in the inclusion of female cultivators by banks. Coverage of female cultivators is the highest, and the resultant gender gap the narrowest, in the southern region (Figure 17.11). The proportion in the southern region was close to 100 per cent in 2011. However, this does not imply that all female cultivators were covered by banks, as one cultivator could have more than one loan account.

Over time, there has been a slow increase in access to direct agricultural credit for female cultivators relative to male cultivators. Banks covered about 47 female cultivators per 100 male cultivators in 2011; the corresponding coverage was 41 per cent in 2001. Female cultivators received about 40 per cent of the direct agricultural credit received by male cultivators in 2011; the corresponding percentage was 27 per cent in 2001.

Predictors of Access to Banking Services

Predictors of Ownership of Bank Deposits

According to Consumer Pyramids, 78.5 per cent of adults in India owned a bank deposit account, a close match with the figure given in Findex.[24] About 71 per cent of women and 85 per cent of men owned accounts, but the proportion of the population operating accounts is not known.[25] There has been a striking increase in the ownership of accounts after the implementation of Financial Inclusion Plans and Prime Minister's Jan Dhan Yojana (PMJDY). About 79 per cent of women reported a deposit account after the announcement of the PMJDY, as compared to 47 per cent earlier.

Here, I analyse the predictors for ownership of bank deposits by applying a linear probability model to the Consumer Pyramids data. I test the hypothesis that women have a lower probability of owning accounts than men. The details of the specification are in Appendix 17.1. The results indicate that the average probability of owning an account is about 14 percentage points lower for

---

[23] It is to be noted that female cultivators accounted for 30 per cent of total cultivators in 2011, partly a reflection of the disparity in land ownership.

[24] This is the average taken from January 2014 to December 2018. While Consumer Pyramids does not spell out the definition of a bank, by way of elimination of other institutions in the database it can be inferred that banks include commercial banks, credit cooperatives and RRBs.

[25] Although the figure for men reported in Consumer Pyramids matches closely with that in Findex, the figure for women is distinctly lower in the former, rendering a much wider gender gap in deposit ownership as per Consumer Pyramids than Findex.

women than for men (Table 17.1, column 1).[26] This finding is in line with the literature that highlights the negative effect of gender on financial inclusion.[27] The probability is lower by 17 percentage points for rural women relative to rural men (Table 17.1, column 1, specification 5). It is even lower for rural women relative to urban men, the differential being 18 percentage points.

Literacy and education enhance the probability of women owning an account (Table 17.1, columns 2 and 3). Women from minority communities have a lower probability of owning an account than Hindu women.[28] Women from backward social groups (Scheduled Castes and Scheduled Tribes, referred to as Social Group B in Table 17.1) have a lower probability of owning an account than "upper" caste (non-SC/ST/Other Backward Class) women.[29]

The effects of financial inclusion policies and PMJDY are evident, as women's probability of owning accounts was higher by about 26 percentage points in the post-September 2014 period than before (Table 17.1, column 3). To differentiate the effect of financial inclusion measures from demonetisation, which was announced in November 2016 and which resulted in a striking increase in bank deposits, I considered only the period between September 2014 and November 2016 (post-PMJDY but pre-demonetisation).[30] Women's probability of owning accounts was higher by about 15 percentage points even during the pre-demonetisation PMJDY period than before (Table 17.1, column 3, specification 8). Evidently, financial inclusion measures increased

---

[26] The linear probability model has been used as it lends itself well to the interpretation of the coefficients and controlling for district-time fixed effects. Although the logit model, which assumes the natural log of the odds $p/(1-p)$ as a linear function of the regressors, is commonly used for testing the outcomes for dichotomous dependent variables, its interpretation is not direct and it also does not allow for controlling fixed effects. Hence, as robustness checks, first, I compared the linear probability and logit models after removing the district-time fixed effects. The results from the two models were qualitatively very similar. Secondly, I also worked out the distribution of the predicted probability values from the baseline specification of the linear probability model and observed that only about 0.02 per cent of the predicted values were beyond the 0–1 range. This implied that the linear probability model was able to produce consistent results.

[27] Deléchat *et al.* (2018) observe that the financial inclusion index for women is lower by 1.1 percentage points than for men for their sample of countries, which includes India. The finding is similar to Kunt *et al.* (2013). The sample of countries in Kunt *et al.* (2013) includes India, and they find that the probability of owning savings and credit accounts is lower for women.

[28] In relative terms, the average probability is lower by about 17 percentage points for Muslim women than for Muslim men (Table 17.1, column 1, specification 6). It is about 18 (17+1) percentage points lower than for Hindu men.

[29] The probability of owning an account for Scheduled Caste/Scheduled Tribe (SC/ST) women is lower by about 15 percentage points than for SC/ST men (Table 17.1, column 1, specification 7). Further, it is 18 (15+3) percentage points lower than for "upper" caste men.

[30] Demonetisation involved the exchange of specified bank notes and resulted in an increase in the growth of bank deposits by households, particularly individuals, in 2016–17 (Saxena and Sreejith 2018).

Table 17.1 *Individual-level predictors of ownership of bank deposit accounts*

Covariates	Ownership of deposit account			
	(1)	(2)	(3)	(4)
	Baseline specification	Specification (2)	Specification (3)	Specification (4)
Gender	−0.144 *** (0.001)	−0.262 *** (0.003)	−0.466 *** (0.003)	−0.183 *** (0.002)
Gender*Rural		−0.052 *** (0.001)	−0.052 *** (0.002)	
Gender*Literacy		0.044 *** (0.004)	0.037 *** (0.004)	
Gender*School education		0.125 *** (0.004)	0.112 *** (0.004)	
Gender*College education		0.138 *** (0.004)	0.126 *** (0.004)	
Gender*Higher education		0.037 *** (0.003)	0.032 *** (0.003)	
Gender*Religion groups (A)		−0.023 *** (0.003)	−0.026 *** (0.003)	
Gender*Religion groups (B)		−0.0006 (0.004)	0.001 (0.004)	
Gender*Social groups (A)		0.011 *** (0.003)	0.006 ** (0.002)	
Gender*Social groups (B)		−0.012 *** (0.003)	−0.006 * (0.003)	
Gender*PMJDY			0.255 *** (0.002)	
Gender*Branch_penetration				0.072 *** (0.002)
Rural women: Rural men (5)	−0.167 ** (0.047)			
Women from Religion groups (A): Men from Religion groups (A) (6)	−0.172 ** (0.064)			
Women from Social groups (B): Men from Social Groups (B) (7)	−0.153 ** (0.054)			
Women in pre-demonetisation PMJDY period: Women in pre-PMJDY period (8)			0.147 *** (0.002)	
No. of observations	6,276,118	6,276,118	6,276,118	5,912,785
R^2	0.27	0.28	0.27	0.27
District–Time FE	Y	Y	Y	Y

Note: See Appendix 17.1 for equations underlying the specifications. Baseline specification

– equation (1); Specification (2) – equation (2); Specification (3) – equation (3); Specification (4) – equation (4). Specification (4) relates to a mapped Consumer Pyramids and *Basic Statistical Returns of Scheduled Commercial Banks in India* data. Specification (5) shows the average differential effect for a rural woman as compared to rural man. It involves running a specification involving Gender, Rural and Gender*Rural. Specification (6) involves running a specification with Gender, Religion group (A), Religion Group (B) Gender*Religion groups (A). Specification (7) involves a specification with Gender, Social group (A), Social group (B) and Gender*Social groups (B). Specification (8) involves running specification (3) by restricting the sample to the pre-demonetisation PMJDY period (between September 2014 and November 2016) containing 2,788,127 observations.

*** $p < 0.01$; ** $p < 0.005$; * $p < 0.1$. Standard errors are clustered by individuals.
Source: Estimated from Consumer Pyramids.

the probability of owning bank accounts among women; and the probability, of course, increased further following demonetisation. Finally, the probability of deposit ownership was higher by about 7 percentage points for women belonging to districts with higher branch penetration (Table 17.1, column 4).

Predictors of Access to Bank Credit

Access to bank credit is extremely limited in India. Only 6 per cent of households report having taken bank credit according to Consumer Pyramids.[31] The incidence of bank loans is only marginally higher for urban households. Also, it is marginally higher for male-headed households as compared to female-headed households; on average, 6.3 per cent of male-headed households access credit as compared to 5.5 per cent of female-headed households.

There is a positive impact of financial inclusion policies on household access to bank credit. About 6 per cent of households reported outstanding bank loans after September 2014 as compared to 3 per cent earlier.

Using household-level data from Consumer Pyramids, I tested the hypothesis that female-headed households have a lower probability of accessing bank credit than male-headed households, *ceteris paribus* (see Appendix 17.2 for the econometric specification). The results showed that on average, the probability of accessing bank credit was lower by about 2 percentage points for female-headed households relative to male-headed households (Table 17.2, column 1).[32] No socio-economic characteristic of female-headed households in the

[31] The percentage closely matches the All-India Debt and Investment Survey's estimate.
[32] A direct comparison of the results for the ownership of bank deposits and access to bank credit may be misleading because: (i) ownership of deposits does not imply *actual* operation unlike credit, which refers to a household reporting an *outstanding* bank loan; (ii) ownership of deposits is at the

Table 17.2 *Household-level predictors of access to bank credit*

Covariates	Access to bank credit			
	(1)	(2)	(3)	(4)
	Baseline speci-fication	Speci-fication (2)	Speci-fication (3)	Speci-fication (4)
Gender_HoH	–0.018 *** (0.001)	–0.018 *** (0.003)	–0.010 *** (0.002)	–0.017 *** (0.002)
Gender_HoH*Rural		–0.003 (0.003)		
Gender_HoH*Religion groups (A)		–0.003 (0.006)		
Gender_HoH*Religion groups (B)		–0.0008 (0.007)		
Gender_HoH*Social groups (A)		0.002 (0.003)		
Gender_HoH*Social groups (B)		0.008 * (0.005)		
Gender_HoH*Physical Assets Index		0.0004 (0.0006)		
Gender_HoH*PMJDY			–0.007 *** (0.002)	
Gender_HoH*Branch_penetration				0.002 (0.003)
FHHs in pre-demonetisation PMJDY period–FHHs in pre-PMJDY period (5)			0.002 (0.002)	
No. of observations	1,924,097	1,924,097	1,924,097	1,820,558
R^2	0.17	0.17	0.17	0.17
District–Time FE	Y	Y	Y	Y

Note: See Appendix 17.2 for equations underlying the specifications. Baseline specification – equation (5); Specification (2) – equation (6); Specification (3) – equation (7); Specification (4) – equation (8). Specification (4) relates to a mapped Consumer Pyramids and *Basic Statistical Returns of Scheduled Commercial Banks in India* data. Specification (5) involves running specification (3) by restricting the sample to the pre-demonetisation PMJDY period (between September 2014 and November 2016) containing 714,081 observations.

*** $p < 0.01$; ** $p < 0.005$; * $p < 0.1$. Standard errors are clustered by households.
Source: Estimated from Consumer Pyramids.

specifications selected significantly explained their access to credit (Table 17.2, column 2).[33]

Financial inclusion policies had a positive correlation with women's ownership of bank deposits and a negative correlation with access to bank credit. The probability of credit access for female-headed households was nearly 1 percentage point lower post-September 2014 than before (Table 17.2, column 3). Given that credit growth slowed down after demonetisation, I restricted the sample to the pre-demonetisation but post-PMJDY period to analyse the effect of financial inclusion policies alone.[34] It turned out that financial inclusion policies showed no significant effect on credit access for female-headed households (Table 17.2, column 3, specification 5).

The penetration of bank branches also showed no effect on credit access for female-headed households, although it increased the access to deposits for women. This finding is in line with the argument that financial inclusion has focused more on deposit mobilisation than on credit provision. It also corroborates a point made in the literature that having branches may be a necessary but not a sufficient condition for credit access, particularly for the underserved sections of society (Chavan 2016). Banks may need more proactive efforts to extend credit to such sections through innovative platforms and products (*ibid.*).

Concluding Observations

After bank nationalisation, redistribution of banking services was upheld as the most important objective of banking policy in India. Banks assumed the role of public institutions, providing basic banking services to underserved sections of the population. Women, being such an underserved section, were also expected to benefit from the increased reach of banking, although the policy did not have an explicit focus on women.

The policy of financial inclusion adopted in 2005 was an attempt to reaffirm

---

individual level, while credit access is at the *household* level. Hence, even if one man or woman from the household reports a loan, it gets counted against the household.

[33] As a robustness check, apart from the household-specific characteristics listed in Appendix 17.2, I also included the following time-variant socio-economic characteristics as explanatory variables in the baseline specification and the specification interacting the baseline variables with *Gender_HoH* (represented by equations 5 and 6 in Appendix 17.2, respectively): (1) average years of schooling of the household; (2) size of the household; (3) total number of females in the household. I observed no qualitative difference between the results from the expanded and the original specifications, underlining the overall robustness of the results obtained from the original specifications.

[34] Unlike deposit growth, credit growth across sectors slowed down after demonetisation and returned to the pre-demonetisation level only after January 2018 (RBI 2019a).

banks' commitment to serving underserved sections while being mindful of their own commercial interests. The profit-maximising nature of the current form of "inclusion" is evident from the greater emphasis on opening branchless banking outlets as compared to physical branches, and mobilising small-sized deposits rather than extending small-sized credit.

Over time, the shares of both women and men in total bank credit have increased. Total bank credit includes credit given to men and women individually, as well as to households, private and public corporations, etc. The increase in women's share, however, has been much slower than the corresponding increase for men, creating a widening gender gap. In 2017, women accounted for only 7 per cent of total bank credit as compared to 30 per cent for men. Even if we are to include credit to microfinance institutions, self-help groups, and joint liability groups as part of "women's credit," women's share in total credit was only 8 per cent. In 2017, the credit received by women was 27 per cent of the deposits they contributed as compared to 52 per cent for men, further underlining the gender gap.

Financial inclusion measures have had a positive effect on women's ownership of bank deposits. The gender gap in ownership of bank deposits has narrowed significantly in India in recent years in comparison with the reduction seen for other BRIICS countries. However, financial inclusion measures have not been able to deliver on two fronts. The first is with respect to usage of deposit accounts by women. In 2017, even though 77 per cent of women in India had deposit accounts in their names, only 34 per cent actually used them. The second is with respect to access to bank credit. Only 5 per cent of women in India reported any form of formal loan in 2017 with their share showing absolutely no increase in the period of financial inclusion.

Views expressed are those of the author and not of the organisation to which she is affiliated. The author benefited from several insightful discussions with S. K. Ritadhi while working on the paper. She gratefully acknowledges his contribution, and the useful comments received from Anwesha Das, V. K. Ramachandran, and an anonymous referee on an earlier draft.

References

Agarwal, B. (1986), "Women, Poverty and Agricultural Growth in India," *Journal of Peasant Studies*, vol. 13, no. 4.

Bandyopadhyay, Tamal (2014), "Mahila Bank: UPA's Rs 1000 Crore Misadventure," *Livemint*, 21 November.

Beck, T. (2015), "Microfinance: A Critical Literature Survey," IEG Working Paper no. 4.

Census of India (2000), *Instruction Manual for Filling up the Household Schedule*, Office of the Registrar General and Census Commissioner, Ministry of Home Affairs, Government of India, New Delhi.

Chakrabarty, K. C. (2011), "Financial Inclusion and Banks: Issues and Perspectives," speech at the FICCI–UNDP Seminar, New Delhi, 14 October.

Chavan, Pallavi (2008), "Gender Inequality in Banking Services," *Economic and Political Weekly*, vol. 43, no. 47, 22 November.

Chavan, Pallavi (2012), "The Access of Dalit Borrowers in India's Rural Areas to Bank Credit," *Review of Agrarian Studies*, vol. 2, no. 2, July–December.

Chavan, Pallavi (2016), "Bank Credit to Small Borrowers: An Analysis based on Demand and Supply Side Indicators," *RBI Occasional Papers*, vols. 35 and 36, nos. 1 and 2, Reserve Bank of India, Mumbai.

Chavan, Pallavi (2017), "Public Banks and Financial Intermediation in India: The Phases of Nationalisation, Liberalisation, and Inclusion," in Christoph Scherrer (ed.), *Public Banks in the Age of Financialisation: A Comparative Perspective*, Edward Elgar Publishing Limited, Cheltenham.

Chavan, Pallavi, and Dutta, Ritam (2019), "A Contemporary Study of Rural Credit in West Bengal," unpublished.

Centre for Monitoring Indian Economy (CMIE) (2019), *Consumer Pyramids dx, People of India, Code Book*, January–April.

Coleman, Susan (2002), "Access to Capital and Terms of Credit: A Comparison of Men- and Women-owned Small Businesses, *Journal of Small Business Management*, vol. 38, no. 3.

Credit Suisse (2016), "The Quick and the Dead," Credit Suisse Securities Research and Analytics, 29 June.

Deléchat, Corinne C., Newiak, Monique, Xu, Rui, Yang, Fan, and Aslan, Goksu (2018), "What is Driving Women's Financial Inclusion across Countries?" IMF Working Paper WP/18/38, International Monetary Fund, Washington D. C.

Gaikwad, M. (2014), "Entry of Bandhan and Bharatiya Mahila Bank into the Indian Banking Sector," *Women's Equality*, nos. 1 and 2, January–June.

Goyal, S. K. (1967), "Banking Institutions and Indian Economy," ISID Working Paper 1, Institute for Studies in Industrial Development, New Delhi, available at http://isid.org.in/pdf/banking.PDF, viewed on 3 April 2020.

Haldar, Antara, and Stiglitz, Joseph (2016), "Group Lending, Joint Liability, and Social Capital: Insights from the Indian Microfinance Crisis," *Politics and Society*, vol. 44, no. 4.

Joshi, Vijay, and Little, I. M. D. (1994), *India: Macroeconomics and Political Economy, 1964–1991*, World Bank, Washington D. C.

Karim, Lamia (2011), *Microfinance and Its Discontents: Women in Debt in Bangladesh*, University of Minnesota Press, Minneapolis.

Kling, J.R., Liebman, J. B., and Katz, L. F. (2007), "Experimental Analysis of Neighbourhood Effects," *Econometrica*, vol. 75, no. 1, January.

Khan, H. R. (2011), "Financial Inclusion and Financial Stability: Are they two sides of the same coin?" address by H. R. Khan, Deputy Governor, Reserve Bank of India at BANCON 2011, 4 November, available at https://rbi.org.in/scripts/BS_SpeechesView.aspx?Id=623, viewed on 9 March 2020.

Kohli, Renu (2018), "Women and Banking: India's Financial Inclusion Suffers from a Gender Gap," *Next Billion*, available at www.nextbillion.net/news/women-banking-indias-financial-inclusion-suffers-from-a-gender-gap, viewed on 9 March 2020.

Kunt, Asli D., Klapper, Leora, and Singer, Dorothe (2013), "Financial Inclusion and Legal Discrimination against Women Evidence from Developing Countries," Policy Research Working Paper no. WPS 6416, World Bank, Washington D. C.

Kunt, Asli D., Klapper, Leora, Singer, Dorothe, Ansar, Saniya, Hess, Jake Richard (2017), *The Global Findex Database 2017: Measuring Financial Inclusion and the Fintech Revolution*, World Bank Group, Washington D. C.

Microfinance Network (MFIN) (2018), *Micrometer*, no. 30, Microfinance Institutions Network.

Mohanty, Deepak (2010), "Perspectives on Lending Rates in India," speech delivered at Banker's Club, Kolkata, available at https://www.rbi.org.in/scripts/BS_SpeechesView.aspx?id=508, viewed on 26 March 2020.

Narain, Sushma (2009), "Gender and Access to Finance," Analytical Paper, World Bank, available at http://siteresources.worldbank.org/EXTGENDERSTATS/Resources/SushmaNarain-AccesstoFinanceAnalyticalPaper.doc, viewed on 26 March 2020.

National Sample Survey Office (NSSO) (2014), "Key indicators of Debt and Investment in India," National Sample Survey 70th Round, Ministry of Statistics and Programme Implementation, Government of India, New Delhi, available at http://www.mospi.gov.in/sites/default/files/publication_reports/KI_70_18.2_19dec14.pdf, viewed on 10 March 2020.

Ramachandran, V. K., Swaminathan, Madhura, and Rawal, Vikas (2001), "Female-Headed Households: A Note on Methodology," paper presented at the Annual Conference of the International Association for Feminist Economics, 22–24 June, Oslo.

Ramakumar, R. (2010), "A Route to Disaster," *Frontline*, vol. 27, no. 24, 20 November–3 December.

Ramakumar, R., and Chavan, Pallavi (2014), "Agricultural Credit in the 2000s: Dissecting the Revival," *Review of Agrarian Studies,* vol. 4, no. 1, February–June.

Reserve Bank of India (RBI) (1991), *Report of the Committee on the Financial System,* Reserve Bank of India, Mumbai.

Reserve Bank of India (RBI) (2001), "Developmental Issues in Micro-credit," speech by Jagdish Capoor, *RBI Bulletin*, Reserve Bank of India, Mumbai, March.

Reserve Bank of India (RBI) (2008a), *Report on Currency and Finance 2006–08,* Reserve Bank of India, Mumbai.

Reserve Bank of India (RBI) (2008b), *Report on Trend and Progress of Banking in India, 2007–08*, Reserve Bank of India, Mumbai.

Reserve Bank of India (RBI) (2015a), *Financial Stability Report*, issue no. 11, June, Reserve Bank of India, Mumbai.

Reserve Bank of India (RBI) (2015b), *Report of the Committee on Medium-term Path on Financial Inclusion,* Reserve Bank of India, Mumbai.

Reserve Bank of India (RBI) (2018), *Report on Trend and Progress of Banking in India 2017–18*, Reserve Bank of India, Mumbai.

Reserve Bank of India (RBI) (2019a), *Annual Report 2018–19,* Reserve Bank of India, Mumbai.

Reserve Bank of India (RBI) (2019b), *Statement of Developmental and Regulatory Policies*, Reserve Bank of India, Mumbai.

Saxena T. K., and Sreejith, T. B. (2018), "Post-Demonetisation Patterns of Deposits with Scheduled Commercial Banks: 2016–17 and 2017–18," *Reserve Bank of India Bulletin*, December 2018.

Shetty, S. L. (2005), "Regional, Sectoral and Functional Distribution of Bank Credit," in V. K. Ramachandran and Madhura Swaminathan (eds.), *Financial Liberalisation and Rural Credit*, Tulika Books, New Delhi.

Singh, Nirvikar (2018), "Financial Inclusion: Concepts, Issues and Policies for India," University of California, Santa Cruz, available at https://mpra.ub.uni-muenchen.de/91047/1/MPRA_paper_91047.pdf, viewed on 10 March 2020.

Subbarao, Duvvuri (2012), "Agricultural Credit: Accomplishments and Challenges," speech at NABARD, Mumbai, 12 July.

Vani, B. P., Bhattacharjee, Manojit, and Rajeev, Meenakshi (2011), "Credibility of Equal Access to Credit: Does Gender Matter?" *Economic and Political Weekly*, vol. 46, no. 33.

Wiggins, Steve and Rajendran, S. (1987), "Rural Banking in Southern Tamil Nadu: Performance and Management," Final Research Report no. 3, The University of Reading, United Kingdom.

Appendix 17.1

Econometric Specification for Individual Access to Bank Deposits

The equation representing the baseline specification is as follows:

$$\text{Bank\_deposit}_{ihdt} = \alpha dt + \beta \text{Gender}_{ihd} + X_{ihdt}\, \varphi + \varepsilon_{ihdt} \text{---- ...} \ (1)$$

The unit of observation is individual 'i' belonging to household 'h' from district–State combination 'd' in time period 't' represented by month–year combination in Consumer Pyramids. 'Bank deposit' takes value 1 if individual 'i' reports ownership of at least one bank deposit at the time of the survey, 0 otherwise. 'α' represents district-time fixed effects controlling for the district-specific time varying factors affecting the ownership of bank deposits.[35] Effectively, I limit the comparison between individuals belonging to a household within the same district during the same time period. 'Gender' takes value 1 if individual 'i' is a woman, 0 otherwise. 'X' represents the vector (other than Gender) of individual-specific socio-economic covariates that may be correlated with ownership of deposits (illustrated in Appendix Table 17.1).

The baseline specification in equation (1) is modified by interacting vector 'X' with 'Gender' to give the following specification:

---

[35] I also controlled for within-household time-invariant factors using the household fixed effects. However, the strength and sign of the coefficients remained largely unchanged between the specifications with and without the household fixed effects. Hence, the specification including household fixed effects has not been reported here separately.

$$\text{Bank\_deposit}_{ihdt} = \alpha_{dt} + \beta\text{Gender}_{ihd} + X_{ihdt}\,\varphi + \text{Gender}_{ihd} * X_{ihdt}\,\theta + \varepsilon_{ihdt}\text{--- ... (2)}$$

I develop a third specification to tease out the effects of financial inclusion measures, termed as Prime Minister's Jan Dhan Yojana (PMJDY):

$$\text{Bank\_deposit}_{ihdt} = \alpha_{dt} + \beta\text{Gender}_{ihd} + X_{ihdt}\,\varphi + \text{Gender}_{ihd} * X_{ihdt}\,\theta + \gamma\text{Gender}_{ihd} * \text{PM JDY}_t + \varepsilon_{ihdt}\text{--- ...(3)}$$

PMJDY_t takes value 1 for 't' from September 2014 onwards and 0 otherwise.

Finally, I capture the correlation of bank branch penetration – as a supply-side factor – with the ownership of bank deposits as follows:

$$\text{Bank\_deposit}_{ihdt} = \alpha_{dt} + \beta\text{Gender}_{ihd} + X_{ihdt}\varphi + \text{Gender}_{ihd} * X_{ihdt}\,\theta + \mu\text{Gender}_{ihd} * \text{Branch\_penetration}_{dt} + \varepsilon_{ihdt}\text{ ... (4)}$$

$\text{Branch\_penetration}_d$ refers to population per bank branch for district 'd' in time 't' taking value 1 if the district has population per bank branch above the median population per bank branch for the corresponding State in 't,' 0 otherwise.[36]

Appendix Table 17.1 *Individual-specific covariates (X) for estimating probability of ownership of bank deposits*

Variable	Description of the variable
Rural	1 if rural; 0 otherwise
Literacy	1 if literate; 0 otherwise
School education	1 if completed up to secondary education; 0 otherwise
College education	1 if completed graduation; 0 otherwise
Higher education	1 if studied up to or beyond post-graduation; 0 otherwise
Religion group (A)	1 if belonged to Muslim/Khasi; 0 otherwise
Religion group (B)	1 if belonged to Sikh/Christian/Jain/Buddhist/any other minority community excluding those included under Religion groups (A); 0 otherwise
Social group (A)	1 if belonged to Other Backward Class/intermediate caste; 0 otherwise
Social group (B)	1 if belonged to Scheduled Caste/Scheduled Tribe; 0 otherwise

[36] Data on bank branches and population figures are sourced from *Basic Statistical Returns of Scheduled Commercial Banks in India* and National Sample Survey, 68th Round (2011–12), respectively, to work out the population per bank branch at the district and State levels. The districts from Consumer Pyramids are mapped to districts from *Basic Statistical Returns of Scheduled Commercial Banks in India*. As the list of districts sourced from *Basic Statistical Returns of Scheduled Commercial Banks in India* does not include districts from the north-eastern region except Assam, the number of observations after the mapping of the districts is lower than that used in all specifications other than (4).

APPENDIX 17.2

Econometric Specification for Household Access to Bank Credit

The baseline specification is as given below:

$$\text{Bank\_credit}_{hdt} = \alpha_{dt} + \beta \text{Gender\_HoH}_{hdt} + X1_{hdt}\,\varphi + \varepsilon_{hdt} \text{----} \ldots (5)$$

The unit of observation is household 'h' from district–State combination 'd' in month–year combination 't'. 'Bank_credit' takes value 1 if the household 'h' reports at least one outstanding bank loan at the time of the survey, 0 otherwise. 'α' represents the district-time fixed effects controlling for the district-specific time varying factors affecting credit access. 'Gender_HoH' takes value 1 if household 'h' is headed by a woman, 0 otherwise. 'X1' represents the vector of household-specific socio-economic covariates (other than 'Gender_HoH') that may be correlated with credit access (Appendix Table 17.2).

The baseline specification in equation (5) is modified by interacting 'Gender_HoH' with vector 'X1':

$$\text{Bank\_credit}_{hdt} = \alpha_{dt} + \beta \text{Gender\_HoH}_{hdt} + X1_{hdt}\,\varphi + \text{Gender\_HoH}_{hdt} * X1_{hdt}\,\theta + \varepsilon_{hdt} \ldots (6)$$

The baseline specification is modified to analyse the differential effect of financial inclusion measures:

$$\text{Bank\_credit}_{hdt} = \alpha_{dt} + \beta \text{Gender\_HoH}_{hdt} + X1_{hdt}\,\varphi + \gamma \text{Gender\_HoH}_{hdt} * \text{PMJDY}_t + \varepsilon_{hdt} \ldots (7)$$

To capture the effect of branch penetration, the following specification is used:[37]

$$\text{Bank\_credit}_{hdt} = \alpha_{dt} + \beta \text{Gender\_HoH}_{hdt} + X1_{hdt}\varphi + \theta \text{Gender\_HoH}_{hdt} * \text{Branch\_penetration}_{dt} + \varepsilon_{hdt} \ldots (8)$$

---

[37] See the previous footnote for details on the data used.

Appendix Table 17.2 *Household-specific covariates (X1) for estimating probability of credit access*

Variable	Description of the variable
Rural	1 if rural household; 0 otherwise
Religion group (A)	1 if household belonged to Muslim/Khasi; 0 otherwise
Religion group (B)	1 if household belonged to Sikh/Christian/Jain/Buddhist/any other minority community excluding those included under Religion groups (A); 0 otherwise
Social group (A)	1 if household belonged to Other Backward Class/intermediate caste; 0 otherwise
Social group (B)	1 if household belonged to Scheduled Caste/Scheduled Tribe; 0 otherwise
Household physical assets index	$\left(\dfrac{x_{hdt}-\mu_{xdt}}{\sigma_{xdt}}\right)+\left(\dfrac{y_{hdt}-\mu_{ydt}}{\sigma_{ydt}}\right)$ where x takes value 1 if household 'h' in district 'd' in time 't' reports saving in gold in the past four months, 0 otherwise; and y takes value 1 if household reports saving in real estate in the past four months, 0 otherwise.[38]

[38] The index is constructed following the definition used in Kling, Liebman, and Katz (2007).

Contributors

Pallavi Chavan, economist working on rural credit, Mumbai

Arindam Das, Joint Director of Research, Foundation for Agrarian Studies, Bengaluru

K. Hemalata, President, Centre of Indian Trade Unions, New Delhi

Indira Hirway, Director and Professor of Economics, Centre for Development Alternatives (CFDA), Ahmedabad

Athary Janiso, Research Scholar, Department of Economics and Finance, Birla Institute of Technology and Science Pilani, Hyderabad

Madhavi Jha, PhD candidate, Centre for Historical Studies, Jawaharlal Nehru University, New Delhi

Abhinav Kapoor, PhD candidate, Michigan State University, East Lansing

Khalid Khan, Assistant Professor, Indian Institute of Dalit Studies, New Delhi

Shruti Nagbhushan, Research Assistant, Foundation for Agrarian Studies, Bengaluru

S. Niyati, Senior Research Fellow, Economic Analysis Unit, Indian Statistical Institute, Bengaluru

Subhajit Patra, Senior Data Analyst, Foundation for Agrarian Studies, Bengaluru

V. K. Ramachandran, Vice Chairperson, Kerala State Planning Board, Thiruvananthapuram

Smita Ramnarain, Assistant Professor, Department of Economics, University of Rhode Island, Kingston

Smriti Rao, Professor, Department of Economics and Global Studies, Assumption College, Massachusetts

Jeta Sankrityayana, Professor of Economics, Sikkim University, Gangtok

Madhura Swaminathan, Professor and Head, Economic Analysis Unit, Indian Statistical Institute, Bengaluru

Jayan Jose Thomas, Associate Professor, Indian Institute of Technology, New Delhi

Sukhadeo Thorat, Chairman, Indian Institute of Dalit Studies, New Delhi

Yoshifumi Usami, Research Fellow, University of Tokyo, Bunkyo City

R. Vijayamba, Senior Research Fellow, Economic Analysis Unit, Indian Statistical Institute, Bengaluru

Index

activity status
daily status, 20, 22, 23, 27, 28, 36, 56
specified activity (SA), 43, 44, 46, 51, 60, 61, 170–72, 174, 180
usual principal and subsidiary status/UPSS, 42–51, 60, 61, 85–88, 171–78, 180, 181, 191, 212
usual subsidiary status, 40, 42–51, 60–61, 169, 170–72
weekly status, 20, 21, 22, 27, 36
agrarian distress, 266–69
agrarian relations, 67–69, 121–28, 221–23, 231–32, 322–26
Agriculture Technology Management Agency (ATMA), 239–40
agricultural employment, 90–92, 101–05, 117–26, 194–96, 217, 229–31, 273, 283–84
Agricultural Wages in India (AWI), 298
agro-ecological zone, 110–17, 221, 233, 331–33, 336
Alabujanahalli village (Karnataka), 23–29, 33, 71–79, 113–30, 222–31, 324–33
Amarsinghi village (West Bengal), 71–79, 113–30, 222–31, 324–33
Ananthavaram village (Andhra Pradesh), 71–79, 113–31, 324–34
Andhra Pradesh, 92, 96, 101, 110–31, 173–76, 219, 223–32, 259, 307–16, 323–26, 358–59
anganwadi worker and helper (AWH), 239, 241, 243–45
animal/milch animal, 43–46, 53–61,170–80, 197, 293–94, 326
artisan, 284, 89
Arunachal Pradesh, 99, 358
Assam, 99, 134–64, 176, 215–19, 307–14, 358
ASHA (Accredited Social Health Activist), 240, 246, 247–48, 249, 251
augmented work participation rate, 41–46, 52–55, 172–73

bank nationalisation, 344, 345–46, 348, 367
Behar, 282–93
Bharatiya Mahila Bank, 349–50
Bihar, 92–106, 114–30, 176, 223–27, 248, 271, 281–94, 307–16, 323–24
bought leaf factory (BLF), 142, 158, 163
Brazil, 352, 356
BRIICS, 352–53, 355, 368
Bukkacherla village (Andhra Pradesh), 71–79, 223–25, 323–32

Calcutta/Kolkata, 135, 143
Canada, 114
care work, 3, 6, 34, 36, 238, 251
see also unpaid work, domestic duty
Caribbean, 136, 137
caste/caste system, 189–90, 202, 224–27
casual worker/casualisation, 91–92, 144–52 156–64, 194, 216–19, 267–68
Census of India, 27, 47, 49, 87, 98, 99, 244, 361
Central Tea Board Act of 1949, Tea Act in 1953, 138, 138, 155
Centre of Indian Trade Unions (CITU), 239, 244
Ceylon, 137, 138
Chhattisgarh, 96, 99, 101, 106, 136, 214, 219
Child Labour (Abolition and Regulation) Act 1986, 145
class/socio–economic class, 23–26, 36, 67–70, 116, 123, 143–52, 221–24, 231, 267–69, 282–84, 295, 326–27
class relations, 67–71, 121–28, 221–23, 266–69, 283–84, 322–26
see also agrarian relations
Colombo, 135, 143
colonial, 136, 140, 143, 152, 282
Committee on Empowerment of Women, 244, 245
Communist Party of India (Marxist) [CPI(M)], 71
community health centre (CHC), 240

construction, 92, 195, 197, 202, 247, 269, 270, 301–05, 313–14

correlation coefficient, 34–35, 122–23, 308–11, 313, 327, 331, 367

credit/bank credit, 343–68

credit–deposit ratio, 356–58

crop/field operation 117–21, 283–92, 299–307, 323–26

Consumer Pyramids Survey, 351

cotton, 152, 153, 228, 282–94, 324–33

cropping pattern, 113–17, 119, 331–33

crop production/crop productivity, 111–13, 128–31, 138–64, 266, 307, 331–33

crop season 25, 26, 33–34, 113–16

dairy/dairying, 42–44, 57–60, 169–73

dairy cooperative, 167

Darrang, 161

days of employment, 11–12, 227–31, 264–66

dearness allowance, 151, 245, 246

debit card, 348, 354, 355

Delhi, 96, 105, 189, 250, 264

deposit/bank deposit, 352–54, 362–65

differentiation/peasant differentiation, 67–70

discrimination, 163, 189–90, 202–03

discouraged worker, 10, 11, 36, 270–71

distress employment, 91, 136, 163, 202, 267, 269, 305, 344

domestic duty, 30–37, 87–93, 176, 180, 181
    see also care work

domestic work, 30, 120

Dooars, 136–64

East/Eastern Africa, 141, 152

education, 34–35, 39, 92–93, 102–05, 106, 198–200, 202, 203, 237–38, 250–52, 362–65

Eighteenth Brumaire, 68

elementary occupation, 196, 197, 200–03

Employment and Unemployment Survey (EUS), 19, 22, 40–43, 46, 49, 51, 54, 56, 57, 86–105, 169–81, 209–17

Employees' Provident Fund (EPS), 241

Equal Remuneration Act 1976, 145

exchange labour, 121, 219

exports, 134–38, 141, 155

factory worker, 140, 162

family labour, 70–80, 93, 121–26, 145, 158–63, 326–29

farm mechanisation/farm machinery, 110–31, 153, 307, 322

female-headed household, 351, 352, 365, 367

feminisation of agriculture, 90–92, 196–98, 221, 229–30

Fifth Schedule, 211, 213, 214, 216, 219

financial inclusion, 347, 348, 350, 351, 352, 354, 356, 361, 362, 363, 365, 367, 368

financial liberalisation, 343, 346–48, 350–51

Findex, 350–55, 351, 354, 355, 362

fishery workers, 197, 200

Foreign Exchange Regulation Act (FERA) 1973, 141, 143, 152

forms of labour, 67, 80, 109, 112, 121, 122, 129, 130
    see also hired labour, family labour, exchange labour

Foundation for Agrarian Studies (FAS), 23, 41, 52, 54, 55, 57, 61, 67, 68, 92, 110, 171, 221, 322
    see also Project on Agrarian Relations in India (PARI)

fuel/firewood, 6, 42, 60, 88, 93, 139, 151, 170, 272, 282, 283, 289, 290, 292, 293–94

gender division of labour, 117, 119–21, 128–31, 271–72, 333

gender wage gap, 285–90, 305–16, 322–34

Gharsondi village (Madhya Pradesh), 71–79, 222–31, 324–34

Goa, 96–106

Gorakhpuri pice, 294

green revolution, 109, 110, 113, 114

gross cropped area (GCA), 114–16

Gujarat, 96–106, 169, 177, 213–19, 307–16

Gulabewala village (Rajasthan), 71–79, 222–31, 323–34

Harevli village (Uttar Pradesh), 71–79, 222–31, 324–33

Haryana, 96–106, 169–77, 232, 281, 306–16

health worker, 237, 238, 247

high-yielding variety (HYV), 109, 114, 115

Himachal Pradesh, 96–106

hired labour, 70–80, 122–26, 131, 156–64, 221–26, 231, 283–92, 322–23

honorarium/honorary worker, 240–44, 246, 248, 249

hours of work, 11–12, 29–37, 170–71, 244, 246, 273

Hunan, 69

immunisation, 243, 247, 248, 254
International Labour Organisation (ILO), International Conference on Labour Statistics, 3–20, 31–32, 36
indenture, 136, 137, 152
Indian Ocean, 136, 137
industry/industry division, 42–51, 134–43 153, 154, 164, 169, 191, 99–103, 194–96, 205, 267–68, 304–05
Integrated Child Development Scheme (ICDS), 239, 242, 243–45
Intensive Agriculture Development Programme (IADP), 109, 115
irrigation, 110–16, 122, 126, 128, 331–33

Jammu & Kashmir, 101, 174, 175, 257
Jharkhand, 101, 136, 213–19
job card, 257, 262, 264, 266

Kalmandasguri village (West Bengal), 71–79, 113–30, 225–32, 324–32
Karnataka, 19, 23, 25, 36, 100–06, 110–30, 141, 145, 158, 161, 227, 307–16
Katkuian village (Bihar), 71–79, 225–32, 323–33
Kenya, 134–43
Kerala, 96–06, 117, 139–61, 232, 259, 307–16, 358
Khakchang village (Tripura), 223–32
Kothapalle village (Andhra Pradesh), 71–79, 223–33

labour absorption, 109, 110, 117, 128, 164, 325, 333
Labour Bureau, 19, 41, 46, 48, 49, 51, 54, 55, 61, 298
labour ratio, 70–77, 127
labour underutilisation, 3, 4, 11–12, 18
Land and Livestock Holdings Survey, 167
landless/landlessness, 59, 61, 113–16, 121, 144, 167, 192, 197, 209, 219, 222, 261, 266, 327–34
landlord/s, 67, 69, 115, 118, 143–44
legislators, 197
liberalisation/neo-liberal economic policy, 146–52, 158–64, 237–38, 250–52, 266–69, 346
Lok Sabha, 244, 245
London, 134, 135, 137, 143, 153

long-term worker/servant, 122, 284–87, 154–62

Madhya Pradesh, 92–106, 169–76, 211–16, 248, 253, 255, 307–16, 359
Maharashtra, 92, 96–106, 176, 211, 219, 223–32, 262, 307–16, 323, 324
Mahatma Gandhi National Rural Employment Guarantee Act (MGNREGA)/NREGA/NREGS, 52–54, 92, 230, 256–73, 308–13
Mahatwar village (Uttar Pradesh), 71–79, 112–30, 323–33
mahua flower, 291
Mainama village (Tripura), 223–32
Malaysia, 137
Mamata, 240
manufacturing, 51, 53, 95, 137–138, 194–95, 266–69
Manipur, 99–107, 216, 316, 358, 359
manual worker, 25–26, 30–33, 67–78, 114–16, 129, 221–32, 298, 326–29
see also hired labour
Marx, Karl, 68, 69
Marxian, 259–62, 266
Maternity Benefit Act, 139
Meghalaya, 96–105, 169, 176, 185, 215, 219, 307, 358
micro finance institution (MFI), 344, 349
mid-day meal/mid-day meal workers, 239, 240, 246, 247, 249–51
migration, 79–80, 136–38, 144
mining, 197, 202
minimum wage, 144–45, 241–42, 243–45, 249, 257–58, 308–13
Ministry of Labour and Employment, 246
Ministry of Rural Development, 310
Ministry of Women and Child Development, 239, 244, 245
Mizoram, 96, 99, 176, 211–19, 358
Mombasa, 143
monthly per capita expenditure (MPCE), 69, 78, 88, 91–95, 96–106, 189, 190, 200–02, 209, 239, 242, 248–51, 285–95, 327
Muhuripur village (Tripura), 225–31
Muslim, 116, 189, 190, 192, 330

Nagaland, 96–105, 176, 358
Nairobi, 143

National Dairy Development Board (NDDB), 167

National Health Mission (NHM)/National Rural Health Mission, 239, 247, 248

National Industrial Classification/Code (NIC), 42, 49–51, 172, 195

Nayanagar village (Bihar), 223–32, 324–33

Nimshirgaon village (Maharashtra), 71–79, 323–33

nutrition, 167, 237, 238, 241, 243, 247, 250

Nomadic Tribes, 224, 225

non-wage benefits, 145, 146, 151, 154, 156, 161, 162

North East/North Eastern, 96, 136, 137, 175, 176, 211, 213–16, 219, 307, 324, 358

occupation category, 52, 98–99, 105, 113–16, 169, 189, 196–98, 202–03, 206–08

Odisha, 101, 105, 211–16, 248, 253, 255, 307–14, 359

Organisation for Economic Cooperation and Development (OECD), 15

Other Backward Classes (OBC), 23, 26, 114, 192–202, 211, 224, 238, 330, 363

own-use production work, 6, 13, 14, 22, 29, 30, 36

paddy, 60, 115–16, 144, 170, 228, 289, 290, 324, 325, 333

Panahar village (West Bengal), 113–30, 229–30, 323–34

panchayat, 27, 262, 263

panel data, 41, 52, 351

para teacher, 238, 240, 241

Patna, 282–94

peasant/cultivator, 25–26, 67–81, 98–99, 145–52, 154–56, 266–69, 283–84, 326

Periodic Labour Force Survey (PLFS), 19, 85, 167–69, 189, 190, 209, 298

plantation, 134–64

Plantation Labour Act (PLA) 1951, 138, 146, 152, 156

ploughmen, 284–99

plucker, 157, 158

potential labour force, 10–11, 14–15

primary health centre (PHC), 240, 247, 250

Prime Minister's Jan Dhan Yojana (PMJDY), 348, 351, 352, 362

professionals, 197

production boundary, 3, 4, 6, 8, 13, 14, 22, 27, 40–43, 93

see also System of National Accounts (SNA)

Project on Agrarian Relations in India (PARI), 23, 52, 67, 68, 110, 221, 322

proletarianisation/proletariat, 67–81, 209

public distribution system, 261

Punjab, 101–06, 110–31, 175, 271, 281

rainfall, 266, 301, 307

Rajasthan, 92–106, 175, 219, 222–29, 248, 255, 259, 307–14, 323–34, 359

regression, 34–35, 39, 328–33, 362–67, 371–73

reproductive work, 258, 271–73, 289, 295

see also unpaid work

Rewasi village (Rajasthan), 71–79, 223–32, 323–34

risk, 163, 167, 266, 344

Russia, 352

salary/salaried, 29–31, 40, 205, 216–19, 240

sampling, 14, 16, 23–26, 46–49, 69

Sarva Shiksha Abhiyan (SSA), 238–41, 249

Scheduled Caste (SC)/Dalit/Adi Karnataka, 23, 25–26, 35, 49, 123–26, 189–202, 224–27, 329, 349, 363–66

Scheduled Tribe (ST), 49, 95, 113, 189, 192, 209–19, 224–27, 238, 329, 349, 363–66

scheme worker, 30, 238–54

self-employed, 22, 29–31, 36, 43–45, 53–56, 92–94, 105, 189, 216–19, 267

self-help group (SHG), 29, 246, 349, 350, 356, 368

services, 4–8, 14, 15, 22, 169

Sikkim, 99, 136, 215, 358, 359

single women, 145, 238

Siresandra village (Karnataka), 23–32, 71–79, 222–32, 324–33

small tea garden (STG)/tea garden, 142, 143, 146, 156, 163

social protection/social security, 241, 242, 247–49, 256, 261–62, 344

Sri Lanka Freedom Party (SLFP), 141

sugarcane, 25, 33, 75, 113, 115, 153, 228, 324–26, 333

Supreme Court, 241, 243

System of National Accounts (SNA)/extended SNA, 3, 4, 13–14, 19–22, 32, 34, 37, 40–43, 93–94, 179, 180

Tamil Nadu, 96–106, 117, 139–61, 169–185, 246, 306–16, 358
tea, 134–46, 151–58, 161–65
technicians, 197, 240
Tehang village (Punjab), 114–31
Terai, 116, 144, 161
Time-Use Survey, 21, 168, 169, 177–81, 185
time-use data/survey, 8, 14–16, 19–23, 26, 28–29, 36, 41, 43, 60
trade/craft workers, 7, 21, 53, 95, 110, 143, 266, 284, 294
trade union, 238, 244, 249
trainee/intern, 4, 6, 7, 13–15, 22, 29
Tripura, 96–107, 176, 222–30, 358, 359

underemployment, 11–13, 227, 232, 298
unemployment, 9–11, 13–15, 18, 19, 31–32, 36–37, 169, 227–29, 266–69, 298, 305
Union Territory, 169, 211, 264
United Kingdom, 114
United National Party (UNP), 142
unpaid work, 7, 8, 21–22, 28–29, 93–94, 238, 242, 93–94, 102–04, 178–79, 251
untouchability, 190
    see also discrimination
Uttar Pradesh, 75, 92–106, 110–30, 175, 232, 307–16, 323, 359
Uttarakhand, 96–106

village study/survey, 23–24, 41, 68–70, 110–12, 221–23, 322–23
volunteer work, 4, 7, 8, 13, 14, 22, 29, 38, 251–54

wage labour, 5, 70–73, 78–79, 126–28, 144–52, 156–62, 216–19, 221, 239, 289, 298–99, 322–23, 327, 329, 332, 334
    see also casual worker
Wage Rates in Rural India (WRRI), 298–99, 315, 324
wage rate/earnings, 40, 54, 126–28, 249, 284–95, 299–321, 323–26, 337
Warwat Khanderao village (Maharashtra), 71–79, 223–32, 323–33
West Bengal, 41–61, 76, 96–106, 110–31, 136–64, 171, 175, 176, 225–29, 307–16, 323
work participation/labour force participation, 19, 21, 27–28, 40, 41, 50–55, 61, 86, 89, 92–93, 171–80, 192–94, 211–14
working-age population, 8, 10, 87, 256, 264–67, 270

Yashoda, 239, 240, 248, 249, 253–55

Zhapur village (Karnataka), 71–79, 222–30, 323–33